Social Research

Third edition

S. Sarantakos

palgrave
macmillan

First published 2005 by
PALGRAVE MACMILLAN
Houndmills, Basingstoke, Hampshire RG21 6XS and
175 Fifth Avenue, New York, N.Y. 10010
Companies and representatives throughout the world

PALGRAVE MACMILLAN is the global academic imprint of the Palgrave Macmillan division of St. Martin's Press, LLC and of Palgrave Macmillan Ltd. Macmillan® is a registered trademark in the United States, United Kingdom and other countries. Palgrave is a registered trademark in the European Union and other countries.

ISBN-13: 978-1-4039-4320-0 (paperback)
ISBN-10: 1-4039-4320-6 (paperback)

This book is printed on paper suitable for recycling and made from fully managed and sustained forest sources. Logging, pulping and manufacturing processes are expected to conform to the environmental regulations of the country of origin.

A catalogue record for this book is available from the British Library.

A catalog record for this book is available from the Library of Congress.
Library of Congress Card Number: 2004054820

10   9   8   7   6   5
14   13   12   11   10   09   08

Printed in China

Brief contents

Full contents

List of boxes

List of figures

List of tables

Preface

This is a compact, concise and comprehensive text of social research written for undergraduate students of the social sciences and related disciplines. It explores critically the diverse and pluralistic nature of social research, integrates popular methodologies and methods and covers a wide area of social inquiry, ranging from positivist analysis to constructionist and feminist research, also stressing hermeneutics, discourse analysis and postmodern research, and introducing applied research (needs analysis, evaluation research and action research). A lengthy and focused study guide (Working with Social Research) is available in electronic form on the publisher's web site.

The text presents research as a dynamic process leading from the choice of the research topic to the writing of the report, and from questions to answers, showing clearly how research progresses from one stage to the next, how decisions are made, how options are chosen and how conclusions are drawn. All methods of social research taught in standard courses are covered in the text, with chapters on feminist research and applied research, which are rarely covered separately in standard introductory texts. As a result, this text will prove useful to students of sociology, social work, psychology, nursing, education, administration, journalism, politics, policing and the social sciences in general, and can be employed at lower as well as higher undergraduate levels.

The book is written in a style that is clear, direct and student-friendly. The direct contribution of students in its development was most helpful. Using the book as their text in a variety of areas, students took the opportunity to comment on its clarity and degree of difficulty, sharing their views with the author regarding the need for additional explanations of complex research procedures as well as for more examples in specific contexts, and for adjustments and improvements to increase its focus and presentation. The input of fellow academics who used the text in their courses was most valuable, although of a different kind.

The third edition is fully revised, expanded, and improved, as well as clearly presented, direct, engaging and student-friendly. This book has many distinctive features, which deserve special consideration. The following are most characteristic:

- The book is compact, concise and comprehensive, and offers a relatively large amount of information in a relatively small space. Using a 'laconic' style based on the motto 'write as much as necessary and as little as possible', a rule stemming from the author's Spartan extraction and early education, the text focuses on substance and discards superfluous talk, unnecessary jargon and confusing 'verbiage'.

- It covers quantitative and qualitative research side-by-side, allowing an easy contrast between these two research strategies, their strengths and their weaknesses. With increasing interest in methodological triangulation in social research, this feature is most useful.

- It contains a strong element of German and Austrian research theory and practice, adding another dimension to the discussion of our standard research.

- It considers the history of social research briefly but adequately, thus helping students to contextualise research and to understand its nature and origins. It offers a separate chapter on feminist research, following its increased popularity and diversity in its procedures; and it includes a new chapter on applied social research, which makes up a large part of research in many areas and especially in social work, social welfare and social policy.

- It introduces statistical programs for social scientists (SPSS) in quantitative analysis, in a simple and straightforward manner that enables students with no mathematical/statistical background to conduct statistical analysis effectively. The latest SPSS version (Version 12) as well as Versions 10 and 11 are considered.

- Last but not least, this text is accompanied by an electronic workbook that contains essay questions, short answer questions, true/false questions, fill-in questions and multiple-choice questions and other elements, which should be a helpful companion to the learning student, and perhaps to the busy lecturer. The workbook can be found in the publisher's web page (www.palgrave.com).

As a basic-level text, the book is oriented towards practice and substance, leaving more demanding theoretical issues for the initiated and advanced readers. In essence, it offers a solid basis for further developments, and prepares undergraduates for a more detailed study of advanced, specialised and theoretically demanding aspects of research, which might be undertaken in other courses, or for which information may be sought in more specialised literature.

In summary, the third edition of this text retains the strengths of the previous editions but it is enriched in content, expanded in coverage, improved in presentation, updated in computer programs, and suitable for more courses, and this without increasing its size. In conclusion, this text is now not only more comprehensive; it also has a wider scope, and is more accessible and more student-friendly than before. Students and teachers who found the text useful in the past will find it now even more attractive, and also suitable for more courses than previous editions.

S. Sarantakos
March 2004

Acknowledgements

The author and the publishers are grateful for permission to reproduce the following copyright material:

- Educational and Psychological Measurement, Inc, Table 5.3

While every care has been taken to trace and acknowledge copyright, the publishers tender their apologies for any accidental infringement where copyright has proved untraceable. They would be pleased to come to a suitable arrangement with the rightful owner in each case.

Foundations of social research

Introduction

CHAPTER 1

THIS CHAPTER

- begins with a brief history of social research
- outlines the main types and motives of social research
- introduces some central political issues of social research
- summarises the ethical standards of social research.

KEY HEADINGS

INTRODUCTION

The aim of this book is to present, in a clear, concise and practical manner, the methods and techniques of social research. These methods and techniques have been developed, modified and practised throughout the history of the social sciences, and constitute the methodological heritage of modern researchers: each method is the result of continuous efforts of many researchers and social scientists, and contains elements contributed by academics from all parts of the world.

With this element of history, that permeates not only the single methods and techniques but also the whole body of methodology of the social sciences, we will begin the discussion of this chapter. Following this, we will explore the types, aims and motives of research, before we introduce the political and ethical parameters of social research.

1 HISTORICAL OVERVIEW

Briefly, social research is the purposive and rigorous investigation that aims to generate new knowledge. It is the intellectual tool of social scientists, which allows them to enter contexts of personal and/or public interest that are unknown to them, and to search for answers to their questions. Social research is about discovery, expanding the horizons of the known, confidence, new ideas and new conclusions about all aspects of life.

As the quest for knowledge, social research has been the ultimate goal of the social scientist, who basically seeks not only to gather useful and valid knowledge, but also to educate the community about the status and validity of certain 'sources' of knowledge. Academics endeavour to explain life and the world, to shake the bases of superstitions, to answer questions regarding all aspects of life from personal fate to physical disasters, and to inform governments how to establish relevant policies and practices.

The nature of this endeavour has by no means been unchanging. Early in the history of social research, the dominant sources of knowledge varied significantly (see Box 1.1); they included common sense, intuition and beliefs (Dimas, 2003; Schndelbach, 2002; Wandmacher, 2002: 5), but for the majority of learned researchers the dominant sources of knowledge were logic, reason, faith, speculation and mysticism. The kind of research presently employed by most researchers, empirical research, was also practised, but only by a minority of researchers; it was the exception and reflected a revolutionary alternative to the practice of philosophers and theologians, who were seen as the legitimate gatekeepers of wisdom, knowledge, and truths.

In empirical research, knowledge was acquired not through logic, reason, faith or speculation but through empirical evidence, namely through evidence based on facts gathered by the researchers. The empirical nature of the research demanded consideration of what researchers experience through their senses and not of what they could logically create through their mind.

The account of the history of social research that follows focuses on the type of alternative inquiry that sought knowledge in empirical evidence and was thus

Box **1.1**

Sources of truth and knowledge

A quantitative research design:

- Common sense: everyone knows that it is so!
- Intuition: I just know it (e.g. 'woman's intuition').
- Beliefs: it is based on personal conviction.
- Tenacity: verification over the years; time has given it validity.
- Tradition: practice through generations ('It has always been so').
- Personal experience: personal testing and experience ('It works for me!').
- Authority: the word of experts ('It is true; professor X said so').
- Divine and supernatural powers: e.g. the revelations of God and of other powers.
- Reason and logic: the intellect can capture truth and knowledge directly.
- Scientific methods: knowledge is derived through empirical procedures.

(Schndelbach, 2002)

different from, and diametrically opposed to, the theological and philosophical tradition. As we shall see, empirical research was practised by Greek philosophers more than two and a half thousand years ago, and grew slowly but steadily, particularly after the mid-1800s.

1.1 The early years

A number of Greek philosophers showed a strong interest in empirical ways of gaining knowledge. Thales (640–550 BC), for instance, applied observation of natural events and offered what could be termed an 'empirical-scientific' approach to the world. Anaximander (611–547 BC), Empedocles (c. 450 BC) and Xenophanes (c. 600 BC) are further examples of empirically thinking philosophers of the distant past. Hippocrates (c. 450 BC) was even more involved in empirical research than his contemporaries; his experiments in health and illness widened the basis of general knowledge, and weaned public opinion away from superstitions such as belief in the powers of demons and bad spirits, focusing instead on the principles of empirical inquiry.

Interest in controlled research that embraced observation and experimentation increased with time, and by 400 BC it was used by philosophers as great and well known as Aristotle (384–322 BC), who saw empirical events as manifestations of fundamental principles of an ordered universe. It was Socrates who was reluctant (as was Plato) to abandon traditional philosophical thinking.

1.2 Forerunners of modern social research

The pioneering work of these Greek philosophers influenced researchers throughout Europe, and was developed more profoundly, particularly during the sixteenth and seventeenth centuries, at the genesis of the *scientific revolution*. However, the success of researchers who sought alternatives to philosophical rules of thinking did not change the course of the quest for knowledge. Old and well-entrenched traditions and practices, and strong loyalties to ideologies of the time, continued to dominate the scene. Empirical research was conducted alongside traditional methods, offering an alternative research model.

This dyadic approach to knowledge continued throughout this period, with traditional philosophical methods being dominant. Social research as we know it today was practised by only a minority of researchers. Closer to our times, during the seventeenth and eighteenth centuries, research was still dominated by reason, tradition, religion and rationalism, but the presence of empirical models in social research became more evident. Examples are Francis Bacon (1561–1626) and Isaac Newton (1643–1727), who used experimentation to unlock the mysteries of nature and to gather 'truths' about social life.

Box **1.2**

Isaac Newton and social research

Isaac Newton (1643–1727) introduced mathematics to experiments as a research tool, and his perception of the process of research led to the formulation of what we know today as the *hypothetico-deductive* model. This model presents social research as an interaction between empirical observation and reason, or, better, between induction and deduction, a notion not very different from what everyone takes for granted in contemporary social sciences.

Newton's ideas are found – in some form at least – in the writings of other theorists, such as Voltaire (1694–1778), and Marquis de Condorcet (1743–1794). John Locke (1632–1704), as can be seen in his *Essays Concerning Human Understanding*, worked towards gaining a precise recording of the world, facilitated through a combination of methods, including observation, measurement and reason.

The emergence of *Political Arithmetic* in England strengthened the image of alternative research methods, to the extent that some writers take it to be the fore-

---

Box **1.3**

William Petty and social research in Ireland in 1672

Petty conducted research in Ireland, and produced the results of his studies in his well-known book *The Political Anatomy of Ireland*, written in 1672 and published in 1691. He carried out his research at the request of Oliver Cromwell, who, after a military victory over the Irish, had a particular interest in the social and economic conditions of Ireland. Cromwell was concerned with the social problems generated by early industrialisation, by a growing capitalism and by increasing urbanisation, and was in need of information that would enable him to prepare effective political plans to organise immigration from England to Ireland, and to rationalise public administration in that country.

runner of modern empirical research. Researchers working within this model used quantitative methods to describe social phenomena and to explain their causes. Well-known representatives of this movement are John Graunt (1620–1674), William Petty (1623–1687), John Howard (1726–1790) and Edmund Halley (1656–1742). Demographic studies, analyses of business trends, poverty studies and studies in prisons (such as those conducted by Howard), employing interviews and participant observation, are a few examples of the work they completed.

1.3 The nineteenth century: the rise of positivism

The changing social and economic conditions of the late eighteenth and early nineteenth centuries had a strong impact on the nature of research employed at that time. An example is the increase in social problems in agriculture and agrarian populations caused by progressive industrialisation and urbanisation, which called for 'realistic', 'specific' and quantifiable data that could provide direct information to the authorities and facilitate the introduction of relevant policies. Social researchers were challenged to intensify their efforts to provide more convincing explanations of these problems and to find solutions to them. Four leading researchers of that time who deserve special attention are Le Play, Quételet, Saint-Simon and Comte.

In France, Le Play (1806–1882) conducted research into typical families of workers (sociography) and constructed family monographs for this purpose. In Belgium, Adolph Quételet (1796–1874) expressed an equally strong interest in empirical research (see Box 1.4). Claude-Henri Saint-Simon (1760–1825) is known as the originator of positivism, although his name has not been used as much as that of Comte, the 'father' of positivism. Saint-Simon used research to find evidence that could strengthen his commitment to fairness and social equality. For him, the role of social scientists was that of secular priests, and science a new religion that could help establish an egalitarian society.

The philosopher who managed to tip the balance in the research endeavour was August Comte (1798–1857). In his writings *Cours de philosophie positive* and *Société positive*, Comte in 1848 denounced the conventional methodology of his time –

Box **1.4**

Adolph Quételet: founder of empirical social research?

Adolph Quételet (1796–1874), an astronomer and mathematician, was most active in empirical research. He was interested in the regularity and constancy of social behaviour, and especially in ascertaining the conditions under which one could predict future behaviour. With this in mind he studied social life empirically, hoping to be able to influence its course and outcome. Using empirical data, he developed life expectancy tables that were of great interest to social scientists – not to mention insurance companies. His well-known book *A Treatise on Man*, published in 1835, provided a strong foundation for modern social research. For some writers, Quételet was the real founder of empirical social research.

based predominantly on metaphysics, speculation and mysticism – and enthroned the positive method as the method of social research. His theory was positivism, the methodology he introduced was the positivist methodology, and the methods he considered appropriate were the scientific ones of experimentation and observation. In Comte's view, knowledge was to be gained only through sensory experiences; hence, only positive phenomena – phenomena registered though the senses – were worth studying. By 'positive' Comte meant phenomena posited or given in direct experience and resulting from scientific observation and scientific method.

Despite strong resistance on the part of the philosophers of that time, and the lack of recognition of Comte's academic work by his colleagues, the social and intellectual atmosphere created by positivism influenced methodological thinking and research practice in Europe as much as in the United States. In psychology, positivism helped to strengthen the notion that the psyche could be seen from a perspective other than the theological, and to explain mental problems through 'scientific' methods and principles. Wilhelm Wundt (1832–1920), for instance, demonstrated his positivist conviction when he established the first psychological laboratory in 1879 in Leipzig, with experiments becoming the central method of psychological inquiry; experimentation (next to psychoanalysis) dominated the psychological thinking and research of that time.

1.4 The twentieth century: research pluralism

The hegemony of positivism

During the late nineteenth and early twentieth centuries, research became not only more popular but also more systematic and more 'scientific'. In the United Kingdom, Seebohm Rowntree conducted a study in 1899 that included all families of workers in the city of York (11,500 families), examining the health parameters of their members. The empirical bias in research is also shown in the work of Charles Booth and Arthur Bowley; the latter conducted a study between 1910 and 1912 that covered five cities, and employed systematic sampling procedures for the first time.

The empiricist tradition of the past – now strengthened by the input of positivism – created great interest among academics and researchers in Europe and elsewhere.

Box **1.5**

Charles Booth: unemployment and poverty in London

Charles Booth conducted studies of poverty and poor families in London in the late nineteenth and early twentieth centuries. The findings were published in the *Life and Labour of the People of London*, which provided empirical evidence that rejected the commonly held belief that poverty was caused by people's bad behaviour and bad habits (drinking, idleness, vice and so on). The study revealed that poverty was caused by unemployment, underpaid work, low wages that were inadequate to sustain a family, large families, and chronic illness. His findings encouraged the introduction of social reforms in England.

During the twentieth century, research centres of various kinds rose to an institutional status. This was clear in Germany and Austria, where public as well as university research centres based on a positivist paradigm grew rapidly in number. It was even more evident in the United States, where social research became institutionalised within many contexts, especially universities (Columbia and Princeton are two examples). Market research and political analyses found in empirical research the right tool to provide them with insights into their domain, and Gallup and Crossley polls became as popular as they are today. The Russel-Sage Foundation, founded in 1909, promoted empirical research into social problems (community studies) in order to improve living conditions in the United States.

The advent and expansion of positivism had two major effects on the theory and practice of research. The first was that social research separated itself once and for all from philosophy and was established as a legitimate and independent discipline. The second was that research became empirical and quantitative, and dominated the social sciences almost entirely.

Challenging the positivist hegemony

The second half of the twentieth century was dominated by a strengthening of the critical spirit that challenged the legitimation of the 'hegemony' of positivism, and resulted in radical changes in the areas of theory and research. Such challenges came predominantly from the campuses of symbolic interactionism, phenomenology, philosophical hermeneutics, Marxism, the Frankfurt School, ethnomethodology (Cicourel, 1974; Garfinkel, 1967) and feminism. Such criticisms encouraged researchers to rethink their methodological orientation and ultimately strengthened a non-positivist or anti-positivist attitude in this context.

Criticism focused on the manner in which reality was addressed and defined, the manner in which knowledge extraction was conducted, the methods employed in data collection and analysis, the ways in which research was designed and executed, the relationship between the researcher and the researched, the positivist perception of gender, and the acceptance of the methods of physical sciences as tools of social research.

Following this, positivism lost significant ground within the domain of social theory, and to a lesser extent in research practice. With regard to the latter, there is a contradiction between verbal and actual allegiance to positivist research. While many researchers criticise positivism, in practice most employ its methodology.

Be that as it may, the fact is that, at this point in time, the domain of social research has a distinct place in academia, one that is separate from philosophy, and entails two major directions, as it did in the far past. One is positivist research, while the other is a diverse model that employs a variety of strategies, ranging from relativism to rationalism and idealism. Both these elements are very strong and influence a sizable proportion of followers.

2 THE STATE OF CONTEMPORARY RESEARCH

This brief historical overview has demonstrated a number of trends (see Box 1.6). The most relevant of these are diversity, direct or indirect ideological engagement

Box **1.6**

Trends in social research over time

- Research has been diverse and pluralistic.
- The two major fronts within the research domain have been positivist (quantitative) and non-positivist (qualitative) research.
- Quantitative research became popular and overshadowed other types of research. However, during the second half of twentieth century the rise of qualitative research reduced its popularity significantly.
- There has been an ideological division over the quality and suitability of social research.
- Research has been associated with personal interests, social problems, ideologies and political interests.
- Research has also served as a tool of social policy and social reconstruction.

of the researchers in the research and its purpose, and some form of control over the process of research. The diversity of research, its political nature and research controls (such as ethics) will be discussed next.

2.1 Diversity of research

Research is diverse and pluralistic. This diversity is associated with a number of criteria such as its focus, its methods, its purpose and its underlying paradigm. Research may focus on people and the physical and social environments, or on hidden structures and meanings. It can aim to increase scientific knowledge or to emancipate people and change their life-world.

Nevertheless, the most significant, most common and also fundamental distinctions in social research are qualitative versus quantitative research. Almost every type of research, regardless of its nature and purpose, is conducted within either a quantitative or a qualitative strategy. But there are many more types, categories and names of research conducted within these two contexts. The most commonly used types are listed below.

Types of research:

- *Basic research* is concerned with the production of new knowledge and with the increase of scientific understanding of the world, and not with the application of its outcomes. It aims purely at the discovery of knowledge; therefore it is also referred to as pure research.
- *Applied research* places a strong emphasis on application and problem solving. When it also entails the personal engagement of the researcher, and elements of change and enlightenment, it is usually referred to as emancipatory research. Social impact studies, action research, evaluation research, and cost–benefit analysis are a few examples of applied research.
- *Longitudinal research* studies social issues on more than one occasion using the same or different samples.
- *Descriptive research* aims to describe social systems, relations or social events.

- *Classification research* aims to categorise research units into groups, to demonstrate differences, explain relationships and clarify social events or relationships.
- *Comparative research* aims to identify similarities and/or differences between research units (Ragin, 1987).
- *Exploratory research* aims to establish the most basic criteria of the research topic, often before the actual study has started.
- *Explanatory research* aims to explain social relations or events.
- *Causal research* aims to establish a causal relationship between variables.
- *Theory-testing research* aims to test the validity of a theory.
- *Theory-building research* is employed to establish and formulate theories.
- *Action research* is 'the application of fact finding to practical problem solving in a social situation with a view to improving the quality of action within it, involving the collaboration and cooperation of researchers, practitioners and laymen' (Burns, 1990: 252).
- *Participatory action research* (PAR) is characterised by the strong involvement and degree of participation of members of the public in the research process (Whyte, 1991).
- *Evaluation research* is employed to assess the suitability, relevance and effectiveness of certain programmes.
- *Feminist research* focuses on the life of women, is conducted by women, on women and for women, and employs a variety of research paradigms.

It must be stressed that diversity is not an indicator of weakness of, or problems with, research procedures. All types of research have a task to perform, and are valuable in their own context and for their special properties.

2.2 Aims of social research

Throughout its history, social research has served a variety of goals. In general this has entailed the generation of knowledge, but more specifically the identification of regularities in social process, which was expected to help us understand the presence, type, extent and causes of problems and the way one could control them (Benini, 2000). But this is not the only purpose of research. Given the plurality and diversity of the philosophical and methodological principles that drive research in theory and practice, its aims are equally pluralistic and diverse. In general, researchers conduct research in order to achieve the goals described in Box 1.7.

The aims of social research presented in Box 1.7 are neither exhaustive nor mutually exclusive. Research projects may be undertaken for a number of reasons and may serve many and diverse aims. These aims depend primarily on the paradigm that guides the project. *Positivist research* strives to achieve the aims listed under point *a*, that is, to explore, explain, evaluate, predict and develop/test theories; while *interpretive research* focuses more on understanding people (point *b*). *Critical research* aims at facilitating a critique of social reality, emancipating people, empowering them to change social reality by suggesting possible solutions and thus liberating them from oppressive and exploitative social structures (point *c*). Still, the boundaries between these three perspectives are rather flexible. There are qualitative researchers, for instance

---

Box **1.7**

The purpose of social research is to:

a. *explore* social reality for its own sake or in order to make further research possible
explain social life by providing reliable, valid and well-documented information
evaluate the status of social issues and their effects on society
make predictions
develop and/or *test theories.*

b. *understand* human behaviour and action.

c. offer a basis for a *critique* of social reality
emancipate people
suggest possible solutions to social problems
empower and *liberate* people.

(see Miles and Huberman, 1994) who include prediction and causal analysis in the aims of qualitative analysis.

In a more general sense, the information and knowledge gathered when pursuing the above aims are also used to achieve other more specific goals of social research, mainly of a practical nature. Researchers (Becker, 1989; Vlahos, 1984) and those having an interest in social research may aim at one or more of the applications listed in Box 1.8. These goals are not mutually exclusive. The choice depends largely on the ideological orientation of the researchers, and their understanding of the role of social sciences in the community.

Box **1.8**

The goals of social research

a. *General goals.* Understanding for its own sake.
b. *Theoretical goals.* Verification, falsification, modification or discovery of a theory.
c. *Pragmatic goals.* Solution of social problems.
d. *Political goals.* Development of social policy, evaluation of programmes and practices, and social criticism; social change and reconstruction; empowerment and liberation.

2.3 Motives of social research

Aims usually refer to the immediate outcomes of the research: for example, to ascertain the extent of a problem, or to establish its causes. Motives relate to more general and overarching goals, and can be intrinsic (that is, related to personal interests of the researcher in the study object), or extrinsic (related to the interests of those contracting the research). Hence, the motives may be different from the aims. However, this does not necessarily mean that the two cannot coincide. Researchers may conduct research, not just for the purpose of ascertaining facts but, more so, in order to improve the quality of life of a group of people.

Some of the motives that are not included in the list of the aims discussed above, which have quite often been identified in research studies and quoted in the literature (Mahr, 1995: 84), are shown in Box 1.9. In the case of contracted research, the motives often given by the sponsors or researchers are not always clear or transparent. There are instances in which the sponsors of a project (or even the researchers) have reasons to hide their real motives, and to mislead the public and certain interest groups. The trained researcher and the critical reader should be able to identify the real motives of research and to act accordingly.

Box **1.9**

Motives of social research

- *Educational*: to educate and inform the public.
- *'Magical'*: to offer credibility to views held by researchers and/or their sponsors.
- *Personal*: to promote the academic status of the researcher.
- *Institutional*: to enhance the research quantum of the institution for which the researcher works.
- *Political*: to provide support to political plans and programmes.
- *Tactical*: to delay decision or action for as long as the investigation is under way.

---

3. POLITICS AND THE PRODUCTION OF KNOWLEDGE

3.1 Introduction

Research produces knowledge, and knowledge is power. Hence, research is the focus of those who have an interest in knowledge, and who wish to own, control and manipulate it so as to produce desired outcomes. It follows that controlling research means controlling power; and therefore controlling research according to plan is an attractive proposition. Consequently, it is important that you become aware of the political nature of research before you start dealing with the details of its structure and process (Sapford and Abbott, 1996).

History has shown clearly and beyond reasonable doubt that the notion of knowledge as power is attractive to all those involved in research and/or having an interest in knowledge and its type and nature. More specifically, political interests in research are associated with the producer of knowledge (e.g. the researcher, research team or research centre), the controller of knowledge (e.g. political systems, research grant committees, interest groups, review commit-tees of professional journals and publishing houses), and the consumer of knowledge (e.g. business organisations, government departments and interest groups).

The manner in which these three sources of political influence affect the research processes varies in a number of ways. They may, for instance:

- promote one type of research while suppressing other types (e.g. favouring research on wife abuse and ignoring evidence of husband abuse)
- support research that would provide evidence for certain political plans and programmes
- suppress the dissemination of knowledge that could work against the interests of certain organisations by controlling the publication outlets
- support the production and dissemination of knowledge that would strengthen economic benefits for business
- control research practice by developing and enforcing relevant professional standards.

3.2 The producer and the construction of knowledge

The researcher has direct access to the construction of the research design, the definition of purpose and motives, the collection and analysis of the sources of information and the choice of the underlying paradigm and methodology. He or she can thus, wittingly or unwittingly, influence the nature of the knowledge produced through the project. Practically, all steps of the research process can be manipulated to serve the researcher's purpose and to produce political gains. A brief list of possible ways of politically biasing research outcomes is given in Box 1.10. These can run through the entire research process, from the choice of the research topic to the publication of the findings.

In order to control those researchers who could manipulate their data in some way, the academic community has taken relevant measures. In certain cases laws have been introduced to control the researcher's professional conduct. In other cases, codes of ethics have been developed to encourage a fair research process, free from deviations such as those listed here.

Box **1.10**

Areas of bias in research

- *The research topic*: choosing topics that produce favourable data and consciously ignoring others.
- *Review of literature*: focusing on supportive sources and ignoring others.
- *The research purpose*: aiming to prove personal convictions.
- *The formulation of the research topic*: choosing indicators etc. that bias the research process to a certain direction.
- *The research design*: choosing sampling procedures and methods of data collection that favour the production of certain data.
- *Fabrication of data*: presenting data that have never been collected.
- *Falsification of data*: changing the content of the answers.
- *Data analysis*: choosing a type of analysis that would favour personal views.
- *Interpretation*: interpreting the findings according to personal beliefs and convictions.
- *Presentation of the findings*: presenting the findings in a manner that does not reflect the real theme of the study.

3.3 The controller of knowledge

Controllers of knowledge are academics and/or members of various interest groups who directly or indirectly control the production and dissemination of knowledge. Most powerful and influential are interest groups, which are often the driving force behind the acquisition and dissemination of knowledge. This is accomplished by determining whether research is to be conducted or not, and whether research findings will be published. The following are a few examples.

- Reviews of applications for research grants can be affected by the personal or ideological bias of the assessor, thus promoting one type of research while suppressing another.
- Reviews of articles, books and other texts submitted for publication can be affected by the personal or ideological bias of the reviewer, so preventing 'undesirable' information from reaching academics and the community in general.
- Researchers, knowing the fate of grant applications and of publication proposals, may feel forced by their circumstances to opt for types of research that are more likely to be funded and have their findings published.
- Advisors influencing the structure of the curriculum in various teaching institutions may advise the institution to delete certain sections (e.g. family studies) and replace them with others (e.g. women's studies), hence generating a need for information in certain areas and suppressing such a need in others.
- Advisors informing government departments on policy issues may guide policy-based research to targets of their personal and ideological interests, ignoring the need for research in other areas.

To overcome these conditions, academics and researchers may take counter-measures, such as developing their own publication outlets and locating funding sources of their own, but the fact remains that options for abusing positions of trust to enhance personal or group interests are still available.

3.4 The consumer of research

The consumer is 'the king', and not only in the domain of business. Research is geared towards producing data where there is a demand for information. This demand may be academic, for example, to explore or test theories, or to measure the presence of an association between variables. However, in many cases, and especially where research is demanding in terms of time, labour and resources, research depends almost exclusively on financial support; this often comes from sponsors who specify the type and nature of research they are prepared to support. Hence, the consumers can play a decisive role, often dictating the type of research to be conducted and the type of findings to be published. In summary, consumers can influence research by

- controlling the *distribution of research funds* so as to support some types of research and suppress others
- controlling *access to the research field*, often disallowing entry to it if they are unsure as to the nature of the findings

- keeping undesirable research findings *hidden*
- controlling *the publication* of undesirable findings, for example by not including them in internal publications or not consenting to their publication when they have ownership of the data, as is the case with certain types of contracted research.

The problem of politicisation of research relates to the professional conduct and ethical standards of the researcher as well as to business interests and personal ideologies of members of the community. As noted above, the academic community has responded to some of these problems by addressing its effects, by establishing publication outlets for less desirable research findings for example, and attracting limited funds to conduct research in less attractive areas. With regard to professional conduct, the responses have been more decisive and more successful. This was accomplished by establishing ethical standards and by enforcing them in all possible contexts, as shown in Box 1.11.

Box **1.11**

Common ethical practices

- Ethical standards are an integral part of any research design.
- Researcher records must be securely kept for future reference and evidence.
- Multiple authorship should be clearly explained, recorded and evidenced.
- Publication of multiple papers from the same data is improper.
- Potential conflicts of interests should be disclosed.
- Respondents must be fully informed about research details that may affect them.
- Informed consent must be ensured and documented in all cases.
- Full justification must be given where ethical standards are thought not to be required.
- Research proposals must obtain approval from relevant ethics committees.
- Problems arising from the research are to be communicated to the ethics committee.

---

4 ETHICS IN SOCIAL RESEARCH

4.1 Introduction

Over the last 30 years, efforts have been made to make research more systematic and more accountable. In the first instance, laws have been introduced which regulate the access to information as well as the behaviour of investigators. Apart from this, codes of ethics have been formulated within research institutions, professional associations and tertiary institutions to ensure that inquiry is conducted according to professional and ethical standards.

International and national professional organisations have established codes of conduct, which their members are expected to follow. Likewise, tertiary institutions have adopted ethical guidelines, and established internal procedures and committees (ethics committees or institutional review boards), which now assess all research projects proposed by their members, ensuring that they adhere to the

Box **1.12**

Ethics in research: the institutional response

- 'It is a basic assumption of institutions conducting research that their staff members are committed to high standards of professional conduct. Research workers have a duty to ensure that their work enhances the good name of the institution and the profession to which they belong' (Australian Vice-Chancellors' Committee).
- 'The primary goals of the Code of Ethics, a symbol of the identity of the ISA, are (1) to protect the welfare of groups and individuals with whom and on whom sociologists work or who are involved in sociologists' research efforts and (2) to guide the behaviour and hence the expectations of ISA members, both between themselves and toward the society at large' (International Sociological Association).
- 'In all their work psychologists shall conduct themselves in a manner that does not bring into disrepute the discipline and the profession of psychology. They shall value integrity, impartiality and respect for persons and evidence and shall seek to establish the highest ethical standards in their work' (British Psychological Society).
- 'This Code establishes feasible requirements for ethical behavior. These requirements cover many – but not all – of the potential sources of ethical conflict that may arise in research, teaching and practice. Most represent *prima facie* obligations that may admit of exceptions but which should generally stand as principles for guiding conduct' (American Sociological Association).

ethical standards of their institution. Feminist groups followed a similar practice; for instance, the Nebraska Sociological Feminist Collective formulated in 1988 a 'feminist ethic' for social science research.

Despite their diversity, codes of ethics focus on the following issues: physical and mental harm to the respondents, covert or hidden research, invasion of privacy, violation of anonymity and confidentiality, deception, coercion, plagiarism, and fabrication or concealment of findings (see Orr, 1999; Pfeifer, 2000). In more general terms, the areas considered in such documents by most organisations and writers alike (e.g. Bailey, 1988; Sproull, 1988; Vlahos, 1984) are the following:

- professional standards and ethical conduct
- the researcher–respondent relationship
- the researcher–researcher relationship
- the treatment of animals in research.

The details related to these broad areas of research practice that concern social scientists are presented in the lists that follow.

4.2 Professional practice and ethical standards

With regard to professional practice, ethical standards require that researchers should

- maintain objectivity in the conduct of social inquiry
- uphold professional integrity
- demonstrate responsibility, competence and propriety
- employ accurate methods of data gathering and analysis
- make use of relevant research methodology
- choose appropriate interpretation of the data
- report their data accurately
- avoid fabrication of data, which is misconduct
- avoid falsification of data, which is misconduct.

Fabrication of data refers to the practice of using data for publication which the researchers never collected. In this case they did not conduct any research to collect the findings claimed. Falsification refers to the practice of changing the content of findings. In this case, research has been collected but the data reported are different from those really collected.

4.3 The researcher–respondent relationship

Of equal concern is the violation of standards relating to the manner in which researchers treat respondents. This includes the possibility of hurting the respondents during the research in some way. Such standards are expected to be adhered to in all cases; a list of the most important is given in Box 1.13. It is now common practice that respondents are informed in writing of all aspects of the research, that they are given the option to take part in the study or to refuse to do so, that they have the right to step out of the research at any time, and that they sign an 'informed consent form'.

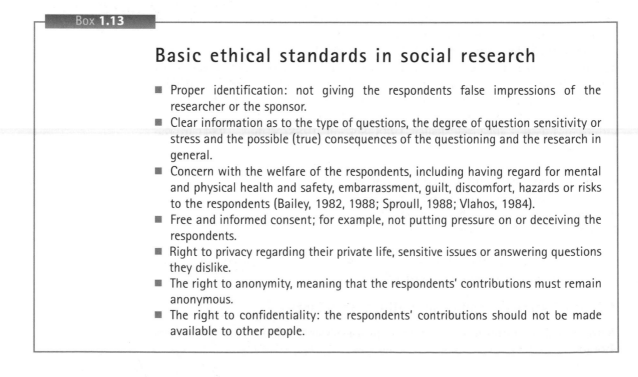

Box **1.13**

Basic ethical standards in social research

- Proper identification: not giving the respondents false impressions of the researcher or the sponsor.
- Clear information as to the type of questions, the degree of question sensitivity or stress and the possible (true) consequences of the questioning and the research in general.
- Concern with the welfare of the respondents, including having regard for mental and physical health and safety, embarrassment, guilt, discomfort, hazards or risks to the respondents (Bailey, 1982, 1988; Sproull, 1988; Vlahos, 1984).
- Free and informed consent; for example, not putting pressure on or deceiving the respondents.
- Right to privacy regarding their private life, sensitive issues or answering questions they dislike.
- The right to anonymity, meaning that the respondents' contributions must remain anonymous.
- The right to confidentiality: the respondents' contributions should not be made available to other people.

Avoiding harm to respondents

It is the researcher's responsibility to ensure that the research will not entail any procedures that can cause harm to respondents. Apart from preventing harm, researchers are responsible for ending research that has proved harmful to the respondents or their assistants. The types of harm that can be experienced by respondents may be physical, mental or legal.

- *Physical harm.* Regarding physical harm, researchers are expected to exclude from their research (a) instruments or procedures that could injure the respondents; (b) subjects who are susceptible to research treatment (e.g. suffering from heart disease or mental disorders); and (c) treatment that may motivate subjects to harm themselves during or after the study. In most cases, social research practices do not include treatment that could harm the participants.
- *Mental harm.* This entails cases where subjects are subjected, directly and/or indirectly, to procedures that cause discomfort, stress of some kind, anxiety, loss of self-esteem, or embarrassment. This can be caused by asking personal questions relating to the subjects or significant others, by formulating questions in a demeaning manner and by treating subjects with disrespect. More critical and more common is mental harm in experimental studies where subjects are manipulated mentally in a manner that gives them impressions that later, during debriefing, are found to be false.
- *Legal harm.* This is as likely to occur as any other type of harm and can have serious personal, emotional, social and economic consequences. This occurs, for instance, when the researcher violates any rights of the respondents, such as their right to privacy, anonymity and confidentiality (see below).

Box **1.14**

Think critically: what is harm?

Researchers wish to avoid any harm to their respondents; but what is really harm? The result of a research instrument (causing fear by confronting the subject with a large spider) or the wider composite of this plus the net outcome of the study: for example, curing arachnophobia? Is harm that which is generally considered to be 'harm' or what the respondent considers harmful? Is the task of the researcher to avoid any harm or only unnecessary harm? There is no agreement among academics on these issues. How useful are ethical prescriptions on this point?

Deception

Deception occurs when researchers encourage people to take part in a study by deceiving them: hiding aspects of research that respondents might find undesirable, or presenting an attractive but false image of the research. Deception occurs when the researcher lies about the research or conducts the study without the knowledge of the respondents. This is the case, for instance, when a researcher visits a family's house ostensibly to conduct an interview about street crime while in reality aiming to investigate household order and family functioning. Deception is allowed only if it is methodologically necessary, and even then the respondents should be adequately informed of the real nature of the study after it is completed.

Ethical standards prescribe that respondents should never be coerced to take part in a study; participation should be free, voluntary and fully informed. This means that respondents should not only know that they are taking part in a study, but also that they give their consent to it and, moreover, that this consent is based on correct facts (informed consent). Researchers respond to the requirement for informed consent in three distinct ways.

- *No consent.* In the first instance, there are cases where the researcher does not offer the option of informed consent. This is the case when the respondents are not supposed to know that they are being studied. Field studies and structured observation where the subjects are not aware that they are being studied are two examples where informed consent is not required. Another example is experiments where knowledge of being studied can affect the results. In these cases, conducting research without consent is allowed if alternative methods of studying the chosen topic are not available.
- *Signed informed consent.* For many researchers, signed informed consent is the common practice, and also the rule. This entails a statement containing adequate information about the nature of the research and other aspects of the researcher–respondent relationship, which is to be carefully read by the respondent, who in turn is to return it signed to the researcher.
- *Verbal consent.* The use of verbal consent is also common. Here the respondent is given a statement containing relevant information about the study, the researcher and the funding body, and consent is given verbally and without signing an informed consent form. This is sometimes the only way of

---

Box 1.15

Informed consent statement

The statement should ...

a. Identify the researcher clearly.
b. Introduce the institution that granted the ethics approval and the funding body, where appropriate.
c. Describe the manner in which the respondent was selected, and the nature/number of participants.
d. Explain the nature and purpose of the research in detail.
e. Clarify the benefits of the research for the subject and/or the community.
f. State specifically the nature and extent of the subject's planned involvement and any risks or discomfort associated with the study.
g. Offer a guarantee of anonymity and confidentiality of the data.
h. Make it clear that the respondent can withdraw from the project at any time.
i. Offer alternative research procedures to be used if preferred.
j. Provide details of the person who can be contacted by the subject in case of conflicts or complaints.

obtaining consent – and hence conducting research – because if the researcher insists on signed consent it will make the study impossible. An example of this is a study of homosexuality, where interviews are often conducted in places such as gay bars or other similar gatherings, and where a request to sign such documents is unreasonable.

Privacy, anonymity and confidentiality

- *Privacy*. Ethical standards prescribe that researchers abstain from delving into the private affairs of the subjects. In the first instance, researchers are not expected to ask personal and sensitive questions if they realise that respondents do not feel comfortable about revealing such information. This is particularly important when respondents are part of a captive audience, feeling obliged to take part in the study. Apart from everything else, this can motivate respondents to give false information. More serious is invasion of privacy when the researcher obtains information about the private life of the respondents indirectly (e.g. during covert observation or field studies). In both cases, the researcher is expected to avoid violating privacy, except for methodologically sound and legitimate reasons.
- *Anonymity*. When anonymity is promised, the name of the respondent does not appear on the research instrument or the data. For instance, questionnaires or interview guides will bear no names. Where informed consent forms are available, they are kept apart from the research instruments, so as to make it impossible to link names with data. Attention should also be paid to demographic data which – particularly in small samples – can betray the identity of the respondent.
- *Confidentiality*. When confidentiality is ensured, the researcher may keep names linked to data, but information made public will neither include the name of the respondent, nor make it possible for the information to be linked with a particular respondent.

4.4 The researcher–researcher relationship

Ethical standards also cover cases in which researchers violate standards relating to intellectual property. Inappropriate use of data belonging to other researchers in a report is unethical and constitutes malpractice. Three examples of such malpractice are listed below:

- *Misleading ascription of authorship*. It is not ethical for researchers to list authors in their report without their permission, to attribute work to persons not involved in the research, or to fail to attribute work contributed by others (e.g. students, trainees or associates).
- *Misuse of authority or role*. It is not ethical to misuse authority or criticise the work of others on the basis on polemic, personal bias or collective interests.
- *Plagiarism*. Researchers should abstain from using other people's work without appropriate acknowledgement.

These ethical standards are a part of what one would consider professional standards, and it is most unlikely that writers of any background would resort to such practices. Apart from anything else, the penalties for such malpractice far outweigh any perceived advantages.

4.5 The researcher–animal relationship

Finally, when dealing with animals care must be taken to ensure that they do not suffer during the research process. More specifically, researchers are reminded that:

- Animals should be kept under acceptable conditions and should not be deprived of basic needs for food, water, sleep and companionship.
- There should be good reasons for subjecting animals to research.
- Animals should not be put under stress or pain, or be injured in any way.

These points are some of the issues contained in guidelines or codes of ethics produced by universities and other sources (e.g. Bailey, 1988; Sproull, 1988; Vlahos, 1984). In a number of cases, malpractice constitutes misconduct that incurs quite serious punitive measures.

4.6 Ethical practice

The application of ethical practices in everyday research is not uniform. Although researchers generally accept the need for ethical standards in principle, the extent to which such standards are accepted, supported and practised varies. Apart from anything else, there is a relative discrepancy between the conceptual allegiance to the principles of ethics and its application in everyday research. Considering both theory and practice, one can easily distinguish between three major groups of practices.

- *Full adherence to ethics.* In this group, researchers accept and practice ethical standards fully, where required. Exceptions are only allowed where methodological reasons make adherence to all ethical principles impossible. The use of hidden methods and situations where respondents are not supposed to know that they are being studied are such examples.
- *Relative adherence to ethics.* This group of researchers argue that full adherence to all ethical principles and in all circumstances is neither possible, practical nor desirable. Being fully ethical and expecting all respondents to hand in a signed consent form would make it impossible to study issues such as homosexuality, family violence, criminal practices, tax evasion, or cheating in examinations. Bypassing ethical standards in certain areas of research is justified by the researchers if the study will produce valuable information that will help society, and also those involved in the study, to improve the quality of their life.
- *Questioning ethics.* There are also writers who resent blind adherence to ethics. It is argued here that ethics must be seen in context of the purpose of the research and also critically. Ethics is another component of the research domain and must be seen as such and not as a factor that determines the feasibility of research. Ethics for the purpose of ethics or as a ritual or profession has little value. Research is not conducted for the sake of ethics but for improving the overall quality of life of people, and ethics should make this quest easier and not difficult or even impossible.

Box **1.16**

The ten commandments on ethics

Thou shalt NOT . . .

1. Include in the study or continue working with a person who demonstrates resistance or discomfort relating to the study or to the research topic.
2. Attempt to convince a person to take part in the study, when this person is not in a position to respond adequately to the research question.
3. Fail to explain all relevant aspects of the study to the respondents before they agree to participate.
4. Promise anonymity and confidentiality if it is likely that this promise will not be honoured.
5. Fail to respect the respondents' privacy.
6. Deceive the respondents in any way.
7. Subject respondents to procedures that may entail physical or mental stress.
8. Include in the study techniques whose degree of safety is questionable.
9 Violate professional research standards, for example by fabricating, falsifying, or concealing data.
10. Accept a contracted research project that violates ethical and/or professional standards.

(Vlahos, 1984; Pfeifer, 2000)

4.7 The limits of limitations

Beyond the basic critical stance to ethics, some critics express concerns as to the advantages of ethical research, and stress the possible disadvantages of strictly applying ethical standards. The most common issues raised on this topic are shown below.

- *Authority*. Who determines what is ethical and what is unethical?
- *Limits*. To what extent are ethical standards to be adhered to? Who sets these limits?
- *Access*. Will research be possible if ethical standards are upheld strictly in all contexts? Will members of criminal gangs sign consent forms, for example, particularly when they admit that they have committed crimes?
- *Essence*. Is 'ethics' a universal concept or impressions of ethicality constructed by people?
- *Objectivity*. Are there objective standards of ethicality?
- *Consistency*. Is the setting of absolute ethical standards consistent with relativist standards (which deny the existence of absolute values), bearing in mind that a sizable proportion of researchers work within a relativist paradigm?
- *Gains*. Who benefits from setting ethical standards? The respondent, the community, the science etc. or those setting and enforcing the standards?
- *Nature*. Is the nature of ethics a real research problem, a political problem or a ritualistic exercise that has to be done in its own right?

- *Benefits.* Is it worth adhering to ethics when this may jeopardise the chance of gaining useful knowledge?
- *Role.* What is the role of ethics? To safeguard the research process or to put strait-jackets on research, often for no real reason at all?
- *Dilemma.* What do researchers do who discover during their study that a respondent is about to commit suicide, or murder another person? Will they alert the police or keep this information confidential?
- *Ethics approval.* Is the assessment of research proposals by ethics committees a worthwhile exercise or just academic ritualism? After all, most ethical standards are almost impossible to police!

Box **1.17**

Thinking critically about ethics and ethical standards

- What is ethical? Is 'ethics' a universal phenomenon?
- Who decides what is ethical and what is not?
- Are there objective standards of ethicality?
- Are ethical standards dealing with 'ethics' or with impressions of ethicality?
- Is the setting of absolute ethical standards consistent with relativist standards, which generally deny the existence of absolute values? How could researchers justify ethics in their research, if they work within a relativist paradigm?
- Who benefits from the setting of ethical standards? The respondent, the community, the science etc. or those setting and enforcing the standards?

WHAT DO YOU THINK? What are the 'correct' answers to these questions?

Despite the logic of some points made above, nothing can ever justify disrespect for ethical standards for whatever reason. As many codes of ethics specify, one of the goals of ethical regulations is to educate researchers as to what is right and permissible and what is wrong and undesirable. The points listed above may serve as a basis for further discussion and justification of ethics in a variety of practical areas of research.

5 SEXISM AND SOCIAL RESEARCH

Sexism is usually associated with any institutionalised, stereotypical or prejudicial beliefs and actions that present one gender as inferior, and discriminate against it. Sexism can prejudice the researcher and bias all phases of research; therefore, sexist influences should be kept out of the research. It is therefore important that we have a closer look at sexism.

Sexism is a subtle and very complex issue. Many writers have made a concerted effort to define it clearly and to operationalise this concept accurately and in

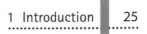

Box **1.18**

Aspects of sexism concerning women

Oppression is expressed in the forms of:

- *Despotism.* Judging males as being by nature most appropriate to lead, dominate and control females.
- *Physicalism.* Considering males strong and competent, and females weak and incompetent.
- *Domesticity.* Assigning women domestic roles, as being by nature most suitable for this.
- *Sexualisation.* Reducing women to sex objects, to serve the needs of males.
- *Ownership.* Believing that men own their wives and may treat them as their property.

Elevation is expressed in the forms of:

- *Protectionism.* Supposing women need to be protected and treated gently and lovingly by men.
- *Generosity.* Believing women need men to care and provide for them, because they are weak and helpless.
- *Emotional bond.* Assuming women must be affectionate and loving, and fulfil the emotional needs of males.
- *Eroticism.* Assumption that women are there to satisfy men's sexual needs, and are therefore loved, adored, deified.
- *Trust.* Supposing that women must be devoted to and trust men for the protection, care and love they receive.

detail. Glick and Fiske (1996), for instance, presented a very impressive account of sexism that distinguished between two forms: hostile and benevolent sexism. In this sense, one could argue that sexism works in a variety of contexts and affects people in a diverse fashion.

In our discussion we employ a similar model containing two opposing elements of sexism, both integral parts of the concept, one reflecting prejudices that put victims (e.g. women) down (oppression), and another than elevates them to something worth protecting and loving, as well as providing for and even dying for (elevation). In both cases, the judgment is based on stereotypes and prejudices associated with gender; hence it reflects sexism and as such must be avoided. Such a practice is evident in practices of a few generations ago concerning women, as shown in Box 1.18.

In technical terms every step of the research process entails procedures that can be constructed and/or presented in a sexist manner. The following are a few examples.

- choosing the research topic
- adopting research paradigm
- appointing the research assistants and other personnel

- attracting key informants and community support
- choosing the sample and the research methods
- negotiating research parameters with and obligations to the sponsor(s)
- addressing the subjects and when asking questions
- debating conflicting views and interests
- writing the report (sexist interpretations, sexist language)
- negotiating the publication of the findings.

What is important for the researcher to know is that sexism should be kept out of all phases of the research. In other words, researchers should ensure that any kind of behaviour that entails stereotypical or prejudicial behaviour associated with gender and discriminating against men or women should be kept out of the research process.

It must be noted that sexism has gradually changed in substance and purpose. After years of regulation and emancipation, its standards have become known to researchers and all those dealing with research. Modern critiques of sexism no longer deal with pointing out gender stereotypes and prejudices but rather with insensitivity to gender discrimination and with resistance to implementing necessary measures that would lead to gender equality.

MAIN POINTS

- Social research has a long history. It has been used extensively for more than 2000 years.
- Research has been diverse and pluralistic, varying in focus, purpose, procedures and theoretical foundations.
- Positivism and positivist research have dominated the research scene for the largest part of the history of the social sciences. Positivistic research is still the most dominant type of research in the social sciences.
- Positivistic research was challenged by a number of schools of thought. The most serious criticisms came from symbolic interactionism, ethnomethodology, phenomenology and philosophical hermeneutics.
- Criticisms came also from Marxism, feminism and other schools of thought.
- There are many types of research. The overarching divisions in social research are qualitative and quantitative research.
- The aims of research vary according to the type of underlying methodology. Positivists aim to explore, explain, evaluate, predict and to develop/test theories; interpretivists to understand human behaviour; and critical theorists to criticise social reality, emancipate, empower and liberate people, and propose solutions to social problems.
- The motives of research are educational, 'magical', personal, institutional, political and tactical.
- Adherence to ethical standards is expected in all forms of research. Ethics relates to professional practice, the researcher–respondent relationship, the researcher–researcher relationship, and the researcher–animal relationship.
- Social research is political; its design and publication of its results entail political elements and/or are guided – directly and/or indirectly – by political interests.
- It is imperative that social research does not include any form of sexist practices.

WHERE TO FROM HERE?

Before you leave this chapter, visit the companion website for the third edition of *Social Research* at http://www.palgrave.com/sociology/sarantakos to review the main concepts introduced in this chapter and to test yourself on the major issues discussed. You will find multiple choice questions, true/false questions, fill-in questions, short answer questions and practical exercises here, as well as a reminder of the aims and main points covered in the chapter, and of course the answers to these questions.

FURTHER READING

Clark, J. (1995) *Ethical and Political Issues in Qualitative Research from a Philosophical Point of View.* Paper presented to the annual meeting of the American Educational Research Association, San Francisco.

Crotty, Michael (Sept–Oct. 1995) *The Ethics of Ethics Committees.* Paper presented at the second Colloquium on Qualitative Research in Adult Education, University of Melbourne.

Goode, E. (1996) 'The Ethics of Deception in Social Research: A Case Study.' *Qualitative Sociology*, 19: 11–33.

Homan, R. (1991) *The Ethics of Social Research.* London: Longman.

Kimmel, A. J. (1996) *Ethical Issues in Behavioural Research: A Survey.* Cambridge: Blackwell.

MacIntyre, A. (1996) *A Short History of Ethics.* London: Macmillan.

Mohr, Marian (1996) *Ethics and Standards for Teacher Research: Drafts and Decisions.* Conference paper delivered at American Educational Research Association Conference, New York.

Platt, J. (1996) *A History of Sociological Research Methods in America. 1920–1960.* Cambridge: Cambridge University Press.

Rosnow, R. L. and Rosenthal. R. (1997) *People Studying People: Artifacts and Ethics in Behavioural Research.* New York: Freeman.

Seiber, J. E. (1992) *Planning Ethically Responsible Research: A Guide for Students and Internal Review Boards.* Beverley Hills: Sage.

2 Varieties of social research

INTRODUCTION

As noted in the previous chapter, social research is complex, diverse and pluralistic. The way research is conducted, its goals and its basic assumptions vary significantly. This diversity appears in well-constructed designs, which ultimately provide the standards and principles of research practice. The two major and most popular forms of research are quantitative and qualitative research. These methodologies guide the work of the vast majority of researchers in the social sciences.

[handwritten note: what is social research.]

In this chapter we shall address these methodologies in detail. In the first instance we shall briefly explore the system of principles that guide social research and generate diversity in its design and practice. Following this we shall present in more detail their structures and processes, their strengths and weaknesses, their usefulness and the degree of flexibility of their boundaries.

1 THE BASES OF THE METHODOLOGICAL DISTINCTION

Diversity in research reflects diversity in the parameters that guide it. More precisely, it means diversity in the ontology and epistemology that underlie the methodology, which in turn guides the research. Simply, methodologies produce different research designs, because they follow in their theoretical structure different ontological and epistemological prescriptions. As shown in Figure 2.1, ontology and epistemology influence methodology, and this guides the choice of research designs and instruments.

The specific way in which ontologies and epistemologies influence the structure and process of social research is explained by the area of study known as the *philosophy of science* (Konegen and Sondergeld, 1985; Machamer, 2002; Nelson, 1990; Poser, 2001). Simply, ontologies inform methodologies as to the nature of reality,

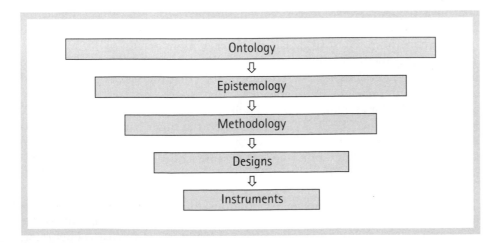

Figure 2.1 The foundations of research

or better as to 'what' social research is supposed to study. Epistemologies on the other hand inform methodologies about the nature of knowledge, or about what counts as a fact and where knowledge is to be sought. Methodologies, finally, following these instructions, prepare 'packages' of appropriate research designs, to be employed by researchers, instructing them as to where to focus their research activity, and how to recognise and extract knowledge (see Table 2.1).

Table 2.1 Theoretical foundations of social research

	Deals with
Ontology	The nature of reality ASKS: What is the nature of reality? Is it objective (out there), constructed, subjective? OR BETTER: What does research focus on?
Epistemology	The nature of knowledge ASKS: How do we know what we know? What is the way in which reality is known to us? OR BETTER: What kind of knowledge is research looking for?
Methodology	The nature of research design and methods ASKS: How do we gain knowledge about the world? OR BETTER: How is research constructed and conducted?
Research	The execution of research designs

Ontological, epistemological and methodological prescriptions of social research are 'packaged' in paradigms which guide everyday research. More specifically, the positivist paradigm, which contains a *realist/objectivist ontology* and an *empiricist epistemology*, guides the strategy of quantitative methodology, and therefore prescribes fixed designs and quantitative methods (see Table 2.2). Similarly, the paradigms of symbolic interactionism and phenomenology, which contain a *constructionist ontology* and an *interpretivist epistemology*, guide the strategies of qualitative methodology and prescribe mostly flexible designs and qualitative methods. We shall explain this later in more detail.

In this sense, methodology occupies a central position in the research process. As noted above, *methodology* is a research strategy that translates ontological and epistemological principles into guidelines that show how research is to be conducted (see, for example, Cook and Fonow, 1990: 72; Harding, 1987a: 2; B. Krüger, 1983; Lather, 1992: 87). Methods, on the other hand are instruments employed in the collection and analysis of data. Finally, ontological, epistemological and methodological principles of the same nature are organised into paradigms, which together with methodologies constitute the domain within which research is conducted.

Briefly, a *paradigm* is a set of propositions that explain how the world is perceived; it contains a worldview, a way of breaking down the complexity of the real world, telling researchers and social scientists in general 'what is important, what is legitimate, what is reasonable' (Kuhn, 1970; Guba, 1990; Patton, 1990:

Table 2.2 Paradigms: theoretical construction of research

	Positivism	Symbolic Interactionism; Phenomenology; Feminism; etc.
Ontology:	Realism/Objectivism	Constructionism
Epistemology:	Empiricism	Interpretivism
Methodology:	Quantitative	Qualitative
Research:	Fixed design	Fixed/flexible design

37). It is a philosophical stance that informs the methodology, provides the arena in which the logic and structure of research are embedded, and guides the process of research (Farber, 2001). Examples of such paradigms are positivism, symbolic interactionism, ethnomethodology and phenomenology.

In general, methodologies are closer to research practice than paradigms; it is therefore understandable that researchers refer to methodologies rather than paradigms when describing their work. Hence, it is more common that researchers report conducting 'quantitative' than 'positivist' research. Reference to the ontological and epistemological nature of a research project is the exception rather than the rule.

Before we continue, it must be noted that there are other types and perceptions of research which do not fit fully within the parameters of qualitative and quantitative methodologies. Structuralism and postmodernism are two examples of how research departs from the two models described above. *Methodological anarchism* (see Feyerabend, 1976, 1981, 1989) is another example. The followers of this paradigm argue that there is no truth in statements about the nature of reality; hence, there are no valid methodological rules as to how research is to be conducted; hence 'anything goes'. Still, the majority of researchers conduct their studies within either a quantitative or a qualitative methodology, or both. These methodologies provide the parameters for a systematic and valid research design, and will be introduced next.

2 QUANTITATIVE METHODOLOGY

2.1 Theoretical background of quantitative research

The theoretical underpinnings of quantitative methodology are those of positivism, as guided by a realist (see Box 2.1) and objectivist (see Box 2.2) ontology and an empiricist epistemology (see Box 2.3). This results in quantitative methodology being an empiricist methodology, and its methods empirical methods. Its main research parameters are presented below.

■ *Perception of reality.* It is characteristic of quantitative methodology that it perceives reality to be objective, simple and fixed. Reality consists of sense

---

Box **2.1**

What is realism?

Realism is the doctrine that ...

■ Universals have an objective or absolute existence.
■ Matter, as the object of perception, has real existence and is neither reducible to a universal mind or spirit, nor dependent on a perceiving agent.
■ The world has a reality that transcends the mind's analytical capacity, and that propositions are to be assessed in terms of their truth to reality.
■ Reality exists independent from our consciousness and experience.
■ The world exists independent from people and their perception, BUT can be made an object of human perception.

(Hügli and Lübcke, 1997: 185)

---

impressions, that is, only of what is perceived through the senses; furthermore, there is one reality in nature, and only one truth. Reality is independent of human consciousness and rests on order, which is governed by strict, natural and unchangeable laws; knowledge of these laws can help to predict and control the outcomes of human action. All members of society define reality in the same way because objects generate the same meanings and people see and name them in the same way.

■ *Perception of human beings*. Human beings are rational individuals who are governed by social laws; their behaviour is learned through observation and governed by external causes that produce consistent results (the same causes produce the same consequences). Human beings are shaped by their social world just as the physical world is governed by fixed laws; they are subject to fixed patterns of life that are empirically observable (the thesis of *nomological thinking*). There is no free will. The world is, however, not deterministic; causes produce effects under certain conditions, and predictions can be controlled by the occurrence of such conditions.

■ *The nature of social science*. Here, science, the tool of knowledge extraction
   – is based on strict rules and procedures, and is fundamentally different from speculation, reason and common sense

---

Box **2.2**

Features of objectivism?

■ Reality and truth exist objectively and can be discovered and adequately measured.
■ Reality is 'out there', has an identity of its own, and exists apart from our awareness.
■ Reality is single, solid and uniform: it generates the same meanings for all actors.
■ Reality is 'found' by the researcher and brought to awareness and to social light.
■ Observance of objective detachment and value neutrality is desirable.

- is deductive, proceeding from the general/abstract to the specific/concrete
- is nomothetic; that is, it is based on universal causal laws, which influence the course of social events and relationships
- relies on knowledge gained through the sense experiences; other sources of knowledge are unreliable. Observation and experience offer the basis of knowledge. The task of the scientist/researcher is to discover the scientific laws that explain human behaviour using quantitative methods, similar to those of natural sciences.

Box **2.3**

What is empiricism?

Empiricism goes back to the writings of the seventeenth and eighteenth centuries, and is directly associated with the work of Francis Bacon (1651–1626), John Locke (1632–1704) and David Hume (1711–1776). Empiricism supports the view that knowledge comes through experience mediated through the senses, and that insight can only be achieved through pure experiences. Empiricism assigns a high value to experience and gives primacy to facts. Hence, observation and experience offer the basis of knowledge. For Hume, opinions are reflections of our impressions of reality. In a more radical form (logical empiricism), empiricism argues that only things that can be verified empirically exist. What cannot be verified does not exist; truths that are not based on experience are meaningless.

■ *The purpose of social research.* The quantitative researcher perceives social research in an instrumental way; research is a tool for studying social events and learning about them and their interconnections so that general causal laws can be discovered, explained and documented. Knowledge of events and social laws allows society to control events and to predict their occurrence and outcomes.

Box **2.4**

Central criteria of quantitative research

1. Use of empirical methods.
2. Objectivity.
3. Value neutrality.
4. Clarity in design and procedure.
5. Distance between researcher and subjects of research.
6. Measurement and quantification.
7. Accuracy and precision.
8. Validity and reliability.
9. Replicability.
10. Representativeness and generalisation.
11. Strict reliance on methods and their results.
12. Rigorous, disciplined, systematic and reality-bound procedure.
13. Strict research design constructed before research begins.
14. Ethical considerations.

2.2 Positivism

Positivism is often taken to be identical to quantitative methodology because it contains the ontological and epistemological prescriptions that show how this methodology should conduct research. Quantitative research is equally often taken to be identical to positivist research for the same reasons. The nature of this paradigm has already been explained in detail and requires no further discussion. Its elements are reflected in the ontological and epistemological descriptions, as well as in the presentation of the theoretical background of quantitative methodology. A brief summary of the main features of positivism is presented in Box 2.5.

Box **2.5**

The ten central principles of positivism

1.   *Objectivism.* Adheres to the notion of objective reality and absolute truths.
2.   *Empiricism.* Claims that knowledge comes through sense experience.
3.   *Quantitativism.* Stresses the value of accuracy, precision and measurement.
4.   *Objectivity.* Discourages subjectivity in the process of social research.
5.   *Value-neutrality.* Maintains that facts should be kept apart from values.
6.   *Anti-rationalism.* Rejects the notion that knowledge comes from reason.
7.   *Universality of science.* Asserts that the methods of the physical sciences are applicable also in the social sciences.
8.   *Deduction/induction.* Employs a design based on deduction and produces inductive generalisations.
9.   *Determinism.* The world is deterministic, following strict causal laws, and if these laws are discovered social life can be predicted and controlled.
10. *Design.* Employs a strict design planned and constructed prior to the commencement of the research

---

2.3 Critique of quantitative methodology

Concerns with quantitative methodology (QM) reflect concerns with the underlying positivist paradigm; hence a critique of the qualitative methodology is a critique of positivism. Critics came from within and from outside this school of thought (e.g. Guba and Lincoln, 1994: 106–7), and raised questions about deep and fundamental aspects of positivism in general and QM in particular. The most important points can be summarised as follows:

- *Reality.* QM defines reality as objective, which is wrong; reality is not objective but interpreted social action.
- *Meanings.* In QM, quantitative measurement is given excessive importance, despite the fact that it often results in 'meanings' that are closer to the beliefs of the researchers than to those embedded in reality.
- *Hypotheses.* Hypotheses formed before the research commences bias the course of the study and restrict research options, forcing upon the respondents opinions or intentions that they might otherwise have not expressed.
- *Experience.* QM restricts experience (a) by directing research to what is

perceived by the senses, and (b) by employing only standardised tools based on quantifiable data.

- *Appearance and essence.* QM fails to distinguish between the appearance and essence of social events; it neglects the essence of life, studies 'appearance' and assumes that appearance is reality.
- *Status quo.* QM employs a theoretical perspective and a type of research that supports the status quo and existing power structures.
- *Methods.* In QM, methods are given a central position, to the extent that they dictate the parameters of research. Often, instead of trying to adjust methods to reality, reality is adjusted to methods. As a result, research is limited only to what can be approached through the existing methods. What cannot be approached through quantitative methods is deemed insignificant, is not considered worth studying, and is not studied.
- *Measurement.* QM perceives reality as a sum of measured or measurable attributes; its primary purpose is to quantify and measure social events, a characteristic often referred to as *quantaphrenia*! This introduces a peculiar and biased perception of the world.
- *The researcher.* QM neutralises the researchers and their influence on the researched, to the extent that they become 'disembodied abstractions', depersonalised (Collins, 1992. 183) and alienated from the world they are supposed to study. This is accomplished through hiding their identity, legitimating a sense of unconnectedness, bracketing out the personal experiences and views of the researcher as well as through refinement and standardisation of methods and techniques. The researcher becomes a 'technician' who serves technocratic goals. In addition, respondents are turned into 'units' or 'objects' and are treated as such. Finally, the researcher is assigned power and control over the respondent.
- *Physicalism.* QM takes the physical sciences as a model (often referred to as *methodolatry* or *physics envy*) and applies their methods in the field of social sciences, treating people as mere natural elements, and seeking the same regularity in social action as in natural phenomena. This is not an acceptable practice.
- *Objectivity.* Reliance on objectivity is unwarranted. Objectivity is neither possible, necessary, nor useful. The perceptions and interpretations of the researcher penetrate the research process in many ways; being subjective offers many advantages in social research, and objectivity can only lead to a technocratic and bureaucratic dehumanisation (Brieschke, 1992: 174).
- *Research procedure.* QM employs a strict research design that determines what is relevant and how it will be studied, and what is meaningful and required, even before the study begins. This restricts the options of the research process, inhibits the initiative and motivation of the researcher, limits the effectiveness of research, and produces artificial data that do not reflect reality as a whole.
- *Context.* QM operates in a mode that separates the object from its context. The personal attributes of respondents become variables, and intensity of feelings and attitudes become numbers and computer data. Such procedures change the structure and process of social life and convert the world into an artificial laboratory.

■ *Gender*. Quantitative research has a gendered character based on the inherent trend to separate the world into fundamental dichotomies, one of which is the masculine versus feminine division. This separation is strengthened by the fact that men are presented as the experts, the 'knowing' subjects, while women are seen as the 'known' (inferior) objects. This ignores and downgrades women, and hence, fails to address reality fully and effectively.

These criticisms are well justified and address the essential elements of the paradigm as seen from the other side of the fence, mainly from the side of qualitative research. Nevertheless, there are those who defend the validity and significance of positivism as a research paradigm (Schrag, 1992). It is argued, for instance, that the positivist basis of quantitative research is still strong although weakening with time, particularly as new theories have been developed or old ones adopted in social sciences from the area of philosophy or psychology. The majority of social scientists still employ a quantitative (positivistic) methodology; as Schrag (1992: 6) put it, 'despite the attacks levelled against it, the positivist paradigm is hard to avoid'.

Box **2.6**

Is the interest in quantitative research really declining?

Here is how prestigious organisations perceive research (emphasis added):

■ 'Research refers to *empirical data collection* in the pursuit of *scientific endeavour* usually in the form of an experiment, survey or evaluation' (Australian Psychological Society, *Code of Ethics*).
■ 'Sociologists work to develop a reliable and valid body of *scientific knowledge* based on research' (International Sociological Association, *Code of Ethics*, Preamble).
■ '*As scientists*, sociologists are expected to cooperate locally and transnationally on the basis of *scientific correctness* alone, without discrimination' (International Sociological Association, *Code of Ethics*).
■ 'Sociologists should strive to maintain *objectivity* and integrity in the conduct of sociological research and practice' (American Sociological Association, *Code of Ethics*, I. A.).

What do these references tell you
about the status of quantitative research?

---

3   QUALITATIVE METHODOLOGY

Unlike quantitative methodology, qualitative methodology is diverse, pluralistic and in some cases even ridden with internal contradictions (Jacob, 1987, 1988). This is due to the fact that it contains elements from many different schools of thought, which are integrated within this research model. This justifies the belief expressed by some writers that there are not one but many qualitative methodologies, and that they cover almost everything that is not quantitative; or even that there is no common denominator in the various qualitative directions in social research (Maindok, 1996: 94). Nevertheless, the central principles of this methodology are taken from a *relativist orientation*, a *constructivist ontology* and an *interpretivist epistemology.* In the following, the most common and important aspects of qualitative methodology will be introduced.

3.1 Theoretical foundations of qualitative methodology

Constructionism

Constructionism focuses on the firm belief that there is in practice neither objective reality nor objective truth. On the contrary, reality is constructed. Although physical reality exists, it is not accessible to human endeavour. Constructionism is about realities and relationships (Gergen, 1994, 1999). Trees, rivers, forests and mountains may exist outside people's consciousness but have no meaning before they are addressed by people. Their meaning is not fixed, ready to be discovered – as objectivists propose – but emerges out of people's interaction with the world. Meanings do not exist before a mind engages them. There is no meaning without mind (Cooper, 1998: 8–9).

Constructing reality means making accounts of the world around us and gaining impressions based on culturally defined and historically situated interpretations and personal experiences. This means that what people perceive as reality is not 'the reality', but what they constructed through experiences and interpretations (Lamnek, 1995; Lueger, 2000: 21–38; Luhman, 1997). In this sense, new structures are virtual structures because they do not realise real social phenomena but represent options of expressions of phenomena (Lueger, 2000: 24). They are latent and symbolic. Finally, in the social world there is no single structure but multiple structures interwoven with each other.

It follows that the construction of reality is an active process of creating a world. The reality people experience in everyday life is a *constructed* reality – their reality – based on interpretation. The presence of an objective reality is not disputed here; objective reality exists but it is not accessible. Hence, impressions

Box **2.7**

Basic assumptions of constructionism

- There is no objective reality; the physical world exists but is not accessible to human endeavour.
- There are no absolute truths.
- Knowledge does not come through the senses alone.
- Research focuses on the construction of meanings.
- Meanings are not fixed but emerge out of people's interaction with the world.
- Meanings do not exist before a mind engages them.
- The world is constructed by the people who live in it.

Box **2.8**

The many faces of reality

- Nature can and will show us another 'face', other laws or categories, and other forms of order, if we approach it at a higher degree of detail.
- The laws of nature and the validity of our observation will often be disintegrated (rejected, deconstructed) when our focus is set at a higher level of competence.
- Order can grow out of disorder if we focus away from details.
- Consideration of details complicates the human understanding of natural phenomena.
- The laws of nature always fall apart as soon as inquiry progresses to higher levels of detail.
- Every law that we might accept at a certain level will in the end be shaken when our knowledge of the details is improved.

(Rescher, 2002: 43–51)

of reality gained by researchers who listen to respondents talking about their lives are constructions of the constructed reality of the respondents; they are impressions of a reconstructed reality.

For instance, an accident at the street corner is an objective reality, but it is not accessible to researchers. The impressions of witnesses are *constructions* of what they thought happened. The information gathered by reporters who interviewed these witnesses is a *reconstruction of reality*, and certainly not 'objective' reality. This allows two major observations. Firstly, there is no single reality but three levels of reality; and secondly, reality does not exist in a frozen state; it is marked by a process-nature, recursivity and reflexivity. Given also that interpretations vary from one person to another, constructed realities are not uniform. Hence there are many forms of constructed realities and they therefore cannot be thought of as the only source of knowledge about reality. They are only variants of reality.

Going a step deeper into this process we can say that interpretation and (re)construction allow the identification of meanings assigned to objects, and this leads to a structuration of the field. Meanings are employed in the various contexts following cultural instructions rather than through the labels which,

Box **2.9**

Popular facets of constructionism

- Two people walked through a rose garden. One saw the roses, the other the thorns.
- Two people looked out through the window. One saw stars, the other saw mud.
- 'All that we see and seem is but a dream within a dream' (Edgar Allen Poe).
- 'If people define situations as real, they are real in their consequences' (Thomas's Theorem).

according to objectivists, are attached to objects. Identification of meanings reduces the degree of complexity by replacing this complexity with a new complexity that is easier to explore and understand.

Central to reality construction is 'communication', which is more than a means of exchanging information. Communication is a selective process of producing meaning in social contexts. This process entails three components: (a) the choice of a piece of information; (b) the choice of the form of information that will be shared; and finally (c) the choice of understanding of this information. Messages are expected to make the content clearly understandable, and to address the point fully. Important in this process of enabling the production of meanings, and of facilitating structuration and communication is, finally, the contextual embedding of objects: objects are meaningful and can be understood only within their context (Lueger, 2000).

Individual and collective generation of meanings

The extent to which people create meanings in interaction with objects varies. At the one end of the continuum, subjects assign such meanings each time they come across a subject; a notion criticised by many writers from within and outside the constructionist domain. More popular is the notion that the assignment of meanings is assisted by cultural mechanisms such as socialisation where people learn to recognise meanings in subjects. Here the construction of meanings is based on culturally defined and historically situated interpretations and personal experiences.

This is most evident in social constructionism. Although it acknowledges the strong contribution of subjects to the construction of meanings, it stresses also the fact that culture and society play an important role in constructing meanings through the process of socialisation. Put simply, subjects do not assign new names and give no new meanings to objects; meanings are generated collectively, are readily available, already constructed by and conveyed through the culture, and are shared and socially constructed, and also sustained and reconstructed through interaction.

The process of socialisation has the task of conveying such meanings and of teaching people where, under what conditions and how to assign them. Such skills and practices create an ability to face the world intelligently and uniformly, and create meanings according to learned standards and principles, assign such meaning to subjects and so make sense of the world. Hence, people learn to recognise objects as trees, cars, stars or forests. However, the construction of meanings is more complex than it appears, and certainly not without consequences, as shown in Box 2.10.

Interpretivism

The processes of construction and reconstruction are laden with personal inputs. Life in a social world makes it necessary for objectivity and rationality to become rather relative concepts. The key process that facilitates construction and reconstruction is *interpretation*. This involves reflective assessment of the reconstructed impressions of the world, and integration of action processes in a general context, which will constitute a new unit.

Box **2.10**

Collective generation of meanings

Although the collective generation of meanings through socialisation and through the media is generally highly valued, this process has been criticised by a number of writers. The main point made is that this process sets people's minds into pre-existing structures and inherited meanings, thus significantly restricting their options and chances in life. Simply, cultures and symbols, created and transmitted from generation to generation, or imposed upon them by their contemporaries, are thought to alienate people from the world they created, and ultimately imprison them in these structures. The media add to this problem by creating images of the world that are fed to the people without their consent or even knowledge, and so control their life. It is argued that the collective generation of meanings subjects people to hegemonic interests.

Interpretivism, as the framework within which qualitative research is conducted, 'looks for culturally derived and historically situated interpretations of the social life-world' (Crotty, 1998: 67). It has its roots in the work of Max Weber (1864–1920), which was concerned with *Verstehen* (understanding) of social life, of Wilhelm Dilthey (1833–1911) and of the Neo-Kantian philosophers Wilhelm Windelband (1848–1915) and Heinrich Rickert (1863–1936). *Verstehen* implies an interpretive stance and is contrasted to *Erklären* (explaining), which is taken to focus on causality. Within this domain, 'interpretive' means to emphasise the production of meanings and to learn the special views of actors, in other words, the local meanings (Pfeifer, 2000).

Verstehen relates to the views, opinions and perceptions of people as they are experienced and expressed in every day life. Here the qualitative researcher is interested in the subjective meaning, namely the way in which people make sense of their world, and in which they assign meanings to it. The researcher may be interested in what divorce means to children, or in what it means to be a woman working in a job traditionally held by men. Methods commonly used in this context are intensive or narrative interviews and content analysis. An emphasis on the subjective meaning is evident in research based on symbolic interactionism and phenomenology.

The qualitative researcher often goes beyond identifying the subjective meaning and explores the processes of constructing social situations and everyday structures that guide and explain personal views and opinions, and focuses on *the mode of production of social structures*. The researcher is interested here in the factors and conditions, cultural prescriptions and the social order in general that generate certain situations and social structures, for instance, the manner in which structures that oppressed women were created, imposed and maintained. An emphasis on this type of research is evident in paradigms such as ethnomethodology and constructionism

Some concerns. The proposition that subjects construct meanings every time they come across objects, and the failure to acknowledge the contribution of social and cultural mechanisms to this process, have led critics to doubt the credibility of constructionism. Apart from this, the point is made that the accuracy and correctness of people's constructions and of their representativeness cannot be tested (Schuetz, 1971: 5). Finally, overemphasis on subjective impressions seems to be as dangerous and counterproductive as overemphasis on objectivism. Interpretivism is not seen as a fool-proof approach to reality; Blaikie (1993: 110–12; 2000) stresses some major criticisms of this epistemology, as shown in Box 2.11.

Box 2.11

Is interpretivism fool-proof?

- When interpretivists attempt to identify the meaningful nature of social life, they often employ a method which is similar to that employed by positivists.
- Adherence to the central elements of interpretivist inquiry (intention, reason, motives) is quite difficult to police; reflective monitoring is not always present.
- It is not possible to know whether researchers gain a true account of the respondent's meanings. Accounts of researcher and respondents may vary and be competing.
- Interpretivism fails to acknowledge the role of institutional structures, particularly division of interest and relations of power.
- Interpretivism cannot address the factors and conditions that lead to meanings and interpretations, actions, rules, beliefs and the like.
- Interpretivism is conservative in that it does not take into account structures of conflicts and hence the possible sources of change.

3.2 Central elements of qualitative research

The brief reference to the main features of the theoretical background of qualitative research highlights the nature of the research focus of this methodology as well as the way knowledge is constructed. In summary, and contrasting qualitative research with quantitative research, the following points are most relevant.

- *Perception of reality.* Qualitative researchers consider reality to be subjective, constructed, multiple, and diverse. Reality is experienced internally (not through the senses), and resides in the minds of the people who construct it; hence each person constructs his/her own reality, which is therefore subjective. Following this, there are as many realities as there are people, and since people perceive the world in different ways, their realities are different.
- *Perception of human beings.* In qualitative research, human beings occupy a central position; they create the meaning systems of events and with these they construct reality. They are not non-participant observers but active creators of their world. For most writers on the subject, there are no general laws of a restrictive nature. In spite of this, patterns and regularities of behaviour emerge as a result of social conventions, established through interaction.

It is the task of researchers to search for the systems of meanings that actors use to make sense of their world.

■ *The nature of science.* In this context, science, as a means of extracting knowledge, is assigned a secondary role. Qualitative researchers assert that:
  – The basis for explaining and understanding people's life is not 'science', as in quantitative research, but common sense; only this way does it become possible to catch the meanings people use to make sense of their lives.
  – The approach employed is inductive, proceeding from the specific to the general and from the concrete to the abstract
  – Science is not nomothetic but ideographic; it presents reality symbolically in a descriptive form.
  – Knowledge is not derived through sense experiences only; understanding meanings and interpretations is more important.
  – Science is not value free; value neutrality is neither necessary nor possible.

■ *The purpose of social research.* In qualitative research, social inquiry has the purpose of helping the investigators to interpret and understand, first, the actors' reasons for social action, second, the way they construct their lives and the meanings they attach to them, and third, the social context of social action. What is important here is not observable social actions but rather the subjective meaning of such actions. The main characteristics of the two methodologies that dominate the social sciences are summarised in Table 2.3.

Table 2.3 The two methodologies: a comparison

Criterion	Quantitative methodology	Qualitative methodology
Reality is	objective, 'out there', to be 'found' perceived through the senses perceived uniformly by all governed by universal laws based on integration	subjective, in people's mind perceived not through senses only diverse; perceived differently created, constructed; not found interpreted differently by people
Human beings are	rational individuals obeying external laws without free will	creators of their world making sense of their world not restricted by external laws creating systems of meanings
Science is	based on strict rules & procedures deductive relying on sense impressions objective and value free	based on common sense & reason inductive relying on interpretations subjective and not value free
Social research	employs quantitative methods aims to explain social life aims to predict the course of events aims to discover social regularities	employs qualitative methods aims to interpret social life aims to understand social life aims to discover people's meanings

3.3 Qualitative paradigms

As noted earlier, qualitative methodology is diverse, and this is evident not only in the ways in which research is conducted but also in the variety of paradigms that are associated with this research strategy. Given that paradigms contain ontological and epistemological principles, and since these principles have already been discussed, we shall focus, very briefly, on only two well-known and popular qualitative paradigms. These are symbolic interactionism and phenomenology.

Symbolic interactionism

Symbolic interactionism was developed by George Herbert Mead, from the Chicago School, whose work was published posthumously by Blumer (1969, 1973, 1979a, 1979b). The main tenets of this theory, which proved useful to symbolic interactionists, are summarised below.

- Social life is formed, maintained and changed by the basic meaning attached to it by interacting people who respond to each other on the basis of meanings they assign to their world. Social life and objects become significant when they are assigned meanings.
- Social life is expressed through symbols. Language is the most important symbolic system.
- The purpose of social research is to study the structure, functions and meaning of symbolic systems.
- The most appropriate method of social research is the *naturalistic* method, which incorporates two major procedures: *exploration* and *inspection* (Blumer, 1969; Vlahos, 1984; Wallace and Wolf, 1986). Exploration studies new areas, looks for details and offers a clear understanding of the research question. Any method is useful here. Inspection, on the other hand, is an analytical method and contains a more intensive and more

---

Box **2.12**

Elements of symbolic interactionism

- 'Human beings act towards things on the basis of the meanings that these things have for them.'
- 'The meanings of such things is derived from, and arises out of, the social interaction that one has with one's fellows.'
- 'These meanings are handled in, and modified through, an interpretive process used by the person in dealing with the things he encounters.'
- 'The actor selects, checks, suspends, regroups, and transforms the meanings in light of the situation, in which he is placed at the direction of his action.'
- 'Meanings are used and revised as instruments for the guidance and formation of the action.'

(Blumer, 1969: 2, 5)

concentrated testing. (Blumer (1969) called this type of approach *sympathetic introspection*.)

■ Data and interpretations depend on context and process and must be steadily verified and, when necessary, corrected.
■ Meanings are established in and through social interaction. They are learned through interaction and not determined otherwise.
■ Meanings are employed, managed and changed through interaction.

The relevance of this theoretical paradigm for qualitative methodology is more than obvious (Denzin, 2000). Most of the principles of this methodology are derived from symbolic interactionism.

Phenomenology

Phenomenology has a long history (Husserl, 1950). Its contribution to qualitative methodology is evident in a number of aspects of its research theory and practice, a number of which share elements of symbolic interactionism. In a brief, perhaps oversimplified, point form, the central contributions of phenomenology to qualitative research are shown below.

■ There is an objective world.
■ Reality is not divided into objects and subjects.
■ The objective world is experienced and becomes real only through consciousness, and not through the senses.
■ Becoming conscious entails reaching out to reality and knowing it; this is called *intentionality*.
■ Social norms reach people without them being aware of it; they guide them about how to see and interpret the world, and people follow them without question. This is called *natural attitude*.
■ Neutralising this natural attitude can be facilitated through *bracketing*: through disconnecting or setting aside preconceptions, ignoring cultural prescriptions, symbolic patterns and meanings, using intuition, universal meanings and structures, and going back to the things themselves.
■ Husserl called the suspension of previously set rules and judgments *epoche*.

Phenomenology not only provides important elements of the constructionist nature of qualitative methodology, but also shows how emancipation and liberation from oppressive structures can be achieved.

3.4 Features of qualitative research

The main features of qualitative research have already been noted during the presentation of the theoretical foundations of this research model as well as when its ontological and epistemological foundations were introduced. These features also represent the central strengths of this research model and its advantages over other forms of inquiry. Briefly, and in point form, the features referred to by most writers on the subject (e.g. Crabtree and Miller, 1992; Flick, Kardorff and Steinke, 2000: 24; Lamnek, 1993; Patton, 1990; J. K. Smith, 1990, 1992), can be presented as shown below.

Qualitative research is:

- *Naturalistic.* It is a research process undertaken in a natural setting (it is field focused).
- *Dynamic.* It focuses on processes and structural characteristics of settings, and tries to capture reality in interaction through intense contact in the field.
- *Subject-centred.* It describes life-worlds 'from inside out', from the view of the subjects.
- *Informative and detailed.* It offers 'thick' descriptions, and allows entry to subjective social constructions of people; it presents the information gathered verbally in a detailed and complete form, not in numbers or formulae (no statistical analysis).
- *Normative.* It employs a value-laden inquiry.
- *Constructionist.* It assumes that the social world is always a human creation, not a discovery.
- *Context-sensitive.* It focuses on contextuality, with the aim of gaining an impression of the context, its logic, its arrangements, its explicit/implicit rules.
- *Reflexive.* It values the reflexivity – the self-awareness – of the researcher.
- *Open.* It stresses the principle of openness; also, it enters the field with no preconceived ideas or pre-structured models and patterns. There is no strict design; no hypotheses; no limits in its focus, scope or operation.
- *Flexible.* Design, methods and processes are open to change.
- *Empathetic.* It aims to understand people, not to measure them.
- *Communicative.* It focuses on communication which is considered a selective process of meaning production in social contexts. Qualitative research operates within communication, of which it is a part.
- *Subjective.* It values subjectivity and the personal commitment of the researcher; it is against objectivity.
- *Interpretivist.* It values the reflective assessment of the reconstructed impressions of the world.
- *Holistic.* It focuses on the whole study object in its entirety.
- *Inductive.* It proceeds from the specific data to general categories and theories.
- *Small-scale.* It studies a small number of people.

A brief analysis of the features of qualitative research reveals that they represent the opposite of quantitative research. Simply, qualitative research is what quantitative research is not, and is not meant to be. A similar observation can be made of quantitative research; it is that what qualitative research is not, and is not meant to be.

3.5 Critique of qualitative research

As noted above, the main features of qualitative research also represent its central strengths and advantages over other models of inquiry. Nevertheless, qualitative research also has its weaknesses. Some of the most common criticisms relate to the following issues (Pfeifer, 2000; Benini, 2000):

- *Efficacy.* Qualitative research is unable to study relationships between variables with the degree of accuracy that is required to establish social trends or to inform social policies.

- *Representativeness.* Qualitative research is based on small samples and hence does not produce representative results.
- *Generalisability.* Since qualitative studies are not representative, their findings cannot be generalised.
- *Objectivity.* The methodological approach does not ensure objectivity, and hence the quality of the findings is questionable.
- *Validity and reliability.* The research structure and procedure do not ensure the validity and reliability of methods.
- *Interpretations.* There is no way of assuring that the researcher fully and correctly captures the true meanings and interpretations of the respondents.
- *Comparability.* Qualitative studies do not produce data that allow comparisons.
- *Replicability.* Given the individualist and subjectivist nature of this research model, replicability of studies is not possible.
- *Ethics.* The nature of research that allows close contact with respondents can lead to ethical problems.
- *Quality of data.* Often, the nature of data collection leads to the production of large amounts of useless information.
- *Anything goes.* The lack of strict research procedures and the high level of subjectivity and relativism give the impression that 'anything goes in this research'.
- *Time.* Qualitative inquiry is very time consuming.
- *Costs.* Qualitative research is relatively very expensive.

The common response to these criticisms is that, first, these points are characteristic to the nature of this research and should be seen in their context as strengths and not as weaknesses; and second, many of these aspects (representativeness, validity, reliability etc.) are different and not inferior. For instance, validity and reliability are observed in qualitative research, but in a way that is different from (not inferior to) those employed in quantitative research (see Chapter 4).

Box **2.13**

The nature of quantitative and qualitative research

Quantitative research	*Qualitative research*
Sets researchers apart from reality	Sets researchers close to reality
Studies reality from the outside	Studies reality from the inside
Uses closed methods of data collection	Uses open methods of data collection
Employs a fixed research design	Employs a flexible research design
Captures a still picture of the world	Captures the world in action
Employs scientific/statistical methods	Employs naturalistic methods
Analyses data only after collection	Analyses data during and after collection
Chooses methods before the study	Chooses methods before/during the study
Produces most useful quantitative data	Produces most useful qualitative data

(See Flick et al., 1991; Lamnek, 1993; Miles and Huberman, 1994)

4 QUALITATIVE AND QUANTITATIVE RESEARCH IN COMPARISON

4.1 Major differences between the methodologies

The discussion above demonstrates very clearly that quantitative and qualitative research models rest on different assumptions about the world and therefore use different approaches to social reality. They are two different ways of addressing different aspects of reality, and both offer legitimate impressions of their study object (See Box 2.13). A more detailed contrast of the two types of research is presented in Table 2.4.

Table 2.4 Perceived differences between quantitative and qualitative methodology

Feature	Quantitative methodology	Qualitative methodology
Nature of reality	Objective; simple; single; tangible sense impressions	Subjective; problematic; holistic; a social construct
Causes and effects	Nomological thinking; cause-effect linkages	Non-deterministic; mutual shaping; no cause-effect linkages
The role of values	Value neutral; value-free inquiry	Normativism; value-bound inquiry
Natural and social sciences	Deductive; model of natural sciences; nomothetic; based on strict rules	Inductive; rejection of the natural sciences model; ideographic; no strict rules: interpretations
Methods	Quantitative, mathematical; extensive use of statistics	Qualitative, with less emphasis on statistics; verbal and qualitative analysis
Researcher's role	Passive; distant from the subject: dualism	Active; equal; both parties are interactive and inseparable
Generalisations	Inductive generalisations; nomothetic statements	Analytic or conceptual generalisations; time-and-context specific

4.2 Methodological symbiosis or incompatibility?

These differences have been interpreted in a variety of ways and have impacted not only on the perceived value of the methodologies but also on the extent of their relevance and applicability. The main question here is whether these methodologies are two incompatible strategies or whether they can be employed together to address the same research question. The most important answers to these questions are shown below (see Hammersley, 1996; Morgan, 1998b).

1. *Diversity and incompatibility.* One very common position to the relationship between quantitative and qualitative methodologies is that they are not only

different but also incompatible paradigms. Methodologies are reflections of the perception of reality and of knowledge acquisition, and hence they are as incompatible as the ontological and epistemological principles that guide them. It is argued that one cannot and should not try to interchange them and their measures. Either we accept and respect the presence and value of ontological and epistemological imperatives that generate the need for methodologies and accept their identity and idiosyncrasy, or we reject them, and with this disregard the methodologies.

The incompatibility of the two basic methodologies has been presented in many contexts, and this has been demonstrated openly in the ongoing mutual criticism of these methodologies, with researchers putting down the methodology of the other camp, which they considered inferior and inefficient.

2. *Diversity but compatibility.* A different position to the relationship between the two methodologies is taken by another group of researchers, who see in principle no difficulties in integrating them into the same project. They acknowledge the differences between the methodologies but recognise their compatibility, which they accept and value, and are content that such a practice is possible, for example, in paradigm triangulation. The question here is not whether these two methodologies can work together for the same purpose within the same context but rather how and to what extent they can be integrated. In practice such a combination can take various forms (Hammersley, 1996). Examples are shown below.

    a. *Successive paradigm triangulation.* This position entails the notion that qualitative and quantitative methodology can be employed together in the same project in succession. For instance, the qualitative methodology is used first and then the quantitative methodology, or vice versa. This is the most common combination of methodologies, and one employed for a long time, even when researchers were as conscious of the methodology question as they currently are. This is the case, for instance, when the researcher conducts a qualitative preliminary study in order to establish some basic parameters (definitions, hypotheses, indicators etc.) that are required to conduct the quantitative study. Similarly, researchers may conduct a quantitative study in order to establish the demographic and/or social context, within which the in-depth qualitative study can be conducted. An example of the later is the author's (1987) two-step study on aging. In this study, a large sample of old people was surveyed to gain demographic and quantitative information about their lives. Following this, a number of typical cases were subjected to a qualitative in-depth study, to ascertain their personal experiences, meanings and interpretations

    b. *Concurrent paradigm triangulation.* In this case, both research paradigms are employed concurrently to investigate the same phenomenon. In some cases, one methodology is given more weight than the other, but sometimes both paradigms are assigned an equal status. This is as theoretically and technically possible as the previous option. An example of such a choice is when the study investigates the effects of unemployment by using (i) standardised questionnaires with unemployed people, and (ii) grounded theory. The emphasis here is not on the methods employed in the project but rather on the methodological context that guides their application. It is obvious that these two approaches address two different aspects of employment. However, these aspects are equally valuable and the findings complementary to each other, producing a more complete and more dynamic picture of the effects of unemployment.

    c.   *Step-wise conversion*. Another example is the use of step-wise conversion, whereby data is gradually converted from qualitative to quantitative. Here statements are categorised and assigned uniform numeric figures, which in turn allow further quantification and quantitative analysis. A study employing unstructured observation that produces a set of brief statements on the same topics from each of the respondents, in which the researcher decides after completing the study to quantify the answers and analyse the data using a quantitative paradigm, is such an example. The conversion of the qualitative data to quantitative form shifts the mode of the study from the qualitative to the quantitative domain. As stated earlier, the use of quantification alone does not convert the methodology. For the conversion to be effective, the whole methodological context must change.

3.   *The best choice*. As noted earlier, the debate on methodology goes beyond diversity and compatibility. In many cases, it entails heated debate as to which is most efficient, producing arguments that merely praise one methodology and condemn the other. Many feminists criticise and reject quantitative methodology; qualitative researchers consider it inadequate; and quantitative researchers see both as a 'soft research option'. This polemic that has dominated social research over the last 25 years seems to be softening somewhat, with many coming to realise that the two methodologies are equally legitimate and equally efficient alternatives.

The differences between the methodologies do not suggest differences in quality but in their nature and purpose. Hence, criticisms and conflicts over the value of the methodologies, such as those presented above, are without logical basis. It is like arguing that ships are not an effective means of transport because they cannot fly; and aeroplanes are not efficient because they cannot cruise through the sea. The fact is that both research models possess certain qualities that make each one suitable for studying particular aspects of reality that the other cannot address equally effectively. Simply, both research models are valuable in their own context, and are highly useful (see Kelle and Erzberger, 1999, 2000).

This appreciation of the specific qualities of these methodological paradigms is reflected in the propositions of many writers who support integration of the two research models in research practice (Bryman, 1984, 1988; Küchler, Wilson and Zimmerman, 1981). It is also seen in the frequent use of methodological triangulation, which is quite common in social research. Within this domain, quantitative researchers, as shown above, employ qualitative research methods together with quantitative ones either concurrently or successively, and have found them extremely useful (see Kelle and Erzberger, 1999, 2000).

Last but not least, the construction of qualitative paradigms combining elements of quantitative research (e.g. feminist empiricism) add to the point that diversity is a strength and not a weakness. Quantitative and qualitative method-ologies are legitimate and useful tools of the trade of social scientists, and both have a purpose. The one complements the other, and both together offer a stereoscopic picture of the world (Sprague and Zimmerman, 1989: 82).

5   QUANTITATIVE AND QUALITATIVE METHODS

Quantitative methods are generally geared towards documenting subject attrib-utes expressed in quantity, extent, or strength, as well as guaranteeing – among other things – objectivity, accuracy, validity and reliability. Their purpose is to measure variables and to produce figures which will allow judgements as to the status of the variables in question, which in turn will allow further processing and comparisons and permit replicability.

The most common methods are surveys, documentary methods, observation and experiments. In many instances, quantitative researchers employ qualitative methods in their studies, adjusted to meet the criteria of quantitative research.

Qualitative methods as a whole are unique and marked by certain criteria. This is so despite the diversity within the qualitative paradigm and the obvious call for equally diverse methods (see Crabtree and Miller, 1992; Flick et al., 1991, 2000; Lamnek, 1993). Some of the main criteria of qualitative methods are lack of strict structure, loosely planned designs geared to capture reality in action, expressive language, collection of thick descriptions, presentation of data in the form of words and pictures, close contact with the respondent, and context sensitivity.

Overall, qualitative research employs 'standard' designs and methods as well as projective procedures (Spitznagel, 1991); nevertheless, the methods employed by qualitative researchers are, in most cases at least, those employed by quantitative researchers, adjusted to meet their methodological standards. For instance, while both research models employ interviews, quantitative researchers usually employ structured interviews and qualitative researchers intensive ones. Similarly, while quantitative researchers usually employ structured observation, qualitative researchers employ participant observation.

Method triangulation. As noted earlier, researchers of both methodological fronts make use of both types of methods as required to address general or specific research needs (that is, to facilitate, enrich or refine the study). Each group of methods possesses certain qualities that are appreciated within and outside their own paradigm.

6   CRITICAL RESEARCH

There have been long controversies about the status of critical research. The basis of these controversies is whether there is a critical methodology that would clearly identify it as a separate form of inquiry. As we shall see later, this issue has not yet been settled, but the overwhelming majority of writers on the subject come down against it.

Critical researchers see the world as being divided and in constant tension, dominated by the powerful, who oppress the people and use the state and its institutions as tools to achieve their purpose. For Marxists, for instance, the state is seen as the extended hand of capitalism. The state, the media, the sciences and the research institutions – to name only a few – not only oppress people but also brainwash them into taking this oppression for granted or to accepting that change is either impossible or too costly. They work for the powerful.

A critical social science 'explains social order so that it becomes the catalyst that leads to the transformation of the social order' (Fay, 1987: 27); it explains social reality, criticises it and empowers people to overthrow it (ibid.: 23). The meth ods used in this context may be quantitative, qualitative or both. Researchers are guided, however, by critical paradigms that guide the choice of methods they use, and use their findings to emancipate people and to influence social policies.

In summary, critical science sees in social research a way of removing false beliefs and ideas about society and social reality, perceives humans as creative and compassionate, and is critical of the power systems and inequality structures that dominate and oppress people in societies. Whether this type of science can be useful or becomes another tool of patronising people and delivering them into the hands of new controllers and experts is another issue (May, 2001).

Nevertheless, the view of the majority of writers on the subject is that, first, critical research is extremely diverse in its theoretical structure, which makes it difficult to set all paradigms under one epistemology and one methodology; second, most aspects of the research procedures employed by critical researchers fall within the parameters of quantitative and qualitative methodology, hence a separate methodology for this group of researchers appears to be unnecessary; third, the critical element of this research model lies – in most cases at least – in the manner in which research findings are treated rather than in the way in which knowledge is acquired; and finally, that critical analysis of the findings, and personal engagement aiming to ensure that the findings are implemented, are not a monopoly of critical researchers. Quantitative and qualitative researchers can be 'critical', and many are.

MAIN POINTS

- It is important to distinguish between perspectives, paradigms, methodologies and methods.
- A methodology is a model entailing the theoretical principles and frameworks that provide the guidelines about how research is to be done.
- A method is a tool or an instrument employed by researchers to collect data.
- The main methodologies in the social sciences are the quantitative and the qualitative kinds.
- Methodologies vary fundamentally from each other, but they are not incompatible. They use the same or similar methods.
- Quantitative methodology takes a strict, objective, neutral and 'scientific' stance and employs a perspective which resembles that of the natural sciences.

- Quantitative methodology has been criticised, among other things, for the way in which it perceives reality, people and research; the methods it uses; the politics it supports; and the relationship it establishes with the researched.

- Qualitative methodology adopts a subjective perception of reality and employs a naturalistic type of inquiry. Its central principles are openness, the process–nature of the research and the object, reflexivity of object and analysis, explication and flexibility.

- Qualitative methodology has been criticised, among other things, for not being able to cope with demands related to reliability, representativeness, generalis-ability, objectivity and detachment, ethics and the value of collected data.

- Quantitative and qualitative methodology are equally valuable and useful in their own context. They are complementary and not mutually exclusive.

WHERE TO FROM HERE?

Before you leave this chapter, visit the companion website for the third edition of *Social Research* at http://www.palgrave.com/sociology/sarantakos to review the main concepts introduced in this chapter and to test yourself on the major issues discussed.

FURTHER READING

Clough, P. and Nutbown, C. (2002) *A Student's Guide to Methodology*. London: Sage.

Greene, J. C. and Caracelli, V. J (eds) (1997) *Advances in Mixed-Method Evaluation: The Challenges and Benefits of Integrating Diverse Paradigms*. San Francisco: Jossey Bass.

Harreé, R. (1972) *The Philosophies of Science*. Oxford: Oxford University Press.

Hughes, J. A. (1990) *The Philosophy of Social Research*. Harlow: Longman.

Morgan, D. L. (1998b) 'Practical Strategies for Combining Qualitative and Quantitative Methods.' *Qualitative Health Research*, 8: 362–76.

Ramazanoglou, G. (2002) *Feminist Methodology: Challenges and Choices*. London: Sage.

Rescher, N. (2002) *Rationalität, Wissenschaft und Praxis*. Würzburg: Königshausen & Neuman.

Seale, C. (1999) *The Quality of Qualitative Research*. London: Sage.

Smith, M. J. (1998) *Social Science in Question*. London: Sage.

Tashakkori, A. and Teddlie, C. (1998) *Mixed Methodology: Combining Qualitative and Quantitative Approaches*. Thousand Oaks, Calif.: Sage.

Feminist research

THIS CHAPTER

- deals with the nature and purpose of feminist research
- discusses briefly its basic theoretical foundations
- depicts its major research positions
- debates its epistemological and methodological position

KEY HEADINGS

INTRODUCTION

Feminist research has emerged as a legitimate, relevant and popular research model. Its quality, and the validity of its findings are beyond contention, and over the years it has produced a significant output that has provided guidelines for policies central to modern societies (Roberts, 1981). Its domain is wide and diverse, and so are its basic methodological principles.

Feminist research is a type of inquiry that deserves its place in this text not primarily because of the nature of methods it employs or the output it produces but rather because of the manner in which it uses conventional methods, the areas on which it focuses, and the manner in which it employs its findings. In this sense, feminist research is an emancipatory type of inquiry. This means that it not only documents aspects of reality; it also takes a personal, political and engaging stance to the world.

In this chapter we shall address the theoretical foundations of this research model, its domain, its nature and diversity, the identity that marks its distinction from other research models, and its epistemological and methodological status. We begin with a brief description of the foundations of feminist research.

1   THE NATURE OF FEMINIST RESEARCH

The foundations of feminist research are those of critical theory, and hence this research model is critical and emancipatory, and perceives reality, science and research within this context. Briefly, feminist research studies the social conditions of women in a sexist, 'malestream' and patriarchal society (Stanley and Wise, 1983: 12), and enlightens people about taken-for-granted sexist practices and the gender-blindness of government and community practices (including publications) that displaced, ignored and silenced women, led to an unequal and discriminating social order, and held them captive for millennia.

Hence, the focus of research that binds together all branches of feminist research is their strong commitment to changing the status of women in modern societies, to studying women, and to employing female feminist researchers: feminist research is research on women, by women and for women. In summary, this emancipatory nature of feminist research is depicted in Box 3.1.

It should also be stressed that feminist research is based on the assumption that the world is socially constructed, displays a relative aversion to empirical positivistic methodology, and rejects the value-free nature of research (Haig, 1997; Punch, 2000). Feminist researchers employ a qualitative and/or quantitative methodology, although they adjust the latter to meet the requirements of the feminist paradigm.

Beyond its emancipatory endeavour, feminist research is a model guided by sound methodologies and producing valuable and high quality research findings. A combination of a variety of theoretical paradigms, as well as methods and procedures adjusted to comply with feminist principles, are the major factors for this. The major criteria of feminist research are summarised below.

Box **3.1**

Feminist research: the quest for emancipation and change

Feminist research . . .

■ Assumes:
- that the powerful dominate social life and ideology
- that research is owned by the powerful (men) at the expense of women
- that men and women differ in their perceptions of life due to their social status.
■ Employs:
- engaging and value-laden methods and procedures that bring the researcher close to the subject
- subjective principles of research, encouraging taking sides and personal commitment to the feminist cause
- a political stance to research topics and procedures.
■ Aims to:
- expose the structures and conditions that contribute to the present situation
- enlighten the community to the factors that generate this phenomenon and propose ways that can help alleviate the problem
- empower women and give them a voice to speak about social life from their perspective
- ultimately contribute towards social change and reconstruction.

2 PRINCIPLES OF FEMINIST RESEARCH

It is often taken for granted that feminist research takes an anti-quantitative attitude and therefore abstains from all quantitative standards and principles of research. Feminists are usually thought to abstain from taking any interest in measurement, validity, objectivity, reliability, representativeness and generalisation. Although some feminists may do so, in the majority of cases this assumption is not correct.

Feminist researchers who follow the interpretivist/constructionist paradigm accept these principles, and ensure that validity, objectivity, reliability and similar standards are considered. We shall see later, when we address these principles, that researchers of both research models adhere to most research principles, in their own way. They may not specify the conditions under which these principles are followed, but nevertheless, they value these principles in their own context.

Feminist research:

■   Is contextual, inclusive, experiential, involved, socially relevant, complete but not necessarily replicable, open to the environment and inclusive of emotions and events as experienced (Nielsen, 1990: 6; Reinharz, 1983).

- Involves an ongoing criticism of non-feminist scholarship, is guided by feminist theory, may be transdisciplinary, aims to create social change, strives to represent human diversity, includes the researcher as a person, frequently attempts to develop special relationships with the people studied and, finally, frequently defines a special relationship with the reader (Reinharz, 1992).
- Puts gender in the centre of social inquiry; making women visible and representing women's perspectives are a major part of feminist critical research (Harvey, 1990: 154).
- Places emphasis on women's experiences, which are considered a significant indicator of reality (Harding, 1987a) and offer more validity than does method; in a wider context feminist research involves primarily the development of women's history, for example by recasting history to take account of women's roles and by reconstructing it in terms of women's rather than men's concerns; or by writing the history of women's realms of experience (Harvey, 1990: 154).
- Discloses distortions related to women's experiences.
- Sees gender as the nucleus of women's perceptions and lives, shaping consciousness, skills, institutions and the distribution of power and privilege.
- Is preoccupied with social construction of 'knowing and being known'.
- Is politically value-laden and critical, and as such is not methodic but clearly dialectical. This implies that it is an imaginative and creative process which engages oppressive social structures (Harvey, 1990: 102–3).
- Is not solely about women but primarily for women, taking up an emancipationist stance.
- It entails an anti-positivistic orientation.
- Employs multiple methodologies and paradigms.
- Includes methods used (a) in research projects by people who identify themselves as feminists or as part of the women's movement; (b) in research published in journals that publish only feminist research or in books that identify themselves as such; and (c) in research that has received awards from organisations that give awards to people who do feminist research (Reinharz, 1992: 6)

These principles are neither clear-cut nor fully accepted by all feminist researchers. An example is objectivity, which obviously is considered to be a part of the identity of empiricist research. Although feminist research rejects objectivity, there are writers who argue that also there is a way of being objective although not of the positivist style.

It is argued, for instance, that although positivist principles such as experimental closure (controlling variables in experimentation), detachment, subject–object dichotomy, and value-neutrality are not accepted, other forms of objectivity are. Examples of objectivity types accepted by some feminists are: dynamic objectivity (Keller, 1985), entailing an emotional bond between the researcher and the subject; openness, where all facts are made known to the respondent, highlighting all contingencies of representation (Harding, 1991); democratic discussion, where all parameters are set out in the open, which encourages cooperation among all researchers as well as criticism from all points of view, and is based on equality of intellectual authority; and anti-sexist practices.

Research principles are addressed in various ways, in their own context, and serve the same or similar purposes as in quantitative research.

Box 3.2

Feminist empiricism

- Employs a realist ontology; a modified objectivist epistemology; a concern for hypothesis testing, explanation, prediction, cause–effect linkages, and conventional benchmarks of rigor, including internal and external validity (Denzin and Lincoln, 1994: 101).
- Accepts objectivist principles of knowledge creation.
- Employs traditional social research, modified to avoid bias, sexism etc. and to meet feminist standards.
- Employs quantitative and qualitative methods.
- Accepts empiricism critically.
- Challenges the notion that the person/identity of the researcher has no effect on the quality of the findings (Harding, 1986: 162).
- Challenges the notion of the adequacy and validity of empirical rules and norms.
- Challenges the notion that science and politics should be kept apart.
- Employs traditional research methods.
- Employs a post-positivist jargon of validity, reliability, credibility and multi-method research strategies (Denzin and Lincoln, 1994).
- Follows primarily more rigorously the existing rules and principles of the sciences (Harding, 1991: 111).
- Criticises not so much the foundations of science, but its practice.

3 FEMINIST RESEARCH POSITIONS

The diversity of research within the feminist paradigm and the boundaries of the attributes of feminist research referred to above are reflected in the research models systematically supported, defended and employed by contemporary feminist researchers, most of which rest on qualitative principles (see Olesen, 1994). Three such examples will be briefly described below. These examples cover the entire domain of social research, ranging from a realist-objectivist empiricism at the one extreme to a subjectivist postmodernism at the other.

3.1 Feminist empiricism

This version of the feminist paradigm accepts within its research model empiricist principles and practices that resemble those of other research models based on an objectivist epistemology, although with some adjustments. The main points of feminist empiricism are shown in Box 3.2.

The central elements of this type of feminist research are legitimate and valid, and are also well accepted by non-feminist researchers. Nevertheless, there are many critical voices. It is argued, for instance, that many principles of this feminist branch are in opposition to basic feminist research standards, which cannot be justified without changing standard feminist thinking. For many writers, also from within the feminist camp, this innovation, necessary and legitimate as it might be, cannot be upheld without serious implications for the overall feminist philosophy.

3.2 Feminist standpoint

Closer to feminist tradition are the feminist standpoint theories of knowledge (Harding, 1987c; Benini, 2000). This research model works on the theoretical proposition that women, due to their personal and social experience as females, are in a better position than men to face and understand the world of women. This relates to the contexts of the world of work, division of labour, mother–child relationships and so on.

Although there are many and different contexts within this model of feminist research (class, ethnicity, race, culture, education and other factors generate different standpoints and hence feminisms), and hence many standpoints, there are some common criteria which guide theory and research in this context. The main points of the paradigms referred to in the literature (Harding, 1989; D. D. E. Smith, 1992: 96) are shown in Box 3.3.

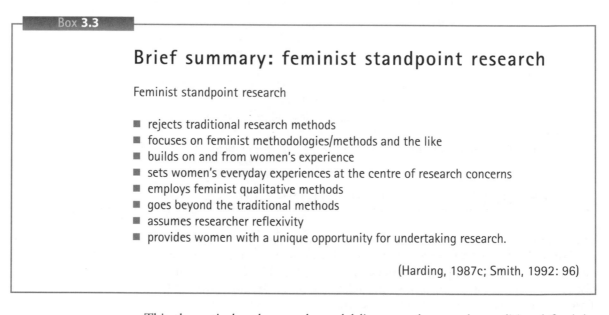

Box **3.3**

Brief summary: feminist standpoint research

Feminist standpoint research

- rejects traditional research methods
- focuses on feminist methodologies/methods and the like
- builds on and from women's experience
- sets women's everyday experiences at the centre of research concerns
- employs feminist qualitative methods
- goes beyond the traditional methods
- assumes researcher reflexivity
- provides women with a unique opportunity for undertaking research.

(Harding, 1987c; Smith, 1992: 96)

This theoretical and research model lies very close to the traditional feminist paradigm, at least with regard to the position of this paradigm in relation to the traditional objectivist and positivist methodology and the postmodernist paradigm, both of which it rejects. This is the type of feminism and feminist research most feminists accept, and this is the impression non-feminists have of what is presented as feminism in all contexts.

3.3 Feminist postmodernism

Postmodern feminism is a newer development within feminist theory and research and has received diverse and contradictory responses from within and outside the feminist domain (see, for instance, Lather, 1991). Postmodern feminists adhere to general philosophical principles that have a strong impact on the way research is to be done. For instance, they view truth as a 'destructive illusion', and the world as endless stories or texts, many of which sustain the integration of power and oppression (Benini, 2000: 164).

Feminist postmodernism has been described by writers (Farber, 2001; Haig, 1997: 182; Nicholson, 1990) as an epistemology that is non-foundationalist, contextualist, and non-dualist, or multiplist, in its commitments. It basically rejects epistemological assumptions of modernism, the foundational grounding of knowledge, the universalising claims for the scope of knowledge, and the employment of dualist categories of thought (Haig, 1997: 182). Brieschke (1992: 174) notes that postmodernist feminism

> has been multi-dimensional, that is, reciprocal and mutual, moving back and forth from self to other(s), concerned with the social structures that enable the self and other(s) to communicate symbolically and intersubjectively. It values and is based upon a sense of connectedness that recognises the inter-dependent construction of both self and other through different ways of knowing. Philosophically, postmodernist paradigms view rationality itself as a social symbolic construction.

Feminist postmodernists are critical not only of conventional research but also of feminist practices, particularly theories of gender and patriarchy, which they consider essentialist (Butler, 1990). They refer particularly to the feminist belief and practice of considering concepts such as 'women' and 'patriarchy' to be universal. Lesbian women and women of colour were the first to raise this issue very strongly, but class and race were equally stressed in the debate.

As stated earlier, despite its innovative approach it has not been received as positively as many other feminist branches. Many of the assumptions it makes about social structures and about women as well as science, truth and knowledge

---

Box **3.4**

Brief summary: elements of feminist postmodernism

Feminist postmodernism:

- is non-foundationalist, contextualist, and non-dualist, or multiplist, in its commitments
- views the world as endless stories or texts, many of which sustain the integration of power and oppression
- views truth as a 'destructive illusion'
- rejects epistemological assumptions of modernism
- rejects the foundational grounding of knowledge, the universalising claims for the scope of knowledge
- rejects the employment of dualist categories of thought
- is critical of conventional qualitative research, and the 'power' of research in general
- is critical also of certain feminist practices which they consider essentialist
- objects to the feminist notion that concepts such as women and patriarchy are universal.

raise doubts as to its relevance to mainstream feminism, to feminist research and to social research in general. Concern has also been raised about its relativist view of social life and the fact that it overlooks serious social problems by overconcentrating on textuality (Farber, 2001)

Feminist postmodernism follows the central principles of postmodernism, which will be discussed elsewhere in this volume.

3.4 Putting it together

Despite the diversity in feminist theory and methodology, feminist researchers share many general and specific standards and principles, reflected in their research theory and practice. Some of these are:

- that women have been marginalised
- that male superiority is perpetuated despite policies, assurances and political promises
- that males and females are considered physically and emotionally different, with men being considered superior
- that there is still a long way to go to establish gender equality
- that the relationship between researcher and researched requires serious reconsideration (Farber, 2001; Pfeifer, 2000).

To reconstruct the research culture and strengthen the effectiveness of feminist research, it was proposed (Farber, 2001; Pfeifer, 2000) that the conduct of research be based on collaborative and non-exploitative relationships, that alienation of researchers from the researched be eliminated, and transformative research be initiated. Accompanying these requirements is the need to set gender at the centre of research as the basic organising principle of research itself and of data analysis and the implementation of findings. The involvement of the researched in the research process has been stressed by many feminist researchers and writers.

Box **3.5**

The impact of feminist research

The advent of feminist research:

- helped to reconstruct the domain of conventional research
- brought to surface neglected aspects of social reality
- added a new view (lens, prism) to the perception of the world
- drew attention to problems in the conduct of social research
- challenged gender ethics, female subjugation and discrimination
- produced evidence that put gender in a new context
- helped to raise women's consciousness and empower them
- freed social research from 'androcentric blinkers'
- offered a legitimate basis for social change in the area of gender
- raised issues that helped to redefine the notion of humanity.

Following these guidelines, the types of research which were considered consistent with feminist research were action research, participatory or collaborative research, needs assessment or prevalence research, evaluation research, and demystification research, where issues and relationships are explained, and the goals of the research are set to be consciousness raising, and emancipating and empowering the oppressed and powerless (Reinharz, 1992: 180–94).

4 FEMINIST RESEARCH METHODS

4.1 The issue

Initially, feminist research employed mainly positivistic methods, using conventional techniques, sometimes in their original form and at other times adjusted by eliminating inherent androcentric bias in method and approach. Nevertheless, this approach gradually changed by distancing itself from conventional methods, while working towards developing distinct feminist methods that would correspond to women's intuitive rationality and also to feminist political commitments (Stanley and Wise, 1983).

If we survey all feminist branches, we find a wide range of views on feminist approaches to methods (Althoff, Bereswill and Riegraf, 2001). One view suggests that there is no research method that is exclusively made for and employed by feminist researchers (Reinharz, 1992; Mason, 1997); rather, methods come from quantitative or qualitative research adjusted to meet feminist principles (Oakley, 1998). Hence, it is not unusual to hear of feminist survey research, or feminist experimental research, feminist field research and other relevant applications. Most common is the use of conventional qualitative research methods (Pilcher and Coffey, 1996), such as in-depth interviews, participant observation and document analysis, but there are also ethnographic and ethnological studies, deconstruction (historical or structuralist deconstruction) and semiological analysis.

4.2 Innovative applications

Despite the remarks above, innovative applications of research strategies as well as new feminist methods have recently been suggested by feminist researchers (Cook and Fonow, 1990). Reinharz (1992), for instance, reported some originality in feminist research in methods as well as in procedure, adding the following examples:

- *Consciousness-raising method.* This is a group discussion technique involving groups. There is no leader or imposed theme of discussion; the discussion is guided by a group facilitator.
- *Group diaries.* Diaries are kept anonymously by members of a group. Emphasis is placed on the group and can involve group interview or memory work, whereby stories are written by the group and read to the members, with discussion and analysis following later.
- *Dramatic role-play.* Views, opinions and feelings are expressed in the form of a drama. The discussion issue is introduced by the researcher; members of

Feminist research focuses on

- consciousness-raising methods
- using intuition or writing associatively
- group diaries
- identification instead of keeping distance
- dramatic role-play
- studying unplanned personal experience
- genealogy and network tracing
- structured conceptualisation
- conversation, dialogue
- photography or talking-picture technique
- non-authoritative and neutral research
- speaking freely into a tape recorder or answering long, essay-type questionnaires.

(Reinharz, 1992)

the group then discuss the main issues and identify general trends or themes. Members of the group improvise, reflecting their feelings in their expressions; this is expected to generate further discussion.

- *Genealogy and network tracing.* This involves inquiring into a woman's history, tracing her relationships, friendships and origin.
- *Non-authoritative and neutral research.* Information is collected and presented to the respondent to make sense of. Emphasis is placed on the respondent and on subjectivity.
- *Conversation, dialogue.* A conversation involving a number of people discussing a topical issue, some impersonating historical figures, without division into questioners and answerers, is used in this method.
- *Using intuition or writing associatively.* This uses a way of 'blending dreams, reading and thought' (Reinharz, 1992: 232), in which the writer appears in a deep non-chronological, non-topical intuitive process; this requires passivity alternating with integration (Reinharz, 1992: 231).
- *Identification instead of keeping distance.* The researcher is expected to identify herself with the subjects, display this identification to the reader and encourage the reader to identify with the writer.
- *Studying unplanned personal experience.* Personal experience, for example illness or an operation (alone or with additional data), is used as the basis of the study.
- *Structured conceptualisation.* This involves recording, analysing and synthesising information related to certain issues, ideas and so on in order to demonstrate how feminists define and understand concepts.
- *Photography or talking-picture technique.* This technique involves a collection of pictures taken at certain intervals to be used in an interview kit; subjects choose pictures to be included in the interview kit and file them in the album according to certain categories. Pictures are used in conjunction with

questionnaires. They can also be analysed and interpreted according to the information they contain, such as sitting order/position, gestures or posture.

■ *Speaking freely into a tape recorder or answering long, essay-type questionnaires.* This technique involves a set of questions sent to the respondent with the instruction to record the answers on tape.

It must be kept in mind that when feminist researchers employ methods which were developed by and for other groups of researchers, they adjust them so that they fit within the critical and emancipatory stance of feminism, and they are directed towards breaking down taken-for-granted concepts and rebuilding them into new entities. 'In so doing they lay bare the essential concepts of the research and use this as the basis for revealing what is really going on' (Harvey, 1990: 101, 102, 152).

4.3 Dialectic method

Another method of feminist research is the dialectic method, whose roots reach back to the Greek philosophers of antiquity. The essence of this method lies in a process of constantly moving between concepts and data as well as between society and concrete phenomena, past and present issues, appearance and essence. In this process, after the initial concept has been chosen, the researcher looks for connections and reflections regarding surface appearances and real situations, forming opinions about the issue in question and thus new concepts, relating them to method and approach, re-examining the new concepts, correcting elements, getting deeper below the surface, and refocusing on the concept in the historical process. This process is continued until the analysis produces a coherent model (Harvey, 1990).

The process entailed in the dialectic method is based on a constant motion of deconstruction followed by reconstruction, which leads to new deconstruction and reconstruction, and so on. A comprehensive description of this process is given by Harvey, as illustrated in the following quotation:

> The dialectical deconstructive–reconstructive process can be construed as a process of focusing on the structural totality or historical moment and critically reflecting on its essential nature. The totality is initially taken as an existent whole. The structure presents itself as natural, as the result of historical progress, that is, it is ideologically constituted. The critical analysis of the historically specific structure must therefore go beyond the surface appearances and lay bare the essential nature of the relationships that are embedded in the structure. This critique ostensibly begins by fixing on the fundamental unit of the structural relationships and decomposing it. The fundamental unit must be broken down until its essential nature is revealed; the structure is then reconstituted in terms of the essentialized construct. The reconstructive process reveals the transparency of ideology. The whole is grounded in historically specific material reality.
>
> (Harvey, 1990: 31–2)

This brief reference to feminist research demonstrates that it employs a comprehensive approach and set of methods, the majority of which are shared with positivists and interpretivists, although their use may be different.

5 FEMINIST CRITIQUE OF CONVENTIONAL RESEARCH

Feminist research is generally different from, incompatible with (Miller and Treitel, 1991: 7) and also critical of conventional social research and science (Fee, 1986; Nielsen, 1990: 7), and the way they treat gender (CSWS, 1986). Quantitative research is thought to present a distorted view of the world (Westkott, 1990), to be dominated by a male ideology, and to suffer problems related to reliability, validity and representativeness (such as non-response, incomplete sampling frames or the hired-hand effect). Feminist research also takes a critical view of objectivity, detachment and hierarchy (Oakley, 1981), and of the conventional practice of using unidirectional instruments executed dispassionately, assigning researchers the role of an objective and detached observer, and devaluing, manipulating and exploiting the respondents. Feminists set the focus of investigations not on standardised ideals of statistical principles but rather on self-defined objectives.

Feminist researchers are equally critical of the use of interviewing practices that many (e.g. Oakley, 1981: 41) find morally indefensible. Interview practice that employs unidirectional methods and is based on a hierarchical relationship between the researcher and the researched is thought to undermine the feminist reassessment of the interrelationship of women with one another (Harvey, 1990: 117). They see in-depth interviews as a better option for many other reasons, but also because they encourage subjectivity and intensive dialogue between equals, which are intrinsic features of feminist analysis of gender experience. Oakley (2000) notes that the opposition to quantitative research is associated with the masculine identity they assigned to it, whereas qualitative research was seen as reflecting female properties, and a female identity.

Feminist research is also critical of the sexist orientation of social research and of social sciences in general. Social sciences are not only based on the writings of their founding fathers, but are also dominated by male stereotypes and attitudes created through the socialisation and professional training of social scientists, the majority of whom are males. Many writers (e.g. Eichler et al., 1985; Eichler, 1988; Reinharz, 1983) have pointed to the many ways in which sexist practices exist and affect social life, and give the following examples:

- *Androcentricity.* The world is perceived and presented from the view of the male. In this context, women are presented as passive objects rather than as acting persons. This can lead to two extreme phenomena, namely *gynopia*, where women are totally invisible, and *misogyny*, characterised by hatred of women.
- *Overgeneralisation/overspecificity.* This occurs when research findings obtained from a specific study are used to explain behaviours of non-specific groups, and vice versa.
- *Gender insensitivity.* This occurs when gender as a factor is totally ignored; for example, when studies of the effects recession has on people neglect gender, or when a study of parents' influence on the socialisation of female children does not differentiate between fathers and mothers.

- *Double standards.* Here, different standards or instruments are used to measure issues related to males and females.
- *Sex appropriateness.* This is a problem derived from the application of double standards and relates to attitudes and expectations that assign behaviour patterns, traits, attributes or roles considered appropriate to a particular gender.
- *Familism.* This is a particular case of gender insensitivity and refers to the common practice of referring to families when in fact the issue in question concerns men, women or members of the family; or when, referring to families, it is assumed that all family members are uniformly affected by a particular issue or problem.
- *Sexual dichotomism.* This is another example of double standards and refers to practices that tend to consider genders as distinctly separate without considering the interrelationships and interdependence that exist between them.

For these reasons, most feminist researchers reject conventional research methods and employ other approaches, such as those referred to earlier. Others employ conventional methods but in a different form and context, retaining their advantages but avoiding their weaknesses. Overall, qualitative methods, adequately tailored to feminist standards and expectations, are the ones employed by the majority of feminists. The difference between feminist and non-feminist research lies not in the type of methods they use, but rather in the way they choose, change and use conventional methods to meet their research goals.

This point has been made clearer over the years even within the confines of feminist theory and research. A number of feminists have come to realise the power of quantitative research and to appreciate the impact it has had – although

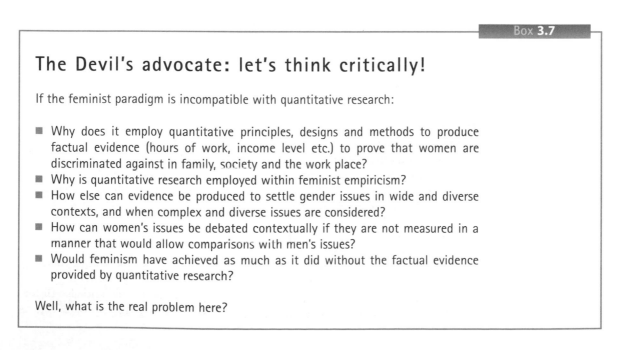

Box 3.7

The Devil's advocate: let's think critically!

If the feminist paradigm is incompatible with quantitative research:

- Why does it employ quantitative principles, designs and methods to produce factual evidence (hours of work, income level etc.) to prove that women are discriminated against in family, society and the work place?
- Why is quantitative research employed within feminist empiricism?
- How else can evidence be produced to settle gender issues in wide and diverse contexts, and when complex and diverse issues are considered?
- How can women's issues be debated contextually if they are not measured in a manner that would allow comparisons with men's issues?
- Would feminism have achieved as much as it did without the factual evidence provided by quantitative research?

Well, what is the real problem here?

indirectly – on the women's cause (Oakley, 1998; see also Maynard, 1994, 1998). How else could it have been demonstrated clearly and beyond reasonable doubt that women were discriminated against in their social, educational, economic, professional and family life, particularly in areas involving quantifiable and measurable issues (income, economic growth, length of employment, facets of household involvement and so on)?

Further, concern has also been expressed with the manner in which qualitative researchers approach reality and construct theory. In a way, leading feminists seem to doubt the approach of both research models, particularly with inductive versus deductive research. As Stanley and Wise (1983: 22) note, researchers cannot have 'empty heads' in the way that inductivism proposes; nor is it possible for theory to be untainted by material experiences in the head of theoreticians in the way that deductionism proposes.

6 IS THERE A FEMINIST EPISTEMOLOGY?

Particularly during the 1970s and 1980s, a number of writers argued strongly in favour of a feminist epistemology (Corman, 1978; Lehrer, 1974; Pollock, 1979, 1986). The main argument behind this view was that the characteristic position of women enabled them to see the world through a feminist lens. If epistemology is the science of perceiving knowledge, it is obvious that women have a case for establishing their own epistemology. Many publications (e.g. Duran, 1995) reflect this in their titles, and writers use this concept freely as if it were correct and legitimate.

Although this argument is still strong, many writers, even from within the feminist camp, do not see it as a viable and logical proposition. After all, epistemologies employed by feminists to access knowledge existed long before the advent of feminism, and were used very extensively by other social scientists. Some relevant views are cited in Box 3.8.

7 IS THERE A FEMINIST METHODOLOGY?

The question of whether feminism has developed distinct methodological principles that could justify the establishment of a distinct methodology alongside the qualitative, quantitative or critical paradigms is by no means new. Claims for a separate place in the ranks of paradigms and methodologies were made long ago, and are still being made. The responses to these claims are diverse, with some arguing in favour and others against such a recognition.

7.1 Arguments in favour of a feminist methodology

Those in favour of a feminist methodology argue, among other things, that:

- Feminism has developed a characteristic approach that is valid and also different from the approaches of the other methodologies. This approach rejects

Box 3.8

Examples of arguments against a feminist epistemology

- Sandra Harding (1986): 'Can there be a feminist standpoint if women's (or feminists') social experience is divided by class, race and culture? Must there be black and white, working-class and professional class, American and Nigerian feminist points?' (p. 26)
- Loraine Code (1991): 'a feminist epistemology is not justified: the economic position is outdated; the positionality of the standpoint is questionable; following a monolithic tradition is not warranted. It is better to work towards transferring the notion of the ruling system, and to challenge the structure of the established epistemological position.'
- Susan Haack (1995): 'Unlike some proponents of a feminist epistemology, I do not think that women are capable of revolutionary insights into the theory of knowledge not available, or not easily available, to men.' (p. 8)
- L. H. Nelson (2002): 'Given the benefits of pluralism in the broader discipline, there now seems little reason to work to develop or to hope for 'a' feminist theory of science. . . . Feminists have found valuable resources in the larger discipline of philosophy of science.' (p. 326)

the male paradigm and the associated methodology and deserves a place in social methodology as a separate and distinct entity.

- A feminist methodology places emphasis on women and their position in society and contrasts it with the emphasis on males that prevails in the other methodologies.
- It explains the world in a unique way (e.g. based on patriarchy), which guides the structure and process of research, the choice and type of methods employed, and the way the results are analysed and interpreted.
- It sees women as the most appropriate researchers for dealing with women's issues, because only women can truly understand women and their unique position. This is what is generally termed feminist standpoint epistemology (Stanley and Wise, 1983).
- A feminist methodology is the sum of feminist methods and deserves to be recognised as such (Reinharz, 1992: 240).
- Feminist research is genuine in that it is marked by seeing reality through a 'female prism', that it rejects the notion of equating 'masculine' to 'universal', recognising the central place men have held in social research and lifting the 'androcentric blinkers' to allow a better vision of reality; it also locates the researcher as a gendered being in the web of social relations (Cook and Fonow, 1990).
- In feminist research, consciousness raising is central not only as a specific research tool but also as a general orientation. Women are in the best position to carry out research on women because, due to their particular position as members of an oppressed group and as scholars, they possess a 'double vision' and are therefore better equipped to identify, understand and interpret

women's experiences. The research process becomes a process of 'conscienti-sation', and through this a research object becomes a research subject and learns to perceive contradictions and to work against oppression (Cook and Fonow, 1990).

- Feminist researchers reject the artificial separation of the researcher and the researched, as well as the implied notion that such a separation produces more valid results. They demonstrate how the research process encourages and reinforces subjugation of women, and challenge the norm of objectivity that it entails and the beliefs that objectivity can be achieved through quan-tification and statistics. Instead, they advocate a dialectic relationship between subject and object of research, a form of participatory research and a 'conscious partiality', that is, the 'researcher's understanding of the connectedness to the experiences of the research subject through partial identification' (Cook and Fonow, 1990).
- Feminist researchers point to areas in which ethical standards are being violated. Such violations create or perpetuate forms of oppression of and discrimination against women, for example using sexist language that perpet-uates female subjugation, using unfair practices related to publication of feminist works, intervening in the respondents' lives and withholding infor-mation from women subjects (Cook and Fonow, 1990).
- The purpose of feminist research is to empower women to transform oppres-sive and exploitative conditions, to provide visions for the future and to attend to the policy complications of research.

Despite the validity of these criteria, there is no agreement as to whether they are sufficient to establish and justify the existence of a feminist methodology. The same authors who presented the above criteria note that there is no agreement among feminists about the right methodology, and go on to say that there is in fact no 'correct' feminist methodology; they conclude that 'at least within the field of sociology, feminist methodology is in the process of becoming and is not yet a fully articulated stance' (Cook and Fonow, 1990: 71). This position does not seem to have changed since then.

Box **3.9**

Think critically: time for a male prism?

- It is generally argued that feminist research should be for women, on women and by women. Does this call for men to make similar proposals on research?
- Feminists reject the 'male paradigm' because it is male; should males reject the 'female paradigm' for being female?
- If the notion of the 'female prism' disqualifies men from studying women, should women be disqualified from studying men for not having the 'male prism'?
- What is wrong with men studying women's issues and vice versa? Doesn't diver-sity in perceptions and procedures produce richer information?

Think about it. There must be a good reason for the feminist position!

7.2 Arguments against a feminist methodology

More conservative are the views of the critics of a feminist methodology, many of whom argue bluntly that such a methodology is not justified. Some of the arguments against a feminist methodology are shown below:

■ Feminists do not have a perspective of their own; rather, they use theoretical and methodological principles of other paradigms, such as Marxism, naturalism, critical theory and psychoanalysis. Without having distinct principles it is not possible to claim a separate methodology.

■ There is simply 'a multiplicity of standpoints, values, outlooks among feminists' (Assiter, 1996: 8). Feminists are very diverse (Marxist feminists, liberal feminists, feminist empiricists, psychoanalytic feminists, poststructural feminists, postmodern feminists etc.) and do not present 'a coherent and cogent alternative to non-feminist research' (Hammersley, 1992a: 202).

■ Many of the criteria and principles on which feminist research is based, and many of the methods they employ, are found in the non-feminist research domain and do not support a convincing argument in favour of a feminist methodology (Hammersley, 1992a: 202).

■ Unique attention to gender is not justified; even post-structural feminists (Alcoff, 1988: 407) argue that such a proposition and practice should be reconsidered and replaced by an emphasis on a plurality of differences.

■ Its objection to positivistic methodological practices, such as the value of method versus experience, its objectivity, its emancipation as a goal of research or a criterion of validity, and the relationship between researcher and

---

Box 3.10

Think critically: why a methodology?

■ What is the real advantage from having a methodology of your own?
■ Do feminist researchers really need a feminist methodology?
■ Will a feminist methodology meet the theoretical principles of all feminists?
■ Will a feminist methodology improve feminist research in any way?
■ Wouldn't a feminist methodology act as a restricting agent upon researchers' decisions?
■ Why should feminist researchers follow malestream practices? (Men have it, why not women?)
■ What is really important in emancipatory research? The methodology or the way methodologies and methods are applied and the purpose they aim to achieve?
■ Doesn't freedom to choose among existing methodologies offer more research options than tying research down to one methodology only?
■ Haven't many feminist researchers accepted qualitative research as most appropriate for guiding feminist research?
■ Will a feminist methodology unite or alienate feminist researchers?

Is the argument about a feminist methodology really worth the trouble?

researched (hierarchy), which many theorists use as a justification for a feminist methodology, are all questionable (Hammersley, 1992a). (For a response to these criticisms, see Geldsthorpe, 1992; Ramazanoglu, 1992.) Apart from this, one major branch of feminist research is based on feminist empiricism, which is not very different from the positivist paradigm.

■ The fact that positivism is considered 'inappropriate' does not justify a feminist methodology as its alternative. Qualitative methodology may be the answer, since its principles seem to be similar to those proposed by feminist critics.

■ Most feminist criticisms of conventional research speak for a qualitative methodology and not for a feminist methodology. These criticisms were introduced by qualitative researchers long before feminist researchers addressed them. After all, most feminist researchers adopt a qualitative paradigm in their research.

■ Many writers argue for a methodology that would be for women, on women and by women. This is neither logical nor valid. The object does not determine the methodology. Will this justify also an ethnic methodology, a racist methodology, ageist methodology and so on? Where will ethnic women belong?

■ Gender has been very frequently placed at the centre of the debate on methodology and on other issues. What is misunderstood here is that gender is not synonymous with women. Men are also a part of it.

■ Feminists argue that the 'male paradigm' is wrong because it is male; is a 'female paradigm' not equally wrong for being female?

■ If the 'female prism' disqualifies men from studying women effectively, and obviously from making judgments about them, does this mean that women are not qualified to study men and to make decisions about them?

■ Why methodology? This is a male invention, a part of the oppressive male paradigm, which feminists reject. Why do feminists want to become a part of an establishment they reject?

The question of whether or not a feminist methodology exists has not been answered fully yet (see, for example, Geldsthorpe, 1992; Hammersley, 1992a; Ramazanoglu, 1992); the debate is still alive. Without denying the value, extent and significance of feminist research, at this stage it is reasonable to argue that current developments in feminist theory and practice cannot support a claim for a distinct feminist methodology. Even prominent feminists are against such a proposition (Harding, 1987c). Referring to the differences of opinion within the feminism ranks, and particularly to feminist postmodernists, Harding (1987b: 188) notes that 'there can never be a feminist science, sociology, anthropology, or epistemology, but only many stories that different women tell about the different knowledge they have'. Blaikie (1993: 125), noting this point, comments that 'in an unstable and incoherent world, the establishment of consistent and coherent theories would be a hindrance to understanding and practice'.

- Feminist research is an established type of research, which has the specific purpose of studying women and their status in the community.
- Feminist research is an emancipatory inquiry focusing on enlightenment and on social change.
- Feminist research employs a variety of methods, adjusted to meet the requirements of the feminist paradigm.
- There are at least three positions within feminist research; these are feminist standpoint, feminist postmodernism and feminist empiricism.
- Feminist standpoint stands closer to the mainstream feminist cause than the other two.
- The three research positions fully cover the range of methodological issues within the feminist paradigm.
- Feminist research borrows methods and designs from other methodologies, especially of a qualitative nature. There are only a few methods that can be characterised as exclusively 'feminist'.
- The characteristic of feminist research is not the methods it employs but their application and purpose.
- The nature of feminist research and the diversity of the paradigm speak against the notion of a feminist epistemology.
- Feminist research operates within an interpretivist-constructionist paradigm.

WHERE TO FROM HERE?

Before you leave this chapter, visit the companion website for the third edition of *Social Research* at http://www.palgrave.com/sociology/sarantakos to review the main concepts introduced in this chapter and to test yourself on the major issues discussed.

FURTHER READING

Alcoff, L. and Potter, E. (1993) *Feminist Epistemologies.* London: Routledge.

Alcoff, L. (1996) *Real Knowing: New Versions of Coherence Epistemology.* Ithaca: Cornell University Press.

Code, L. (1991) *What Can She Know? Feminist Theory and the Construction of Knowledge.* Ithaca: Cornell University Press.

Harding, S. (1998) *Is Science Multicultural? Postcolonialisms, Feminisms, and Epistemologies.* Bloomington: Indiana University Press.

Harding, S. (1991) *Whose Science? Whose Knowledge? Thinking from Women's Lives.* Ithaca: Cornell University Press.

Nelson, L. H. (1990) *Who Knows: From Quine to a Feminist Empiricism.* Philadelphia: Temple University Press.

Oakley A. (2000) *Experiments in Knowing: Gender and Method in the Social Sciences.* Cambridge: Polity.

Stanley, L. and Wise, S. (1993) *Breaking Out Again: Feminist Ontology and Epistemology.* London: Routledge.

4 Principles of social research

THIS CHAPTER

- focuses on the basic rules of research
- presents the main types of measurement in detail
- introduces the nature of validity and reliability in research
- considers the role of representativeness and generalisation
- examines the relevance of these principles for qualitative research.

KEY HEADINGS

INTRODUCTION

Regardless of its diverse and pluralistic nature, structure and process, social research is generally expected to adhere to certain standards and principles. The nature of these standards and principles may vary, but their presence and necessity are taken for granted. For most researchers, this is a reflection of the nature of social research, which requires it to be based on sound and reliable criteria.

Quantitative researchers do not hesitate to state their allegiance to principles, of which those shown in Box 4.1 are most important.

In this chapter we shall explore and discuss these research principles and demonstrate how they are employed and justified by researchers. Most of these principles will be discussed in other chapters directly and/or indirectly and more extensively. It is worth noting that these principles are often referred to by other names; qualitative researchers, for instance, use different concepts when addressing the principles of their research model.

Box **4.1**

Principles of quantitative research

- Precision in measurement
- Replication
- Validity
- Reliability
- Objectivity
- Ethics
- Representativeness
- Generalisability

1 MEASUREMENT

1.1 Introduction

The research process usually begins with the theoretical preparation or formulation of the research topic (a step which is as complex as it is diverse). This will establish the foundations for the remaining parts of the study; it is therefore very important and deserves special consideration. Before we enter this discussion, however, we need to consider another general and fundamental element of the research process and one of the principles of social research, namely measurement. Measurement is a central element of social research and also fundamental for the procedures that will be introduced in the next chapter, where the preparation step of the research is considered.

In the first part of this chapter, we shall first introduce the concept, nature and types of measurement and a number of issues associated with it. We shall look at measurement as an element of social research, and explore its nature, types and major characteristics.

1.2 Nature of measurement

Social research, irrespective of its type and nature, entails a degree of measurement. This involves categorising and/or assigning values to concepts, and is

Box **4.2**

Measurement facilitates:

- adequacy in description and assessment, offering a full account of the concept
- uniformity in description and assessment, over time and among researchers
- comparisons between complex concepts, enabling the identification of fine distinctions
- consistency in the assessment of concepts, over time and among researchers
- accuracy and precision in procedures, by taking into consideration all aspects of concepts
- replicability in social research, by the same or different researchers, in the same or different contexts.

diverse in nature and level of operation. It is also a very useful procedure because it serves to ensure high quality in social research. Most of all, measurement is undertaken to facilitate adequacy, uniformity, comparisons, consistency, accuracy and precision in describing and assessing concepts.

Generally, measurement may be quantitative or qualitative. Quantitative measurement concentrates on numerical values and attributes. Qualitative measurement refers to labels, names and qualities. Qualitative measurement describes attributes by using common concepts or symbols or introducing new ones; a common procedure involves description of categories and classifications. The classification of 'residence' into 'urban' and 'rural', for instance, is a qualitative measurement. In the view of some writers, qualitative measurement does not qualify as 'measurement' since it does not demonstrate the main criteria of measurement, such as precision, reliability and validity; rather, it is a process of labelling, classification and description. Nevertheless, as we shall see soon, this view is not fully accepted.

1.3 Variables

Definitions

Variables are empirical constructs that take more than one value or intensity; for example, sex (male, female), marital status (single, married, divorced, widowed, deserted), age and education are variables. The opposite of variables are constants. Constants take only one value or intensity. The researcher determines at the outset of the study which concepts will act as constants and which as variables.

The construction of variables follows a systematic procedure that adheres to the rules of measurement. Failure to meet these requirements will result in distortions and inaccuracies in measurement, and hence in false results. Two very important rules are that variables must *relate to one concept only* and *must be measurable*.

There are many types of variables. These types vary according to a number of criteria, such as their nature (geographic variables, demographic variables etc.), their position within the research context (dependent variables, independent variables etc.), or other factors. The following types are most common:

■ *Dependent and independent variables.* An independent variable (IV) is a variable that is set to cause changes in or explain another; a dependent variable (DV) is a variable that is set to be affected or explained by another variable. For instance, in a research study of 'family status and scholastic achievement', the independent variable can be family status, and the dependent variable scholastic achievement. This distinction is not associated with the nature of the concepts but rather with the nature of the research design. The same variable (e.g. scholastic achievement) can be an independent variable in one project (when studying the question: does scholastic achievement affect alcohol consumption?), but a dependent variable in another (when studying the question: does gender affect scholastic achievement?).

■ *Extraneous variables.* These are variables which are 'outside' the research question, argument or hypothesis; they are distinct from the dependent or independent variable. For instance, in a study investigating the validity of the theory that race (IV) is associated with scholastic achievement (DV) (e.g. with whites doing far better then blacks), the real reason for the changes in scholastic achievement may be not race (IV) but income and prejudice, which were unexpected and unplanned, and not calculated in the research equation of the original theorists. In this case, income and prejudice are extraneous variables. Hence, looking for the presence of possible extraneous variables is always a logical and necessary procedure in social research, before the relationship between IV and DV is confirmed.

■ *Discrete and continuous variables.* Discrete and continuous variables differ from each other in terms of scale continuity; the former are not continuous but use whole units only, whereas the latter are continuous and can be fractioned indefinitely. In discrete variables (also called binomial variables), measurement uses whole units, with no possible values between adjacent units. For instance, marital status is a discrete variable; it can be 'single', married', 'divorced', 'widowed' or 'cohabiting'. Similarly, gender is a discrete variable. Gender can be either 'male' or 'female'. In both examples, there is nothing between the values. In contrast, 'weight' is a continuous variable; it can use smaller increments of units, for example it can be 73.2, 78.1 or 85.6 kg. Discrete variables are counted, not measured; continuous variables are measured, not counted. Examples of discrete variables are ethnicity, race, sex, marital status, cause of death or blood type. Examples of continuous variables are height, distance, time, age, temperature or IQ scores.

■ *Demographic variables.* Demographic variables deal with demographic data such as age, residence, religion, marital status, family size, race, education and sexual preference. Remember, a demographic variable can be dependent or independent, discrete or continuous, depending on the nature of the research design.

There are many more distinctions in variables, most of which are common when advanced statistics are used. For example, there are 'quantitative' and 'qualitative variables'. Qualitative variables use nominal scale measurement; racial origin, ethnic origin, religious affiliation or sex are qualitative variables. Quantitative variables use either ordinal or metric scales. There is also often a distinction between conceptual (or nominal) and operational variables.

1.4 Levels of measurement

Measurement can be performed at four levels, which among other things vary with regard to the degree to which they match the characteristics of the real-number system. The four levels of measurement and four corresponding scales are: the nominal, the ordinal, the interval and the ratio level. Nominal-level measurement has the lowest and ratio-level measurement the highest match with the real-number system.

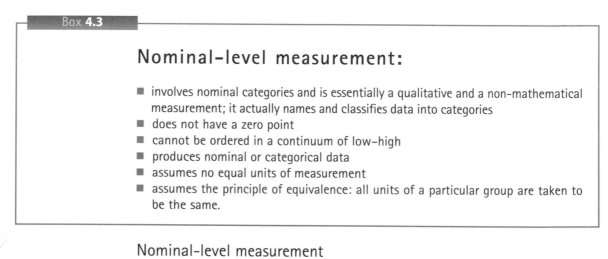

Box **4.3**

Nominal-level measurement:

- involves nominal categories and is essentially a qualitative and a non-mathematical measurement; it actually names and classifies data into categories
- does not have a zero point
- cannot be ordered in a continuum of low–high
- produces nominal or categorical data
- assumes no equal units of measurement
- assumes the principle of equivalence: all units of a particular group are taken to be the same.

Nominal-level measurement

This is the simplest, the lowest and the most primitive type of measurement. At this level, measurement involves classification of events into categories that must be distinct, unidimensional, mutually exclusive and exhaustive; the resulting scales are 'naming' scales. Such a measure indicates that there is a difference between the categories considered.

Such differences refer to nature but not to magnitude. Thus, dormitory No. 10 is not twice as large as dormitory No. 5. In a similar fashion, numbers assigned to categories have no mathematical meaning, are used only for identification and cannot be added, subtracted, multiplied, divided or otherwise manipulated mathematically. Classifying the respondents in categories such as male–female, black–white, young–old, single, married, cohabiting, separated, divorced, remarried or widowed, or Catholic, Protestant, Anglican or Orthodox is based on nominal measurement. Classifying respondents according to their place of birth, religious affiliation, political affiliation, car type and place of residence are additional examples. Further examples of nominal measurement are: nationality, type of shoes, skin colour, type of music and brands of drinks.

It must be noted that only statistical measures designed for nominal measurement, can be employed in this context.

Ordinal-level measurement

Measurement at the ordinal level involves not only categorising elements into groups but also ordering data and ranking variables in a continuum ranging according to magnitude, that is, from the lowest to the highest point (transitive relationship). Here, numbers offer more information since they not only indicate

Box **4.4**

Ordinal measurement:

- refers to ranks based on a clear order of magnitude of low and high signifying that some elements have more value than others
- assigns numbers actual mathematical meaning as well as identification properties.
- is essentially a quantitative measurement
- shows a relative order of magnitude.

differences between categories but also rank them; however, they do not allow mathematical operations such as addition or subtraction.

With regard to the last point, order of magnitude allows categories to be ranked (who is first, second, last) but does not indicate the amount of difference between the groups (how much above or below a certain category neighbouring categories are). So the difference between the first and second may be different from that between the sixth and seventh categories. The intervals are not necessarily equal.

Examples of such forms of continuum employed in ordinal measurement are: status (low, middle, high); size (smallest, small, big, biggest); quality (poor, good, very good, excellent); class (low, middle, high); achievement (poor, moderate, high); income (low, middle, high). Ranking occupations is another example.

Interval-level measurement

This level of measurement, as well as demonstrating the properties of ordinal-level measurement, provides information about the distance between the values, and contains equal intervals, ordering subjects into them. This method allows the researcher to assess differences between respondents and to obtain more detailed information about the research topic.

Interval-level measurement allows the researcher, first, to establish whether two values are the same or different (as in nominal measurement), second, to determine whether the one is greater or smaller than the other (as in ordinal measurement), and third, to ascertain the degree of difference between them. Nevertheless, it does not have a true zero point, and if a zero is used it is set arbitrarily, is done so for convenience and does not mean absence of the variable.

Box **4.5**

Interval-level measurement:

- includes equal units
- is essentially a quantitative measurement
- facilitates differentiation and classification
- incorporates ordering of subjects
- specifies the numerical distance between the categories.

For example, if the IQ of two students is 105 and 125 respectively, in nominal terms this means that they have a different IQ; in ordinal terms that the first student has a lower IQ than the second; and in interval terms, that the IQ of the second student is 20 points higher than that of the first student, but not, say, one-fifth greater than the other student.

In mathematical terms, at this level numbers assigned to categories are used to count and rank, but can also be added to and subtracted from each other. This indicates that interval-level measurement is superior to the other two. However, given that there is no true zero, they cannot be multiplied or divided. Statistical measures for nominal, rank and interval data can be used. Examples of this type of measurement are degrees of temperature, calendar time (day, week, month), attitude scales and IQ scores.

Ratio-level measurement

Measurement at this level includes all the attributes of the other three forms, plus the option of an absolute true zero (0) as its lowest value, which in essence indicates the absence of the variable in question. Simply, it is an interval-level measurement with an added true zero. Hence all attributes of interval-level measurement also apply here. Ratio-level measurement allows the researcher to make statements about proportions and ratios, that is, to relate one value to

Table 3.1 Levels of measurement: a summary

Criteria	Nominal	Ordinal	Interval	Ratio
Properties of measurement	Naming	Naming and ranking	Naming, ranking and equal intervals	Naming, ranking, equal intervals & zero point
Nature of measurement	Categorical	Ranking	Scoring	Scoring
Mathematical functions	None	None	Addition and Subtraction	All four functions
Relevant statistical tests	Lambda test χ^2 test	Spearman's ρ M-W U test Sign test	Pearson's r t-test; ANOVA	Pearson's r t-test; ANOVA
Nature of under-lying construct	Discrete	Discrete or continuous	Continuous	Continuous
Examples	Marital status, gender, race, residence, ethnicity	Income, status, achievement, social class, size	temperature, calendar time, IQ scores, attitude scales	Length, weight, distance, number of children age
Typical answers to questions	Male, Female Single, Married, Irish.	Always; often; sometimes; never.	Scores Likert scales Degrees	Years Kilograms Kilometres

another. For instance, a comparison of speed of response of two students to a stimulus – say, 10 seconds and 20 seconds – allows the researcher to conclude that the first is twice as fast as the second.

In the social sciences this level of measurement is employed mainly when measuring demographic variables; however, it is considered inappropriate for measuring attitudes and opinions. This is because a zero (0) option in an attitude scale means no attitude, or no opinion, which is misleading; even having 'no opinion' is in itself an opinion.

In terms of mathematics, numbers arrived at through ratio ordering indicate counting as well as ranking, and can also be added, subtracted, multiplied or divided. Examples of this type of measurement are those given for the interval level above, with the addition of a 0 point in the continuum. Other examples could, for instance, come from the following areas: number of family members, weight, length, distance, number of books that subjects own, reaction time and number of products produced per hour.

Measuring variables

Variables are not measured at one specific level only. Whether a variable will be measured one way or another depends very much on how it is conceptualised and on what type of indicators have been used during measurement. The same variable can be measured in a variety of ways. Age, for instance, can be measured nominally, if it is defined in broad and discrete categories, such as infancy, adolescence, adulthood, middle age and old age; or as young and old. It can be measured also at the ordinal level, when respondents are ranked according to age from the oldest to the youngest.

Age can also be measured at the interval level, given that units are equal, and that we can determine how many units of difference there are between age levels. Interval-level measurement tells us not only whose age is higher (as in ordinal-level measurement) but also how much higher it is. Age can, finally, be measured at the ratio level, since it has an absolute (non-arbitrary) zero. One cannot be younger than 0; and a 20-year-old person is twice as old as a 10-year-old person.

Box **4.6**

Arbitrary and true zeros

The use of true zero as the distinguishing characteristic of ratio scales has caused some confusion. This is due to the fact that it often is difficult to distinguish true zeros from arbitrary zeros. Zeros are not always 'true'. True zeros are meaningful; arbitrary zeros are not. For instance, when we measure temperature, a zero degree reading does not mean no temperature at all! And in measuring attitudes, a zero does not mean no attitude at all (having no opinion on an issue is an opinion!). These zeros are not true zeros, they are arbitrary zeros. However, when measuring income, number of cars, or number of children, a zero indicates no presence of these criteria: it means no children, no income, no cars. These are true zeros; and only measurement using these true zeros can be conducted at the ratio level.

Despite the degree of freedom researchers enjoy when measuring variables, there is a rule of thumb according to which variables are measured at the highest level possible. Overall, discrete variables are measured at the nominal or ordinal level, and continuous variables at the interval or ratio level.

Putting it together

All levels of measurement are effective and useful in their own context and in terms of the purpose for which they have been developed. However, nominal-level measures are the least precise, followed by ordinal-level measures, and then by interval-level measures, with ratio-level measures offering the highest degree of precision. Measuring at the interval and ratio level has many advantages, but not all variables can be measured at these levels (Wang and Mahoney, 1991).

Measurement is a very important and relatively complicated process, but it is associated with many problems and errors. It is limited by the nature of our social world and the variables in question, the perceptions of researchers and their personal bias. Its value depends on the accuracy of the instruments used and the model of operationalisation employed.

2   REPLICATION

Replication applies to quantitative research, where it is required that studies should be conducted in such a fashion that they can be repeated by other researchers to allow validity checking and so more comparisons. With regard to the former, this principle is supposed to guarantee the absence of subjective influence by the researcher and full objectivity in the procedure. The results here are expected to reflect the views of the respondents fully, so that the same outcomes are achieved each time the study is repeated. With regard to the latter, researchers who conduct the same studies in the same or in a different context should be in a position to use the research instruments of the previous study without difficulty, so that the full study can be replicated. This permits valid comparisons and more legitimate generalisations.

Replication is a requirement of quantitative research. In qualitative studies this issue is treated differently. In general, most qualitative researchers do not consider it necessary to adhere to such a requirement, seeing it as irrelevant and impossible. The nature of qualitative research – the lack of interest in representativeness, the use of ad hoc sampling arrangements, and the strong interest in the views of the subjects rather than of the whole community – places replication outside the reigns of this type of research. For many, qualitative research and replication are incompatible.

3   SCALES AND INDEXES

3.1   Introduction

Scales are techniques employed by social scientists in a variety of contexts, particularly in the area of attitude measurement. They consist of a number of items (statements or questions) and a set of quantified response categories. Each item is chosen so that people with different points of view about it react to it in a different way. Scales are employed because they offer (see Benini, 2000):

- *High coverage.* Scales allow a complete coverage of all significant aspects of the concept.
- *High precision and reliability.* Scales allow a high degree of precision and reliability.
- *High comparability.* The use of scales permits detailed and accurate comparisons between sets of data.
- *Simplicity.* Scales help to simplify collection and analysis of the data.

Scales are constructed in a series of complex steps and then statistically tested. Construction and statistical testing are very involving and demanding tasks; they are therefore not easily accessible to the novice, and are certainly beyond the scope of this text. Even experienced researchers prefer to employ already existing and well-tested scales rather than develop new ones. It is worth referring however to a few basic guidelines of scale construction, as handed down to us by two experts Edwards (1957), and Likert (1932). These are shown in Box 4.7.

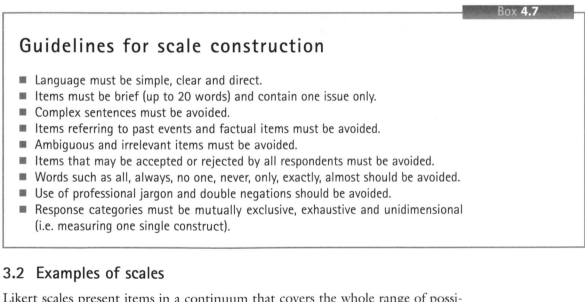

Box **4.7**

Guidelines for scale construction

- Language must be simple, clear and direct.
- Items must be brief (up to 20 words) and contain one issue only.
- Complex sentences must be avoided.
- Items referring to past events and factual items must be avoided.
- Ambiguous and irrelevant items must be avoided.
- Items that may be accepted or rejected by all respondents must be avoided.
- Words such as all, always, no one, never, only, exactly, almost should be avoided.
- Use of professional jargon and double negations should be avoided.
- Response categories must be mutually exclusive, exhaustive and unidimensional (i.e. measuring one single construct).

3.2 Examples of scales

Likert scales present items in a continuum that covers the whole range of possible responses, allowing respondents to choose the answer that fits their opinion. The following is an example of the type of questions employed in Likert scales.

Qu. 57. Gay marriage is as good as heterosexual marriage. (Please circle the number in front of the answer of your choice.)
1. Strongly agree
2. Agree
3. Undecided
4. Disagree
5. Strongly disagree

Another example is the Bogardus Social Distance Scale, which helps to test how close people allow others, for example strangers, to come to them. The content of this scale is shown in Box 4.8.

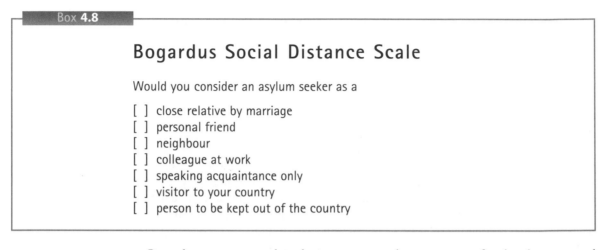

Box **4.8**

Bogardus Social Distance Scale

Would you consider an asylum seeker as a

[ ] close relative by marriage
[ ] personal friend
[ ] neighbour
[ ] colleague at work
[ ] speaking acquaintance only
[ ] visitor to your country
[ ] person to be kept out of the country

Over the years, researchers have constructed an armoury of scales that are used to test topics of interest. These scales are made available to researchers for a small charge to use when studying the relevant topic. There are books of several volumes that contain such scales, details about their creators, their fields of application and other useful information.

3.3 Indexes

An index is a measure containing a combination of items, the values of which are summed up to provide a numerical score. Indexes are used to describe and measure global concepts accurately by considering a number of specific and representative aspects of the concepts. They represent a summary figure and a composite measure in which each item measures one element of the concept, and provides information on this element or part.

An example is the *Quality of Life* index for the city of Vienna. Such an index may include the following items: employment opportunities, recreation opportunities, weather, pollution level, medical services, educational opportunities, childcare services, safety, crime rate and racial problems. These items will be transformed into questions/statements and the index presented for evaluation. Each question will be scored and the total will present a single measure.

The items of an index can be given the same weight (unweighted index) or different values (weighted index). The latter option is taken when, for instance, some index items are thought to be more important than others. In the example given above, employment rates, safety and crime rates may be considered more important for the quality of life than the weather or childcare, and may, therefore, be given a higher value (and a higher score) than the other items. In other cases, the unweighted index is employed.

Indexes are useful measures and can be employed in every aspect of life, such as the economy, politics, education, social life, teaching and religious observance. They are constructed using theoretical principles or mathematical formulae. In either case, they are compound measures, and as such they do not differ greatly from scales (Pfeifer, 2000).

4 VALIDITY

4.1 Validity in quantitative research

Validity is the property of a research instrument that measures its relevance, precision and accuracy. Validity tells the researcher whether an instrument measures what it is supposed to measure, and whether this measurement is accurate and precise. Hence, it is a measure of the quality of the process of measurement, and one that reflects the essential value of a study, and which is accepted, respected, and indeed expected by the researchers and users of research. In general, a measure is expected to be relevant, accurate and precise.

- *Relevance.* An instrument is considered to have absolute validity when it measures what it is supposed to measure and nothing else – no more, no less. If a researcher wanted to know the distance between two cities, kilometres or miles would be a relevant instrument. Similarly, a scale of kilos is a relevant instrument when measuring a person's weight, but is not relevant if used to estimate the person's intelligence.
- *Accuracy.* Validity also entails a degree of accuracy. Accuracy refers to the ability to identify the true value of the item in question. For instance, if you step on your bathroom scales (which measure whole kilos only), and you obtain a reading of 70 kilos (which is your real weight), the scale is accurate. However, if the reading were 68 kilos, the scale would have been inaccurate (and hence invalid).
- *Precision.* Validity requires also that a measure is precise. Precision implies accuracy, but in addition it requires that measurements employ the smallest possible measure. For instance, for a dietician who wants to measure the weekly weight gain or loss of a patient undergoing a special medical treatment, scales that read whole kilos only (68, 69, 70 kilos, and so on) are not precise enough. They are required to read fractions of a kilo.

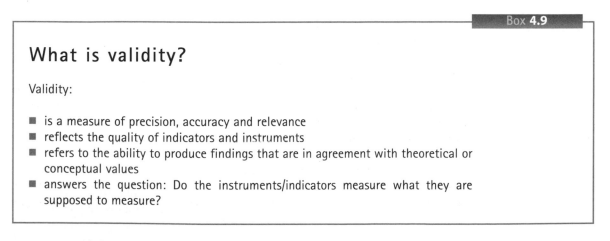

Box **4.9**

What is validity?

Validity:

- is a measure of precision, accuracy and relevance
- reflects the quality of indicators and instruments
- refers to the ability to produce findings that are in agreement with theoretical or conceptual values
- answers the question: Do the instruments/indicators measure what they are supposed to measure?

4.2 Testing validity

In quantitative research, there are two ways of checking the validity of an instrument; these are empirical validation and theoretical validation. In this context, tests of internal and external validity are employed. In the former, the validity of a measure is checked against empirical evidence. In the latter, the validity of an instrument is ascertained through theoretical or conceptual constructs. In both cases, validity is claimed if the test results are acceptable.

Empirical validation

Empirical validation tests pragmatic or criterion validity. If an instrument has, for instance, produced results indicating that students involved in student union activities do better in their exams, and if this is supported by available data, the instrument in question has pragmatic validity. Again, validity here is assumed if the findings are supported by already existing empirical evidence. In this case the validity is *concurrent validity*.

If new findings support the predictions of the measure in question, this measure is said to be valid. For example, if a study found that an eventual introduction of advanced statistics into the social sciences degree would result in a significant drop-out of older students, and if meanwhile this prediction is supported by new findings, the measure has validity. This is known as *predictive validity*.

Theoretical validation

Theoretical or conceptual validation is employed when empirical confirmation of validity is difficult or impossible. A measure is taken to have theoretical validity if its findings comply with the theoretical principles of the discipline, that is, if they do not contradict already established rules of the discipline. There are several types of theoretical validity.

Face validity

An instrument has face validity if, 'on the face of it', it measures what it is expected to measure. For example, a questionnaire aimed at studying sex discrimination has face validity if its questions refer to discrimination experienced by people because they are male or female. The standards of judgement here are based on general theoretical standards and principles, and on what other researchers consider to be the case.

It should be noted that when there are no common standards and principles, and when there is disagreement as to what is generally right to expect this instrument has no face validity. An instrument employed within a study aiming to establish whether people are religious or not that contains only questions related to the respondents' smoking habits is not valid, because it is theoretically known that smoking is not associated with religiosity.

Content validity

A measure is considered to have content validity if it covers all possible dimensions of the research topic. If a researcher in a study of religiosity employs a questionnaire that contains questions only on 'church attendance', this research instrument has no content validity. This is because it focuses only on religious practice and neglects other parts of the concept, such as religious beliefs and religious commitment.

Construct validity

A measure can claim construct validity if its theoretical construct is valid, in other words, if it measures the constructs it is supposed to measure. Validation concentrates here on the validity of the theoretical construct. For example, if an instrument tests the attitudes of two groups of students known to have different views on the issue in question, and this instrument finds them to be different – that is, it verifies the known difference – this instrument is said to have construct validity.

Internal validity

Internal validity refers to the extent to which the research design impacts on the research outcomes. Internal validity checks ensure that the findings of the research have not been affected by instruments or procedures, and that they are the results of the independent variable. Examples of factors that can threaten internal validity, for example in experimental research, panel studies or trend studies, are given below (see Farber, 2001):

- Unexpected structural changes might occur during the course of the study, subjecting respondents to different conditions.
- Normal developmental changes are to be expected in longitudinal studies where data collection occurs in, say, five-year intervals.
- Diverse methods may be used over the course of the study, subjecting respondents to different research instruments.
- Different sampling procedures may be employed during the course of the study, leading to selection problems.
- There may be diverse personnel in the study, with different levels of competence, experience, knowledge and attitude.
- Changes or alterations in recording techniques may lead to inconsistent records.

In such cases, the respondents are exposed to factors that can affect the information collected in the study.

External validity

External validity refers to the extent to which research findings can be generalised, and is mostly relevant to explanatory studies. The following are a few examples of how conducting the research can threaten external validity (see Farber, 2001).

- *Testing.* Being chosen to take part in the study can stimulate respondents to become more familiar with the study object and hence become more knowledgeable than the average population.
- *Sampling.* Inadequate or biased selection may lead to unrepresentative samples.

- *Multiple exposure.* Exposure to a variety of research instruments might cause an interaction effect and associated problems.
- *Measures.* Inappropriate measures may produce unrealistic responses.

Regardless of the type of validity, its contribution to research is most important, and researchers make a concerted effort to include relevant tests in their studies.

4.3 Validity in qualitative research

Validity is a methodological practice not only of quantitative but also of qualitative research (Lancy, 1993; Maxwell, 1992; Miles and Huberman, 1994; Steinke, 2000). Qualitative researchers aim to achieve validity, which they consider to be a strength of their research, since it frees data from interference and contamination, control or variable manipulation (LeCompte and Goetz, 1982); this is facilitated in a number of ways, particularly through their orientation towards, and study of, the empirical world (Blumer, 1979a: 49), through construction of appropriate methods of data collection and analysis (Volmerg, 1983: 124) or through specific measures such as communicative, cumulative, ecological or argumentative validity (see Köckeis-Stangl, 1980).

Validity is an integral part of qualitative research (Lancy, 1993; Steinke, 2000; Volcott, 1990) although it often appears under a different name. Some speak of 'credibility', 'trustworthiness' and 'authenticity' instead; others use concepts such as objectivity, reliability, credibility, transferability, confirmability, verification, quality, standards dependability, corroboration, referential adequacy, truth and honesty; while others employ the original name but qualify it in some way. They speak, for instance, of intersubjective validity, supplemental validity, and paralogic validity, or even trustworthiness, ironic validity (Lather, 1993: 677), paralogic/neo-pragmatic validity (Lyotard, 1984), rhizomatic validity (Derrida, 1976), and sensual validity, or situated validity (Lather, 1993). In some contexts, the quantitative researchers' question 'Does the research instrument study what it is supposed to study' is replaced by the question 'Do the researchers see what they think they see?'

To guarantee validity in their work, qualitative researchers apply a number of measures. These vary from case to case, with some researchers proposing one set of measures and others suggesting another. Some of these types of validation, referred to by a number of writers (see Drew et al., 1996; Lamnek, 1993; Pfeifer, 2000; Terhardt, 1981: 789), are presented below.

- *Cumulative validation.* A study can be validated if its findings are supported by other studies. The researcher can compare the various findings and make a judgement about the validity of the studies.
- *Communicative validation.* This form of validation entails the involvement of the participants – by checking accuracy of data, evaluation of project process, change of goals etc. (in the Delphi format), by employing expert external audits, and by using triangulation – in order to achieve a multiple perspective (Kardorff, 2000: 245–6), and to confirm authenticity.
- *Argumentative validation.* This form of validity is established through presentation of the findings in such a way that conclusions can be followed and tested.

■ *Ecological validation.* A study is held to be valid if carried out in the natural environment of the subjects, using suitable methods and taking into consideration the life and conditions of the researched.

Other 'tactics'

In a different manner, Miles and Huberman (1994) suggest 'tactics' for testing or confirming findings which, although not direct forms of validity, have a similar function. Some are similar to those presented above (e.g. cumulative or communicative validation); others are close to the form of validation employed by quantitative researchers. Proposals for an integrated effort to safeguard validity in qualitative research have been offered by other writers (Lincoln and Guba, 1985; Drew et al., 1996: 169–71). The important point here is that validity is not a criterion of quantitative research but a common basis for most types of research. A view supported by many workers in this area is that investigators do not need to demonstrate validity but rather methodological excellence, that is, research performance in a professional, accurate and systematic manner.

These types of validation are considered to be as effective as those employed in quantitative research. For some writers they are even more effective. Lamnek (1993: 154–9), justifies this point on the ground that, in qualitative research and studies:

■ The data are closer to the research field than in quantitative research.
■ The collection of information is not determined by research screens and directives.
■ The data are closer to reality than in quantitative research.
■ The opinions and views of the researched are considered.
■ The methods are more open and more flexible than in quantitative research.
■ There is a communicative basis that is not available in quantitative research.
■ A successive expansion of data is possible.

Observing the developments in the area of validity in social research, it becomes obvious that in qualitative research quality assurance has been given increasingly

Box **4.10**

Validity in ethnographic research

'(1)The researcher should refrain from talking in the field but rather should listen as much as possible. He or she should (2) produce notes that are as exact as possible (3) begin to write early, and in a way (4) which allows readers of his or her notes and reports to see for themselves. This means providing enough data for readers to make their own inferences and follow those of the researcher. The report should be (5) as complete and (6) as candid as possible. (7) The researcher should seek feedback for his or her findings and presentations in the field or from his or her colleagues. (8) Presentations should be characterised by balance between the subjects and (9) by accuracy in writing'

(Wollcott, 1990: 127–8)

high priority (see for example Lincoln, 1995; Seale, 1999; Steinke, 1999). Important innovations have been introduced to ensure validity. Some central points in this area have been those described above, but apart from this the notion of an open and clear description of the procedures of data collection and interpretation, the presentation of relevant materials, the reproduction of transcripts, field notes, and even an emphasis on replication have been highly significant (Matt, 2000: 585).

5 RELIABILITY

Reliability refers to the capacity of measurement to produce consistent results. Reliability is equivalent to *consistency*. Thus, a method is reliable if it produces the same results whenever it is repeated, and is not sensitive to the researcher, the research conditions or the respondents. Reliability is also characterised by precision and objectivity (see Box 4.11). As in validity, so in reliability there are two major aspects of interest in this context; these are *internal* reliability and *external* reliability. Internal reliability means consistency of results within the site, and that data are plausible within that site. External reliability refers to consistency and replicability of data across sites.

The purpose of reliability testing is to ensure that the instruments in question are robust and not sensitive to changes of the researcher, the respondent or the research condition. This, apart from implying that the instrument allows replicability, demonstrates that reliability is concerned with objectivity, accuracy, precision, consistency and stability. These criteria are employed as in validity.

Box **4.11**

What is reliability?

Reliability:

- is a measure of objectivity, stability, consistency, and precision
- measures the quality of indicators and instruments
- refers to the ability to produce the same findings every time the procedure is repeated
- answers the questions: does the instrument/indicator produce consistent results? Is the instrument free of bias associated with the researcher, the subject or the research conditions?

5.1 Reliability in quantitative research

There are at least three types of reliability, all of which are considered by social researchers. These are:

- *Stability reliability*, relating to reliability across time. Here the question is whether a measure produces reliable findings if it is employed at different points in time.

- *Representative reliability*, which relates to reliability across groups of subjects. The question here is whether the measure will be reliable if employed in groups other than the original group of subjects.
- *Equivalence reliability*, which relates to reliability across indicators and to multiple indicators in operationalisation procedures. The question here is: will the measure in question produce consistent results across indicators?

There are also several methods for testing reliability of an instrument. The most common methods are the following:

- *Test-retest method*. The same subjects are tested and retested with the same instrument. If the same results are obtained the instrument is reliable.
- *Split-half method*. Responses to the items of an instrument are divided into two groups (e.g. odd/even questions) and the scores correlated. The type and degree of correlation indicate the degree of reliability of the measurement.
- *Inter-item test and item-scale test*. Inter-item correlations or item-scale correlations indicate the degree of reliability of the instrument.
- *Alternate-form reliability*. Reliability is tested by administering two similar instruments in one session, and is assessed by the degree of correlation between the scores of the two groups.

These tests are regularly used and entail a considerable amount of statistical analysis and interpretation. Instruments are tested before they are put to use, and the results are normally disclosed to the academic community every time these instruments are referred to and their findings published. The advent of computer-based statistical analysis has made this task easier, more accurate and more enjoyable than before, and is being consistently used by quantitative researchers.

A closer analysis of reliability shows that it is related to validity. Actually, reliability without validity is of little use. Even the most reliable instrument is useless if it is not valid. For instance, the scales that show the student's weight is exactly 65 kg every time the student steps on them are of no value if the student's actual weight is known to be 99 kg. Hence, it is useful to measure and interpret reliability results together with validity scores.

5.2 Reliability in qualitative research

Qualitative researchers give little – if any – attention to reliability in the way that quantitative ones do. They have many reasons to object to these practices (see Box 4.12). They do consider reliability an important parameter of research but, to adhere to it, they employ methods that are radically different from those employed in quantitative research.

Qualitative researchers use measures of reliability that in their view are more effective, such as increasing the variability of perspectives in research, or setting up a list of possible errors or distortions which they aim to avoid (McCall, 1979). Overall, qualitative researchers strive for rigour but employ different methods to achieve it. In the majority of cases, they avoid the use of the concept 'reliability'; instead they use concepts such as *credibility* and *applicability*, or *auditability*.

Objectivity is replaced by: *confirmability* (Guba and Lincoln, 1989); *coherence*, that is, the extent to which methods meet the research goals; *openness*, the degree to which otherwise suitable methods are allowed to be used; and *discourse*, that is, the extent to which researchers are allowed to discuss the researched data and interpret them together and evaluate the consequences of such findings (Bogumil and Immerfall, 1985: 71). References to *trustworthiness, dependability, credibility, transferability* and *confirmability* also seem to be popular (Flick, 1998: 231–2)

Box 4.12

Qualitative research and quantitative reliability

In their quest for validity, quantitative researchers are thought to:

- control the environment
- employ high levels of measurement and standardisation
- restrict the researcher-researched relationship
- create artificial situations which are different from those they intend to study
- alienate the researcher from the research environment, which is counterproductive.

Overall, the quality of qualitative research is assessed in more general terms than that of quantitative research. It is done by such means as demarcating statements of the subjects and interpretations of the researcher; following procedures that would guarantee that multiple researchers produce comparable results (e.g. through appropriate training); and increasing the documentation of the results (Flick, 1998: 224).

Both aspects of reliability, the internal and the external, are considered in qualitative research. How these dimensions of reliability are addressed in practice varies from case to case. One common view (Flick, 1998: 231–2) proposes the following paths:

- prolonged engagement and persistent observation
- peer review or debriefing
- analysis of negative cases
- checking 'the appropriateness of the terms of reference of interpretations and their assessment'
- member checks (communicative validation)
- external auditing.

In a similar manner, Drew and associates (1996: 169) suggest that the following steps should be followed if internal reliability is to be achieved:

a. Use low inference descriptors.
b. Use multiple researchers whenever possible.
c. Create a careful audit trail (a detailed record of data that can be used by other scholars to check internal validity).

d. Use mechanical recording devices where possible (and with permission).
e. Use participant researchers or informants to check the accuracy or congruence of perceptions.

With regard to external reliability, the same authors propose the following five steps:

a. Specify the researchers' status or position clearly so that readers know exactly what point of view drove the data collection.
b. State the identity of the informants (or what role they play in the natural context) and how and why they were selected (while maintaining confidentiality).
c. Delineate the context or set boundaries and characteristics carefully so that the reader can make judgments about similar circumstances or settings.
d. Define the analytic constructs that guide the study (describe specific conceptual frameworks used in design and deductive analysis).
e. Specify the data collection and analysis procedures meticulously.

Regardless of the significance of these approaches to reliability, a number of writers argue that qualitative research does not provide as high a degree of reliability as quantitative research. However, this view is not shared by others who argue that both models of reliability testing are correct in their contexts. They are different but they serve their particular purposes.

5.3 Validity and reliability

Validity and reliability are both quality measures of research instruments, and although they are quite different in their nature and purpose, some students find

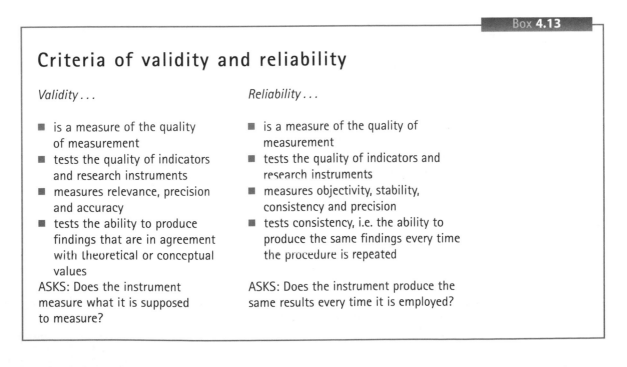

Box **4.13**

Criteria of validity and reliability

Validity...

- is a measure of the quality of measurement
- tests the quality of indicators and research instruments
- measures relevance, precision and accuracy
- tests the ability to produce findings that are in agreement with theoretical or conceptual values

ASKS: Does the instrument measure what it is supposed to measure?

Reliability...

- is a measure of the quality of measurement
- tests the quality of indicators and research instruments
- measures objectivity, stability, consistency and precision
- tests consistency, i.e. the ability to produce the same findings every time the procedure is repeated

ASKS: Does the instrument produce the same results every time it is employed?

it difficult to distinguish between the two. An example may help to clarify the difference. If a male student weighs himself 20 times and every time he receives a reading of 65 kg (which is also his true weight), the scale is both reliable and valid. If all recorded readings were 40 kg, the scale is reliable but not valid. And if he obtains 20 different readings (40 kg, 45 kg, 63 kg etc.), the scale is neither valid nor reliable.

The validity and reliability of a measure are closely interrelated. Nevertheless, the one cannot predict the other. A reliable instrument is not necessarily valid. Even the most reliable instrument can be invalid. As noted above, reliability alone cannot assess the quality of an instrument fully. The validity score is the most important.

6   OBJECTIVITY IN SOCIAL RESEARCH

6.1 The debate

Objectivity is the research principle that requires that all the personal values and views of the investigator must be kept out of the research process. The purpose of this is to minimise personal prejudice and bias, and to guarantee that social reality will be presented as it is, and not as the investigator interprets it, imagines it or wants it to be.

Although this is a long-standing principle, the question of whether social inquiry ought to be objective or not has not been answered uniformly by the academic community. Over the years academic views on this issue have been divided, with two lines of thought occupying the two extremes of the argument. The one is known as *value neutrality*, and the other as *normativism*. The former was the position of quantitative researchers, and the latter the stance of qualitative and other researchers.

Box **4.14**

What is objectivity?

Objectivity is the empiricist doctrine that the research process and design must be free of personal bias and prejudice. It rests on the belief that facts and values should be kept apart, and that research should focus on what really is and not on what ought to be. Objectivity reflects value neutrality.

Value neutrality

The notion of value neutrality reflects the requirement that investigators ought to minimise the effects of their own biases. Social researchers are seen as 'technicians' or consultants and not as reformers; or better, as neutral observers and analysts and not as philosophers or moralists. The researcher's personal views and value judgments are to be kept out of research. In a more general context, objectivity subscribes to a number of principles and convictions, three of which are the following:

- The social sciences are value free; their goal is to study what is and not what ought to be. Research should aim to achieve the highest possible degree of objectivity.
- Social scientists should be value free; they should rule out value judgments, subjective views, personal bias and personal convictions.
- Value judgments should be reserved for policy makers, and not for social scientists.

Normativism

Normativism is critical of the value and usefulness of objectivity and proposes that value-neutrality is not justified. More specifically it proposes that (Abercrombie et al., 1988; Fay, 1980; Mills, 1959; Wadsworth, 1984):

- Objectivity is unattainable, unnecessary and undesirable.
- Social science is normative; its goal is to study what ought to be and not only what is.
- People's orientation is based on and constructed with values, which direct thinking and action, and cannot be neutralised, isolated or ignored.
- Being normative and disclosing the inevitable bias or personal beliefs is less dangerous than pretending to be value free.

6.2 Objectivity in quantitative research

Quantitative research accepts and supports objectivity, and considers it one of the most important principles of social inquiry. This is obvious, given that quantitative research operates within an objectivist epistemology. For quantitative researchers, objectivity is regarded as a virtue that every social researcher should try to achieve. Although they are aware that it is difficult to reach a high degree of objectivity, the endeavour to reach the highest possible level is taken for granted.

The logic of objectivity rests here on the argument that research has the task of capturing and presenting reality as it is and not as it is interpreted, imagined or wanted to be by the investigator. If one is interested in why female students

The logic of objectivity

- The purpose of research is to discover objective truths.
- Objective truths can be verified only when contrasted with objective reality.
- The task of verification is completed by researchers.
- It is important that verification is conducted objectively and focuses on objective reality.
- The subjective views and personal values of the researcher can only distort the process of verification, and cannot enhance the objectivity of truths.
- Hence, subjectivity distorts the process of discovery of objective truths and must be excluded from research.

get higher grades in science courses, one expects the researcher to set aside personal views and try to establish the real reasons. If one disregards objectivity and constructs a research design that is biased by personal beliefs and ideologies, the sampling procedures will be affected as much as the choice of methods of data collection and analysis and, obviously, the findings and conclusions. The results will be flawed and will not correspond to reality. Five such researchers may produce five different sets of answers to the same question. Objectivity serves to restrict the influence of such personal biases and prejudices in the research process and to allow reality to come forward as it is, without manipulation.

6.3 Objectivity in qualitative research

Qualitative researchers fundamentally reject the notion of objectivity. Given that qualitative research rests within the parameters of an interpretivist epistemology, this is self-evident. Hence, involving personal views and interpretation in the research process is not only acceptable but advisable, and is considered an advantage.

The logic behind this position is that there is no objective reality to begin with. Hence, it is not possible to capture objective reality in the way that objectivism proposes. Researchers capture one aspect of reality – their reality – and this is what they can describe and present. Apart from this, value neutrality is considered to be unattainable, unnecessary and undesirable. One cannot consider intrinsic evaluation, feelings, beliefs and standards as insignificant or uninfluential. Social scientists ought to have a standpoint on social issues, and they must produce value judgments if they wish to solve social problems. Qualitative research encourages intersubjectivity, closeness between the elements of the research, and involvement of the researcher in the whole research process (Becker, 1989; Stergios, 1991).

Further, adherence to objectivity is taken to support the status quo. Hence believing in and trusting what is objective means believing in what people learned to consider objective, and failing to challenge it. Objectivity legitimises beliefs and practices that people take for granted. Women for instance learned to take the world of males as objective, and came to accept it (see Keller, 1985; Reinharz, 1992). It follows that abandoning objectivity will free thinking from 'inappropriate' constraints and 'unconscious' mythologies. Through disengaging thinking from notions of what is generally considered to be objective, one can capture reality more effectively.

This position does not mean that qualitative researchers abandon the academic requirement to be responsible, truthful and transparent in their work. It is often argued that in qualitative research objectivity is 'emergent'; that is, it evolves out of the subjectivity of the parties of interaction. Qualitative research uses an intersubjective concept of objectivity in as far as its aim is to break away from subjectivity through generalisation.

Some researchers, instead of speaking of objectivity, speak of transparency: openly stating the course and elements of the research process, and letting others judge its quality. Others (Rorty, 1985: 10; J. K. Smith, 1992: 101) consider objectivity as equivalent to solidarity, namely the degree of agreement among colleagues and researchers. Simply, objectivity is achieved if colleagues agree with the research process, accept the results and praise the researchers for their achievements.

In this sense, a form of objectivity is accepted and practised, although under different labels and within the parameters of the overarching paradigm. Guba and Lincoln (1989), for instance, confirm that any qualitative study of rigour is expected to contain what they call truth value, applicability, consistency and neutrality. The latter is another word for objectivity and is expected to provide

---

Box **4.16**

Where and how objectivity is practised

Research parameters	How objectivity is practised
Reality	By perceiving reality in objective terms, as an objective reality that must be reproduced as it is, without distortions of any kind
The researcher	By respecting value neutrality, i.e. being free of personal values, bias, and prejudice, and studying 'what is' and not 'what ought to be'
Research topic	By conceptualising the research topic in an objective manner; selection of indicators and definitions should be free of personal bias, experiences, and views
Methodology	By choosing the appropriate methodology in a process free of personal preferences, ideologies or bias
Design construction	By constructing the design using professional standards, avoiding personal bias, and assuring compliance to ethical standards throughout the study
Sampling	By choosing the sample in compliance with research standards and practices, excluding personal bias and preference
Data collection	By choosing relevant methods and gathering data using professional standards, and by focusing on 'what is' and not on 'what ought to be'
Administration	By guiding arrangements towards facilitating the completion of the study, using fair and professionally acceptable standards and not personal or ideological preferences
Data analysis	By describing relevant methods clearly and by conducting analysis in a manner that reflects professionalism, and avoiding personal biases and preferences
Interpretation	By including clear and detailed justification of conclusions, revealing personal perceptions and interpretations of data and reality for verification
Reporting	By constructing the report in a manner that clearly outlines the data and the personal interpretations of the writer; personal views etc. should be made clear.

confirmability. For many qualitative researchers, some form of neutrality is a central element of qualitative research, although the nature and extent of that 'objectivity' are different from that of quantitative researchers.

Finally, in feminist research, which is openly a qualitative kind, some forms of objectivity are accepted and practised. Examples of objectivity are: dynamic objectivity (Keller, 1985); openness, where all facts are made known to the respondent, highlighting all contingencies of representation (Harding, 1991); democratic discussion, where all parameters are set in the open, which encourages cooperation among all researchers as well as criticism from all points of view, and is based on equality of intellectual authority (Longino, 1990); and anti-sexism practices.

7 REPRESENTATIVENESS

Representativeness has always been a central target of researchers who aspire to gather data that would allow them to speak for the whole target population. As we shall see later, one of the most important aspects of sampling is to ensure representativeness, and researchers have devised many methods to ensure that social research will meet this requirement. Apart from this, sampling procedures are considered proper if they are representative for the target population.

Representativeness is associated with the nature of principles of the underlying methodology, and hence the status of this attribute within a research project depends on the nature of the methodology.

Box **4.17**

What is representativeness?

Representativeness is a research principle that reflects the capacity of social research to produce findings that are consistent with (representative of) what appears in the target population; this is a property of sampling. The aim of representativeness is to ensure that all relevant groups of the target population are adequately represented in the research sample. The degree of representativeness determines the extent to which the findings of a study can be generalised.

Quantitative research

Representativeness has a central place in, and is one of the aims of, quantitative research. Several procedures have been developed and are currently employed to ensure the representativeness of the sample and the study in general. Most of these procedures deal with the nature of sample selection as well as with sample's size and composition. Statistical techniques have been developed to assist with this process. Standard errors, for instance, are calculated, and techniques used that can assist in achieving a sample size that will allow the study to claim representativeness.

The logic of employing this research principle lies in the fact that – as noted above – it is associated with the quality of the results. Representative studies speak for the whole population. Non-representative ones do not; they do not support generalisations.

As already mentioned, representativeness is affected by theoretical frameworks; some provide more suitable conditions for constructing a representative study than others. However, it is also affected by errors in the design and/or execution of the research; some are accidental errors (caused by uncontrollable mistakes), while others are systematic errors caused by faulty designs that allow a disproportional representation of some parts of the population in the sample.

Qualitative research

In qualitative research, representativeness, as we introduced it above, is considered irrelevant and unimportant for several reasons. First, it is not consistent with the principles of the qualitative paradigm, and second, the size of the sample and the nature of qualitative sampling procedures do not allow any claims for representativeness. Nevertheless, this does not mean that qualitative researchers are not interested in representativeness. There are researchers who consider it to be an indispensable element of qualitative research and take precautions to ensure it (e.g. Miles and Huberman, 1994).

Such precautions include, for instance, avoidance of 'sampling non-representative informants, e.g. by over-relying on accessible or elite respondents', and of 'generalising from unrepresentative events or activities', or 'drawing inferences from non-representative processes'. Miles and Huberman (1994: 265) advise that weak non-representative cases should be expanded, and suggest the following ways to do so:

- Increase the number of cases.
- Search purposely for contrasting cases.
- Sort the cases systematically and fill out weakly sampled case types.
- Sample randomly within the total universe of people and phenomena under study.

The last suggestion brings qualitative research as near as one can get to quantitative research and is a controversial suggestion indeed. Although it brings qualitative research closer to a legitimate claim for representativeness, it also takes it further away from the very principles of this research paradigm.

8 GENERALISABILITY

Literally, generalisability is the ability to generalise something. In social research it means generalising the findings beyond the boundaries of the group studied. It is the other side of representativeness: high representativeness is associated with high generalisability, and vice versa. Hence, the earlier discussion on representativeness is relevant to our discussion of generalisability. It is obvious that researchers endeavour to be able to claim generalisability in their studies, regardless of the nature of this attribute, and so they design their sampling procedures for this purpose.

Box **4.18**

What is generalisability?

In social research, generalisability refers to the capacity of a study to extrapolate the relevance of its findings beyond the boundaries of the sample. In other words it reflects the extent to which a study is able to generalise its findings from the sample to the whole population. Obviously, the higher the generalisability, the higher the value of the study.

There are several forms of generalisation. The two representative types are *scientific* (*inductive*) generalisation and *naturalistic* generalisation. The former refers to the extrapolation of the validity of the findings of a study of representative cases to the whole population. Naturalistic generalisations are more diverse and include several variations. Analytical generalisations, exemplar generalisations, and case-to-case transfer (transferability) (Firestone, 1993) are a few examples. These are basically theory-related generalisations. They can also rest on the argument that the typical cases studied are representative of a species, and hence findings concerning these typical cases can be considered applicable within this species.

Quantitative researchers mostly employ scientific or inductive generalisations, using probability theory to construct the samples, and statistical methods and techniques to estimate the level of generalisability. Qualitative researchers employ naturalistic generalisations, and in order to achieve this, they use typical cases as their sample. The manner in which generalisability is justified within qualitative research varies considerably. Some writers employ *multi-site research* (i.e. sample triangulation) to achieve generalisability. Obviously, choosing typical subjects from a variety of backgrounds ensures representativeness and hence generalisations.

Other writers explain generalisability by means of criteria such as *conceptual power, fittingness* and *comparability* (e.g. Schofield, 1993). Fittingness relates to the degree of fit between the case studied and the case to which researchers want to generalise their findings (ibid.: 211). Focusing on this point is a way of 'claiming' generalisability. Comparability refers to the assessment of the relevance of the findings by checking similarities and differences between the studied site and the sites to which the findings are to be generalised. The question here is whether the site studied is *typical* of the others. Multi-site research entails the study of the same issue in more than one site, thus establishing the relative representativeness of the sites.

MAIN POINTS

- The principles of research are precision in measurement, accuracy, validity, reliability, objectivity, replication, representativeness and generalisability.
- Some form and degree of measurement is included in all types of research.
- There are four levels of measurement: nominal, ordinal, interval and ratio levels.
- Variables are measured at the highest level possible.

- Validity is the ability to produce accurate results and to measure what is supposed to be measured. It is an attribute of quantitative and qualitative research.
- Quantitative research employs many types of validation: for example, empirical, theoretical, face, content and construct validity.
- In qualitative research, validation takes the form of cumulative, communicative, argumentative or ecological validation.
- Reliability is the capacity to produce consistent results. It is an attribute of both quantitative and qualitative research
- Objectivity excludes personal values from research, and is valued in quantitative research.
- Representativeness is an important characteristic of social research that is closely adhered to in both quantitative and qualitative research.

WHERE TO FROM HERE?

Before you leave this chapter, visit the companion website for the third edition of *Social Research* at http://www.palgrave.com/sociology/sarantakos to review the main concepts introduced in this chapter and to test yourself on the major issues discussed.

FURTHER READING

Beere, C. A. (1990) *Gender Roles: A Handbook of Tests and Measures.* New York: Greenwood.

Bolton, B. F. (2001) *Handbook of Measurement and Evaluation in Rehabilitation.* Gaithersburg, Md.: Aspen.

Bowling, A. (1997) *Measuring Health: A Review of Quality of Life Measurement Scales.* Buckingham: Open University Press.

Caria, M. (2000) *Measurement Analysis.* London: Imperial College Press.

Chen, S.-Y. (1997) M*easurement and Analysis in Psychological Research: the Failing and Saving of Theory.* Aldershot: Arebury.

Edwards, A. A. (1957) *Techniques of Attitude Scale Constructions.* New York: Appleton-Century-Crofts.

Ginevan, M. and Splitstone, D. E (2004) *Statistical Tools for Environmental Quality Measurement.* Boca Raton, Fla.: Chapman & Hall.

Kirk, J. and Miller, R. L. (1986) *Reliability and Validity in Qualitative Research.* Newbury Park, Calif.: Sage.

Krebs, D. and Schmidt, P. (1993) *New Directions in Attitude Measurement.* Berlin and New York: W. de Gruyter.

Laster, P. E. and Bishop, L. K. (2000) *Handbook of Tests and Measurement in Education and the Social Sciences.* Lanham, Md.: Scarecrow.

McDowell, I. and Newell, C. (1996) *Measuring Health: A Guide to Rating Scales and Questionnaires.* New York: Oxford University Press.

Michell. J. (1999) *Measurement in Psychology: Critical History of a Methodological Concept.* New York: Cambridge University Press.

Plake, B. S. and Impara, J. S. eds (2001) *The Fourteenth Mental Measurements Yearbook.* Lincoln: Buros Institute.

Robinson, J. P., Shaver, P. and Wrightsman, L. S. (1999) *Measures of Political Attitudes.* San Diego: Academic Press.

Spector, P. E. (1992) *Summated Rating Scale Construction: An Introduction.* Newbury Park: Sage.

Thorndike, R. M. (1997) *Measurement and Evaluation in Psychology and Education.* Upper Saddle River, N.J.: Merrill.

Zeller, R. A. and Carmines, E. G. (1980) *Measurement in the Social Sciences.* Cambridge: Cambridge University Press.

Research planning

Research design

- reviews the process of social research
- gives examples of its structure and place in social research
- reviews its relevance for qualitative and quantitative research
- clarifies their application by giving examples of design construction
- shows how to construct your own research project.

INTRODUCTION

This is where the actual research process begins; with a committing interest in certain answers, and of course with many questions. The questions that come up first are, 'Where do I begin', and 'What do I do next?', or better, 'What is the first step towards doing research?', and then 'What follows right after that?'. This chapter will help you answer these and many other questions relating to how actual research is initiated and planned, and what type of decisions must be made in order for the research to achieve its purpose.

In the discussion that follows, we shall see that the first step towards doing research is to develop a plan that will present a summary of its main elements: what will be studied and how, when and where the research will take place; then, how it will be executed; and, finally, how the data will be analysed and published. We shall also see how this planning of research is applied in real situations, including a student's project.

1   THE RESEARCH PROCESS

The manner in which research will be conducted is determined by the methodology that underlies the research. Qualitative and quantitative researchers conduct their research in different ways. Nevertheless, the overall models they employ share the same general structure. All researchers, despite their differences, follow the same basic path of research. The five basic criteria of the research process are shown below.

a.   Research is conducted in the form of steps, guiding the researcher from the beginning to the end of the inquiry.
b.   These steps are: first, the choice of the research topic and methodology; second, the methodological construction of the topic; third, sampling; fourth, data collection; fifth, data analysis and interpretation; and sixth, reporting.
c.   Quantitative researchers move from step to step progressively, ensuring that each step is fully completed before they move to the next. Qualitative researchers are more flexible about this.
d.   The design of the research model is constructed before the start of the research, although in certain contexts flexibility on this is also accepted.
e.   There is a degree of order in the process of moving from step to step, varying according to the underlying paradigm.

The six steps of the research process (criterion 'b' above) and the questions they intend to answer are briefly described in Box 5.1. Designs are usually presented in writing, constituting a document that is shared among the members of the research team, or are thought out clearly, and retained in the researcher's mind. This is particularly so for simple studies conducted single-handedly by the (experienced) researcher.

Box **5.1**

Steps of the research design

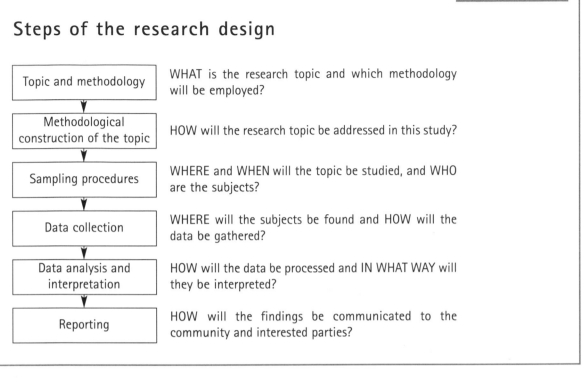

Topic and methodology	WHAT is the research topic and which methodology will be employed?
Methodological construction of the topic	HOW will the research topic be addressed in this study?
Sampling procedures	WHERE and WHEN will the topic be studied, and WHO are the subjects?
Data collection	WHERE will the subjects be found and HOW will the data be gathered?
Data analysis and interpretation	HOW will the data be processed and IN WHAT WAY will they be interpreted?
Reporting	HOW will the findings be communicated to the community and interested parties?

2 DESIGN AND EXECUTION OF RESEARCH

2.1 The research design

Research entails two major stages: one is the stage of planning, and the other is the stage of execution. During the first stage, researchers construct a design, a plan of the research, and during the second they collect and analyse the data. The former is conducted in the researcher's office, the latter in the field.

The design explains in some detail how the researcher intends to conduct the work, namely how the questions asked in each research step shown in Box 5.1 will be addressed. This implies that the researcher will go through the research steps, one by one, and describe adequately the activities to be undertaken in each step.

There are many forms of design. Some focus on the process of data collection only (e.g. Diekmann, 1995: 274), while others extend their boundaries to cover data analysis (e.g. Ragin, 1994: 191). Most writers and researchers, however, see the research design in a wider context, covering all aspects of research from the selection of the topic to the publication of the data (e.g. Flick, 2000b). This is how designs will be perceived and addressed in our discussion.

2.2 Purpose of the research design

The purpose of research designs varies according to the nature and purpose of the study, the type of population, the structure of the research, the number of researchers and research assistants, and the ideological affiliation of the researcher, among other factors. For most writers on the subject (e.g. Berger et al. 1989; Flick, 2000a; Pfeifer, 2000) the purpose of the research design reflects the goals described in Box 5.2.

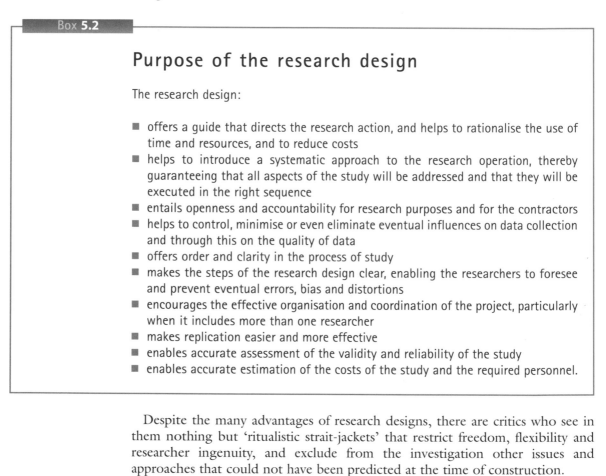

Box **5.2**

Purpose of the research design

The research design:

■ offers a guide that directs the research action, and helps to rationalise the use of time and resources, and to reduce costs
■ helps to introduce a systematic approach to the research operation, thereby guaranteeing that all aspects of the study will be addressed and that they will be executed in the right sequence
■ entails openness and accountability for research purposes and for the contractors
■ helps to control, minimise or even eliminate eventual influences on data collection and through this on the quality of data
■ offers order and clarity in the process of study
■ makes the steps of the research design clear, enabling the researchers to foresee and prevent eventual errors, bias and distortions
■ encourages the effective organisation and coordination of the project, particularly when it includes more than one researcher
■ makes replication easier and more effective
■ enables accurate assessment of the validity and reliability of the study
■ enables accurate estimation of the costs of the study and the required personnel.

Despite the many advantages of research designs, there are critics who see in them nothing but 'ritualistic strait-jackets' that restrict freedom, flexibility and researcher ingenuity, and exclude from the investigation other issues and approaches that could not have been predicted at the time of construction.

Despite this, research designs are an integral part of the research process. Quantitative researchers employ designs as much as qualitative researchers do, as we shall see next.

3 RESEARCH DESIGN IN QUANTITATIVE RESEARCH

3.1 Basic criteria for quantitative research design

In quantitative research, social inquiry follows a well-constructed design that covers in detail all the steps of the investigation. In this sense, research is perceived as progressing in a sequence of steps that are closely interrelated and develop from the first to the last, and in which the success of each depends on the successful completion of the preceding step. The features that mark the identity of the quantitative design are listed in Box 5.3.

Box **5.3**

Features of the quantitative research design

A quantitative research design:

- contains six major steps (see Box 5.4)
- sees the steps as relatively separate and independent parts of the research
- is constructed before the research commences
- is presented precisely and in great detail
- is rigid, leaving no flexibility or choice for change during execution
- is a one-way process, allowing no revisiting of steps that have already been completed
- presumes that successful completion of a step depends on the success of previous steps
- is based on objectivity, requiring that all decisions are made using professional standards and allowing no scope for the personal preferences or decisions of the researcher.

Briefly, quantitative researchers employ the model of research design introduced in Box 5.1, although with some adjustments, as we shall soon see.

3.2 Structure of quantitative research design

As noted earlier, the structure of the steps of the quantitative research design varies according to the nature and purpose of the study, the complexity of the topic and population, and the number and expertise of the members of the research team. The general rule is that too many instructions limit the flexibility that every researcher wants to enjoy, while too few guidelines leave many questions unanswered, and allow too much freedom to research assistants, which may cause distortions.

Quantitative research favours the more restrictive option, precisely because it does not allow flexibility and freedom in the research process. The steps and specific tasks associated with each step of this research model are given in Box 5.4. Note also the direction of the flow (arrows) of the research process.

It is worth stressing that the research design is to be perceived as a dynamic process, with the steps being interrelated and with each affecting the other, and being fully understood within that context.

3.3 Steps in quantitative research design

The content of a research design outlined above will be discussed in detail in the remaining chapters of this book, for it constitutes the essence of social inquiry. In this section we shall introduce briefly the meaning and content of the various steps, using an example to demonstrate their application in a real research context.

Box **5.4**

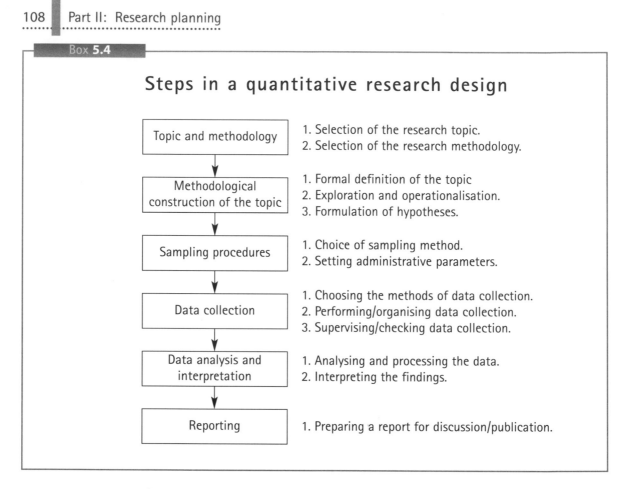

Steps in a quantitative research design

Topic and methodology	1. Selection of the research topic. 2. Selection of the research methodology.
Methodological construction of the topic	1. Formal definition of the topic 2. Exploration and operationalisation. 3. Formulation of hypotheses.
Sampling procedures	1. Choice of sampling method. 2. Setting administrative parameters.
Data collection	1. Choosing the methods of data collection. 2. Performing/organising data collection. 3. Supervising/checking data collection.
Data analysis and interpretation	1. Analysing and processing the data. 2. Interpreting the findings.
Reporting	1. Preparing a report for discussion/publication.

Step 1. Topic and methodology

The research begins with the selection of the topic to be studied and the research methodology (qualitative or quantitative). At this stage, the researcher makes explicit what is to be studied, and what methodology will be employed.

a. *Selection of research topic.* Here the topic of the study is formally stated. Any topic that is amenable to social inquiry can be chosen. For instance:

Topic: Parental divorce and children's attitudes to marriage.

The question here is whether the experience of parental divorce by children has any effect on the way young people perceive marriage.

b. *Selection of methodology.* The researcher must decide which methodology will direct the study. The choice is usually between quantitative and qualitative research. For instance:

> Methodology: Quantitative methodology (resting on a positivist paradigm).

The researcher decides to use a quantitative study, either because this methodology is more suitable for the intended study or because the researcher has already established a methodological affiliation and predisposition to carry out predominantly, or even exclusively, quantitative research.

Step 2. Methodological construction of the topic

This step aims to make the research topic clear and specific and eventually to reduce it to the actual topic of analysis. In this context the topic will be defined more accurately, explored and operationalised, and hypotheses will be formulated.

a. *Formal definition of the topic*. Here, the researcher will explain clearly and accurately the topic as it will be analysed in the research. For instance:

> Definitions:
>
> Parental divorce: Legal dissolution of parental marriage.
> Attitudes to marriage: Personal stand on marriage.
> Children: Biological children aged 20–25 years of age.

Note how concepts have been specified and reduced. Divorce applies here to married couples only (not cohabiting); and the study focuses only on children between 20 and 25 years of age, and not children of all ages.

b. *Exploration*. This entails a thorough study of existing information on the subject; here the researcher will specify how this will be facilitated. For instance:

> Exploration: Basic information will be gathered through literature review.

c. *Operationalisation*. This entails a process of converting the research topic to a form that can be measured. Operationalisation is a process of translating abstract concepts into measurable indicators. Most quantitative researchers use operational definitions of some kind. In our example this will proceed as follows:

> Operationalisation:
>
> 1. Parental divorce is assessed according to whether the parents of the respondent have been divorced or not.

> 2. Attitudes to marriage will be measured by means of two scales; one relating to whether children have positive or negative attitudes to this lifestyle, and one regarding whether they intend to marry or not.

d. *Formulation of hypotheses.* Here the researcher will state whether a hypothesis is required, and if so, which one. (A hypothesis is an assumption about the possible outcome of the study and provides a guideline for the research.) In our example, the following two hypotheses are appropriate:

> Hypotheses:
>
> 1. Experience of parental divorce is associated with negative attitudes to marriage.
> 2. Experience of parental divorce is associated with rejection of marriage as a personal choice.

Step 3. Sampling procedures

In this part of the design, the researcher will specify where and when the study will be conducted, and who will take part in it, in other words, who will be the subjects. In our example a sample will be taken, and will be selected as follows:

> Sampling: The sample will be chosen by means of probability sampling. The sample will include 300 male and 300 female children of divorced parents, taken from the records of the 15th district court, covering cases of the last 12 months.

Step 4. Data collection

For this step, the researcher will specify how subjects will be approached, how data collection will be accomplished, and how data will be returned to the researcher. It will also note how research personnel and conditions will be handled so that the data will be gathered without bias and distortion. In our example, this step could be briefly described as follows:

> Data collection: Data collection will proceed by means of interviews, and will be conducted by students, previously trained by their lecturer, using the resources of their institution. Standard measures of data collection will be applied.

Step 5. Data processing

The design will specify how the collected data will be analysed and processed, including methods of analysis and processing, and the means of accessing the resources required. In our example, the researcher may decide as follows:

> Data processing: Data will be grouped, and subjected to statistical analysis by means of computers in order to uncover trends regarding children's attitudes to marriage as a personal choice. Resources will be provided by the teaching institution.

Step 6. Reporting

In this step, the researcher will specify how the findings will be communicated. This refers not only to the nature of the report but also to the channels of publication. In our example, this will be as follows:

> Reporting: An internal, self-published report will be sent to the institution that supported the project, and to the sponsor. A series of articles will be prepared for publication in professional journals.

General comment

It goes without saying that the brief references to the content of the steps of the research design, presented through our example, are abbreviations of the real design. In real case research the descriptions are much more diverse and much more detailed. All the steps of this process will be introduced later, and will be discussed separately in detail.

4 RESEARCH DESIGN IN QUALITATIVE RESEARCH

4.1 Introduction

Qualitative researchers employ research designs as much as quantitative researchers do. After all, 'no design is a design'. They set the path of their research in some way and form, and are committed to a design, although in their own way (Berg, 1995: 14; Bouma, 2000: 2; Miles and Huberman,1994: 16, 17). All know what they intend to study, what settings to investigate, how and when, which actors to approach, which processes to consider, what types of events to register and what instruments to employ (Benini, 2000).

Nevertheless, the extent to which qualitative designs describe the content of the steps, the degree of rigidity of their instructions and the design of the flow of the research process vary considerably, presenting at least two types of qualitative designs: the *fixed* and the *flexible* designs.

4.2 Fixed qualitative designs

The fixed model of qualitative design employs a relatively structured approach, resembling the quantitative model. The steps are the same as those of quantitative research, as is the direction of the process, which is a one-way-path, from the choice of the topic to the conclusions (see Box 5.5). Two important points must be kept in mind when this research model is considered.

First, this model is employed when the researcher has a clear idea about the nature of the research topic and is interested in the way which people respond to it. Hence, methodological parameters can be specified at the outset without knowing the responses of the subjects. Second, it is employed when data analysis is conducted partly or entirely after data collection. This is, for instance, the case when data are recorded mechanically, and are analysed after collection. The model of the quantitative design discussed above applies also to this research model.

Box **5.5**

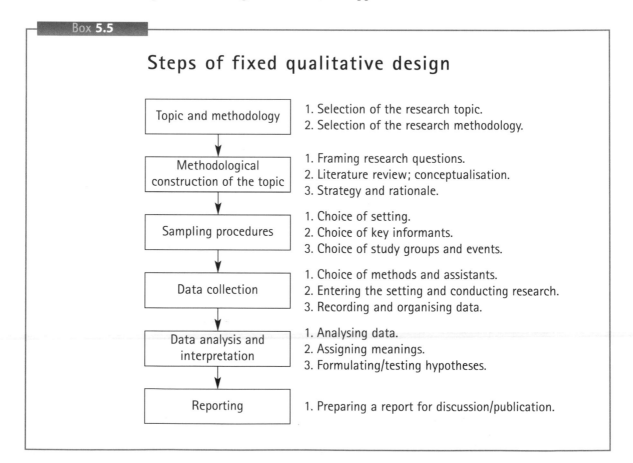

Steps of fixed qualitative design

Topic and methodology	1. Selection of the research topic. 2. Selection of the research methodology.
Methodological construction of the topic	1. Framing research questions. 2. Literature review; conceptualisation. 3. Strategy and rationale.
Sampling procedures	1. Choice of setting. 2. Choice of key informants. 3. Choice of study groups and events.
Data collection	1. Choice of methods and assistants. 2. Entering the setting and conducting research. 3. Recording and organising data.
Data analysis and interpretation	1. Analysing data. 2. Assigning meanings. 3. Formulating/testing hypotheses.
Reporting	1. Preparing a report for discussion/publication.

An example of a fixed qualitative research model is a study of the experiences of women employed in traditionally male jobs, using in-depth interviews with a sample of women from three selected areas of employment. The interviews, which were constructed before the beginning of the study, were conducted by three interviewers, were audio-recorded, and transcribed, and the resulting text was subsequently analysed using content analysis.

4.3 Flexible qualitative designs

More common is the flexible model of qualitative research. The flexible qualitative design:

- Contains six major steps (see Box 5.6).
- Is constructed before the research commences.
- Is presented in a general and non-specific manner, allowing interpretations, leaving space for further decisions to be considered.
- Allows freedom of unlimited movement between the steps of data collection and data analysis in both directions, using new information to fine-tune concepts, sampling and analysis. Qualitative inquiry does not employ a one-way research process.
- Is not based on objectivity; it follows strictly professional standards; it allows for personal preferences of the researcher.

A presentation of the steps of the flexible qualitative design, including the central tasks to be accomplished in each step, is given in Box 5.6.

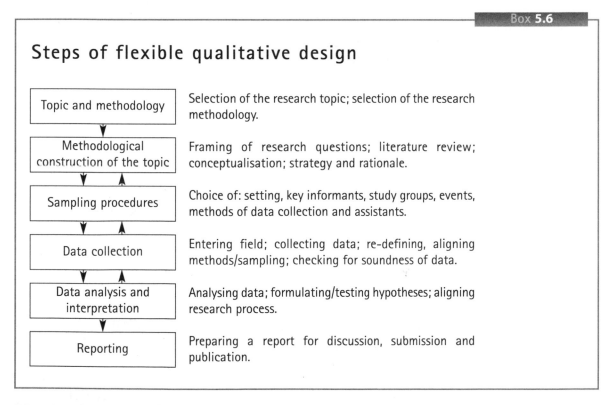

Box **5.6**

Steps of flexible qualitative design

Topic and methodology	Selection of the research topic; selection of the research methodology.
Methodological construction of the topic	Framing of research questions; literature review; conceptualisation; strategy and rationale.
Sampling procedures	Choice of: setting, key informants, study groups, events, methods of data collection and assistants.
Data collection	Entering field; collecting data; re-defining, aligning methods/sampling; checking for soundness of data.
Data analysis and interpretation	Analysing data; formulating/testing hypotheses; aligning research process.
Reporting	Preparing a report for discussion, submission and publication.

4.4 Quantitative and (flexible) qualitative designs

The differences between fixed qualitative and quantitative designs are minimal; they lie in the content of each step and particularly in the nature of the research focus and methods used, not in the structure of the design. The differences between quantitative and flexible designs are more obvious and more significant. Even when the same concepts and elements are used, their content, purpose and nature often vary considerably. The basic differences between these two research models are shown in Table 5.1.

In conclusion, designs are an integral part of any systematic investigation, and serve to guide the course of the research process. They are set by the researchers themselves, and in reality contain directions or reminders about how it was decided to conduct the research. In qualitative research, designs are carefully constructed and more flexible than in quantitative research, and serve the same purpose equally well in their context. The content and complexity of their designs may vary but their presence in the process of everyday research practice cannot be denied.

Table 5.1 Research designs: a comparison

Procedure	Quantitative models	Qualitative (flexible) model
Research topic	Selection of Research Topic Selection of Methodology	Selection of Research Topic Selection of Methodology
Methodological construction of the topic	Definition: precise, accurate and specific Employs operationalisation Hypotheses: formulated before the study	Definition: general, and loosely structured Employs sensitising concepts Hypotheses: formulated through/ after the study
Methods, sampling and projections	Well planned and prescriptive Sampling: well planned before data collection; is representative Measurement/scales: employs all types Arranging printing of documents Appointing assistants (if required)	Well planned but not prescriptive Sampling: well planned, often during data collection; is not representative Measurement/scales: mostly nominal Planning field visits Appointing assistants (if required)
Data collection	Uses quantitative methods Employs assistants	Uses qualitative methods Usually single-handed
Data processing	Mostly quantitative and statistical analysis Inductive generalisations	Mainly qualitative; often collection and analysis occur simultaneously Analytic generalisations
Reporting	Highly integrated findings	Mostly not integrated findings

5 RESEARCH DESIGN IN CRITICAL RESEARCH

The majority of researchers working within a critical paradigm employ a quantitative or qualitative research design. This applies to both the steps and the content of the steps of the design. Researchers may change the latter, but such changes are not significant enough to alter the methodological nature of the research design.

What makes critical research different is not necessarily its technical construction but rather its focus, its degree of engagement and emancipation, its purpose and particularly the politicisation of its process and results. Critical researchers choose topics that are topical and of political significance, and those that are consciously or unconsciously neglected, and work towards emancipating the community in general and the people affected by the problems, and towards changing and reconstructing the social order.

Here the research paradigm entails elements of activism, engagement, ideology and commitment to change, which bias its process and focus. These attributes are most important and serve many goals, particularly with regard to minorities and oppressed groups. In a sense, any research design can become a part of critical research, when it focuses on engagement, critique, change and emancipation.

6 EXAMPLES OF RESEARCH DESIGNS

In this section we shall introduce a few examples, to help you understand fully how research is constructed. We shall demonstrate how a quantitative design was constructed to investigate family values among students, and then how a common format of qualitative research is designed, before we demonstrate how a project is planned, which undergraduate or postgraduate students are often expected to complete. We begin with a quantitative design.

6.1 Quantitative research design: an example

A few years ago, the author decided to conduct a study on family values. The reason for this was the great number of people deciding not to marry as well as the significant proportion of married people divorcing. Given that this phenomenon is evident in most parts of the Western world, it was decided to include several countries in the project. With this in mind, a plan was developed that was to guide the research process. The parameters of this plan were identical to those introduced earlier in this chapter. Below are brief descriptions of the steps of this research design.

Selection of topic and methodology. The topic was 'Family values' and the methodology selected was quantitative. This was because family values were to be measured precisely so as to allow comparisons between the various groups of respondents within each country and between the countries. Also, the topic was expected to be operationalised and this required quantification and precise and accurate measurement. A claim for a relative representativeness and for generalisations made quantitative research a better option.

Methodological formulation of the topic. After the topic had been defined and the methodology chosen, the topic was slightly reduced by focusing the study, first, on young people below the age of 25 and, second, on people with a relatively similar background. Following an extensive literature review, major trends within this context and a number of scales were identified. The Familism scale was one of these. Overall, the topic was operationalised and its dimensions identified; the first four were family, heterosexual marriage, gay marriage and feminism. Indicators were chosen and ultimately translated into questions. It was hypothesised that among students below the age of 25,

H1 Attitudes to family values are very positive.
H2 Attitudes to heterosexual marriage are positive.
H3 Attitudes to gay marriage are negative.
H4 Attitudes to feminism are positive.

Sampling. In order to maintain a consistent background among the respondents, it was decided that they would be students of tertiary institutions. The countries were Austria, Greece, Japan, Australia and the United States. Researchers from these countries were chosen to take part in the study. The relevant questionnaires were constructed and translated into the various languages, and team members took the responsibility of obtaining ethical approval from the relevant ethics committees as well as the collection of the data.

Data collection. Questionnaires were distributed to students, who signed informed consent forms, working within the parameters of ethical standards. Students were chosen using probability sampling procedures. The questionnaires were collected by the team members and forwarded to the author for analysis.

Data analysis. Over 5,000 questionnaires were collected and subjected to quantitative analysis regarding trends in each dimension of the topic as well as among the various countries. Correlations between aspects of the topic and a series of other variables to establish more detailed results were also conducted. Very briefly, the first two hypotheses were verified by the study; the third and fourth hypotheses were not.

Reporting. So far one conference paper and one article have been published. More publications are currently in preparation.

6.2 Fixed qualitative designs: an example

While working on gay couples, the author decided to explore further the social relationships of children of gay parents (Sarantakos, 2000b). The opportunity emerged when four such couples with children of primary-school age moved out of the city and settled in a country town and in the same area. The project became even easier, firstly because the parents welcomed the proposed project, offering their support when and where needed, secondly because their children attended the same school, and thirdly because the parents and their children were open about their family style. Hence, teachers and students knew of the status of the children. Within these parameters, the research evolved as shown below.

Selection of topic and methodology. The topic was 'Social relationships of children of gay couples'. A qualitative methodology was chosen, primarily because the purpose of the study was to explore the topic in general terms, being open to any type of information. The aim of the study was to facilitate descriptions rather than quantitative data.

Methodological formulation of the topic. A more specific definition of the topic evolved through exploration, discussion with colleagues and the parents of the children, and more serious thinking about the topic. The focus of the study shifted to relations with children at school, particularly during playtime. The research interest changed to how children of gay parents fit into a school environment during their class-free time, how other students react to them as children of gay parents, and how they in turn respond to their schoolmates.

Sampling. It was decided that the study would include the children of gay parents as they interacted with other children, and would be conducted every day for two consecutive weeks in the school playground, in the morning before classes began, and during lunchtime.

Data collection. It was decided that the method of data collection would be non-participant unstructured observation. The playground was in front of the school building and this made it easy to observe the children from a distance. Given the number of children and the expected complexity of interactions, it was decided to video-record the children as carefully as possible, and to process and analyse the data after collection.

Data analysis. It was decided to employ qualitative analysis (mainly descriptive) when analysing the data. Beyond this, the videos were to be viewed by other researchers as well as the parents of the children. This was expected to offer opportunities for explaining behaviours more extensively and perhaps more accurately.

Reporting. The results regarding the behaviour of the children of gay parents were most illuminating, and raised many more questions than they answered. Reports were written employing the qualitative model (see Chapter 17).

6.3 Flexible qualitative design: an example

Flexible qualitative designs provide a context within which research procedures are conducted as required by the research outcomes. They entail a dynamic process that builds itself as it goes. The parameters of this design require some knowledge of the underlying principles, so the example we will use here is one that is employed by many researchers who employ a flexible design. This is grounded theory. Below, we shall outline the rationale of this approach, and then describe how a researcher can construct a flexible design and also what the various steps will contain.

Introduction to grounded theory

Grounded theory is both a method, technique or research design, and the outcome of the research. It is not just a tool of data analysis either, for it entails all aspects of a research model, beginning with the selection of a question and ending with an answer. It is 'grounded' because it is related to, emerges out of, is created through and is 'grounded' in empirical data. Grounded theory was developed by Glaser and Strauss (1967).

Since its inception, grounded theory has changed somewhat, and different versions of this model have been developed. The notion of certain elements (concepts, categories) varies among its supporters, and its allegiance to interpretivism has also been questioned (Charmaz, 2000).

Characteristics of grounded theory

Grounded theory is embedded within the interpretivist paradigm; hence it demonstrates all the characteristics presented in previous chapters on this. Strong emphasis is placed on the researcher as an element of the research process. This underlines the importance of an interpretation of reality that places as much emphasis on the object of analysis as on the interpreter. Researchers are seen here to operate like artists: approaching reality in an unprejudiced manner and forming and shaping it accordingly.

Being grounded in data means that grounded theory is close to everyday behaviour and action. Everyday knowledge is an unrenounceable resource, and a central element of its structure and approach. Primary experience is very significant for the development of grounded theory, which is marked by the parameters of openness and flexibility, and focuses on the development, comparison and testing of concepts and key and core categories.

The development of concepts is a process not a structure; it is constantly changing. This is facilitated through a sequence of processes which are continuous until saturation is achieved. These are: first, induction (development of temporary/conditional hypotheses); second, deduction (derivation of implications of hypotheses); and third, verification (testing of the validity of these hypotheses).

Being a qualitative research model, grounded theory demonstrates all the criteria of the qualitative paradigm, such as interpretivism, openness, flexibility, communicativity and naturalism. What makes grounded theory different from qualitative models such as the fixed model is the emphasis it places on the following points:

- The whole research process is guided by the knowledge gathered during the study (the emerging theory) and not by conventional practices.
- The nature of sampling and the respondents, as well as sample size, are decided according to the information gathered during the study.
- Sampling refers not only to people but also to events and to settings.
- Analysis is not conducted after but during data collection. There is a constant interplay between collection and analysis, continued until saturation has been achieved.

While there are certainly differences in other aspects of this research model, the above mentioned are the most important.

Box **5.7**

Basics of grounded theory

- It questions the notion of starting research with already established prescriptive guidelines.
- It aims to develop theory through the research, not to subject research to theory.
- It is most suitable in areas where theories are not available or the field is dominated by many contradictory theoretical positions.
- It follows a qualitative paradigm and is almost exclusively employed by qualitative researchers, but it can equally be employed within a quantitative model.
- It is applicable to any field and any setting, being equally suitable and effective.
- The research design is not a direct one-way path but a circular one, which allows moving back and forth between data collection and analysis.
- It employs a purposive sampling procedure (theoretical sampling) guided by the information collected during the study, and completed when theoretical saturation is reached.
- It employs a variety of methods, from observation to interviews and documentary analysis.
- Analysis proceeds from open coding to axial coding and to selective coding, which produce concepts, categories, typologies and theory.
- The characteristic of this research design is that it is guided not by the researcher or other general professional practices and standards but by the theory that emerges during the research.

(Pfeifer, 2000: 193)

The research process

In general terms, the major steps in qualitative research based on grounded theory are not different from those employed in the flexible qualitative model. Their content and purpose, however, are different. As shown in earlier examples, these steps are as shown in Box 5.8 (Strauss and Corbin, 1998).

The procedures of data analysis will be considered in more detail in Chapter 15. In technical terms, the analysis follows a systematic path leading from open coding to axial coding, to selective coding and then to the creation of a conditional matrix. The main elements of the research process in the grounded theory model can be described as follows:

a. *Constructing categories.* Through open coding and by segmenting information, the researcher establishes categories of information, and looks for properties/subcategories within the categories, attempting to dimensionalise the properties.

b. *Interconnecting categories.* Employing axial coding, researchers search for a central category or a central phenomenon, and then attempt to identify the presence of causal conditions that impact on the phenomenon, explore the specific

Box **5.8**

Research design in grounded theory

Research steps	*Tasks*
Step 1: Selection of the research topic	Choosing the research topic and the relevant methodology.
Step 2: Construction of the research topic	Outlining the boundaries of the topic and of the methodology; searching for material, asking generative questions, etc.
Step 3: Theoretical sampling	Choosing the setting, the event and the respondent(s) to be addressed first. Settings, events and respondents will change as the research progresses.
Step 4: Data collection and analysis	Data gathering and open coding; examining, and comparing data; conceptualising data, leading to identification of concepts; adding new data; refining concepts. Axial coding; integrating/re-integrating data and constructing categories. Inter-connecting, contextualising categories, giving attention to causes and consequences; Adding new data; comparing categories, formulating propositions. Selective coding; identifying the core category, relating it to other categories, validating their relationships, and further refining and developing them. Testing propositions/hypotheses; theoretical saturation; leading to theory.
Step 5: Reporting	Preparing a report.

strategies employed to cope with these influences, analyse the context of the causal factors and study their consequences.

c. *Forming a story that integrates categories.* Selective coding helps to identify a central line that integrates the categories identified in the axial coding process, leading to the emergence of conditional propositions.

d. *Developing and testing propositions.* This process leads to the establishment of a logical system containing the historical, social, and economic factors and conditions that influence the central phenomenon, which can be visually displayed in a conditional matrix. This eventually leads to the establishment of a substance-level theory, which will be subjected to further empirical testing.

Why use this research model?

The value of this theory and its acceptability among social scientists is demonstrated by the extent to which it is applied in real social research. Bryman and Burgess (1994: 6), referring to the popularity of grounded theory, note that it is 'widely adopted as an approving bumper sticker in qualitative studies'. Others (e.g. Pfeifer, 2000) note that researchers see in grounded theory certain advantages, or rather a combination of strengths, which make it a useful research tool and one that offers advantages over other qualitative methods. It is noted on this that grounded theory:

- is theory neutral (it can be used by researchers with a diverse epistemological background)
- is a model suitable to both qualitative and quantitative research (Glaser and Strauss, 1967: 17)
- possesses mechanisms that help researchers to avoid feeling swamped by the data
- generates rich data from the personal experiences of people
- has the capacity to develop theories
- is a powerful research model with a rigorous procedure.

However, grounded theory does not hold a 'monopoly of rigour', exclusivity of access to the personal experiences of respondents, or exclusively to the capacity to develop a theory. Moreover, there are several weak points in this research model that require due attention. Lamnek (1988), for instance, makes the following points:

- The notion of entering the research scene without preconceptions is sociologically very questionable.
- The notion of personal involvement in the research raises the point of subjectivity and the level of validity of the findings.
- The extent to which new information is expected to be added is not very clear.
- There is not enough explanation of how hypotheses are to be verified.
- The process of data collection is not very clear. There is no information about what should be included in the study, that is, what is useful, suitable, theoretically relevant and so on.
- The validity of data needs to be defined in some way, when data are considered as offering empirical validation of the relationships contained in the theory.
- The method of theory building (especially of formal theory) is not precise.
- The notion of the theory being 'grounded in data' betrays empiricist principles and objectivist elements of research, which are incompatible with its qualitative paradigm.

7 DESIGNING YOUR PROJECT

This example is for those of you who will be expected to design and execute a project as a part of your studies. Those who do not fall into this category can take this opportunity to see how to construct a design that will guide a real study. If you are one of those who need to design a project, this example will help you construct the skeleton of the design, and then fill it in with more specific details as you go.

The structure you will construct will contain all parameters required to stimulate your thinking, to set time and resource parameters, to refine and further adjust the definition of the topic, and to choose the methods of sampling, data collection and analysis while you are studying them.

For instance, you may choose the topic and the methodology; you may also choose the sampling procedure and other methods; if you are confident that these are the methods you want to employ, you may pay more attention to them while going though them during your study. Your choice may motivate you to ask relevant questions, before finalising the construction of the design. The discussion that follows offers an example of such a design.

7.1 Pre-design decisions

Remember, whatever the research topic and the methodology, you need a research design. This may be fixed, rigid and strict, or it may be flexible, dynamic and unfolding. Nevertheless, it will be a design. But before you begin with the construction of your research design, it is worth considering some basic issues that require your attention. The following are a few examples.

Pay attention to:

- *Priority*. Institutional guidelines as to how research is to be conducted and presented are to be given priority.
- *Supervisor(s)*. Keep in close contact with your supervisor(s). They have a better understanding of the nature of the research and hence can provide useful suggestions.
- *Breadth and depth*. Be modest and realistic with your research ambitions. Don't bite off more than you can chew.
- *Computers*. Use electronic assistance wisely. Remember, computers will give you what you give them. In qualitative research, transcribing data may be more time consuming than doing the analysis. You are the judge!
- *Time*. Use time constructively, by planning your research systematically, for example by using a time-set design that will guide you through the research within time parameters.
- *Resources*. Whatever their nature and amount, resources must be used wisely. Make sure that they are assessed within the parameters of the research, the nature of the topic and the time available. Adequate resources do not always guarantee success in a project.
- *Limits*. How confident are you that you will be given permission to enter the research field? If this is an issue in your research, make sure, before you even think of constructing the design, to check:

- whether permission can be obtained
- whether a request for permission is required
- whether this will limit the publication of your findings (will you own the data?)

7.2 Your design

Topic and methodology

Choose your topic by taking into account factors wider than your personal interest. This is true also for methodology. With regard to the latter, consider seriously the points made in Chapter 2. Both methodologies are effective tools of research but they serve different goals. Make sure you choose the one that is suitable to your research.

The choice of topic is equally critical. Like methodologies, topics tie you down to a domain and research path that will be critical for you throughout the research. Make sure that the topic is not only within your research interests but also within your research possibilities. Here are some relevant points to consider when choosing the topic.

Choosing a topic

- The topic should be within the area of your expertise. Basic knowledge of the topic and its theoretical and methodological environment will significantly reduce later difficulties and unwelcome surprises.
- It should lend itself to rigorous empirical analysis and allow the application of the types of research described earlier (Chapter 1).
- You need to be able to handle the topic within the time parameters of the institutional regulations. Remember to assess the research topic within the context of your study (thesis, dissertation etc.) rather than of the world. Additional aspects of the topic can be addressed at a later time.
- You need to consider the constraints of resources as well as accessibility to the research field. As noted above, topics that are hard to access can cause serious problems and delays in your research. Be sure about both accessibility and suitable resources before you choose the research topic.
- The topic must be researchable, first in general terms, and second by means of the methodology you chose. You cannot study issues that are not accessible to empirical analysis (such as life after death!), and must bear in mind that methodologies are constructed to study particular aspects of reality.

Methodological formulation of the topic

This step allows you not only to take your research further by refining it and making it clear and specific. It also allows you to correct decisions you made in the previous step. If for instance your topic is found to be too general or – even more importantly – too large for the project, you have a chance at this point to reduce it in content and focus. Below are a few important tasks that you need to perform to establish sound foundations for your project.

How do I do it?

- *Explore your research topic.* Have you read enough to be able to speak with some confidence about the theoretical and conceptual parameters of the topic? A thorough literature review is a minimum requirement. Additional steps such as talking to experts (academics who know more about this topic) or to people associated with the research topic may give you some new insights into the domain of the research.
- *Define the research topic accurately.* Particularly if you are working within a quantitative paradigm, it is important that you define the research topic clearly and specifically, so that there is no doubt about its nature and dimensions. This will not only help you to avoid possible misunderstandings and methodological errors; it will also enable you to make comparisons more easily and accurately.
- *Operationalise the topic.* If you have decided on a quantitative study, you can hardly avoid operationalising the topic of your study. Read the next chapter to see what this involves. This will help you to measure general concepts such as alienation, religiosity and power. You will need to create indicators and other elements that will make measurement easier, more accurate and more precise.
- *Any hypotheses?* This may be an optional device for some, but an essential part of the game for others. Here you simply make a logical and educated guess as to the outcome of the study. When using inferential statistics, hypotheses are required.

Sampling

Having established the basic parameters of the research, you now have to make another decision. This concerns the people you will include in the study and other related factors. The questions below are brief reminders of the relevant tasks.

Sampling: questions to be answered

- Which sampling procedure will you employ to choose the appropriate sample?
- When and where will the respondents be studied?
- How large should the sample be?
- Is a sampling frame required? If so, is one available?
- How representative should the sample be?
- Are the required time, funds and staffing available? If so, how can they be rationally employed?
- How is non-response going to be dealt with in the study?
- Do any issues of ethics and objectivity need to be considered at this stage, and how will such requirements be met?

Data collection

At this stage of the research design you must explain clearly and unambiguously how the required information will be collected. The following points need to be considered:

Data collection: questions to be answered

- Which method(s) will be employed to gather the data?
- Will assistants be required during this stage of research?
- Do documents need to be printed and distributed in some way to respondents?
- What kind of qualities will the assistants need to have?
- Is training required for the assistants (e.g. interviewing skills)?
- What kind of procedures have been introduced to deal with possible non-responses?
- Is there a need to check data collection for fairness, accuracy, reliability and so on?

Data analysis

As in the previous steps, you have to make important decisions and answer many relevant questions. In most cases these questions mainly concern technical and administrative issues. Other questions relate to the essence of analysis, which depends on the type of methodology chosen. These issues are discussed in detail in Chapters 15 and 16, and require no further attention here. There are however questions about aspects of the research that require attention at the planning stage to enable you to make relevant decisions. Some of these questions are listed below.

Data analysis: questions to be answered

- Will the analysis be quantitative or qualitative?
- If the analysis is quantitative, will computers be needed?
- If so, are the computers equipped with appropriate programs?
- Will you need help in data entry and processing?
- Are funds available for these services?
- In qualitative research, will you need assistance with transcription of the results or other tasks?

Reporting

The nature and content of the report will very much depend on the requirements of your institution. This relates to the format of presentation, as well as the report's size, the number of copies required and other aspects. The report depends also on the nature of the study, the underlying methodology and the nature of the data. All relevant requirements to be met if a research report is to be presented in accordance with professional standards are explained in Chapter 17.

In conclusion, it should be noted that the discussion in this chapter is as much related to preparing a research design at a professional level as to constructing a design for a one-off project, thesis or dissertation. All parts of this text relate to this task.

- The research process is often presented in the form of a model. The research design provides a path that guides the process from beginning to end.
- Research is assumed to proceed in a set of steps that are executed in a prescribed order.
- The use of a research model guides research planning and action, and brings many advantages to the research project.
- Quantitative researchers employ fixed designs; qualitative researchers employ both fixed and flexible designs.
- The steps of a research model are preparation, research design, data collection, data processing and reporting.
- Research preparation entails selection of methodology, selection and definition of the research topic, exploration, operationalisation and formulation of hypotheses.
- Data collection entails decisions and action regarding the collection of the information required to address the research question.
- Data processing entails grouping, presentation, analysis and interpretation of the findings.
- Reporting refers to the process of publishing the findings.
- Grounded theory research falls within the parameters of qualitative research.
- Grounded theory perceives research units as autonomous, sees scientific interpretation of reality as the work of an artist, sees continuity from everyday thinking to scientific thinking, and assumes openness of social scientific formation of concepts.

WHERE TO FROM HERE?

Before you leave this chapter, visit the companion website for the third edition of *Social Research* at http://www.palgrave.com/sociology/sarantakos to review the main concepts introduced in this chapter and to test yourself on the major issues discussed.

FURTHER READING

Bechhofer, F. and Paterson, L. (2000) *Principles of Research Design in the Social Sciences*. New York: Routledge.

Bordens, K. S. and Abbott, B. B. (1999) *Research Design and Methods: A Process Approach* (4th edn). Mountain View, Calif.: Mayfield.

Budestam, K. E. and Newton, R. R. (2001) *Surviving your Dissertation: A Comprehensive Guide to Content and Process*. Thousand Oaks, Calif.: Sage.

Creswell, J. W. (2003) *Research Design: Qualitative, Quantitative, and Mixed Method*. Thousand Oaks, Calif.: Sage.

de Vaus, D. (2001) *Research Design in Social Research*. London: Sage.

Denscombe, M. (1998) *The Good Research Guide for Small-scale Social Research Projects*. Buckingham: Open University Press.

Hakim, C. (2000) *Research Design: Successful Designs for Social and Economic Research* (2nd edn). London: Routledge.

Hart, C. (2001) *Doing a Literature Review*. London: Sage.

Mitchell, M. and Jolley, J. (2004) *Research Design Explained*. Belmont, Calif.: Thomson/Wadsworth.

Punch, P. D. (2000) *Developing Effective Research Proposals*. London: Sage.

6 Initiating social research

THIS CHAPTER

- describes how the research process begins
- defines the tasks required at this step of research
- introduces operationalisation of concepts and triangulation
- explains this process in both quantitative and qualitative research
- clarifies the nature and role of hypotheses in social research.

KEY HEADINGS

INTRODUCTION

In the previous chapter it was shown that the research process proceeds through a number of steps, beginning with the identification of the research topic, and moving through the process, until data collection, analysis and processing are completed. In this sense, the steps have a specific purpose, are assigned certain tasks, and can be addressed as prescribed.

In this chapter, we shall address the first step of the research design, focusing on the individual tasks that are assigned to it. Particular emphasis will be given to the many ways in which the research topic is prepared so that the researcher can study it successfully and in detail. Associated with this is the question of the methodology, which has to be selected at this point.

We begin our discussion with the first step of the research process, and more particularly with the selection of the research topic.

1 SELECTION OF THE RESEARCH QUESTION

One of the first issues the investigator has to make clear and specific is the focus of the research. This implies the identification first of the research question, and second of the methodological framework within which the topic will be studied. Simply, the researcher has to answer very clearly the questions: 'WHAT will be studied in this project?' and 'HOW will this be studied?' Although the latter is a very complex question, it is important to know at least whether the study will be qualitative or quantitative.

Research theory and practice (see Pfeifer, 2000; Puris, 1995) concur that there are at least three major issues associated with the selection of the research topic that deserve attention, and that the researcher must be aware of. First, what can be studied in a research project? Second, who selects the research topic? Third, what factors influence the decision to study a certain research question? These points will be addressed briefly below.

1.1 The nature of the research question: 'What can be studied?'

In practice, social scientists can investigate virtually any social issue. The research topic can be related to people, groups, ideas, ideologies, attitudes and opinions, structures and processes, methods and practices, and the causes and effects of social events. Units of study can be taken from any level, that is, from the individual-to-individual level, individual-to-group level, or group-to-group level. A research project can operate at one or more levels.

The only restrictions of this freedom relate to issues of relevance, researchability, feasibility and ethics. *Relevance* refers to whether the study of the research topic is relevant to the purpose of the study. *Researchability* refers to whether the research topic is approachable methodologically. Topics that do not lend themselves to methodological scrutiny, such as whether there is a God or whether there is life after death, are not suitable and cannot be studied empirically. While research can approach the perceptions people have of God or life after death, a direct empirical study of these issues is not possible. *Feasibility* relates to whether the research is possible, that is, whether the researcher has access to the research subject as well as the means and resources that are required to complete the study. *Ethics*, finally, refers to whether the proposed study is ethically justifiable and follows ethical standards and principles in its design, execution and the application of the findings.

Any topic that is relevant, researchable, feasible and ethical can be studied. However, it should be noted that of these four factors only the second and third are directly relevant to the question: 'What can be studied?' Obviously topics that are not relevant or are not based on ethical standards can still be studied. There are two levels of rules regarding what researchers should study: one relates to what researchers *can* study, and the other refers to what researchers *should* study. Both sets of rules are important.

1.2 Who chooses the research question?

The researcher. It is generally taken for granted that the right to choose the research topic rests with the investigators, who generally study issues that lie within the area of their personal expertise and interests. These interests are related to external factors, such as income, prestige or promotion, advancement of knowledge or improvement of social conditions (extrinsic motivation); or to internal factors, such as the research issue per se (intrinsic motivation).

Social conditions. In a number of cases, the choice of research topic is determined by social conditions. Here, research has a social function and must be carried out irrespective of the personal preferences and interests of the investigator. It is argued here that the researcher is a part of the community, has a public responsibility and duty to serve, and that research is guided by the needs of that community. Hence, the choice of research question should be governed by social conditions and the needs of society, and the researcher has a responsibility to address issues of social significance. In practical terms, researchers are expected to select a research topic that requires serious attention, even if they are not personally interested in it. In a way, this occurs in some cases of contracted research, where economic support is provided for certain topics only.

The sponsor. Complex and demanding research topics are usually funded by sponsors who not only provide the resources, but also determine the area of study, and often the research topic. Many researchers work for specific employers, who in turn determine the research topic. Contract research will also have limited freedom of choice; in certain cases the researcher is employed to investigate a specific topic, and that remit cannot be changed.

1.3 Selection in a social context: important factors

A number of factors usually affect the choice of a particular research question. These factors may be influenced by practical or theoretical aspects, or by personal views and interests (Pfeifer, 2000; Puris, 1995). Some of the factors affecting the selection of a research topic are shown in Box 6.1.

Box **6.1**

Factors affecting the choice of the research topic

- *Financial constraints.* Topics funded by sponsors are more likely to be studied than those that receive no support.
- *Time.* Studies that take up too much time are less likely to be chosen by researchers than others that are equally important but require less research time.
- *Availability of assistants and experts.* Lack of research assistants may force researchers to opt for topics that can be studied without their help.
- *Research paradigm.* Topics studied within popular paradigms (e.g. feminist research) may be preferred to topics investigated within other paradigms.
- *Expertise.* Researchers normally study topics that are within their professional interest and expertise.
- *Ideology.* Researchers study issues that are consistent with their ideological affiliation. Feminists study women, and Marxists study the status of workers in capitalist societies.
- *Access to the research subject.* Issues that are difficult to access are less popular research topics than those that are easily accessible.
- *The need for data.* The need for information on certain subjects attracts the interest of researchers not only through their own volition but also because these issues attract funds, and hence assistants and other resources.

In many cases, the decision of a research topic is influenced by several factors, although one may be more influential than others.

1.4 Basic questions

After the research topic has been chosen, the investigator usually explores further methodological issues related to the researchability of the topic and related factors. The extent of such an exploration depends on factors related to the nature of the topic; however, some questions are thought to be particularly important in this context (see for example Pfeifer, 2000; Puris, 1995). Examples of such questions are given below.

- What is the research unit? Before embarking on the next stage, the researcher should know exactly what the research unit of the study will be. 'Research units' are quite often defined very differently; thus the researcher should make it clear at the outset that the research will deal with a certain unit, in a certain context, with certain characteristics. It is important to stress that this is the unit the investigator will refer to when conclusions, statements or generalisations are made.
- What is the level of research? Research can be conducted at several levels, for example:
  - first-level research, that is, the relation between individuals
  - second-level research, that is, the relation between individuals and groups

    – third-level research, that is, the relations between groups.
An investigation may be carried out at more than one level. It is the task of the researcher to define these levels adequately during the first step of the research design.

- Will objectivity be observed? The attitude of the researcher to objectivity should be made clear at the outset. If measures to ensure objectivity have been taken, these should be stated. If objectivity is considered irrelevant, this should be made known. Researchers must state clearly whether they take the role of a 'detached observer', an 'empathetic observer', a 'faithful reporter', a 'mediator of languages', a 'reflective partner' or a 'dialogic facilitator'. Each role entails a different degree of objectivity. Hence, the degree of commitment to objectivity should be defined clearly at this stage of the project.

- Can observance of ethical standards be guaranteed? Ethical issues should be considered at all stages of the research design, and measures taken to guarantee that the respondents will not be adversely affected in any way by the research or the publication of the findings. At this stage, there are several ethical questions that are extremely relevant, for instance those listed in Box 6.2.

When all questions have been answered satisfactorily, the researcher will proceed to the next step.

Box **6.2**

Ethical considerations when choosing a research topic

- Can this topic be addressed without violating ethical standards?
- Can confidentiality and anonymity be guaranteed?
- Can it be ensured that the study of this topic will not endanger the respondents and their families?
- Can this study hurt the researcher?
- Can it be ensured that all members of the research team will adhere to ethical standards?
- Will the study of this topic necessitate any type of unfair dealing, illegal or unethical activity?
- Can the research arouse outside interest (e.g. from the authorities) that could harm the participants?
- Is it likely that ethics approval from the proper authorities will be obtained?

(Benini, 2000: 27–8)

---

2 SELECTION OF THE RESEARCH METHODOLOGY

2.1 Introduction

The manner in which research will proceed depends on many factors, but the underlying methodology is the most important. For this reason, it is imperative that at this stage the researcher defines and outlines clearly the type of methodology that will guide the research project. In some cases just stating that the investigation will be based on a quantitative or qualitative framework might suffice. In other cases more information may be required.

This is for instance the case when researchers need to state the paradigm that guides their theory and ideology. Such extra information would be required, for example, where the research adopts a Marxist, feminist or symbolic interactionist approach. Explaining the theoretical and ideological basis of the project offers a better understanding of the research, provides a clear and sound basis for developing the research design, and allows a fair and valid interpretation and assessment of the findings.

Whether the methodological framework will be quantitative or qualitative, whether the orientation of the framework will be critical, empowering or descriptive, and whether the definition of the framework will be general or specific and detailed depends on many factors. Some of these are related to the research object and others to the theoretical perspective that guides the thinking and operation of the researcher. We already know that any decision is acceptable and legitimate if it is justified in terms of methodological standards; and in this sense there is no right or wrong methodological framework.

The choice of methodology is usually made after the research object is selected, but in many cases it is chosen earlier. It is common for researchers to work mostly within a specific paradigm, for example they may be Marxists, feminists or structuralists, and hence their methodological affiliation is a constant and not a variable.

2.2 Criteria of choice

It has already been shown that social research can be conducted within a quantitative or qualitative context, and that both types of research are equally legitimate. Hence, when we are talking about the choice of methodology, the question is not about its *quality* but about its *suitability*.

Normally, although ideology plays an important role, the choice of a suitable methodology is directed by theoretical principles. This issue has been addressed by social scientists and methodologists alike, who have taken positions on this issue and have produced sets of criteria to guide their choice . Berger et al. (1989: 152) argue that the choice of methodology is usually influenced by factors such as those listed in Box 6.3.

In general, the conditions under which a quantitative methodology is employed are very clear. Its nature and the homogeneity of its approach leave no doubt as to when this research model is to be employed. In brief, that is when the project is interested in:

- observable phenomena
- quantification and measurement
- objectivity
- large samples
- validity and reliability
- description, relationships and causality
- statistics as a tool of data analysis

Factors affecting the choice of a methodology

Factors that may affect choice include:

- the underlying theoretical paradigm
- the appropriateness of the method for the theoretical goals
- the adequacy of the method for the research object
- the overall purpose of the project
- the nature of the expected outcomes
- the realisation of methodological rules which determine its structure, possibilities and limitations
- examination of the prerequisites and conditions that must be considered when performing mathematical-statistical tests.

- representativeness and generalisability
- replication, precision and accuracy.

In a similar manner, qualitative methodology is employed when researchers seek to understand how people make sense of their environment and the factors and conditions that shape their lives (Bogdan and Bilkin, 1992; Drew et al., 1996: 162). More specifically, Flick and associates (1991) relate the choice of qualitative methodology to factors such as those listed in Box 6.4.

Factors in favour of a qualitative methodology

A qualitative methodology is chosen when:

- The standard of knowledge in the area of the research subject is inadequate and provides no sound basis for a quantitative study. The qualitative research in this case takes the form of an exploratory study.
- There is a need to study reality from the inside, that is, to understand it from the point of view of the subject.
- The study object is so complex that a quantitative method is of little use (Kleining, 1991).
- There is a need to capture reality 'as it is', that is, in interaction.
- The researcher intends to present the information gathered, not as numbers or formulae but verbally, in a detailed and complete form.
- The researcher wishes to approach reality without preconceived ideas or preconstructed designs and patterns.
- The investigator perceives researcher and researched as elements of the same situation and the research design as a whole unit.
- The researcher wishes to capture the meaning and regularities of social action.

In conclusion, regardless of the reason for opting for one or the other methodology, at this stage of the project, the researcher is expected to make a decision as to which of them will guide the study, and to justify this decision.

3 METHODOLOGICAL CONSTRUCTION OF THE RESEARCH TOPIC

Following the choice of methodology, and having already decided which topic to study, the researcher will focus on the research question and work to refine and adjust it so that it can be approached methodologically. In some cases this 'refinement' and 'adjustment' is very simple, or even not necessary at all. This is the case, for instance, in flexible qualitative research, where definitions are usually formulated fully during the research. In other cases, for instance in quantitative research, it can be very complex indeed, and involves, as we shall see later, very complicated methods and highly sophisticated procedures.

In quantitative research, during this step, additional information is gathered to further clarify the object of study; to refine the research question, making it more specific and preparing it for investigation; to develop a framework for the research project; and to link the research question with research methods and procedures.

More specifically, when constructing the research topic the following tasks are to be considered:

- definition of the topic and associated variables
- exploration
- operationalisation
- formulation of hypotheses.

Depending on the state of knowledge, quantitative researchers usually consider all four tasks in their research, although to different degrees. In qualitative research, however, researchers take differing views on this. For some, these tasks are not to be constructed at the outset but to be developed during the research. For others, the design should be flexible and not commit them in advance. For most qualitative researchers, operationalisation is inconsistent with the essence of qualitative methodology.

4 DEFINITION OF THE TOPIC

The first point to be considered at this stage is the definition of the topic and of the related variables. The nature of definition depends on a number of factors, of which the type of methodology is important. Quantitative researchers usually define the topic accurately and specifically; qualitative researchers prefer to define it loosely and in general terms. However, both will define their topic in a way that makes it clear, explicit and distinguishable from other objects, and so makes the study possible.

For example, if the research question is about 'Family and delinquency', quantitative researchers are expected to explain what they mean by both 'family' and 'delinquency', and define these concepts accurately. In doing so, the researcher will not necessarily develop a new definition for each concept, since there are many well-accepted definitions available for both concepts. However, since there are many types of families and of delinquency, researchers will specify the kind of issues they intend to investigate.

For instance, whether they will study: (a) one-parent families, *de facto* families, homosexual families, reconstituted families, extended families, ethnic families, city families or country families; (b) families of married couples, unmarried couples or both; (c) families with parents of all ages or of specific age groups; (d) families with children or without children; (e) families with children of a specific age, and so on.

When defining the topic, researchers will reduce it significantly. They may, for instance, reduce the concept 'family' into 'families in which at least one partner is over 25 years of age', 'families with children under five years of age', or 'families with teenage children'. Quite frequently, researchers begin their definition with the statement that 'for the purpose of this study family is defined as . . .' and then describe the type of unit they intend to deal with in their study. In a similar fashion, the researcher will define 'delinquency'. These definitions are expected to be specific enough to enable the researcher and the respondent to differentiate between the issues in question and other matters that are excluded from the study.

As stated earlier, especially with regard to quantitative studies, defining the topic makes it concrete and specific and more understandable, and through doing this the study is 'prepared' for an effective methodological operation to follow. The topic in the previous example, 'Family and delinquency', might read, after definition: 'Children of working-class families and delinquency rate (property crimes)'. At this stage in the research design, both concepts (family and delinquency) are clearly defined, and have become concrete and specific.

The process of defining the research question is predominant in quantitative research. In qualitative investigations, definitions are loosely structured; it is expected that additional information will be collected during the study and will help to refine concepts and define them more clearly in a more concrete and specific manner. The more information is gathered and the more respondents are included in the study, the clearer the definitions become. It must be kept in mind that qualitative researchers are interested in people's interpretations of objects and events, and this includes their definitions.

5 EXPLORATION

5.1 Introduction

Some exploratory work is undertaken in any study, irrespective of its methodological framework or its purpose. In some cases this work is elementary, and serves as a guide for the formulation of hypotheses and/or for the operationalisation of the concepts. In other cases, exploration is a major part of the research study. The latter is, for instance, the case in certain forms of qualitative research.

Exploratory studies are most frequently carried out when there is insufficient information about the research topic, so that the formulation of hypotheses and the operationalisation of the question are difficult or even impossible. More specifically exploration is undertaken for reasons (see Becker, 1989; Puris, 1995) such as those given in Box 6.5.

5.2 Types of exploratory studies

Exploratory studies can take many forms, depending on the nature of the main study, the purpose of the research, the study object, the state of knowledge in the area of investigation and, more specifically, the purpose of exploration. As a prelude to a quantitative study, exploration is usually found to take one or more of the following forms (Vlahos, 1984):

- review of available literature
- expert surveys
- analysis of case studies.

Most projects employ more than one type of exploratory study, with literature research being predominant. This also constitutes the first step of exploration, when more types of exploration are employed. Library research or literature review will determine whether additional exploration is required and, if so, what type of exploration will be necessary.

Box **6.5**

What is exploration for?

- *Feasibility.* Exploration will show whether a study of the issue in question is warranted, worthwhile and feasible.
- *Familiarisation.* Exploration will familiarise the researcher with the social context of the research topic, with details about relationships, values, standards and factors related to it, and with methods.
- *New ideas.* An exploratory study may help to generate ideas, views and opinions about the research object, which are useful when constructing the research design.
- *Formulation of hypotheses.* Exploration will show whether variables can be related to each other, and if so in what way, direction and degree.
- *Operationalisation.* Exploration can help to operationalise concepts, by explaining their structure and by identifying indicators.

Literature review. This involves a secondary analysis of available information already published in some form. It can be a study of the research object alone, with the aim of collecting information about its structure, process and relationships, thus increasing the familiarity of the researcher with the research object and strengthening the credibility of the project.

In addition, it can consider previous research, to link that with the study currently planned. It may also be geared towards a historical or comparative analysis of the issue in question so that the current study can be placed in a historical context. Finally, it may review a theory or the methods and techniques most suitable for the study, simply by looking at the ways other researchers have approached the topic, and by evaluating their suitability and effectiveness.

Traditionally, the place for literature review is the library; hence it is often referred to as library search. The advent of the Internet has expanded the current frame of search by adding the virtual library, not only expanding the boundaries beyond the local libraries but also making a search fast and easy.

Expert surveys. Expert surveys involve interviews with experts who have substantial knowledge and experience in the research area, although their views might not have been published. This unpublished information is often very relevant to the research object, and can only be obtained through such interviews.

Case studies. When information collected through literature review and expert surveys is insufficient, researchers collect first-hand information through case-study research. Single cases relevant to the issue are selected and studied, in order to collect information for the main study.

It must be noted that case studies, as a concept, can be a research design as well as a method of data collection. The former is more appropriate for qualitative studies; the latter is mostly used as a prelude to quantitative research in the context of exploration. Both types of case-study research will be discussed later.

6 OPERATIONALISATION

6.1 Operationalisation in quantitative research

Often, even the best definitions do not prepare concepts clearly enough to make further research possible. Using definitions in research can be misleading and cause confusion, bias and distortions. Try, for instance, to investigate with some degree of objectivity, certainty and accuracy concepts such as love, patriotism, morale, oppression, ambition, pride, motivation, esteem, joy, anxiety, temperament and learning ability without explaining them further. Even concepts such as social class are difficult to use directly in research because they incorporate many elements (Ellis, 1993), and can therefore be understood and interpreted differently by the respondents. Asking people straight questions about which social class they belong to is found to produce biased and inaccurate answers, with a large proportion of respondents ranking themselves as middle class.

The fact is that concepts are complex and diverse. Some entail one dimension, others are multi-dimensional. Some (e.g. gender, weight, height, age, distance) are directly observable, and their empirical reference obvious and easy to ascertain. Others (e.g. intelligence, ethnicity, class, alienation, norms, cohesion, values) are not empirically observable, and their empirical reference is neither obvious nor easy to establish.

Box **6.6**

What is operationalisation?

Operationalisation is the process of converting concepts into their empirical referents, or of quantifying concepts for the purpose of measuring their values, such as occurrence, strength and frequency. It is employed when concepts are vague, unclear or abstract, and thus involves a process of translating abstract concepts into synonymous empirical referents; in this way it facilitates a precise measurement.

When concepts are complex and hence difficult to describe (often referred to as constructs), researchers use known concepts that are directly observable and accessible to allow access to the unknown ones. These known and observable concepts, which serve as a means to understand and describe unobservable ones, are called indicators. They are observable characteristics or empirical equivalents to the concepts they represent, and make measurement not only possible but also valid (Laatz, 1993). The process of identifying the indicators is called operationalisation (see Box 6.6). The notion of operationalisation is based on the principles of operationalism developed in the nineteenth century, according to which a concept is identical with its empirical equivalents (for example, intelligence is identical with IQ scores).

Central procedures

The central concepts that characterise operationalisation are measurement, dimensions, indicators, measures, sampling and design (Laatz, 1993). In simple terms, operationalisation contains four major elements: identifying the dimensions of the concept, selecting indicators, identifying empirical referents, and quantifying the variable (see Box 6.7). The process of operationalisation is simple and straightforward, and can be displayed graphically as shown in Figure 6.1.

Box **6.7**

Major elements of operationalisation

- Identification of dimensions that reflect the nature and complexity of the concept. Dimensions refer to aspects of the concept.
- Selection of indicators that reflect the presence/absence and strength of the dimensions of the concept.
- Identification of empirical referents, that is, the range of values the indicators can assume, and assignment of scores that represent the degree of presence or absence of the concept or variable.
- Quantification of the variable, that is, identification of the continuum of values the variables can assume, and assignment of scores as above – here, for the main variable.

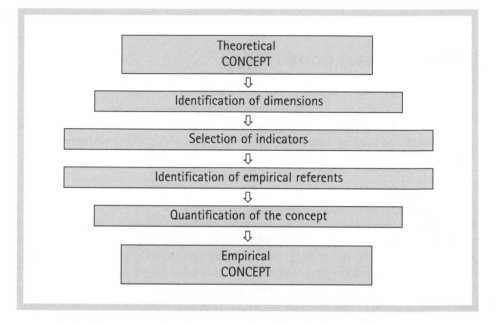

Figure 6.1 Operationalisation

Examples of operationalisation

Using the concept 'social class' as an example, operationalisation will begin with identifying the dimensions of the concept (e.g. economic, occupational and educational status), and will continue by choosing the indicators of the concept's dimensions (e.g. income, occupation and education), identifying the empirical referents (e.g. amount of money per year, type of job and years of study) and quantifying the concept (e.g. establishing, as a result of the estimation of the value of the indicators, what constitutes a upper, middle and lower social class).

In this sense, the researcher who investigates the distribution of people within the class system of their community will not ask the respondents directly about which class they think they belong to, but rather about the amount of money they earn, the type of job they have and the years of study they completed. Indicators and referents serve here as a bridge between theoretical and empirical concepts. This not only makes it easier for the respondents to answer; it also facilitates more accurate and more valid responses.

Box **6.8**

Operationalising social class

Concept	Dimensions	Indicators	Empirical referents
Social class	1. Economic status 2. Occupational status 3. Educational status	1. Income 2. Occupation 3. Education	1. Amount of money 2. Type of job 3. Years of formal study

Let us now apply this in another example. A researcher wishes to measure the degree of religiosity of politicians in the United Kingdom. It is important that religiosity is measured as accurately as possible. Hence, a more detailed operationalisation is required. Employing the above design we proceed as shown in Figure 6.2.

Basic questions in operationalisation

The basic questions that need to be addressed during the process of operationalisation are:

- What is the concept to be studied?
- What are the dimensions that need to be addressed?
- What are the most appropriate indicators that describe each dimension fully?

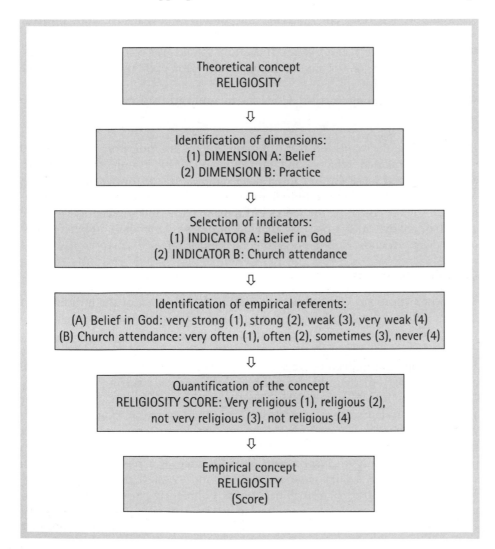

Figure 6.2 The process of operationalisation

- Does operationalisation measure what it is supposed to measure?
- Are the instruments of measurement reliable?

Apart from attempting to establish clarity and precision, these questions encourage the researcher to check the validity and reliability of operationalisation.

Rules of operationalisation

The basic rules of operationalisation are associated with the selection and quantification of the empirical referents, and are as follows:

- *The rule of empirical relevance.* Indicators should adequately reflect the concept they are intended to measure. Indicators should be synonymous with the concept.
- *The rule of correspondence.* Indicators should correspond fully with the concept, and only one concept, and should be exhaustive and mutually exclusive.
- *The rule of empirical adequacy.* Indicators should have the capacity to measure all aspects of the concept adequately, with each one addressing one dimension only.
- *The rule of quantification.* Uniform quantification procedures should be employed.

In most cases, the transition from the concept to the indicators is simple and direct. Age, gender, religion and ethnicity are a few examples. Educational achievement and sociability are additional examples. In the former the indicators will be scores achieved in the central areas of study; in a primary school environment, this may perhaps be the scores in English, maths and social studies. In the latter (sociability), indicators may include number of friends, number of visits received from friends, club membership and similar items.

Choosing indicators

The most critical part of operationalisation is the selection of the indicators. It is quite often difficult to define concepts clearly and to translate them into conceptual constructs that are synonymous with and cover all aspects of the concept.

Dimensions and indicators are selected in many ways. In some cases they are chosen by means of theoretical principles, in other cases through speculation. In both cases it is assumed that a relationship between concepts and their empirical equivalents exists. Experience is another source of indicators. Analysis of real definitions is yet another. However, the most secure way of choosing indicators is to use exploratory studies, especially case-study analysis based on primary experience with respondents. For instance, if a researcher wished to study class status in a small rural community, and to select the relevant indicators, a qualitative study of a small part of the population would be most appropriate. This study would focus on what people thought constituted 'social class', and what in their view assigned members of the community a high or a low rank in the class context.

6.2 Operationalisation in qualitative research

Qualitative researchers do not employ operationalisation. Instead, when there is a need for creating such concepts, sensitising concepts are used. The general view of operationalisation is that it is an inadequate research instrument; many researchers point to a number of deficiencies. Most critics of operationalisation (see, for example, Lamnek, 1993) refer to the following problems:

- *Inadequacy.* Operationalisation is often based on common sense, and therefore it links concepts not with reality but with other concepts, leaving reality untouched. Operationalisation is considered an inadequate way of approaching reality.
- *Incompleteness.* Operationalisation does not and cannot cover all aspects of the concept in question just by using existing knowledge. If sufficient knowledge about the concept was available, there would be no need for research. Thus, operationalisation can only cover some aspects of the concept.
- *Subjectivity.* The structure of operational definitions often depends on the personal understanding of the researcher. For this reason the same concept can be operationalised in many different ways by various researchers. Such forms of operationalisation may be of little use.
- *Concept and scores.* Quite often, concepts are taken to be equivalent to the scores of tests arrived at through operationalisation (e.g. IQ scores and intelligence), an assumption that is not always true.
- *Timing.* First, operationalisation is completed before the research has started. For this reason, instead of explaining and enriching the concepts in question, it reduces the options of the research and limits its scope. Second, concepts are not explored through the 'researched' but through the researcher, before the study is completed. Third, operationalisation is conducted too early in the research process.
- *Validity.* These problems call into question the validity and reliability of the whole study.

This view is supported by many qualitative researchers. For some, the best form of operationalisation is no operationalisation at all. However, the views of qualitative researchers on this issue are not fully uniform.

It is characteristic of these criticisms of a quantitative measure that they come from within a qualitative paradigm, and hence are bound to be negative. For quantitative researchers operationalisation is a powerful tool, fully supported by its paradigm, and almost always employed in a variety of ways and to a certain degree by nearly all researchers, wittingly or unwittingly. Still, its methodological significance should not be overestimated. One should remember that operationalisation is valuable only if used properly, aiming to establish ideal structures and offer operational definitions that approximate the concepts included in the study. The results obtained through operationalisation should finally be interpreted in the context of the indicators used.

Box **6.9**

Operationalisation: an example

Assume we are to study the class structure in a small country town. The intention of the study is to ascertain whether the community is divided into classes, and if so how the various classes compare with each other, using quantitative methods. How do we address 'class' in this town? To answer this question we proceed as shown below.

1.   *Identification of dimensions.* A review of literature related to class in the region reveals that class entails at least three major dimensions: the *economic, occupational* and *educational* status. A combination of these dimensions is considered to constitute a person's position in the class system.
2.   *Selection of the indicators.* Next we search for indicators: criteria that reflect the presence and extent of each of these dimensions. Examples of such indicators commonly employed by researchers in this context are *income* for economic status, *years of education* for educational status, and *type of occupation* for occupational status. Hence, measurement in this case will focus on these indicators.
3.   *Identification of empirical referents.* The next task is to identify criteria that will allow us to quantify the indicators and so allow measurement and comparisons. These criteria are the referents. This means that the indicators will be translated into their empirical equivalents (referents). The obvious referent for income is money; the referent for education is 'years of study'; and for occupation it is the score assigned to the various occupation groups. (Such scores are readily available.)

     Following this, income will be divided into nine groups, each with a fixed amount and together covering the range of income earned by respondents; similarly nine occupation groups will be established according to the status assigned to jobs, and educational groups will be constructed according to the years of study completed by each respondent. Each indicator will then be ranked from very low, through moderate, to very high, and numerical values will be assigned to each of the groups, ranging from 0 to 9. The pattern of quantification will be held uniform for all indicators. We shall see later that each indicator will be translated into a number of questions, and each question will provide the required information for the quantification expressed in general or average scores. If a respondent obtained, for instance, the scores 6, 4, and 3 for the indicators of class, this person would have obtained an average class score of 4.3.
4.   *Quantification of the variable.* The procedure employed in the previous step will also be employed to quantify 'class'. Its continuum may be divided into the following nine groups: lower low, middle low, upper low class; lower middle, middle middle, upper middle class; and lower upper, middle upper, and upper upper class. Each group will be ranked from low (score = 1) to high (score = 9). The scores 1–3 will indicate low class, 4–6 middle class and 7–9 upper class. In our example, the class score of 4.3 will indicate a lower-middle class position.

7 MULTIPLE OPERATIONALISM: TRIANGULATION

7.1 Introduction and types of triangulation

Triangulation refers to the practice of employing several research tools within the same research design. Initially, triangulation was used to reflect what was known as *multiple operationalism* or *convergent validation*, and since it usually entailed three paths of action, it was named triangulation. This procedure allows the researcher to view a particular point in research from more than one perspective, and hence to enrich knowledge and/or test validity. Triangulation can be applied in all aspects of the research process. It can relate to the methods of data collection, the manner in which data are employed, the investigator, the critical stance and the theoretical perspective (Blaikie, 1988). The following are the most commonly used types of triangulation:

- *Method triangulation*. This combines several methods in the same study. It employs a mixed-method design to investigate different aspects of the same phenomenon (Crawford and Christensen, 1995). It can employ methods of different methodological affiliation (inter-method triangulation), or of the same methodological affiliation (see Denzin, 1989).
- *Time triangulation*. This method entails the use of research at different times, for example, surveying students during the first and last week of their first session. This is known as successive triangulation, as against concurrent triangulation, where diverse methods study the same topic at one point in time. Examples of time triangulation are longitudinal studies, such as panel studies and trend studies. Mixed triangulation is possible when studies triangulate, say, methods and/or samples concurrently and consecutively (e.g. using multiple methods during the exploration and several samples in the main part of the trend study).
- *Paradigm triangulation*. Here a number of different paradigms (e.g. positivist and interpretive) are employed to study the same phenomenon. A qualitative study, for instance, may be employed in a manner that produces quantifiable data, and after data collection the data is quantified, analysed and interpreted within a quantitative perspective.
- *Investigator triangulation*. In this form, triangulation combines the expertise of more than one investigator in the same study (Flick, 2000c). This is a useful method in qualitative research where flexibility and openness are accepted. In quantitative research, investigator triangulation can be applied during the construction of the research design, especially during the interpretation of findings.
- *Sampling triangulation*. Here two or more samples are employed within the same project. Such triangulation is found in experiments when experimental and control groups are treated in a distinct manner that allows testing of causal relationships, often increasing the number of control groups to enhance the explanatory power of the instrument.

It goes without saying that these types of triangulation are not mutually exclusive. More than one form can be employed when required.

7.2 Purpose of triangulation

Triangulation is employed for a number of reasons. Using three methods, for instance, is thought (see Flick, 2000c; Burgess, 1984) to allow the researcher:

- to be thorough in addressing all possible aspects of the topic
- to increase the amount of research data, and hence increase knowledge
- to enrich the nature of research data
- to facilitate a study, where one procedure serves as a stepping-stone for the other
- to allow comparisons (e.g. in longitudinal studies)
- to achieve a higher degree of validity, credibility and research utility
- to overcome the deficiencies of single-method studies.

From a feminist stance, triangulation is thought to 'express the commitment to thoroughness, the desire to be open-ended and to take risks', as well as to 'increase the likelihood of obtaining scientific credibility and research utility' (Reinharz, 1992: 197). Combining quantitative and qualitative research on the same topic allows a stereoscopic view of its structure and process, so avoiding the deficiencies of each of these models.

7.3 What is triangulation worth?

Although the use of triangulation is generally thought to produce more valid and reliable results than the use of single methods, there are researchers who see little – if any – value in this research practice. Problems and conditions of triangulation have been discussed by many writers (e.g. Lamnek, 1993; Silverman, 1985: 105–6), who argue that expanding the spectrum of research does not necessarily guarantee better results.

In addition to problems emerging from the theoretical justification of triangulation and the positivistic bias it seems to entail, it is argued that there is no evidence to suggest that studies based on triangulation necessarily produce more valid results. Even if all the diverse methods support each other's findings, they might all be invalid. In simple terms, the findings of a study based on several

Box **6.10**

Critique of triangulation

- Triangulation and single-method procedures alike can be useless if they are based on the wrong conditions and wrong research foundations.
- Triangulation can be used as a way of legitimising personal views and interests.
- Triangulation is difficult to replicate.
- Triangulation per se is no more valuable than a single-method procedure, which can be more suitable, useful and meaningful to answer certain questions.
- Triangulation is not suitable for studying every social phenomenon.

(Lamnek, 1993: 245–57)

methods are not necessarily 'better' than the findings of a single-method study. Finally, critics ask: What happens if multiple methods employed in the same study produce different findings? Which method is valid? Beyond this, if methods from different methodological contexts are employed, to what extent can their results be compared?

8   FORMULATION OF HYPOTHESES

8.1   Introduction

A hypothesis is an assumption about the status of events or about relations between variables. It is a tentative explanation of the research problem, a possible outcome of the research, or an educated guess about that outcome. For some methodologists any logically justifiable assumption can be a hypothesis; for others such an assumption should be scientifically justifiable, and created on the basis of sufficient theoretical or empirical evidence. Hypotheses are generally answers to research questions and can be generated in many ways. They can be developed through existing theories, through research findings of other studies, evidence, commonly held beliefs or intuition.

Hypothesis construction is an integral part of quantitative research and is employed by researchers, although more frequently in some areas (e.g. psychology) than in others. Its purpose is to offer a clear framework and guide when collecting, analysing and interpreting the data. More specifically, hypotheses are expected:

- to guide the social research, by offering directions to its structure and operation
- to offer a provisional answer to the research question
- to facilitate statistical analysis of variables in the context of hypothesis testing.

In many cases hypotheses serve as a testing tool for the relationships between variables. In this sense, a hypothesis contains a possible solution to the research problem; its validity will be tested by the evidence gathered by the study. At the time of construction, hypotheses cannot be described as true or false; they can only be relevant or irrelevant to the research topic. If we were to study, for instance, the effects of education on religiosity, a relevant hypothesis could be: 'a high level of education is associated with low religiosity'; equally possible could be: 'education is conversely related to religiosity'; 'education is positively correlated with religiosity'; and 'there is no relationship between education and religiosity'. Every stance taken within the hypothesis is correct, as long as it is relevant to the purpose of testing.

Both quantitative and qualitative researchers employ hypotheses, although in different forms, at different research stages and for different purposes. While the former see hypotheses as a step towards research, the latter perceive hypotheses as emerging out of the research. In the following section we shall consider hypotheses as employed by quantitative researchers. The nature and construction of hypotheses in qualitative research will be discussed later.

8.2 Types of hypotheses

There are many forms and types of hypotheses, mainly depending on their structure, goals and nature. A few examples of types of hypotheses are described briefly below.

- *Working hypotheses.* A working hypothesis is a preliminary assumption about the research topic, most commonly made when there is not sufficient information available to establish a hypothesis, and as a step towards formulating the final research hypothesis.
- *Statistical hypotheses.* A statistical hypothesis is a statement or set of statements developed by means of statistical principles related to the probable distribution of certain criteria of the population. Statistical hypotheses are used as part of the process of verification, lend themselves to statistical testing, and are expressed in the context of a null hypothesis and an alternative hypothesis. Statistical testing should determine whether a statistical hypothesis is accepted or rejected.
- *Null hypothesis (H_o).* This is one of a set of two hypotheses (the other is the *alternative hypothesis*) formulated by the researcher to be used in the context of hypothesis testing.
- *Alternative hypothesis.* This is the other of the set of two hypotheses referred to above (see '*null hypothesis*'), and states the opposite of the null hypothesis. In statistical tests of null hypotheses, acceptance of H_o means rejection of the alternative hypothesis; and rejection of H_o means acceptance of the alternative hypothesis.

8.3 Criteria of hypothesis construction

Hypotheses can be presented in any form except that of a question. However, they have to meet a number of standards, which are listed below. While some methodologists are convinced that all these criteria should be met, others require that only a few of them are necessary. In general, hypotheses are required (Pfeifer, 2000) to:

- describe variables or establish a relationship between variables
- be empirically testable (capable of being proven right or wrong)
- focus on one issue only
- describe variables or relationships between variables
- be clear, specific and precise.

Hypotheses can be formulated in a *descriptive* or *relational* form; in the former they describe events, in the latter they establish relations between variables. They may also be *directional* or *non-directional*, depending on whether or not they make a concrete suggestion about the research question. Whether hypotheses are formulated in one or other of the forms listed above depends very much on the nature of the study as well as on the manner in which hypotheses will be addressed.

8.4 The trouble with hypotheses

Although hypotheses are used widely, their role in social research has been criticised on many grounds. Apart from the criticism that they make no positive

Box **6.11**

Types of hypotheses

Type of hypothesis	Examples of hypotheses
Descriptive	'Many single parents live in poverty'
Relational	'The gender of single parents affects their quality of life'
Non-directional	'Marriage is associated with happiness'
Directional	'Married people are happier than unmarried people'

contribution to the research process, it is argued that they bias the research design (e.g. data collection, data analysis and interpretation), restrict its scope, limit its approach, and hence predetermine the outcome of the research.

More specifically, it is argued that when hypotheses precede the research, they reflect previous 'knowledge' of what they are supposed to study, and this affects the researcher's perception of, and action within, the research project. The hypothesis in fact prescribes the path of research and the aspects that are to be considered in the investigation, and so sets blinkers and strait-jackets on their operation. This is obviously contrary to qualitative principles that consider it imperative that researchers suspend previous knowledge in favour of openness regarding specific meanings and understandings of the subject in question (Meinefeld, 2000: 266).

Despite these criticisms, many investigators employ hypotheses in their research, implicitly or explicitly. It is argued in this context that:

- Hypothesis testing is employed when very specific aspects of relationships are tested.
- Hypotheses highlight existing aspects of the research topic on which the analysis is focused.
- In most cases hypotheses are based on information collected through previous research or exploratory studies.
- Previous knowledge is not necessarily detrimental to a study.
- The notion of suspending all previous knowledge and of openness is thought to be artificial if not impossible.

The last point is quite challenging; how can a well-trained researcher 'ignore' previous knowledge, especially about techniques of data collection and of research in general? After all, the purpose of science is to build on existing knowledge. Let us expand this point for a moment. Do qualitative researchers suspend their knowledge of methodology, their academic maturity and ability to interpret, gained through long previous studies and experience in the area? Previous knowledge and expertise are highly valued and are expected to be acknowledged in the research report. It is not surprising that there are qualitative researchers who do not fully accept the idea of suspending previous knowledge. Moreover, not all qualitative researchers abstain from using hypotheses testing (Meinefeld, 1997; Hopf, 1996).

- Research initiation entails the selection of methodology, selection and definition of the research topic, the decision to conduct an exploratory study, operationalisation and formulation of hypotheses.
- The step of research initiation is undertaken by all researchers, although qualitative researchers are less strict about detailed procedures than quantitative researchers.
- The research topic is usually chosen by the researcher but can also be determined by social circumstances or the sponsor.
- The choice of methodology is guided by the underlying theoretical paradigm and the nature of the research topic.
- The goals of exploratory studies are to explore the feasibility of a study, to familiarise the researcher with the research topic and the respondents, to bring new ideas to the research, and to facilitate operationalisation and the formulation of hypotheses.
- Operationalisation is the process of quantifying variables for the purpose of measuring their strength and frequency. It entails selection and quantification of indicators, and quantification of the variables.
- The rules of operationalisation are the rule of empirical relevance, the rule of correspondence, the rule of empirical adequacy and the rule of quantification.
- Triangulation is the procedure in which data collection is accomplished through more than one avenue.
- A hypothesis is an assumption about the possible outcomes of the study. Hypotheses are expected to be clear, specific, precise and empirically testable, to describe one issue at a time, and not to contain statements that are contradictory.
- Qualitative researchers do not employ operationalisation, and do not construct hypotheses prior to the commencement of the research.

WHERE TO FROM HERE?

Before you leave this chapter, visit the companion website for the third edition of *Social Research* at http://www.palgrave.com/sociology/sarantakos to review the main concepts introduced in this chapter and to test yourself on the major issues discussed.

FURTHER READING

Cooper, H. M. (1998) *Synthesizing Research: A Guide for Literature Reviews*. London: Sage.

Fink, A. (1998) *Conducting Research Literature Reviews: From Paper to the Internet*. London: Sage.

Gash, S. (2000) *Effective Literature Searching for Research*. Aldershot, UK: Gower.

Hart, C. (1998) *Doing a Literature Review: Releasing the Social Science Imagination*. Thousand Oaks, Calif.: Sage.

Sampling procedures

THIS CHAPTER

- outlines the nature and types of sampling
- clarifies the rationale and principles of sampling
- introduces quantitative and qualitative sampling
- elaborates on the meaning and computation of the sample size.

KEY HEADINGS

INTRODUCTION

One of the most significant issues investigators have to consider when designing a project is the type and number of the people who will be included in the study. In this context, they have to consider a number of very important questions, such as:

- Will the whole population or a sample be studied?
- If sampling is preferred, which sampling procedure is most suitable?
- How large should the sample be?
- Is a sampling frame required?
- If so, is one available?
- How representative should the sample be?
- How will possible problems, errors and distortions be prevented?
- What kind of administrative arrangements are required for the selection of the sample?
- Are the required time, funds and staffing available, and if so, how can they be rationally employed?
- How will non-response be dealt with in the study?
- Are there any issues of ethics and objectivity to be considered at this stage, and how will such requirements be met?

The answers to these questions are many and the options diverse. One option is complete coverage of the population (saturation survey), whereby all units of the target population will be studied. In this case the target population is also the survey population. Another option, and the most common, is sampling, whereby the target population is investigated by studying a small part of it, namely a sample.

Box 7.1

Some basic concepts of sampling

Target population. The population for which information is required.

Survey population. The part of the target population that is studied.

Sample. The part of the survey population that is to be studied.

Sampling. The procedure employed to extract samples for study.

(Sampling) Units. The persons, groups, systems etc. chosen to be studied.

Saturation survey. A survey that includes all units of the target population.

---

1 REASONS FOR SAMPLING

It was mentioned above that sampling enables the researcher to study a relatively small part of the target population, and yet obtain data that are representative of the whole. Although this is one good reason for researchers to employ this procedure, there are many more that can be put forward in favour of sampling. Those listed in Box 7.2 are the most common (Becker, 1989; Benini, 2000):

Why use samples?

- *Necessity.* In many cases a complete coverage of the population is not possible.
- *Effectiveness.* Complete coverage may not offer substantial advantage over a sample survey. On the contrary, it is argued that sampling provides a better option since it addresses the survey population in a short period of time and produces comparable and equally valid results.
- *Economy of time.* Studies based on samples take less time and produce quick answers.
- *Economy of labour.* Sampling is less demanding in terms of labour requirements, since it covers only a small portion of the target population.
- *Overall economy.* Sampling is also thought to be more economical, since it involves fewer people and requires less printed material, fewer general costs (travelling, accommodation etc.) and of course fewer experts.
- *More detailed information.* Samples are thought to offer more detailed information and a high degree of accuracy because they deal with relatively small numbers of units.

Despite these advantages, sampling is associated with a number of problems, which deserve to be mentioned. The two most obvious problems are, first, that sampling requires more intense and complex administration, planning and programming than saturation surveys; and second, that sampling implies a reduction in the size of the target population and, hence, fewer potential respondents; this raises questions regarding representativeness and generalisation of the findings that cannot be ignored.

The response to these logical concerns about sampling is simple and convincing. Sampling may require administration and programming but overall both are less demanding when dealing with a sample (e.g. 5,000 people) than with a whole population (e.g. 5 million). Finally, samples are chosen in such a way that the demand for representativeness and generalisation is not compromised. In this sense, studying fewer people can be a strength and not a problem.

2 PRINCIPLES OF SAMPLING

Samples are expected to be representative. To achieve representativeness, sampling procedures are expected to follow certain standards and methodological principles. Particularly with regard to quantitative research, researchers and writers alike consider those listed in Box 7.3 to be very important (see Pfeifer, 2000; Selltiz et al., 1976).

Box **7.3**

Principles of sampling

- Sample units must be chosen in a systematic and objective manner.
- Sample units must be easily identifiable and clearly defined.
- Sample units must be independent of each other, uniform and of the same size, and should appear only once in the population.
- Sample units are not interchangeable; the same units should be used throughout the study.
- Once selected, units cannot be discarded.
- The selection process should be based on sound criteria and should avoid errors, bias and distortions.
- Researchers should adhere to the principles of research (discussed in Chapter 4).

Additional or alternative standards and principles will be introduced when considering specific types of sampling, especially when dealing with sampling in qualitative research. Researchers who work outside quantitative parameters have raised questions about sampling, in particular about objectivity and the rigid formulation of its principles, but this does not detract from the validity of these elements.

3 TYPES OF SAMPLING

Sampling procedures vary considerably. Samples may be constructed through self-selection (respondents decide to take part in a study, for example, in response to media calls for volunteers) or, as is most common, through the researcher. There are also sampling procedures based on probability standards (random or probability samples), and on non-probability standards (non-probability samples). In the following sections we shall discuss probability and non-probability types of sampling. The main criteria for these samples are listed in Box 7.4.

3.1 Probability (random) sampling

Probability sampling is the procedure in which the choice of respondents is guided by the probability principle, according to which every unit of the target population has an equal, calculable and non-zero probability of being included in the sample. There are several forms of probability sampling, but simple and systematic random sampling are the most common. These two types of probability sampling and the methods they employ will be considered below.

Simple random sampling

The characteristic of this type of random sampling is that the sampling units, apart from having an equal chance of being selected, are independent from each other. Their chance of being selected does not depend on the selection of other units. This distinguishes simple random sampling from systematic random

Criteria of probability and non-probability samples

Probability sampling	*Non-probability sampling*
Employs probability theory	Does not employ probability theory
Is relatively large	Is small, often covering a few typical cases
Size is statistically determined	Size is not determined statistically
Size is fixed	Size is flexible, but can also be fixed
Sample is chosen before the research	Sample is chosen before and during the research
Controls researcher bias	Does not control researcher bias
Involves complex procedures	Involves simple procedures
Has fixed parameters	Has flexible parameters
Involves high costs	Involves relatively low costs
Planning is time consuming	Planning is not time consuming
Is designed to be representative	Representativeness is limited
Planning is laborious	Planning is relatively easy
Treats respondents as units	Treats respondents as people
Facilitates inductive generalisations	Facilitates analytical generalisations
Is employed in quantitative research	Is mostly for qualitative research

sampling, which will be discussed later. The three most common methods of simple random sampling are: the lottery method, the random numbers method and the computer method.

The lottery method

Choosing respondents by the lottery method entails a procedure that can be described as follows:

Step 1. Identify or construct a sampling frame, that is, a list of the units of the target population. Such frames may for instance be the electoral role, student records, rating records or similar lists. Include the names and addresses of sample units in alphabetical order and numbered accordingly.

Step 2. Determine the sample size, that is, the number of units required for the study.

Step 3. Place a number of small discs or balls in a container, numbered to correspond to the names contained in the sampling frame. If 500 names are listed in the frame, there should be 500 balls or discs in the urn, numbered from 1 to 500.

Step 4. Mix well and remove one ball from the urn. The number of this ball is registered and the corresponding name in the sampling frame is noted. This is the name of the first respondent. The ball is either returned to the urn or left out; either method may be employed. Continue this process until sufficient names have been selected. (If an already drawn number is selected it is ignored). The selected respondents constitute the sample.

Example A. A researcher is interested in the attitudes of first-year university students (N = 6,000) to feminism. How will a sample be constructed using the simple random sample procedure and the lottery method? Below are the necessary steps:

1. A list of the names and addresses of all first-year students is obtained from the university administration, arranged in alphabetical order, with the names numbered (this is the sampling frame).
2. It is decided that the sample size will be 500.
3. An urn with 6,000 balls, numbered from 1 to 6,000, is obtained.
4. The balls are mixed and the first is drawn. If the number on that ball is 679, the name on the list that corresponds to that number is identified and recorded, together with the address and telephone number (if required). This process of drawing and recording names is continued until the number of recorded names reaches 500, which is the required sample size.
5. The 500 names drawn following this procedure constitute the sample, which will be studied in this survey.

The random numbers method

This method is similar to the lottery method, except that the urn and balls are replaced by random number tables, which are available in separate publications or in the appendices of statistics texts. Choosing the sample by using the random numbers method involves the following steps:

Step 1. Identifying or constructing a sampling frame.
Step 2. Selecting appropriate tables of random numbers.
Step 3. Picking numbers from the tables randomly and registering them; the names in the sample frame that correspond to these numbers constitute the sample.

Example B. Taking the same example as we used in describing the lottery method, we select the sample using the method of random numbers. We proceed as follows:

1. A list of all first-year students' names is obtained, numbered and ordered accordingly.
2. The sample size is determined; this is 500.
3. An adequate number of lists of random numbers that contain all numbers included in the sampling frame are used. If, for instance, there are 6,000 students on the list, it should contain numbers up to 6,000. Such lists are readily available in various forms, sizes and number combinations.

4. Pointing randomly with a finger or pencil at the list of random numbers, the operator notes the number that is under the finger or the pencil point.
5. The name in the student list that corresponds to that number is identified. This is the name of the first respondent. This process continues until the required number of students has been collected.

The computer method

In this method, we instruct the computer to give us a set of numbers equal to the number of sample units, for example, 500 numbers ranging between 1 and 6,000. Having the numbers, we follow the model employed in the previous methods. This technique is employed when the sampling frame is not in the computer; but if it is electronically available, we instruct the computer to choose, say, 500 names from the list with a simple command. Obviously the computer requires a small program to complete this task.

Example C. The sample for the 'students and feminism' study is to be selected by the computer method. We proceed as follows:

1. The appropriate sampling frame is obtained.
2. The sample size is determined; this is 500.
3. The computer is instructed to randomly select 500 numbers from 1 to 6,000.
4. The respondents are identified as in the previous examples.
5. These respondents constitute the sample for the study.

Although all three sampling methods are efficient and commonly used, the electronic construction of samples has become more popular than in the past due to increased computerisation and accessibility to public records and electronic telephone books; moreover, computers have become an integral part of the research context. Where appropriate records are available and suitable, the computer can choose not only numbers but also names, addresses and other contact details, and can even phone respondents on request. Drawing numbers from the hat and similar techniques are becoming methods of the distant past.

Systematic random sampling

Systematic random sampling is a procedure in which the sampling units are *not only chosen randomly* – as in simple random sampling – but in which this random choice is *also integrated with the choice of another sampling unit*. This is what distinguishes this type of sampling from simple random sampling, and what qualifies it to be termed systematic. The actual choice of units is orchestrated through a system of computation that aims, first, to maintain randomness in selection, and second, to spread the sampling units evenly throughout the list of respondents (the sampling frame). The system is based on the *sampling fraction method*.

In this method, units are drawn from a sampling frame by means of the sampling fraction (symbolised by k) that is equal to N/n, where N is the number of units in the target population and n the number of units of the sample. For instance, if the target population is 4,800 and the intended sample size 600, the sampling fraction is 8 ($k = 4,800/600 = 8$). To select a sample by using the sampling fraction method, we proceed as follows:

Step 1. Identify or construct a sampling frame.

Step 2. Determine the sample size.

Step 3. Compute the sampling fraction k (as above, $k = N/n$).

Step 4. Randomly select a number between 1 and k. In the above example, since $k = 8$, the random number would be between 1 and 8; let us say 6.

Step 5. Record the random number (6) and every eighth number after 6, until 6,000 is reached, e.g. 6, 14 (6 + 8 = 14), 22 (14 + 8 = 22), 30 (22 + 8 = 30) etc.

Step 6. Locate the names in the sampling frame that correspond to the selected numbers.

The respondents thus identified constitute the sample.

Example D. The local Telecom office wants to survey the 11,000 customers who joined a half-price programme six months ago and assess their degree of satisfaction with this programme. We are to conduct this survey, and in the first instance we need to draw up a sample using the systematic random sampling procedure. The intended sample size is 500. A list of the customers in question is available. How do we choose the 500 respondents?

1. Obtain the sampling frame from the Telecom office.
2. Compute the k fraction; this is 11,000/500 = 22.
3. Randomly select a number between 1 and 22; in this case, 18.
4. Compute the numbers for each of the 500 respondents by progressively adding 22 to 18 and to the resulting sums. The numbers will be 18, 40 (18+22 = 40), 62 (40+22 = 62), 84 (62+22 = 84) and so on.
5. Locate the names in the sampling frame that correspond to these numbers. These are the customers who will be included in the sample.

This has been a very popular and also reliable method of sampling, but as in other cases, the use of computers in this area has displaced it somewhat; in practice it is now used mostly by those still employing manual sampling procedures.

Stratified random sampling

Stratified random sampling is a *probability sampling procedure* in which the target population is divided into a number of strata, and a sample is drawn from each stratum. The resulting sub-samples make up the final sample of the study. The strength of this procedure is in that it allows all population groups to be represented in the final sample. The division of the population into strata is based on one or more significant criteria, such as sex, age, ethnic background, race or economic status.

The sample size can be proportionate or disproportionate to the units of the target population. This means that the samples taken from each stratum can be either proportional or disproportional to the size of the samples. As indicated above, a stratified sample is employed when there is a need to represent all groups of the target population in the sample, and when the researcher has a special interest in certain strata. In this sense, the method is very economical, and offers a high degree of representativeness. A stratified sample is drawn as follows:

Step 1. The target population is divided into a number of strata, according to the number of the significant groups in the population.
Step 2. The sampling frames for each of these groups are identified; if these are not available, relevant frames must be developed.
Step 3. Employing one of the methods discussed above, a sample is drawn from each group. This can be proportionate or disproportionate to the number of units in the population.
Step 4. The individual samples are merged into one; this constitutes the sample for the study.

Example E. We are asked to study the attitudes of our community to the government's foreign aid policy. Stratified sampling has been chosen in order to include in the study all ethnic groups. To obtain the names of the respondents, we proceed as follows:

1. Sampling frames are identified or prepared for each ethnic group in the community.
2. A decision on whether a proportionate or non-proportionate stratified sampling should be employed is made.
3. The number of subjects to be chosen from each ethnic group is determined. This is 60 per cent for Asians, 20 per cent for Africans, 15 per cent for Greeks and 5 per cent for Germans.
4. One of the methods discussed above (e.g. the lottery method, random numbers, sampling fraction) is used to choose the sub-samples (i.e. the separate samples from each ethnic group).
5. The sub-samples are merged into one sample.

The resulting respondents constitute the final sample. In this way, the researcher can expect a relative representativeness of the major ethnic groups in the study, which is, as would be expected, higher than if the target population was not stratified.

Multi-stage sampling

In multi-stage sampling, the selection of sample units begins with the choice of a large sample, and *proceeds with new samples taken in succession from those previously selected*, thus facilitating the construction of a more suitable and more effective choice. More specifically, a large sample is chosen, using a random sampling procedure, and then another sample is taken from within this sample, excluding excess and unrelated units. For instance, if the study is to focus on professional women, all men and non-professional women contained in the first sample will be discarded. If required, another sample is chosen from the second sample for similar reasons. This process is continued for as long as required, with each additional drawing making the sample more specific, more focused, more relevant to the research object, and more representative. The characteristic of this type of sampling is that data collection is conducted only from the final sample.

The process of choosing a sample through the multi-stage sampling method proceeds as follows (see Pfeifer, 2000):

Step 1. A sampling frame for the target population is identified.
Step 2. A large probability sample is chosen; the units of this sample are usually referred to as primary selection units. A sample from the primary selection units is then chosen.
Step 3. After the criteria of the respondents have been identified (in terms of gender, ethnicity, marital status etc.), another sample is drawn from within this sample. In most cases, a second sample is sufficient to meet the requirements of the study. Otherwise, the procedure is repeated until the targeted sample size is reached.
Step 4. The final group constitutes the sample of the study.

> *Example F.* We are to study the attitudes of nurses to the proposal that compulsory reporting of suspected domestic violence injuries should be abolished. The sample is to be determined by means of multi-stage sampling procedures. To obtain the sample we proceed as follows:
>
> 1. A list of nurses from all hospitals in the region is obtained.
> 2. From this list, 2000 nurses are chosen.
> 3. Using hospital unit as criterion, 600 nurses are chosen, representing all major hospitals of the country.
> 4. These 600 nurses are finally screened, first using gender as a criterion, and then specialisation, age, and length of employment, resulting in a balanced sample of 150 respondents. A non-probability method is used.
> 5. These respondents constitute the final research sample.

The use of several screenings and drawings is not only time-consuming but also expensive. Hence, multistage sampling procedures are employed only when absolutely necessary. An obvious case for such a sampling procedure is a heterogeneous population where there is not enough information to permit the construction of a representative sample without screening.

Cluster sampling

Cluster sampling is a procedure in which the researcher *chooses the study units progressively*, beginning with clusters and moving to smaller groups within them, before the final sampling units are considered. This sampling method is employed primarily when a sampling frame is either unsuitable or not available. Cluster sampling is also employed when alternative methods are too expensive, and particularly when clusters are an important research factor. Such clusters include schools, classes, soccer teams, hospitals, small business and other well-integrated groups with a common identity. The following is an example.

Example G. We are interested in the attitude of technical-school teachers to a recent government report on subsidies to these educational institutions. The study is to be conducted by means of a survey. Cluster sampling will be used in order to allow schools affected by the new proposed measures to respond. To compile the sample we proceed as follows:

1. A list of all technical schools is constructed (sampling frame), or obtained from the relevant authorities if available (and if accessible).
2. The number of schools required for the study is determined by employing appropriate standards.
3. Schools are chosen from the sampling frame by means of one of the sampling methods introduced above (the lottery method, sampling fraction etc.).
4. The number of teachers required for the study is determined and then divided by the number of schools to determine the number of teachers to be chosen from each school (proportionate or disproportionate numbers to be considered).
5. The required number of respondents from each school are chosen, using one of the methods introduced above.
6. The sum of all teachers chosen this way constitutes the sample.

It should be noted that, although it is clearly a distinct technique, cluster sampling operates in a manner similar to that of stratified sampling and, even more so, of multi-stage sampling. Some writers employ this method to choose subjects spread in large areas, as with area sampling. In either case, this sampling procedure has its own identity in dealing with clusters, and is systematically employed when conditions require it.

Multi-phase sampling

The sample selection within this procedure is identical to multi-stage sampling, with the difference that in this sampling procedure, *each sample is adequately studied before the next sample is drawn.* This offers an advantage over other methods, because the information gathered at each phase helps the researcher to focus the selection more effectively and more constructively in later phases.

Example H. A social worker is interested in the division of labour among homosexual couples. The sampling procedure is to be multi-phase sampling. To compile the sample we proceed as follows:

> 1. A sampling frame of homosexual people is constructed, and 500 are randomly chosen.
> 2. These respondents are interviewed about the nature of their relationship, their age, and other demographic criteria.
> 3. Of these respondents, 300 (150 gay and 150 lesbian couples) are chosen randomly who have a permanent partner and at least one child living in the same household.
> 4. This stratified sample will be the final sample to study the division of labour among homosexual couples.

You will have noted that the use of sequential samples is employed very constructively and effectively by researchers to facilitate research where it is not otherwise possible, and to achieve what single-sample studies cannot.

Area sampling

Area sampling is a procedure in which *multi-stage sampling is applied in geographical area*s. More specifically, the samples are chosen as follows:

Step 1. Framing the area.
Step 2. Dividing it into large parts.
Step 3. Randomly selecting a number of representative parts.
Step 4. Dividing the selected parts into units that are small enough to be studied directly.
Step 5. Drawing a representative sample of units from each part.

This will be the sample for the study. A typical example is given below.

> *Example I.* A journalist is interested in the views of people, living in country towns, on a proposed Euthanasia Bill. The proposed sampling procedure is to be area sampling. In this typical case, sampling proceeds as follows:
>
> 1. A sampling frame of country towns is established, and a sample of five towns is drawn.
> 2. The chosen towns are divided into suburbs, and four suburbs from each of the five towns are chosen randomly, resulting in 20 suburbs to be studied.
> 3. The streets in each chosen suburb are listed and a sample of five streets is chosen from each. This gives 100 streets registered for consideration.
> 4. The households in each of the chosen streets are now listed, and ten households are chosen from each street for study. This gives 1,000 households.
> 5. The sample will include the heads of all households chosen in the final draw.

This sampling procedure is employed when the researcher has reasons to believe that other sampling procedures may not allow all geographical areas to be represented in the study.

Spatial sampling

This procedure is employed when the study *addresses people temporarily congregated in a space*, and the data have to be collected before the crowd is dispersed. An example of such cases is the study of the views of people demonstrating in a city square about tax policies. Due to the nature of the population, there are neither sampling frames nor sufficient time available to permit the use of other methods. Apart from this, data collection has to be conducted so that a relatively representative coverage is achieved, randomly and in a systematic way before the crowd disperses. The way this is usually done is shown in the following example.

> *Example J.* In a sit-in at the local university, students have occupied the main administration building and refuse to leave. The Department of Sociology quickly decides to investigate certain aspects of this demonstration, including the reasons for participating in it, and the type of students joining such a demonstration. The choice of the respondents proceeds as follows:
>
> 1. Ten interviewers line up at the front of the room where students are gathered.
> 2. As instructed, the interviewers address the person who happens to be in front of them, and ask the study questions.
> 3. Then, they all move five steps forward and approach the person who is now in front of them.
> 4. They proceed further, in the same way, until they reach the back of the room.
> 5. The students interviewed constitute the sample for the study.

Obviously, the details of the procedure can be changed to meet the actual circumstances of the situation. For instance, if a crowd is large, the interviewer might have to walk a longer distance, say ten steps. Also, it may be necessary for the interviewer to seek specific people; for example, the first will be male, the second female, and so on, or to include a variety of respondents (young, old, ethnic, non-ethnics and so on).

3.2 Non-probability sampling

As the name indicates, non-probability sampling procedures do not employ the rules of probability theory, do not ensure representativeness, and are mostly used in exploratory research and qualitative analysis. Some of these techniques can, with some adjustment, be converted into probability methods. Accidental sampling, purposive sampling, quota sampling and snowball sampling are examples of non-probability sampling techniques; they are presented below.

Accidental sampling

This procedure employs no systematic techniques to choose the respondents. Instead the sample units are *those people who 'accidentally' come into contact with the researcher*. For instance, the researcher may stand at a street-corner, in front of a school or church, or at the main exit of a shopping centre, and ask a number of people passing by to take part in the study. They are chosen 'by accident' – they just happen to be there at that time – hence the name of the sampling procedure (there are several other names for it, including 'convenience sampling', 'chunk sampling', 'grab sampling' and 'haphazard sampling'). An example is given below.

Example K. The local chamber of commerce in a small country town want to study people's reasons for shopping in the four large supermarkets. The sampling procedure is accidental sampling. The study proceeds as follows:

1. Two interviewers stand at the door of each supermarket with instructions to address 100 shoppers passing by with relatively full supermarket trolleys, asking them the relevant questions.
2. The completed forms are returned to the researcher on the same day for evaluation.

The researcher here is not interested in representativeness, objectivity, validity or similar considerations, but in getting information that would reveal certain aspects of the lifestyle in question, and in certain cases give information about typical cases.

Purposive sampling

In this technique the researchers purposely *choose subjects who, in their opinion, are relevant to the project.* The choice of respondents is guided by the judgement of the investigator. For this reason it is also known as judgemental sampling. There are no particular procedures involved in the actual choice of subjects. Here is an example:

Example L. A researcher is interested in the problems of immigrants in a particular community. To explore this topic, it is decided to interview key informants such as the local priests, club secretaries and functionaries of ethnic welfare groups. In the investigator's view, these people can offer adequate and useful information that will give a picture of the problems facing immigrants.

In such cases the important criterion of choice is the knowledge and expertise of the respondents, and hence their suitability for the study.

Quota sampling

Quota sampling is a procedure in which *the researcher sets a 'quota' of respondents to be chosen from specific population groups*, defining the basis of choice (gender, marital status, ethnicity, education etc.) and determining its size (e.g. 60 parents of toddlers; 35 policewomen; 66 teachers and so on). The choice of the actual respondents is usually left up to the interviewer.

More specifically, the researcher considers all significant dimensions of the population and ensures that each dimension will be represented in the sample. This is usually referred to as dimensional sampling and is particularly useful when the sample is small. In such cases, this procedure guarantees that at least one case from each dimension of the population will be included in the sample.

> *Example M.* The Health Commission is interested in identifying the state of health of workers employed in mining industries around the country. Instead of going through the process of compiling sampling frames in each industry, and then choosing the respondents, the researcher decides to use quota sampling. This proceeds as follows:
>
> 1. Interviewers are sent to each major mining industry.
> 2. The interviewers are told to study, in each unit: 10 workers aged below 20; 10 workers aged 21–30; 10 aged 31–40; 10 aged 41–50; 10 aged 51–60; and 10 aged over 60.
> 3. The interviewers are also told to consider length of service in their selection. Each of the above quotas must contain the same proportions of workers employed in these industries for more and for less than two years.
> 4. The persons who took part in the study constitute the sample.

Quota sampling is quite common in the social sciences because it is less costly than other techniques, does not require sampling frames, is relatively effective, and can be completed in a very short period of time. It is limited, however, especially with respect to representativeness, control of sampling and fieldwork requirements, which in such studies are not relevant. It must be noted, however, that the choice of the respondents can be determined more strictly, by employing probability rules, hence requiring sampling frames and specific methods of selection, while retaining the quota factor. This would convert the procedure to a probability sampling, which is quite possible.

Snowball sampling

In this approach, the researcher *chooses a few respondents*, using accidental sampling or any other method, and *asks them to recommend other people* who meet the criteria of the research and who might be willing to participate in the project. This process is continued with the new respondents until saturation – that is, until no more substantial information can be acquired through additional respondents – or until no more respondents are available.

> *Example N.* The author (Sarantakos, 2000b) was interested in the lifestyle of same-sex couples and wanted to investigate the establishment of such relationships, as well as their structure, process, stability and quality of life.

Given that there were no records on homosexual couples to be used as sampling frames, snowball sampling was used. The sampling design was as follows:

1. A number of same-sex couples identified through accidental sampling in Australia, New Zealand, Austria and Germany were located and interviewed.
2. These respondents were asked to recommend further homosexual couples.
3. After these new couples were interviewed, inquiries for further same-sex couples were made, and additional respondents were secured.
4. This process was continued until the sample was saturated.

This method is employed when the lack of sampling frames makes it impossible for the researcher to achieve a probability sample, when the target population is unknown, or when it is difficult to approach the respondents in any other way. In many cases, snowball sampling is the only way of securing a sample for a study.

Theoretical sampling

Theoretical sampling is not a form of 'sampling' in the sense we introduced it above. In the words of its creators (Glazer and Strauss, 1967: 45), theoretical sampling is the '*process of data collection for generating theory*'. The focus here is on data collection rather than on the choice of respondents.

In very simple terms, in theoretical sampling the sample units are not simply 'chosen' by the researcher prior to the commencement of the study but determined by the knowledge that emerges during the study (Burgess, 1984; Strauss, 1991). The researcher chooses the first respondent, collects relevant information and knowledge about the research topic, and on the basis of this decides which person to study next. The direction of 'theory' that develops during the research process determines who the next respondent will be, a decision that could have not been made at the start of the study. Theoretical sampling is interconnected with data gathering and serves to enable comparisons in time and place so as to discover variations in concepts and to integrate categories in terms of their properties and dimensions (Strauss and Corbin, 1998: 201).

In theoretical sampling, the study does not continue until all respondents have been contacted but rather until the process of study indicates that saturation has been reached; that is achieved when data collection no longer generates new data, when the categories are 'well developed in their properties and dimensions', and when the relationships among these categories are 'established and validated' (Strauss and Corbin, 1998: 212).

Example O. Assume we are interested in establishing some firm ideas about the coping strategies employed by a group of people who have lost their jobs as a result of a factory closure on the outskirts of the city. We are also interested in how they perceive and experience their new roles and their lives in their family and the community. How do we go about choosing the unemployed people? A very elementary description of the relevant parts of the study is given below.

Box **7.5**

The nature of theoretical sampling

Theoretical sampling:

- Entails an ongoing process. The sample here is not chosen and fixed at the outset and before the commencement of research, but chosen in an ongoing process that goes right through the whole study.
- Involves 'places, people and events'. Theoretical sampling takes into account the fact that people think and act differently, depending on many factors. Taking these factors into consideration helps the researcher to test, verify and contrast emerging concepts, categories and theory.
- Is guided by the emerging theory. Theoretical sampling is self-regulated in the sense that it guides data collection and analysis towards developing a theory, which in turn directs the nature and content of sampling.
- Is concerned with developing and validating theory. It is geared towards assuring that the emerging theory is adequately tested, so that it can be granted validity and high quality.
- Ends when theoretical saturation has been reached. It is not the identification of the respondents but the completion of the research that brings sampling to an end.

(Benini, 2000)

1. Approach one of the people affected by the closure of the factory and discuss the issue as planned.
2. Analyse the collected data and, while working on the main issue of the research, look for hints indicating that new aspects of the issue and additional information are available, and which people can provide such information.
3. Approach such a person. Continue the interview with the new person, explore the new facet of the issue and search for further information that would contribute to theory development and indications of where such information is available (i.e. what kind of person could provide such data).
4. This process of gaining new information and new informants will continue until saturation is achieved (i.e. until no more new information is found).

You may have noticed that this procedure resembles that of snowball sampling, except that here the hints as to new respondents are not given directly by the previous respondent but by the new information and the demands of the developing theory. This process will be understood better when the data analysis of grounded theory research is presented later in this text.

4 SAMPLING PROCEDURES IN QUALITATIVE RESEARCH

It has quite often been argued that qualitative researchers do not use sampling procedures. This is not correct. It is more accurate to say that they employ sampling procedures that correspond to the philosophy of this type of research, and that are less structured, less quantitative and less strict than the techniques quantitative researchers employ.

Normally, qualitative studies employ a form of non-probability sampling, such as accidental or purposive sampling (Kuzel, 1992), as well as snowball sampling and theoretical sampling. Qualitative sampling is biased by the nature of the underlying qualitative framework, which is perceived as an investigative process, not very different from detective work, where 'one makes gradual sense of a social phenomenon, and does it in large part by contrasting, comparing, replicating, cataloguing and classifying the objects of one's study' (Miles and Huberman, 1994). Sampling here comes after factors and conditions become clear and directive; making decisions about sampling before the study has begun is neither proper nor useful.

Nevertheless, qualitative research has no strict, agreed rules for sampling employed by all researchers. Sampling procedures employed by qualitative researchers include those mentioned above (accidental, purposive, snowball sampling and so on) or a version or combination of quantitative sampling procedures. In all cases, sampling is closely associated with theory. It is therefore either theory-driven 'up-front' (Miles and Huberman, 1994: 27), where subjects are chosen before data collection, guided by theory, or progressively, during data collection. The latter is known as *theoretical sampling*, and is connected with grounded theory.

Irrespective of the type of sampling chosen, several sampling parameters must be considered before a qualitative study can begin. Although qualitative sampling is a function of the research process itself that is decided on while the research is in progress and depends on the outcome of the study, researchers do have to decide at the outset at least about a number of issues, such as the informants or respondents who will be studied, the setting where research will take place, the events and processes to be considered in the investigation, and the time when research will be conducted. In any case, sampling procedures in qualitative research are inevitably related to a number of issues and choices, a few of which are listed below.

- *Kind of people*. The kind of people (actors) who will be included in their study, at least those to begin the study with.
- *Time*. The study may be conducted on working days, on weekends, during the school holidays, in summer or winter, in the afternoons, in the evenings or at any other time.
- *Kind of event*. The kind of event or processes to be studied; whether it will be a routine event, a special event, an unexpected event, or all types of events.
- *Setting*. The context in which the research will be conducted (e.g. the home, the club, the work place, a friend's house).

In summary, the sampling procedures employed by qualitative researchers demonstrate a number of characteristics; those presented in Box 7.6 are considered by a number of writers (e.g. Berger et al., 1989; Lamnek, 1988; Miles and Huberman, 1994) to be most significant.

Criteria of qualitative sampling

Qualitative sampling is directed:

- not towards large numbers of respondents but rather towards typical cases
- not towards fixed samples but towards ones that are flexible in size, type or subjects
- not towards statistical or random sampling but towards purposive sampling
- not towards 'mechanical' sampling but towards theoretical sampling
- towards fewer global settings than quantitative sampling
- not towards choosing a sample before the study has started, but (often) while the study is in progress
- not towards a strictly defined size but a sample whose number will be adjusted while the study is in operation
- not towards representativeness but rather towards suitability.

As stated earlier, the range of qualitative research has significantly widened in scope and purpose during the past ten years, allowing researchers more choice than before. It is interesting, then, to note that a trend is gradually becoming more evident within certain circles of qualitative research, whereby the sampling repertoire includes a wide range of methods and procedures, including tools such as *a priori* determination, complete collection, theoretical sampling, extreme case sampling, typical case sampling, maximal variation sampling, intensity sampling, critical case sampling, sensitive case sampling, convenience sampling, primary selection and secondary selection (Flick, 1998). Obviously, sampling is equally valuable in both research domains; only their structure and purpose are different.

5 INTERNET SAMPLING

The popularity of and easy access to the Internet has affected the conduct of social research in many ways. This is clearly shown in sampling, which has begun to adjust its techniques to new ways to approach people in the community. Internet sampling has become a part of the research armoury of modern researchers, with more and more research bodies using it as their preferred sampling procedure.

In simple terms, Internet sampling is a procedure that is administered, partly or fully, through the Internet. This entails procedures which enable the researcher to bring questionnaires to the attention of prospective respondents, by either directly forwarding them the questionnaire, or informing them of the availability of the survey and asking them to participate. This is facilitated through email or web pages.

Email. Researchers who gain access to email lists act in one of two ways. They may send a message to the address, asking the email holder to volunteer and take part in the survey. This is usually conducted as a part of the usual spamming, uninvited email. The other approach is for researchers to attach the questionnaire to an email sent to all members of an email list, with an invitation to participate. In a number of cases, participation is associated with a variety of rewards.

Web pages (URL). The same procedure is employed when respondents are sought in the web page, where readers are asked to complete a questionnaire, and if they agree they are directed to the questionnaire. Internet users will come across the researcher's message or the advertisement of an advertising agency, or both, and will respond according to their interests.

In a sense, Internet recruiting of respondents is not very different from advertising a study in the media, or contacting people on the phone. As in the latter approach, Internet sampling has to deal with problems of representativeness; the number of Internet users is limited, and is significantly lower among older people. Researchers make an effort to overcome this weakness by enlarging the population basis of prospective respondents, for example by means of sample triangulation, but the problem remains. The extensive use of spamming and the resulting anger of Internet users at this annoying interference often makes the response to uninvited invitations far from pleasant. As noted above, offering rewards for full participation may be one answer to the problem.

6   SAMPLE SIZE

The question about appropriate sample size in social research is given due attention by researchers of all schools of thought (Krämer and Thieman, 1987). However, the focus of relevant estimations varies significantly, with some showing an interest in pure quantity, others in quality and others again in both. A wise rule in this case is: the sample must be 'as large as necessary, and as small as possible'. This critical figure is reached in some cases through logical estimates, and in others through statistical computation, as we shall see next.

6.1 Non-statistical estimations

Sample size is directly associated with two major factors: the paradigm that guides the research, and the nature of the target population. These are the major determinants of the size of the sample, at least in logical terms. In quantitative research, both are seriously considered when the sample size is addressed. In qualitative research, the paradigm guides the process, but the nature of the data obtained will determine the size, and this is unpredictable. The study will stop when saturation is achieved, and this emerges out of the data and not out of logical thinking or other calculations. There are, however, qualitative researchers who follow the quantitative paradigm, and estimate their sample size in advance. Hence, the matter is not that simple!

Be that as it may, quantitative researchers and some qualitative researchers will come to a decision regarding the size of their sample before the study begins. The guiding factors in this context are associated with the type of population, the type of methodology employed, the availability of time and resources, the aim of the research, the type of instruments used, the accuracy required and the capacity of the research team. More particularly, the parameters listed in Box 7.7 deserve consideration.

It is worth noting that large samples do not always guarantee a higher degree of precision, validity and success in general. The quality of the results depends on several factors and the sample size is only one of them.

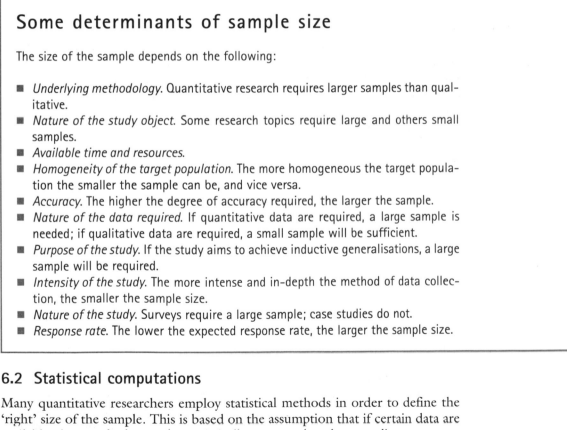

Box **7.7**

Some determinants of sample size

The size of the sample depends on the following:

- *Underlying methodology.* Quantitative research requires larger samples than qualitative.
- *Nature of the study object.* Some research topics require large and others small samples.
- *Available time and resources.*
- *Homogeneity of the target population.* The more homogeneous the target population the smaller the sample can be, and vice versa.
- *Accuracy.* The higher the degree of accuracy required, the larger the sample.
- *Nature of the data required.* If quantitative data are required, a large sample is needed; if qualitative data are required, a small sample will be sufficient.
- *Purpose of the study.* If the study aims to achieve inductive generalisations, a large sample will be required.
- *Intensity of the study.* The more intense and in-depth the method of data collection, the smaller the sample size.
- *Nature of the study.* Surveys require a large sample; case studies do not.
- *Response rate.* The lower the expected response rate, the larger the sample size.

6.2 Statistical computations

Many quantitative researchers employ statistical methods in order to define the 'right' size of the sample. This is based on the assumption that if certain data are available, the sample size can be statistically computed so that sampling errors can be reduced to a minimum or to an acceptable or expected level. There are several methods employed by statisticians and social researchers, some of which are quite complicated and beyond the limits of this treatise.

In general, the logic of many statistical methods relates sampling error to the standard error (SE): if the standard error is reduced, the sampling error is also reduced. The standard error depends on the size of the sample: with increasing sample size the standard error is decreased. Thus an acceptable standard error can be achieved by changing the sample size. This method manipulates the size of a sample by increasing or reducing it, until it corresponds to a standard error that is considered acceptable. This is then the ideal sample size.

The standard error varies inversely with the square root of the sample. If, for instance, we intend to halve the standard error, we have to quadruple the sample size. Thus, if we wish to determine the sample size that will reduce sampling errors, we start with a sample size taken at random, compute the standard error and increase the sample size until the relevant standard error is at an acceptable level. This manipulation works well with small samples, where increases in sample size result in increases in accuracy (i.e. decreases in sampling error), but it does not work equally well with large samples. Above a certain point, the increase in size required to achieve a significant decrease in the error is so large and therefore so costly that it makes such an increase not worth the effort.

In the main, the method employed depends on whether the estimation is directed towards means or proportions. In the former, investigators are interested in ascertaining trends and average scores in the area of study. For example, how large should my sample be to study the average amount of money spent by female students on alcohol per year? In the latter, researchers endeavour to estimate the proportion of people acting in a certain way. For instance, what is the proportion of female students who support affirmative action in this country? There are statistical techniques available to estimate the relevant sample size in both cases.

6.3 Estimating sample size through tables

There is an easier way of estimating the 'right' sample size, without needing to use formulae and computations. This is done by means of tables. The researcher who wishes to know how large the sample should be needs only to look at the table and, considering the necessary factors, such as p, q, Z and E, computes the figure that corresponds to the required sample size. Simply, p is the population estimate, q is the difference between p and 100, Z is the chosen confidence level, and E the maximum deviation from the true proportions considered by the researcher as acceptable.

Such tables are many and diverse and are constructed as shown above, that is, by means of the relevant formulae, this time for every possible combination of p, q, Z and E values. The more factors considered and the more detailed the values of these factors, the more detailed and accurate the table and, unfortunately, the more cumbersome the identification of the sample size figure. In tables with many factors and factor values, for instance, one has to decide on the right factors and values, search for the right column and row, and determine the required figure. When there are fewer factors, the tables are easier to use but offer limited information. Such tables may, for instance, offer advice about a certain p/q combination, one confidence level (95 per cent or 99 per cent) and one option for degree of accuracy.

Parten (1950: 314–15), for instance, published two tables, one for the 0.05 confidence level and one for the 0.01 confidence level. The tables offer sample size estimates for dichotomous population percentages (p and q) for two levels of confidence and for error limits ranging from 0.25 to 10. They provide useful information and save time and energy when deciding the required sample size.

Krejcie and Morgan (1970) offered an even easier table for estimating sample size (see Table 7.1). The only information needed to estimate sample size is the size of population. Consequently, their table gives figures for populations ranging from 10 to 1,000,000 people and the corresponding figures for the required sample size. This table computes the sample size by means of another formula, which takes into consideration chi-square for 1 degree of freedom, the population size, the population proportion, which is set at 0.50, and the degree of accuracy, which is set at 0.05, by using a formula developed by the research division of the National Education Association (USA), published in 1960.

Table 7.1 Table for determining sample size from a given population

N*	Sæ	N	S	N	S	N	S	N	S
10	10	100	80	280	162	800	260	2800	338
15	14	110	86	290	165	850	265	3000	341
20	19	120	92	300	169	900	269	3500	346
25	24	130	97	320	175	950	274	4000	351
30	28	140	103	340	181	1000	278	4500	354
35	32	150	108	360	186	1100	285	5000	357
40	36	160	113	380	191	1200	291	6000	361
45	40	170	118	400	196	1300	297	7000	364
50	44	180	123	420	201	1400	302	8000	367
55	48	190	127	440	205	1500	306	9000	368
60	52	200	132	460	210	1600	310	10000	370
65	56	210	136	480	214	1700	313	15000	375
70	59	220	140	500	217	1800	317	20000	377
75	63	230	144	550	226	1900	320	30000	379
80	66	240	148	600	234	2000	322	40000	380
85	70	250	152	650	242	2200	327	50000	381
90	73	260	155	700	248	2400	331	75000	382
95	76	270	159	750	254	2600	335	1000000	384

*N is the population size   æS is sample size

Estimating the required sample size by using this table is just a matter of reading numbers! (See Table 7.1.) For example, to specify the required sample size you need to know the size of the target population. For a population of 260 people the suggested sample size is 155; for a population of 1,600 the sample size is 310, and for a population of 20,000 the sample size is 377.

A word of caution: the statistical procedures presented above provide a handy tool for estimating the sample size required in each case when a study is to be carried out and when the sample is to be representative. Although these procedures are statistically sound, they relate to estimations based on assumptions and conditions, on which the estimates depend. As shown above, the sample size depends on the values of p, Z and E, chi-square and so on – values that are often difficult to estimate. How can we be sure, for instance, that p is 10, 25 or 48, or that σ is 50, particularly when our knowledge of the population is restricted? Guessing the value of the standard deviation of a population for which we intend to estimate the unknown mean is again a daring estimation. Figures obtained through these procedures must be interpreted within their boundaries.

MAIN POINTS

- Sampling is the process of choosing the respondents and the units of the study in general.
- Sampling is a common practice and an indispensable research tool in social sciences.
- As the alternative to conducting a saturation survey, sampling offers many advantages.
- In quantitative research, sampling units are chosen prior to the commencement of the study, objectively and systematically; are easily identifiable and clearly defined; independent from each other; not interchangeable; and free of errors, bias and distortions.
- The two distinct types of sampling are probability and non-probability sampling.
- In probability sampling, all units have an equal, calculable and non-zero probability of being included in the sample.
- Non-probability sampling does not adhere to the rules of probability.
- Qualitative researchers employ non-probability sampling procedures such as theoretical sampling, accidental sampling, purposive sampling, quota sampling and snowball sampling.
- Usually, one sample is sufficient to conduct a study, but multi-sample studies are also common.
- Sample size is defined using statistical and non-statistical methods.

WHERE TO FROM HERE?

Before you leave this chapter, visit the companion website for the third edition of *Social Research* at http://www.palgrave.com/sociology/sarantakos to review the main concepts introduced in this chapter and to test yourself on the major issues discussed.

FURTHER READING

Fink, A. (1995) *How to Sample in Surveys.* Thousand Oaks, Calif.: Sage.

Henry, G. T. (1990) *Practical Sampling.* Newbury Park: Sage.

Lavrakas, P. (1993) *Telephone Survey Methods: Sampling Selection and Supervision.* Beverley Hills: Sage.

Maisel, R. and Hodges Persell C. (1996) *How Sampling Works.* Thousand Oaks, Calif.: Sage.

Sudman, S. and Blair, E. (1999) 'Sampling in the Twenty-first Century.' *Journal of the Academy of Marketing Science*, (27)2: 269–77.

Methods of data collection

Multiple-sample studies

INTRODUCTION

As noted when discussing sampling procedures, the number of samples per study varies from one case to another. Overall, while the vast majority of investigations employ only one sample, there are some that employ two or more. The purpose of using more than one sample varies from case to case, but in general it serves to ascertain changes over time and facilitate comparisons as well as establishing causality, triangulation and hypothesis testing. Within these parameters, there are at least five types of study that deserve to be mentioned. These are

- experiments, which study two or more samples, in most cases concurrently
- panel studies, which analyse the same sample at different points in time
- cross-sectional studies, which investigate different samples concurrently
- trend studies, which study different samples at different points in time
- focus groups, which examine several natural or constructed groups.

In this chapter we shall address the five types of multi-sample study and explain their value for social research. In most cases, the main characteristic of these methods of data collection is the way they use samples. However, the difference goes beyond the methods. It is also the research design that is important. As we shall see, particularly with regard to experiments, the research logic and the manner in which information is collected and causation is checked are equally characteristic of this research model.

1   EXPERIMENTS

1.1 Introduction

Experiments are a part of everyday life. Since the dawn of humanity people have experimented in many ways to ascertain the best ways of coping with everyday problems and to improve the quality of their life in general. Cooks have experimented with various methods and ingredients to improve the quality of food; husbands and wives with communication methods to improve the quality of marriage; children with techniques to win the attention of their parents; teachers with various teaching methods to convey mathematical principles to mentally disabled children more effectively; and businessmen with a variety of methods to gain access to a large segment of the market.

This everyday practice was adopted and improved by physical scientists and became the standard method of discovering knowledge. From the physical sciences experiments moved to psychology. They were introduced in this area by Wilhelm Wundt (1832–1920), a German psychologist, and William James (1842–1910), an American philosopher and psychologist, and became one of the major procedures employed in this area to discover knowledge. The step from psychology to sociology and other social sciences was a small one. Although experimentation is more common in psychology than in other social sciences, it is currently being used by researchers of diverse affiliations and backgrounds.

Experiments are almost exclusively used within a quantitative model. Qualitative experiments are practically unknown, and little has been written about their nature, structure and usefulness, let alone their theoretical and methodological properties (Kleining, 1991). In this section, we shall explore experiments as a method of data collection, and in particular their nature, structure, types and process, as they are employed by quantitative researchers in the social sciences. A brief note on qualitative experiments will be made at the end of this section.

Box **8.1**

Minimum properties of causation

An association is 'causal' if it is statistically proven to entail:

- *Correlation.* A strong association between the variables.
- *Consistency.* The association between cause and effect must be consistent.
- *Time order.* The cause precedes the effect, and not vice versa,
- *Contiguity.* Cause and effect must be contiguous, that is close together in both time and space.
- *Exclusion of spuriousness.* The relationship must not be spurious; in other words, the effect is not the result of extraneous intervening variables but of the causal variable alone.
- *Rationale.* There must be a rationale that explains and justifies causality.

1.2 Strengths and weaknesses of experiments

Like other methods, experiments demonstrate many strengths and also some weaknesses. The most common strengths and weaknesses of experimentation are listed below.

Strengths:

- *Replication.* Experiments are constructed in a manner that allows replication, assuming that repeating the procedure will not lead to different results.
- *Prediction.* Their structure and process, and their detailed and rigorous design allow reasonable predictions to a higher degree than many other methods.
- *Causality.* Experiments possess all the methodological parameters required for establishing causality.
- *Precision.* Rigorous planning and checking of the status of variables, and the validity and reliability of methods allow a high degree of precision in all steps of the research process.
- *Convenience.* The size of the samples, the detailed and accurate preparation of the experimental conditions, and the detailed research design make experiments a most convenient research method.

Weaknesses:

- *Control.* Depending on the circumstances, experiments may not allow the degree of control that is required to exclude unwanted or unintended influences outside the independent variables.
- *Representativeness.* Samples are usually too small to produce representative findings.
- *Process.* The research process is too technical and too artificial to allow generalisations.
- *Ethics.* There are cases in which conditions dictate that ethical standards are of secondary importance.

Experiments are employed because they have advantages over other methods of data collection, and for many researchers the advantages outweigh their shortcomings. As noted above, they are most popular in psychology and some other areas.

1.3 The nature of experiments

Experiments are used to ascertain the presence, type and degree of a causal relationship between two variables. An association is considered to be causal if it entails the criteria listed in Box 8.1 (see B. Bergman, 1991; Dimas, 2003: 91).

As a rule, experiments involve some degree of manipulation of the surroundings and an assessment of its effects on certain targets. Manipulation of the environment takes place in a very systematic form, and is based on controlling for, ruling out or closing off all factors except those included in or related to the stimulus (known as closure). This aims to eliminate every possible influence other than the induced stimulus, in order to facilitate an accurate measurement of the effects of this stimulus.

The purpose of experiments is twofold, namely to test hypotheses and to develop theories. In its most elementary form, an experiment consists of the choice of the subjects, the establishment of the controls and conditions required for the test, the pre-testing of the dependent variable, the re-testing of the dependent variable after the stimulus has been introduced, and the evaluation of the results (see Box 8.2)

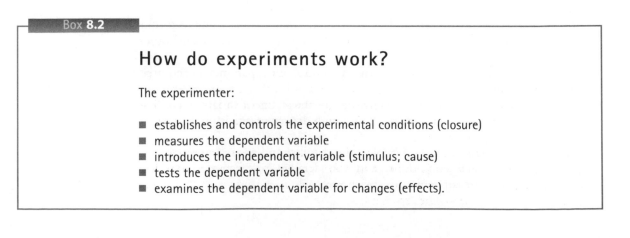

Box **8.2**

How do experiments work?

The experimenter:

- establishes and controls the experimental conditions (closure)
- measures the dependent variable
- introduces the independent variable (stimulus; cause)
- tests the dependent variable
- examines the dependent variable for changes (effects).

Central to experimental studies is the systematic procedure employed to ensure that the relationship between independent and dependent variables remains intact and free of distortions. This procedure entails the Max–Con–Min rule (Stapf, 1995: 240–1), which prescribes that it is a task of the experimenter to

- *maximise* the effects of the independent variable on the dependent variable
- *control* outside distorting influences, and
- *minimise* the effects of non-systematic (chance) variables.

Experiments adhere to strict principles of quantitative methodology, perhaps more strict than in other contexts. More obvious are these principles when referring to:

- the way in which variables are measured (must be consistent and method-ologically sound)
- conditions under which variables are measured (to be held constant, especially through closure)
- the replicability of the study
- the comparability of the findings
- the expectation that repetition under controlled conditions is a basis for testing causality.

These are clear reflections of the strict quantitative structure of the methodology that underlies this research process.

1.4 Steps in experimental research

Experiments are carried out in a manner that, in principle, is no different from that employed in other areas of research. The steps of the research model presented in the introductory chapters of this book apply also in the area of experimentation. Some differences between this general model and that employed in the process of experimenting do exist in relation to the content of some steps, but only with respect to details. The experimental research process can be described as shown in Box 8.3.

In the following sections we shall look more closely at some aspects of experimental designs, examine some important elements of experimentation in more detail, and compare them with those of other methods.

1.5 Experimental sampling

Characteristics of the sample

Selection of the subjects in an experimental design is usually undertaken by means of the probability sampling procedures discussed earlier in this book. The experimental sample demonstrates the following characteristics:

- It includes two study groups: the *experimental* group and the *control* group. The experimental group is the one that will be exposed to the independent variable, namely to the stimulus; the control group is the group that is not subjected to the independent variable.

The experimental research process

Step 1. *Selection of the topic and methodology.* Asks: What will be studied? Which methodology will be used?

Step 2. *Methodological construction of the topic.* Asks: What is the detailed definition of the topic? What are the variables? How will they be operationalised? What is the hypothesis?

Step 3. *Sampling and methods.* Asks: How many groups will be constructed and tested? How will the respondents be chosen?

Step 4. *Data collection.* Asks: What methods will be employed to collect the data? How will the methods be conducted? How will closure, and other principles be adhered to? Is there a need for a laboratory or for assistants? Are computers or other equipment needed? How will they be procured? How will the data be collected? How will extraneous influences be controlled? Are issues of ethics being observed?

Step 5. *Analysis and interpretation.* How will data be analysed and interpreted?

- The two groups must be checked for any systematic differences.
- The subjects in the experimental and control groups must be the same or similar with regard to the research topic.
- The selection of the subjects should be free from sampling bias.

These criteria aim to ensure that the sampling procedure produces a representative sample free from bias and distortion, and that it establishes two similar sub-samples.

Methods of sampling

There are at least three methods of sample selection in experiments. These are randomisation, subject matching and group matching. The choice of the appropriate sampling procedure depends on many factors, including theoretical/methodological considerations, experimental conditions, data required, nature of the research question and nature and type of subjects.

- *Randomisation.* In this method, two subjects are selected randomly from a sampling frame, and one is placed in the experimental and the other in the control group. This process is repeated until sufficient subjects are selected.
- *Subject matching.* From the sampling frame, pairs of adequately matched subjects are chosen, and one is placed in the experimental group and the other in the control group. Again, this continues until the planned number of subjects is reached.
- *Group matching.* In this method, pairs of matched groups – that is, groups with subjects of the same or similar characteristics (e.g. average age, education, status, achievement or performance) – are chosen, and one group is used as the experimental group and the other as the control group.

All three methods are widely used, and all have their strengths and limitations. The subject-matching method is affected by the inherent difficulty of matching subjects; when similarity is the principle of selection, it is not easy to define consistently what is or is not similar. Group matching is equally affected by this problem; in addition, the use of averages (where employed) results in individual differences not being considered. Randomisation is more objective and freer from bias than the other two methods, and is especially useful if subject matching is not possible. But it still replaces individual judgment with 'objective' selection, and quite often it is not possible to argue that such a method guarantees the establishment of similar groups, especially when the samples are relatively small.

1.6 Arrangement of experimental conditions

In order to be able to make definite statements about the causal relationship between the independent and dependent variables, the experimenter should ensure that factors other than the independent variable do not affect the dependent variable. All possible factors that could have an influence on the progress of the experiment should be controlled. Where control of these factors is not possible, the experimenter should be in a position to assess the influence of such factors and to consider their effects when interpreting the findings.

'Arrangement' usually refers to group composition, the process of selection, the structure of the setting in which the experiment is to be performed, time of the test, nature of the stimulus (independent variable) and its meaning for the subjects, time between pre-test and post-test, opportunity for manipulation or conditioning during the time between pre-test and post-test, strict supervision, instructions given during the experiment and similar factors and conditions that might have a differential impact on the subjects.

1.7 The process of experimentation

Experiments begin with the establishment of first contact with the subjects and continue with manipulation and measurement of the variables. The three basic steps of data collection in experiments are as follows:

Step 1. *Pre-test*. This step is called pre-test because it takes place before the subjects are exposed to the experimental treatment. The pre-test includes measurement of the dependent variable, usually of both the experimental group and the control group. This measurement is taken as a basis for assessing the eventual changes of the dependent variable during the experiment.

Step 2. *The test*. During this step the subjects are exposed to the independent variable. This may entail taking part in a discussion, reading a book, taking a certain medicine, consuming an amount of alcohol, watching a film, attending a lecture or visiting a club. The nature and duration of the stimulus varies with the nature of the experiment and the independent variable. In some cases it might take only a few minutes, in other cases significantly longer.

Step 3. *Post-test*. After the experimental treatment has been completed, the subjects are tested again. This is referred to as post-test because it takes place after the experimental treatment. During this test the dependent variable is measured again in order to ascertain its present status. Following this, the results of the pre-test and post-test are compared and any variations in the results are recorded.

Example A. A journalist is interested in testing the hypothesis that the media have a strong impact on the attitudes of students towards immigrants, using experiments as the method. How will she proceed? The necessary steps are shown below:

1. The experimental and control groups are chosen, by using one of the methods described above.
2. The experimental conditions are established.
3. Both groups are pre-tested to measure the attitudes of the subjects towards immigrants, by using attitude scales and by computing attitude scores for each subject.
4. The members of the experimental group are shown a film dealing with immigrants, their life and ambitions. This film is not shown to the members of the control group.
5. Both groups are post-tested by re-measuring their attitudes to immigrants using attitude scales, and computing the attitude scores for each subject.
6. The results of the pre-tests and the post-tests are compared to ascertain whether there are any significant differences.

1.8 Analysis and interpretation of experimental data

The analysis and interpretation will concentrate on data collected through the pre-test and post-test. These data will be analysed and compared and the differences computed, most likely by using statistical methods; an attempt will be made to establish a causal relationship between the variables in question. For instance, if the results of the pre-test and post-test of the control group show no difference while those of the experimental group are significantly different, and given that other factors were controlled, it may be concluded that the independent variable was the cause of the change.

1.9 Types of experiments in quantitative research

Regardless of the design they employ, experiments appear in various forms. Some of these forms are used predominantly by psychologists, others by sociologists and other social scientists. The following three types are the most common forms of experiments in the social sciences.

- *Laboratory experiments.* These are conducted in a laboratory, where all external factors can be controlled.
- *Field experiments.* These are performed in natural situations, such as city blocks, bars, meeting places of migrants, villages, churches and classrooms.

■ *Demonstration experiments.* Demonstration experiments may be field or laboratory experiments but with one group (the experimental group) only. Although they help to 'demonstrate', highlight or illustrate trends in or aspects of human behaviour, they are not true experiments because, first, they do not contain a control group, and therefore no comparisons can be made, second, they do not select subjects randomly, and third, there is no clear timing for the experimental treatment, since it can continue for as long as the subjects remain in the treatment (Pfeifer, 2000).

1.10 Experimental designs

Psychologists and social scientists use several types of experimental design. The differences between them lie mainly in the number of experimental and control groups employed in each experiment, in the use of pre-tests (whether in the experimental group only or in both groups), and in the way in which the independent variable is treated. The aim of the experimenters who introduce the various types of designs is to eliminate or at least control the effect of any factors that could affect the process and/or the results of the study. The most common designs are listed below.

■ *Before–after design.* This employs only one group, the experimental group, which is pre-tested, exposed to the stimulus and post-tested. The differences between the pre-test and post-test scores indicate the possible effects of the independent variable on the dependent variable.
■ *Classical experimental design.* Here, two groups are employed, the experimental and the control group. Although both are adequately prepared for the experiment, pre-tested and post-tested, only the experimental group is exposed to the independent variable. This is the most common form of experiment.
■ *After-only experiment.* This is identical to the classical experimental design, except that neither the experimental group nor the control group is pre-tested.
■ *Solomon two-control-group design.* This design employs one experimental group and two control groups. In principle, one control group and the experimental group are treated as in the classic experimental design. The second control group is not pre-tested, but is exposed to the independent variable and post-tested.
■ *Randomised group design.* Here, the design includes two experimental groups and one control group. This design is similar to the classic design, except that it includes two experimental groups.
■ *Solomon four-group design.* This design employs two experimental groups and two control groups. One experimental and one control group are treated as in the classic experimental design. The second experimental group and the second control group are not pre-tested but are exposed to the independent variable and are post-tested.

There are many other experimental designs (e.g. factorial design) which are extensively used in the area of psychology. In sociology and other social sciences such complex designs have little use. Social scientists are more likely to use field or quasi-field experiments rather than laboratory experiments or multi-group and multi-design experiments.

1.11 Field experiments

Field experiments (also known as naturalistic experiments) are experiments like those described above; they differ from other experiments in that they are conducted in natural situations, that is, in the field. 'Field' here is the context in which the subjects live their lives: their home, school, street, shopping centre, church and so on, which have not been constructed for the purpose of experimentation, and also not controlled by the researcher.

There are two types of field experiment: true field experiments and quasi-field experiments. The former require complete adherence to the principles of experimentation, while the latter do not. The choice of each of these forms depends on the nature of the study and particularly on the degree of accessibility to experimental parameters. For instance, where a true field experiment is possible, it will be employed; otherwise, a quasi-field experiment is undertaken. Similarly, when there is no need for detailed statistical information, and general knowledge of the issue in question is more than adequate, quasi-field experiments can be employed.

The following is a quasi-field experiment: in a supermarket, one of the cashiers is advised, when handing change to the customers to add $20 to it. If the customer accepts the overpayment without comment, the cashier would re-count the change and return the proper amount to the customer. The researcher records the way in which customers react to the overpayment, and the number and type of people who accept or question it.

Although this method is popular and its results are accepted, the nature of such experiments has often been questioned. Some critics argue that there are insufficient parameters to justify them as experiments; or that they are surveys. The decisive factor here is whether the experimental conditions are adequately structured and controlled. If so, they qualify as experiments.

True field experiments are difficult to construct, for many reasons. First of all, the choice of similar groups or subjects in natural environments is quite difficult and sometimes impossible. Hence, it is difficult to determine the cause of any change in the behaviour of the subjects, since its origin cannot be determined. This might force researchers to limit field experiments to areas in which similar units are available. This of course reduces their applicability markedly.

Apart from this, it is argued that it is difficult to choose natural environments that are similar or comparable. The problem here is as serious as in the previous case. Also, we cannot assume that comparable environments affect the research units in a similar way. Finally, it is argued that field experiments are very complex, time-consuming and costly.

1.12 Social experiments

Most social experiments are examples of true field experiments. They are commonly used in educational, medical and psychological research, as well as by those working in the areas of social policy and programme evaluation. Characteristic of social experiments is that they choose their subjects by employing

systematic random sampling procedures, and make no attempt to control experimental conditions and extraneous influences (Orr, 1999: 10). Such control is
considered impossible in social experiments.

Overall, social experiments are applied in the social context and compare social
groups to ascertain whether certain factors have an impact on the community.
For instance, low-income families may be randomly chosen and assigned to
experimental and control groups; the families of the experimental group are
offered certain incentives while the families of the control group are not. The
research question here is whether the families of the experimental group change
in any way, and more importantly whether it can be assumed that incentives have
an impact on low-income families.

Another example is related to programme evaluation. Before a programme is
introduced, a large sample of respondents is chosen randomly and then pre-tested
to establish the level of their response to certain central criteria (pre-test). Six
months after the programme has been introduced, the same respondents are
tested again (post-test) to establish changes in their response to the pre-tested
criteria. The presence or absence of changes will allow some form of assessment
of the programme in question.

1.13 Validity of experiments

Experiments are among the most valid instruments of social research, due to their
attention to methodological parameters and to controlling possible causes of
distortions. Still, there are many difficult factors that are generally thought to
raise questions about the validity of experiments (Berger et al., 1989; Farber,
2001; Suls and Rosnow, 1988). These are:

- *Maturation.* The change in the dependent variable may not be caused by the
  independent variable but rather by maturation of the subjects.
- *Conditioning.* Pre-testing might sensitise subjects and predispose them
  to develop an interest in the experiment and respond atypically to
  experimentation.
- *The history effect.* Historical events might occur during the time between the
  pre-test and post-test, and might affect the responses to the latter.
- *Changes in samples.* These are changes due to mortality, spatial mobility or
  general unavailability of subjects and/or experimenters.
- *Instrumentation.* There is a possibility that changes in the dependent variable
  are due to changes in the nature of the tests during pre-testing and post-test-
  ing rather than to the effects of the independent variable (measurement
  decay).
- *Interaction.* Changes in the dependent variable might be caused by a combination of several factors, which may or may not include the independent variable.
- *Sampling.* Changes in the dependent variable might be caused by sampling
  problems.
- *The Hawthorne effect.* Changes might be caused by the fact that subjects
  know that they are being studied (also referred to as the reactivity effect).
- *Modelling.* The dependent variable might change because the experimenter
  expects the subjects to behave in a certain way and the subjects wish to please
  the experimenter.

■   *Ecology*. Changes in the dependent variable might have been caused by the 'ecology', or the experimental setting and measurement.

This is not to be taken as a criticism of experimentation. Knowledge of such risk areas, which can affect the validity of experiment, empowers the researchers to construct an experiment on sound foundations so that distortions can be avoided.

1.14 Experiments in qualitative research

Nature of qualitative experiments

Although semi-structured experiments of some kind have been employed sporadically in the social sciences, used in a systematic manner and within a qualitative paradigm, qualitative experiments are still in their infancy. Neither the theorists, the methodologists nor the practitioners have made an effort to demonstrate that qualitative experiments are possible, or to demonstrate clearly when, under what conditions and how they should be conducted. Researchers who employ them do so using their own understanding of what they consider a qualitative experiment (Benini, 2000). Overall, qualitative experiments are not seen as legitimate, logical or straightforward procedures that should be taken seriously. There are several reasons for this.

In the first instance, it is argued (Kleining, 1986; see also Lamnek, 1995) that experiments are no longer as popular as they used to be; criticisms based on principles of the philosophy of science and qualitative research as well as on 'technical' grounds seem to have contributed to this. Qualitative methodologists do not seem to have made a serious effort to develop a suitable methodology for qualitative experiments.

Apart from this, the method of experimentation has over the years become synonymous with quantification, measurement, statistics, control, intervention, objectivity, standardisation and similar qualities; to conduct experiments outside these parameters appears to be unthinkable. Quite simply, a 'qualitative experiment' seems to be a contradiction in terms!

Still, the need for qualitative experiments and the contribution they could make to social sciences has been recognised by some researchers who have either conducted experiments that are close to what we would call non-quantitative experiments, or made a contribution to the discussion of this topic (Kleinig, 1986; Lamnek, 1995), and described the manner in which qualitative experiments are conceptualised and practised.

Rules of experimentation

By definition, a qualitative experiment is expected to adhere to the rules of qualitative methodology, which are inconsistent with the kind of experiments described in the previous section. Similarly, the object of study must be chosen in a manner that will be consistent with a qualitative model; in other words, the objects of study must be accessible to the tools of qualitative methods. Appropriate objects for qualitative experiments include individual or collective relationships and behaviour, and everything related to such relationships. Obviously, as Kleining (1982) and other writers (e.g. Lamnek, 1995; Pfeifer, 2000) have noted, there are established rules for doing qualitative research that can be applied in the area of qualitative experiments; of particular importance are four rules which are summarised as follows:

- The researcher does not intend to test hypotheses but to develop new ones.
- The object is not defined rigidly but remains open and flexible, allowing future revisions and adjustments. More precise definitions are developed after the study is completed.
- The rules here are flexibility, openness and structural variability. This relates, for instance, to the choice of methods and sampling procedures.
- The emphasis of analysis and evaluation is on identifying commonalities rather than on stressing differences. The principle of dialogue is egalitarian not critical/authoritarian. In Kleinig's view, the process of analysis is a circular one, in which the author moves around the object of analysis throughout the experiment, looking for answers. To this is added the dialectic process of discovery: an answer raises a question, which demands a new answer, which leads to a new question which calls for an answer, and so on. This is continued until the research object is explained.

Although the conceptual ramifications of qualitative experiments are not difficult to establish and defend – at least on theoretical grounds – in reality this becomes quite a difficult task. Experiments are what they are because of their nature, and taking away many of their central principles (causality, objectivity, statistical analysis etc.) deprives them of their methodological identity. Apart from this, in some cases the criteria of qualitative research are superficial, leading to confusion, particularly to neophytes of social research. For instance, stressing similarities rather than differences makes little sense for at least two reasons. First, how can one ignore the differences in a study when changes in group structures and comparisons make questions about these differences almost inevitable, and certainly most interesting? Second, why is a study of differences in multiple-group investigations of little or no importance? Hopefully, with the passing of time and with the increasing interest of qualitative researchers in experiments, many of the characteristics of this type of research – so far sketched only lightly – will be given due attention.

2 PANEL STUDIES

2.1 Introduction

The characteristic of panel studies are, first, that they study the same sample on more than one occasion; second, they study the same topic; and third, they employ the same methods. For instance, the author studied 330 cohabiting couples in 1980, and interviewed them again on two subsequent occasions, 1985 and 1992 (Sarantakos, 1992). The period between the various stages of the study can vary from case to case; some studies use two stages, while others use more.

The length of the time interval between the stages depends on factors such as the nature of the study object and the research purpose. Issues that change quickly may require shorter intervals than those changing only over long periods of time. Finally, short intervals are most useful when the study is concerned with the chronological unfolding of social events and changes, which studies with long intervals may not be able to register.

When considering whether to employ a long panel study, there are a number of factors that must be taken into account as they can potentially affect the quality of the study. A few examples of such factors are shown in Box 8.4.

Box 8.4

Where do panel studies usually go wrong?

- *Loss of subjects.* This may be due to death, moving away, being unable to take part in the study and so on (the longer the study, the more likely it is that subjects will become inaccessible).
- *Conditioning.* Subjects develop an interest in, and hence learn more about, the study object over time, and therefore are no longer representative of the population.
- *Instrument bias.* Instruments may be employed in different ways in the various stages. Presentation, timing and conditions of data collection may vary.
- *Respondent bias.* The subjects become accustomed to the research instrument and its questions, and are therefore better able to respond to the study's question in subsequent stages.
- *Study conditions.* Data collection, even if performed in exactly the same way in the various stages, can be seriously affected by the personal and family conditions of the subject. Put simply, conditions of study can hardly be exactly the same for each respondent in all stages.
- *Costs.* The longer the study, the greater the cost.

Researchers have developed strategies to control these and other factors that affect the validity of panel studies, but such factors cannot be fully eliminated. For instance, loss of subjects can cause a serious problem if those who depart are of particular importance for the study; they may constitute a cohort that is no longer represented. Similarly, the more subjects learn about the study's subject matter, the less they represent the target population.

2.2 Variants of panel studies

Panel studies are also used in other forms. In most cases, these variants are either not sufficiently different to deserve special attention, or are not 'studies' but tools or instruments used within other studies. Below are a few examples.

Cohort studies. Cohort studies are panel studies that focus on cohorts; that is, they study the same cohort on several occasions. One may study all those born in a city suburb in 1990, conducting surveys every two years, recording the changes on a number of issues, and so identifying changes over time. The previous discussion on panel studies applies also in such cases.

Multi-stage studies. Here the researcher initially selects a number of respondents (primary selection units), and then draws from within that sample a smaller sample of respondents who meet the criteria for the study. The initial sample may contain ethnic students in a large university; the second sample contains only those who had a relationship with a citizen of the host country. The process of reducing the number of respondents by focusing on specific criteria and by forming new samples can continue for as long as it is required. For instance, provided that the size of the second sample was large enough to allow further treatment, the researcher could draw a third sample, by choosing a small and balanced group of male and female students, who would ultimately be studied.

The main advantage of this sampling procedure is that it allows the establishment of a sample that is directly related to the research object. With every additional selection, the sample becomes more focused and more relevant to the research question, and the results can be expected to be equally relevant and more representative.

Multi-phase studies. In a multi-phase sampling procedure, the choice of samples and sub-samples is the same as in multi-stage sampling. First, the primary selection units are chosen; then a sample is drawn from them, and so on. However, in a multi-phase sampling procedure, each sample is adequately studied before another sample is drawn from it. Consequently, while in multi-stage sampling, only the final grouping is studied, in multi-phase sampling, all samples are researched. This offers an advantage over other methods, because the information gathered at each phase helps the researcher to choose a more relevant and more representative sample.

2.3 Cross-sectional studies

Cross-sectional studies employ samples from different sectors and compare them by using a set of criteria related to the theme of the study. Examples of such studies would include a study of workers in three different sectors of heavy industry to establish differences in working conditions and pay, a study of entry criteria in the medical schools of three universities, and a study of performance criteria of police officers in one rural and one city area. In the context of descriptive studies, the purpose of cross-sectional studies is to establish differences between the sections. It can also produce data which will permit the establishment of causal relationships.

2.4 Trend studies

Trend studies are like panel studies in that they are conducted at different points in time; they differ, however, in that they do not use the same sample but different samples. Structurally and in methodological terms they are the same, and the points made about panel studies apply also to trend studies.

For instance, one may be interested in establishing the criteria which young people consider important when they choose their future spouse, and particularly in whether these considerations change over time. To address these points, one may draw a large sample of young males and females and collect relevant data. Ten years later, one might repeat the same study, this time with a new sample of young males and females, and compare the data collected at these two points in time.

The fact that trend studies use different samples has many advantages. First of all, they avoid problems such as loss of subjects, conditioning and so on that are associated with panel studies. Selection of respondents is also easier, and entails much lower costs. However, these advantages are countered by disadvantages, particularly regarding the comparability of the populations in question, comparability of samples, continuity in the application of methods, and establishing causality. It is important to note, however, that when comparisons between groups over time are considered, trend studies are the only method available. In the example mentioned above, the employment of a panel study would have been most inappropriate; using the same sample at both points in time would have not answered the question of how young people choose a spouse because, by the time the study was repeated, the respondents would have no longer been young.

2.5 What is wrong with panel studies?

The nature of these studies is associated with many problems that the researcher must take into consideration. These stem from the intensity of the study, which assumes people will remain in it for a long period of time and agree to being studied more than once. More specifically, the problems listed in Box 8.5 are reported to deserve special attention (see, for example, Bailey, 1982; Stergios, 1991).

Nevertheless, these are very useful methods, and are widely used in the context of industry, household studies, service industries, sociological and psychological studies. Knowing their weaknesses and taking precautions to prevent them from affecting the research can improve their value and usefulness in social research.

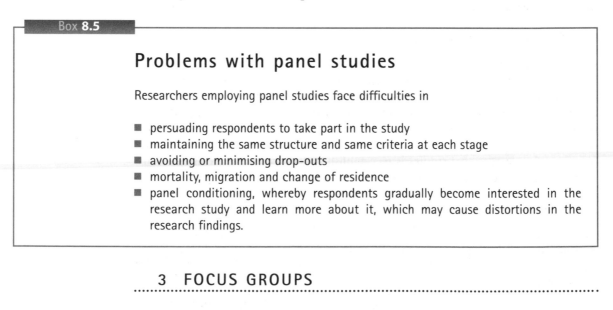

Box **8.5**

Problems with panel studies

Researchers employing panel studies face difficulties in

- persuading respondents to take part in the study
- maintaining the same structure and same criteria at each stage
- avoiding or minimising drop-outs
- mortality, migration and change of residence
- panel conditioning, whereby respondents gradually become interested in the research study and learn more about it, which may cause distortions in the research findings.

3 FOCUS GROUPS

3.1 Introduction

Focus group research can best be described as a loosely constructed discussion with a group of people brought together for the purpose of the study, guided by the researcher and addressed as a group. Due to the use of interviewing techniques, it is also referred to as 'focus group interviewing' (e.g. Berg, 1995); and because it addresses the group rather than specific members, it is also known as 'group discussion' (H. Krüger, 1983). Given that more than one group is usually included in the study, and that each group constitutes a separate sample of respondents, focus groups can be seen as a multi-sample study.

In its most common application, this method entails: first, the selection of people with a particular interest, expertise or position in the community; second, the formation of the group by bringing these people together in the same venue; third, the introduction of the discussion topic by the researcher, who acts as a facilitator and arbitrator; fourth, guiding the discussion so as to address the research topic; fifth, encouraging discussion among the members of the group rather than between them and the researcher; and sixth, observing and recording the discussion. The emphasis on discussion among the group members where the researcher acts as a facilitating observer (not an interviewer) is the essence of the method, and one that distinguishes it from a group interview.

This method was introduced by Kurt Lewin in 1936 in the United States, in the context of small-group experiments, and later in other areas of research, including market research and opinion research. Currently it is used in four distinct contexts: as a preliminary (pre-research) study leading to quantitative research; as a self-contained and principal method of research; as a supplementary (post-research) method; and as a part of a multi-method study (McQuarrie, 1996; Morgan, 1997).

The focus group method appears in two forms, the unstructured or semi-structured form and the structured form, which are employed by qualitative and quantitative researchers respectively (Stewart and Shamdasani, 1990). Its popularity is reported to be steadily increasing (Morgan, 1996).

3.2 The purposes of focus groups

The purpose of focus groups varies with many factors, and particularly its paradigm. In a quantitative context, this method appears in a variety of forms. As a pre-research method it can help to prepare the main study by providing sufficient information about the study object, about operationalisation by defining indicators, and about preventing possible errors. As a main study it offers information about group processes, spontaneous feelings, reasons and explanations for attitudes and behaviour as adequately as any other method. As a post-research method it explains trends and variances, reasons and causes, attitudes and opinions (e.g. Dreher and Dreher, 1991; Mariner, 1986)

In another form, group discussion is employed to bring about changes in the group and its members, as a result of the direction and intensity of the discussion. It can further provide valuable information about group processes, attitude changes and manipulation, the attitudes and opinions of group members, the group or the public, the effectiveness of certain methods and so on. It can also enable the testing of group strategies in solving problems (Flick, 1998). Finally, the study of focus groups can 'generate diversity and difference either within or between groups, and so reveal . . . the dilemmatic nature of everyday arguments' (Lunt and Livingstone, 1996: 96).

Overall, this method does not aim to analyse the group but rather to provide a forum that facilitates group discussion, to brainstorm a variety of solutions and to establish a mechanism of opinion formation. Within the context of the group, it is expected that, through mutual stimulation, a group environment will encourage discussion; increase the motivation to address critical issues; enable the facilitator to lead the discussion towards focal points and topical issues; and allow significant points of view to be presented in a real, emotional and summated form as spontaneous expressions (in other words, producing the opportunity for a controlled presentation of personal views). In this way, important information can be gathered in a relatively short period of time.

Within a qualitative research model, group discussion offers access to the construction of meanings while participants interact with each other within the group, the breadth and variation of those meanings, and the way in which the group negotiates them. This is expected to occur when group members, first, address, describe or explain issues introduced by the leader or a member of the group; second, compare different points of view, third, evaluate views and outcomes of discussion, and judge relevant arguments; and fourth, make decisions, draw conclusions or present alternative points of view, while trying to achieve a possible consensus.

3.3 The discussion process

The conduct of group discussion has been described in different ways. The basis of diversity is the nature of the underlying paradigm, although the nature of the topic plays a role in this context. Some (e.g. Mucchielli, 1973) contend that there are three major steps in group discussion – warm-up, confrontation and relaxation – while others list six or even more steps. Lamnek (1993) refers to the steps: being a stranger, orientation, adjustment, intimacy, conformity and fading out of the discussion.

In more general terms, group discussion as a method of data collection unfolds in a manner parallel to that of our other models of social research. Nevertheless, there are some special points that mark this particular model (see especially Berger et al., 1989: 339–44; Dreher and Dreher, 1991: 186–8; Flick et al., 1991). The following deserve special attention.

Choice of the group. The choice of groups varies significantly. In some cases, natural groups are chosen; in other cases, they are constructed by choosing appropriate respondents. The choice of the participants is equally guided by theoretical principles. Although structured selection is employed, it is more common for participants to be selected by the researcher according to their expertise and social attributes. Depending on the purpose of the study, in some cases the group is chosen to be homogeneous and in other cases diverse.

The size of the group is usually large enough to provide a basis for a reasonable discussion and to allow personal contacts among the participants, but not so large as to make such contacts difficult. In practice, the group size is between five and ten, although significant deviations from this are not uncommon. Likewise, the number of groups included in a study varies. The research model, the nature of the topic and the purpose of the study will determine the number of the groups as well as whether they will be addressed concurrently by using several facilitators, or consecutively. In practice, the number of groups employed in a study ranges from as few as ten to as many as 50.

Introduction of a goal-directed discussion. The discussion usually begins with a few general points to familiarise the participants with the group, moving on to a 'discussion-generating question' related to the research topic. The group leader will intervene as required, directing the discussion to the research goals and keeping its course interesting and balanced, that is, equally distributed among all members of the group. How the direction of the discussion will proceed from here is a question that depends on the nature of the underlying paradigm. Quantitative researchers will expect adherence to objectivity and distance between the leader and the members of the group, as well as strict and uniform procedures. Qualitative researchers will give little – if any – attention to these issues.

In physical terms, the environment in which the discussion will take place is chosen to be conducive to a comfortable and stimulating debate, without disturbances. Rooms are to be arranged so that they are not affected by noise or other forms of disturbance, and to facilitate eye contact.

Guiding the discussion. The discussion will be facilitated by the group leader in whatever way the situation requires. Discussions that are slow to start will be helped to gain momentum through additional questions, probes and other appropriate means; non-talkers will be encouraged to participate and those who dominate the discussion will be kept on track. Motivation, encouragement, stimulation and control will bring about a balanced environment that is conducive to group discussion. The nature of the mechanisms employed to ensure a fair and balanced discussion will vary with the underlying paradigm.

3.4 The leader

The leader occupies a central position in the context of group discussion, and is normally a facilitator rather than a controller. The extent to which this method achieves its purpose depends to a large extent on the research context; within these parameters, the quality of this facilitator is very important. Leaders are generally expected to have the attributes listed in Box 8.6.

The leader's role will very much depend on factors such as the research topic, the nature of the group, and the underlying theoretical framework.

Box **8.6**

The qualities of the facilitator

Facilitators are required to have:

- adequate theoretical and methodological knowledge of the research topic, and general intellectual capacity
- experience with group work as well as the ability to guide the discussion effectively
- the capacity to create an environment that will encourage involvement, control dominating participants and keep the discussion moving in the right direction
- leadership qualities
- the ability to develop a warm atmosphere among the members of the group.

3.5 Recording

There are many ways to record data produced in group discussions. Electronic recording is the most common. This has obvious advantages but may affect the readiness of some participants to speak, and requires a lot more time for viewing or listening to the tapes, and/or transcribing them. Manual recording is an alternative but it is equally limited by the innate difficulty of coping with intensive and multi-sided discussions. Having two leaders, with each of them taking notes in turn or one recording the data and the other acting as the facilitator, may be a solution.

The nature and content of recording depend on the nature of the study, available resources and the nature of the expected information. In one context the data may be quantitative and standardised. In other contexts it may be qualitative, entailing 'thick' descriptions.

3.6 Limitations of focus groups

The value of focus groups as a method of studying group discussion relies heavily on both the 'group' and the 'leader'; hence success depends very much on these two factors. It is therefore understandable that problems of this method noted in the relevant literature relate almost exclusively to these two points (Berger et. al., 1989: 339–44; Dreher and Dreher, 1991: 186–8; Flick et al., 1991; Mahr, 1995; Puris, 1995), which are listed below.

Weaknesses of focus groups

- Being in a group might make participants hide their real opinions, especially if their views can have effects on their personal life or professional career.
- Recording of the data can be problematic.
- Domination of the discussion by some members might affect the direction and outcome of the discussion.
- Some members may not participate in the discussion.
- There may be attempts to go along with the leader for many reasons (e.g. to 'get it over with', or to please a leader who holds an important position in the respondents' personal, political or professional life).
- There may be difficulties with keeping discussion on track.
- Group members may have reasons to offer a collective front and deceive the leaders.
- The findings may not be representative.

Although these points are relevant and legitimate in their context, they should be taken as a reminder of the areas in which focus groups can 'malfunction' and not as discounting of the quality of the method. An experienced researcher will arrange the context and process of discussion so that distortions and problems will be prevented.

3.7 Focus groups and feminist research

Most feminist researchers are open to types of research that employ a qualitative research model, and which lend themselves to a feminist analysis. In this sense, focus groups offer a most suitable research tool; with few exceptions, they can provide a useful method for all feminist groups. Empiricist feminists can use this method effectively, but many of its attributes are most consistent with the work of those employing qualitative research models. Such attributes are: first, the opportunity to study women in natural environments; second, the close relationship between the researcher and the research; third, the role of the researcher as a facilitator and not as controller, implying lack of hierarchical structures; fourth, the opportunity for the participants to state and discuss their views among themselves, making their voices heard; and fifth, the opportunity to discuss group processes and collective meanings in context.

MAIN POINTS

- Studies often employ more than one sample. They may employ the samples at the same research stage, or at different stages.
- Experiments, panel studies and focus groups are examples of multi-sample studies.
- Experiments measure the effects of a stimulus on a subject in a controlled environment.
- Sampling in experiments is accomplished by means of randomisation, subject matching and group matching.
- Experiments follow a set of steps. In a typical case experimentation involves a pre-test, a test and a post-test. There are several experimental designs.
- There are laboratory experiments, social experiments and field experiments.
- The validity of experiments depends on a number of factors, such as maturation, conditioning and instrumentation, the history effect, changes in samples, interaction, sampling, ecology, modelling and the Hawthorne effect.
- Longitudinal studies employ more than one sample within the same study.
- Panel studies and trend studies are two common types of longitudinal studies.
- Focus groups facilitate collection of data by means of group discussion.

WHERE TO FROM HERE?

Before you leave this chapter, visit the companion website for the third edition of *Social Research* at http://www.palgrave.com/sociology/sarantakos to review the main concepts introduced in this chapter and to test yourself on the major issues discussed.

FURTHER READING

Boniface, D. R. (1995) *Experiment Design and Statistical Methods for Behavioural and Social Research.* London: Chapman and Hall.
Boruch, R. (1997) *Randomized Experiments for Planning and Evaluation: A Practical Guide.* Thousand Oaks, Calif. Sage.
Bullock, R. (1998) *Research in Practice: Experiments in Development and Information Design.* Sydney: Ashgate.

Cobb, G. W. (2002) *Introduction to Design and Analysis in Experiments.* Emeryville, Calif.: Key College.

Collins, C. A. (1999) *Statistical Experiment Design and Integration: An Introduction with Agricultural Examples.* New York: Wiley.

Galavotti, M. C. (2003) *Observation and Experiment in the Natural and Social Sciences.* Boston: Kluwer Academic.

Gooding, D. (1990) *Experiments and the Making of Meaning: Human Agency in Scientific Observation and Experiment.* Boston: Kluwer Academic.

Krüger, R. A. (1998),) *Moderating Focus Groups.* Thousand Oaks, Calif.: Sage.

Krüger, R. A. and Casey, M. A. (1998) *Focus Groups: A Practical Guide for Applied Research.* Thousand Oaks, Calif.: Sage.

Menard, S. (1991) *Longitudinal Research.* Newbury Park, Calif.: Sage.

Morgan, D. L. (1998a) *Planning Focus Groups.* Thousand Oaks, Calif.: Sage.

Orr, L. L. (1999) *Social Experiments: Evaluating Public Programs with Experimental Methods.* Thousand Oaks, Calif.: Sage.

Patzer, G. L. (1996) *Experiment–research Methodology in Marketing: Types and Applications.* Westport, Conn.: Quorum.

Robson, C. (1994) *Experiment, Design and Statistics in Psychology.* Harmondsworth, Middlesex: Penguin.

Spinello, R. A. (2003) *Case Studies in Information Technology Ethics.* Upper Saddle River, N.J.: Prentice-Hall.

Travers, M. (2001) *Qualitative Research through Case Studies.* London: Sage.

Wilkinson, S. (1999),) 'Focus Groups: A Feminist Method'. *Psychology of Women Quarterly*, 23, pp. 221–44.

Yin, R. K. (2003) *Case Study Research: Design and Methods* (3rd edn). Thousand Oaks, Calif.: Sage.

Field research 9

- deals with research conducted in the field
- explicates the main characteristics of field research
- discusses the nature and design of ethnographic research
- presents a brief discussion of case studies.

INTRODUCTION

The methods grouped together in this chapter have in common the fact that they are conducted in the field. In this sense, they share an interest in natural settings and first-hand information, but also a qualitative methodological approach. This is the reason that, although they have been used for some time by social anthropologists and ethnologists, they became popular among social researchers only after qualitative research gained ground in the social sciences.

The methods which we shall address in this chapter are field research, ethnographic research and case studies, methods that are referred to as 'naturalistic research' by some and 'low-constraint methods' by others. Researchers hold differing views about the identity of these methods as well as about the distinction between field research and ethnographic research. However, the important point in our discussion is their nature and purpose, and this is what we shall address in the following pages, beginning with field research.

1   FIELD RESEARCH

1.1 Introduction

Field research is the systematic study of ordinary events and activities as they occur in real-life situations. It is a naturalistic inquiry that takes place in the 'field', that is, in a natural setting that is not constructed for the purpose of conducting research (Lincoln and Guba, 1985). It is a quasi-longitudinal form of research, in that it takes a long time to complete. It is also highly flexible, as its design allows for changes as the research progresses (Burgess, 1982).

Field research has the purpose of exploring real-life situations, behaviour patterns and the reasons behind social interaction, and more particularly of seeing life through the eyes of, and from the perspective of, those living in the field. The methods employed by field researchers are many and diverse; the most common are systematic interactions and observations, and semi-structured or structured interviews.

In some contexts, field research serves quantitative studies as an exploratory study. More important is field research as a main study, where it can be a descriptive study, a hypothesis-testing study or a theory-testing study. Field research is not just a set of methods of data collection but also a model that employs a number of techniques of data collection and analysis.

1.2 Types of field research

Several types of research are conducted in the field. In point of fact, every study conducted under natural conditions is a field study, provided of course it is conducted in a particular way. However, there are studies conducted in the field that are sufficiently distinct to deserve special consideration as specific forms of research. At least two such types of field research will be addressed in this discussion. These are *particularistic* and *holistic* field research. They constitute the two extreme positions in the range of field research.

Box **9.1**

Main criteria of field research

Field research

- is a systematic study of events and activities occurring in natural settings
- is longitudinal, in that it is conducted over a long period of time
- employs a flexible design, allowing for changes where required
- aims to study real life situations and the factors that drive their course
- endeavours primarily to understand life through the eyes of the people
- employs a variety of methods of data collection and analysis
- may serve as a step to quantitative research, but is more often a separate study
- employs a qualitative research model
- is particularistic, when it studies aspects of social life
- is holistic, when it studies entire cultures.

Particularistic field research. This type of field research focuses on social issues and situations, aiming to understand their structures, processes and outcomes as they occur and as displayed in the behaviour of those involved in the study, but without particular reference to overarching contexts such as culture. People's behaviour is viewed as their personal response to their immediate environment and not as a cultural expression. An example of this type of particularistic field research is when a researcher joins a primary school as an assistant teacher, and in this role studies the way in which female and male first-year teachers resolve everyday gender issues in their class. The question here is whether female teachers are more/less gender-biased than male ones.

Holistic field research. This type of research focuses on cultures as whole entities, their structure and characteristics per se as well as in comparison with other cultures. It may focus on primitive cultures that have survived time and exist in some form in modern societies; alternately, it may look at modern cultures or subcultures and compare them with others. Its concern is with cultures as entities and not necessarily with their parts. An example of holistic field research is a study of Turks in Vienna (Austria), which depicts the main cultural elements of Turkish culture within a European context, its main standards regarding institutions, religion, family, affinity, role of men and women and the like, and the way the culture copes with external strains imposed by the host culture. The focus here is not on individuals but on the culture of Turks, which in some ways is more traditional and restrictive than in Turkey.

Mixed models. Particularly during the last thirty years, a successful attempt has been made to combine these two research models by expanding the particularistic type of research and including elements of the holistic model in its theory and design. Although in most cases the focus remains the same (i.e. aspects of social life), explanations are sought within a cultural context. This contextualisation of aspects of social life became a fashion in many research paradigms, to the extent that it has been taken as characteristic of qualitative research as a whole (although unfortunately this is not always the case). With regard to field research, writers on women's issues have employed such contextualisation very successfully to demonstrate how many gender issues are anchored in cultural prescriptions and standards, and hence are taken to be 'correct' and 'normal'.

For reasons of simplicity, in this text we present the particularistic type of field research under its commonly used name, namely *field research*, while for the holistic model we use the already established concept of *ethnographic research*.

1.3 Design of field research

The design of field studies varies with the nature of the underlying paradigm. In the quantitative model, it is relatively rigid and deterministic, while in a qualitative paradigm it is relatively open and flexible. The main characteristics of design construction discussed earlier in this volume apply in this model also. Briefly, the basic steps of the field research design are given below.

Step 1: Topic and methodology

At this stage, the researcher will state which topic will be studied, and within which methodology it will be constructed and researched.

Step 2: Methodological definition of the topic

When quantitative methodology is employed, the topic will be clearly defined, reduced, and specified and operationalised to some degree. In qualitative research, such specifications will be rather general and flexible.

Step 3: Sampling procedures

In quantitative research the sample will be determined precisely before the study commences. In qualitative research it may be less rigid and may be left partly open to be completed during the study.

Step 4: Data collection

In quantitative research data collection proceeds as given in the research design. In the qualitative model, data collection will be less predictive, based on openness and flexibility. Below are brief descriptions of what usually happens during this stage of research.

a. *Entering the field.* Here the researcher takes the first step and enters the field; this is what in qualitative research is referred to as 'going native'. Important tasks to be completed at this stage of research are gaining entry and acceptance, establishing the research environment, and building up contacts and rapport. Gaining entry is not usually a difficult task; however, there are cases in which it is very demanding or even impossible to pass the 'gatekeepers' of the field. Identifying key persons, negotiating accessibility, choosing methods of contact and settling into the group are also among the tasks of this step of research.

b. *Gathering data.* Data collection begins with an exploration which might simply involve identification and description of issues related to the research subject, but may also entail analysis of some kind, as well as evaluation of the findings. Collection and analysis are conducted in a qualitative fashion; the task may, however, also include some quantitative procedures and computations.

Data collection mainly entails observation of the setting, people and behaviours. More specifically it may include observation of various aspects, ranging from surroundings and structures to household contents and colours, to temperatures and weather. The nature and type of the respondents, including age, ethnicity, gender, marital status, relationships and attitude to the research topic are some of the issues considered in the observation. In addition, data collection relates to content and context of speech and communication, including verbal communication, body language, and emotional expressions. Data collection may involve interviews and face-to-face interaction which result in a multiplicity of data. All in all, data collection results in rich information or thick description, all arranged in a manner that allows easy handling.

c. *Taking notes.* Observation, interaction and communication are constantly transformed into notes of some kind that are systematically organised for future use. These notes refer to all the daily experiences of the researcher, some relating to observations, and others to encounters, conversations, ideas and impressions. Files are stored in folders either as hard copies on paper, or in electronic form. They may be organised in chronological order, from the beginning to the end of the study (chronological files), or according to content (content files). The former include data collected during the first contacts with the respondents, and progress through time, until the end of the study. The latter contain files developed around key concepts; every time information is collected, it is processed conceptually and filed in the appropriate folder.

In this way, information on key concepts grows with time: filed and re-filed continuously right through the study, as new information is added to the system and as files get bigger and difficult to handle. Eventually, files may become very large and the information complex and diverse, requiring internal reprocessing and re-assignment. This often leads to the development of new and refined concepts, to make filing easier, more detailed and more meaningful. In this sense, filing entails a large degree of processing, analysis and interpretation as new information is collected. When information is stored in chronological order, analysis will begin with reading, sorting out and identifying concepts and meanings, before integrating data into logical cohorts of information.

d. *Leaving the field.* When data collection is complete, field work is brought to an end. The researcher leaves the field, normally without breaking the relations with the members of the community abruptly, but rather after preparing the field for the departure and after assuring future cooperation and a promise to communicate the findings to the respondents.

The process of leaving begins with a gradual disengagement, which may take some time, largely depending on the nature of the study and particularly on the degree of the researcher's involvement in the respondents' lives. When relations have been impersonal, exit from the field is easy; the researcher leaves as soon as the data collection is complete. In other cases, gradual disengagement and leaving need to be planned thoughtfully and far in advance so that both the researcher and the subjects are at ease with this event.

There are cases where the researcher leaves quietly with no announcements or ceremony. Where the research procedure did not include personal relations over a long period of time, this can be one method of exit. In most cases, where the research involved closer relationships with subjects and also with key informants and gatekeepers, and where the respondents were actively involved in the research process, the exit from the field is more formal and more demanding.

Researchers often organise a meeting with the people they worked with during the research and announce the closure of the study, thanking the subjects for their cooperation. In such cases, leaving the field is often deeply felt by many long-standing subjects, and the researcher is expected to be prepared to deal with such issues. To leave of one's own accord and without informing the respondents in some way is rather unusual.

Step 5: Data analysis

Depending on the paradigm, data analysis may commence during the collection of the data. This is the case in qualitative research of the flexible kind, where the analysis begins as researchers make sense of observations, relationships and settings, when they distribute notes to concept files, and when they decide how next to progress and what kind of choices to make to clarify events and processes. In other cases, analysis focuses on converting large amounts of notes to clear statements and conclusions. Here, data analysis begins with reading and processing notes and with filing them in a constructive manner.

This process also involves the formulation of typologies: that is, grouping similar experiences, events and other elements so as to discover meaning. As the researcher is observing, talking and filing, typologies emerge, reflecting a realistic impression of life in the setting. Typologies are developed in key areas of the setting, covering aspects such as the nature of the setting and of the relationships, types of people, interactions and so on. The development of typologies helps construct

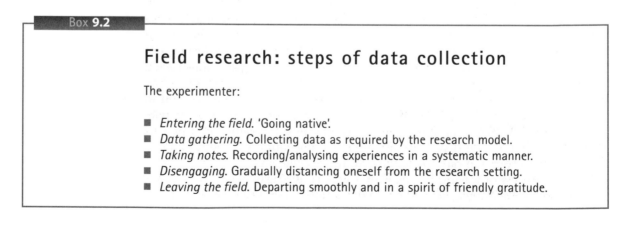

Box **9.2**

Field research: steps of data collection

The experimenter:

- *Entering the field.* 'Going native'.
- *Data gathering.* Collecting data as required by the research model.
- *Taking notes.* Recording/analysing experiences in a systematic manner.
- *Disengaging.* Gradually distancing oneself from the research setting.
- *Leaving the field.* Departing smoothly and in a spirit of friendly gratitude.

meaning in the setting, focus observation/interaction on important aspects of life, and narrow down perception and analysis. Data analysis here follows the paths of qualitative analysis, which will be discussed in more detail later in this volume. Basically, this process leads to the development of meaningful typologies, hypotheses and eventually theories.

Step 6: Writing up

Although researchers adhere to the general standards of presentation applied in qualitative research when writing up field-research reports, they have much greater freedom in writing than is permitted to other qualitative researchers, not to mention quantitative researchers. As we shall see later in this text, reports are usually prepared within three models: the member-centred format, the writer-centred format and the mixed format.

To a large extent, this pattern of research is employed by most field researchers. Briefly, it suffices to say that here, as in other forms of research, the research model employed is the one introduced earlier in this text. The specific content of the research steps will be determined by the underlying methodology, as described in Chapter 2.

2 ETHNOGRAPHIC RESEARCH

2.1 Introduction

Literally, ethnography is the science of 'ethnos', that is, nation, people or culture. The specific definition of this discipline, as well as its name, varies significantly among social scientists in the various parts of the world. While some retain the name and definition as stated, others use the terms social anthropology, cultural anthropology or ethnology instead. And while some use these concepts interchangeably, others consider them to be separate disciplines. Beyond this, ethnography has been seen as the science of cultural description, a description and interpretation of a cultural or social group or system, the study of cultures with the purpose of understanding them from the native point of view, entering a setting with the purpose of doing field research by using ethnography like field research: street ethnography; church ethnography; cricket ethnography, and 'the practice [that] places researchers in the midst of whatever it is they study' (Berg, 1995: 86).

In general, ethnography and ethnology were considered to be the areas of interest of anthropologists who were generalists and interested in relationships between people and the physical, socio-political, personal, cultural and historical aspects of their life, and they were kept out of the area of social sciences. Ethnographic studies were thought to be the prerogative of anthropologists, mainly because these workers were dealing with primitive cultures. However, with recent developments in the social sciences, and especially with the advent of feminism and women's studies, ethnographic research, particularly critical ethnography, has become rather popular (see, for example, Anderson, 1989; Hammersley, 1991, 1992b; Hammersley and Atkinson, 1983; Taylor, 2001; Warren and Hackney, 2000).

Ethnography is commonly used when researchers are interested in the nature, structure and process of cultures, particularly when they are exploring the cultural determinants of human behaviour; assessing the significance of cultural context for behaviour and human products; and when there is a need to gain an insight into a particular culture before a detailed and specific study is undertaken. In this section, some of the aspects of ethnographic research will be outlined.

2.2 Criteria of ethnographic research

The main criteria of ethnographic research do not differ from those encountered in field research. However, there are some differences in their content and purpose, mainly generated by the nature, context and purpose of ethnographic research. As noted earlier, field research is generally considered to be particularistic in its approach while ethnographic research is holistic, and ethnographic research is one form of field research. A brief summary of these and other basic criteria of ethnographic research is given in Box 9.3.

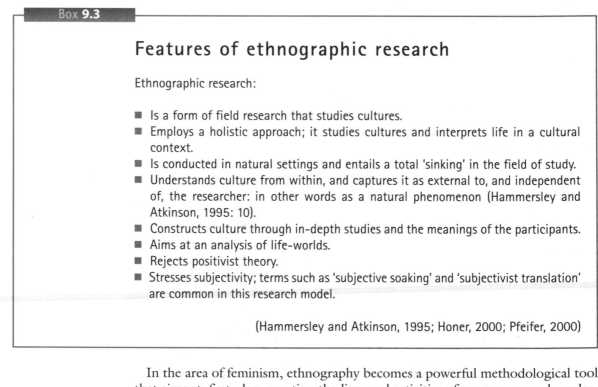

Box **9.3**

Features of ethnographic research

Ethnographic research:

- Is a form of field research that studies cultures.
- Employs a holistic approach; it studies cultures and interprets life in a cultural context.
- Is conducted in natural settings and entails a total 'sinking' in the field of study.
- Understands culture from within, and captures it as external to, and independent of, the researcher: in other words as a natural phenomenon (Hammersley and Atkinson, 1995: 10).
- Constructs culture through in-depth studies and the meanings of the participants.
- Aims at an analysis of life-worlds.
- Rejects positivist theory.
- Stresses subjectivity; terms such as 'subjective soaking' and 'subjectivist translation' are common in this research model.

(Hammersley and Atkinson, 1995; Honer, 2000; Pfeifer, 2000)

In the area of feminism, ethnography becomes a powerful methodological tool that aims at: first, documenting the lives and activities of women; second, understanding the experience of women from their own point of view; and third, conceptualising women's behaviour as an expression of social contexts (Reinharz, 1992: 51).

2.3 Methodology in ethnographic research

Ethnographic research uses a number of methods, most of which are employed by other researchers in the context of different paradigms and methodologies. In technical terms it is not significantly different from field research. However, the approach and the way in which methods are employed are different.

The methods employed in ethnographic research are of two kinds, *descriptive* or *critical*. Critical ethnographic research is common in social sciences. It analyses critically the interconnections between social practices and overarching macro-cultural principles. The purpose of this research depends on the paradigm that underlies the project. If the research employs a positivistic paradigm, the purpose of the ethnographic research may be to describe, explain and categorise social events, whereas if it is used in an interpretive paradigm it may aim at understanding the dynamics of a sociocultural system as well as of how people interpret their world. In critical studies, ethnographic research aims to emancipate, empower and liberate people.

In general, the overall design of ethnographic research falls within the parameters of field research. In this context, ethnographers use field work of many kinds, for instance, personal participant observation, interviews, document analysis, filming and recording. This is often assumed to entail a rejection of positivist thinking and research. However, as Atkinson and Hammersley rightly note,

> [to reject positivist methods] is not to say that quantitative methods are rejected in total by ethnographers; indeed, structured forms of data collection and quantitative data analysis are frequently employed to some degree or other in ethnographic work. What is rejected is the idea that these methods are the only legitimate, or even the most important ones.
>
> (Atkinson and Hammersley, 1994: 251)

2.4 The research plan

As noted above, the research design employed in ethnographic research is no different from that employed in field research. Only the nature and content of the individual steps vary, to serve the special interests of the research. An example of such a research plan is presented by Berg (1995) who lists the following steps:

a. *Accessing a field setting (getting in)*. This is facilitated through contacts with 'gatekeepers' and informants or other persons who assist with this task. Entry to the setting can be overt or covert: researchers can enter the scene openly and officially, or anonymously, without members knowing their real identity.
b. *Becoming invisible*. The guiding rules here are: do not expose identity, research plan or aim; interact and observe/record, but do not influence; ensure the safety of self, notes and subjects.
c. *Watching, listening and learning*. Here the researcher observes/listens to the physical setting, the participants, relationships and preferences; locates subgroups; takes notes, films events, records communication; works with notes, coding etc.
d. *Disengaging (getting out)*. This implies exiting, dissolving relationships, emotional disengagement.

This plan is brief and indicative of the way in which action in the field is planned and managed. However, there are a number of points in this plan that do not apply to all types of ethnographic research. Steps b and c are two such cases. With regard to Step b, not all ethnographers remain invisible. There are many studies where researchers sink into the web of culture, live as indigenous people for a long period of time, and present themselves as outsiders and researchers, disclosing not only their identity but also the nature and purpose of their study. With regard to Step c, data collection entails more than watching and listening. Interviewing and interaction are often as common, useful and effective in ethnography as observation.

Last but not least, this list refers to one part of the research plan only. It does not include theoretical, conceptual and methodological considerations.

2.5 Strengths and weaknesses

In general, ethnographic research is a type of field research; hence the discussion presented in the previous section of this chapter also applies here. However, there are certain issues in this debate that refer primarily to ethnographic research. A brief summary of these strengths and weaknesses are summarised below.

Strengths:

- holistic perspective
- use of the sociocultural context as the explaining source
- high degree of flexibility
- capacity to identify contradictions and inconsistencies
- high quality of the researcher–participant relationship
- closeness to the participants
- high external validity
- high sensitivity to subtle nuances of meaning and significance
- capacity for longitudinal study: studying issues over time.

Weaknesses:

- inability to provide evidence supporting causality
- inability to ensure validity and reliability
- lack of replication
- inability to ensure objectivity
- no free access to the field, or to personal and subjective information that constitute the basis of the study
- difficulty with going native, which often affects studies and leads to problems
- interviewer effect that causes obvious distortions
- distortion of the natural setting by the very presence of the researcher.

An issue that is disputed in this context concerns validity, which obviously cannot meet the standards of quantitative research. Still, as noted earlier in this volume, qualitative researchers claim validity of their findings on the basis of different standards. With regard to ethnographic research, validity is claimed on the grounds of the criteria listed in Box 9.4.

Ethnographic research has been used extensively by qualitative researchers, and is gradually becoming even more popular. Many of its weaknesses are associated

Box **9.4**

How do ethnographic researchers ensure validity in their work?

- By refraining from talking; they listen instead.
- By producing exact and accurate notes.
- By writing early and in a way that brings readers to the field.
- By not forcing readers to accept the writer's view; they let them make their own inferences.
- By producing notes that are as complete and as candid as possible.
- By seeking feedback from the field and/or colleagues.
- By constructing presentations that are balanced between the subjects.

(Wolcott, 1990: 127–8)

with its qualitative nature, and if it is evaluated within these parameters the deficiencies noted above have little impact on the status of this research model.

3 CASE STUDIES

3.1 Introduction

A case study is 'an empirical inquiry that investigates a contemporary phenomenon within its real-life context when the boundaries between phenomenon and context are not clearly evident; and in which multiple sources of evidence are used' (Yin, 1991: 23). Case-study research involves individual cases, and studies over an extended period of time (Kromrey, 1986: 320). Case studies are not a method of data collection but a research model, and employ a number of methods of data collection and analysis in a variety of contexts (Bromley, 1986).

Case studies research is by no means uniform. Many case studies are developed within a qualitative paradigm; others employ quantitative principles. Stake (1995: 237) refers to three different types of case study: the intrinsic, the instrumental and the collective case study.

An *intrinsic case study* is normally conducted for its own sake; in other words, to learn about this case only. There is no expectation that the results will be generalised to explain similar cases. An *instrumental case study* is used to inquire into a social issue or to refine a theory. The results have a wider application, beyond the study itself. A *collective study* includes a number of single studies investigated jointly for the purpose of inquiring into an issue, phenomenon, group or condition. It normally includes several instrumental studies.

Despite the diversity that characterises case studies, some common standards are found in all types. The relevant literature refers most frequently to the characteristics of case studies listed in Box 9.5.

Box **9.5**

Basic criteria of case study research

- It is conducted in natural settings.
- It is suitable for pursuing depth analysis.
- It studies whole units not aspects of units.
- It entails a single case or a few cases only.
- It studies typical cases.
- It perceives respondents as experts, not as sources of data.
- It employs many and diverse methods.
- It employs several sources of information.

Case studies are employed in both quantitative and qualitative research, although to a different extent and for different reasons. In general, case studies are employed as pre-research, as the main study and as post-research. In quantitative research they are employed as pre-research, that is, as an exploratory study. In qualitative research they appear as main studies, as research enterprises of their own that aim to develop hypotheses or even theories. Case studies investigate social life within the parameters of openness, communicativity, naturalism and interpretativity, as informed by the interpretive paradigm, as explained earlier in this volume.

3.2 Research design

The design normally prescribes, among other things, the logical sequence in which the study is to be carried out, as well as the elements of the study, its methods of data collection and analysis and all administrative procedures that need to be considered for the study to be carried out without problems or delays. In case-study research the design is contained in the case-study protocol, which will be described next, and which does not differ significantly from the research model introduced earlier in this volume. More specifically, the following points of the research design deserve further attention (see Becker, 1989; Yin, 1991).

Step 1: Choosing topic and methodology

The first step towards conducting a case study analysis is the selection of the research topic and the case(s) to be studied. Here the focus of the study (the aspects of the case that will be considered) needs to be explained. Any aspect can be studied, provided that it can be addressed fully within the case, ranging from behaviour and interrelations, to persons and groups, to processes, organisations and whole cultures (Yin, 1991). The choice of the topic is always made within the parameters of the overarching paradigm.

Step 2: Methodological construction of the topic

When quantitative research is employed, the topic will be refined and translated into variables and indicators, and its argument will be expressed in the form of hypotheses. When qualitative research is employed, this process will be less advanced and more open, and the definitions will effectively remain as originally constructed, except when a rigid design is employed. In the latter event, the design will borrow a number of elements from the qualitative model. Overall, the minimum points that would be considered within the qualitative paradigm in this case are whether the research question is concrete enough to be studied methodologically, whether it is accessible through case research, whether such a study will yield worthwhile results, and whether the research topic is compatible with the qualitative paradigm.

Step 3: Sampling procedures

Having determined what will be studied and how it will be addressed methodologically, the researcher will specify which case(s) will be included in the investigation. The options are to have one case (a single-case study) or more than one case (a multi-case study). Similarly, the approach can be holistic or embedded.

In qualitative research, when more than one case is studied, the research may begin with one case chosen on the basis of its suitability for the research; the first case is normally chosen as a typical case, that is, a typical example of a category of cases. Additional cases are chosen by means of snowball sampling, or other methods such as theoretical sampling. In this case, expansion of cases follows the principles of the emerging theory, and may include similar or different cases.

In other cases of qualitative research, sampling may be guided by typicality (choosing typical cases) and theory, but also by demand (contracted research), convenience, personal interest, accessibility or relevance to topical issues. The characteristic of qualitative case studies is that, as in other cases, the rule of representativeness and generalisability of the findings are judged within their own domain. The primary guides in this process are balance and variety as well as opportunity to learn. Typicality is not always the guiding principle. Factors considered in the choice may include persons, events and places, as well as advice from members of the community. Despite the interest in typical cases, the choice is made in a manner that ensures 'variety but not necessarily representativeness, without strong argument for typicality, again weighted by considerations of access and even by hospitality. . . . Here, too, the primary criterion is opportunity to learn' (Schwandt, 1994: 244). The minimum parameters to be considered in this case are whether the case or cases are suitable, accessible, researchable and methodologically adequate, and whether the study is ethically permissible.

Step 4: Data collection

First of all, the procedure and methods of data collection have to be chosen. Putting it simply, how will the data be extracted from the case(s) chosen? Which method(s) will be considered? And, are these suitable and legitimate (i.e. compatible with the underlying paradigm)? These questions must be answered clearly and satisfactorily in this step of research. Following this, the researcher will take the steps described below:

a. *Gaining access.* This entails getting permission to investigate the case (where required), meeting the appropriate people and establishing contacts.

b. *Data collection.* Data collection proceeds according to the nature of the study and the underlying framework. In most cases employing a qualitative model, the researcher attempts to identify trends and tease out meanings, making sense of the situation under study. Pre-coding of data, exploring the site thoroughly, identifying and recording data, interpreting and reinterpreting, reflecting, revising and so on are the tools of the process that allows access to data.

c. *Recording of data.* This entails taking notes, filing, re-filing, revising, organising and re-organising; or simply recording data chronologically and preparing them for analysis when the study is complete. The latter is practised but not very popular.

d. *Partial data analysis.* A degree of analysis of recorded data is a part of the research process that is employed in all types of case studies. Even deciding which parts of interaction or observation to consider worth recording and filing, as well as how to categorise them and in which folders to store them, implies an elementary level of analysis. In many cases this goes a few steps further, setting the parameters for the final stage of the analysis. Depending on the paradigm that guides the research, initial analysis during data collection varies from very low to very high. In a number of cases, analysis is completed while collecting the data.

e. *Disengagement.* This step has more to do with maintaining positive relationships with the respondent(s) than with the quality of the data collected. Still, a formal departure serves to announce the end of the study and to give an opportunity to the researcher(s) to express their appreciation for having been allowed to conduct the study.

Steps 5 and 6: Analysis, interpretation, reporting

The extent of analysis that is conducted at this stage depends very much on the paradigm that guides the research, and on the extent to which analysis was conducted during data collection. In general, some conclusions will be drawn and statements made regarding their overall significance for theory and research. Whereas single or few cases give a poor representation of a target population, and poor grounds for advancing grand generalisation, a single case as a negative example is seen as being able to establish limits to grand generalisation. Reports will be prepared as required for studies of their nature (see Chapter 17).

It is worth stressing the usefulness of the general research model introduced in Chapter 4. Whatever the research model, inquiry goes through the six steps of the model. Their content might vary, but the fact remains that they mark the path of the research process.

3.3 Data analysis

In case-study research, analysis may involve a number of methods that in essence attempt to address the initial propositions of the study. There are several techniques employed in case-study analysis; the most common are listed below (Pelz, 1981; Yin, 1991).

- *Pattern-matching*. This technique compares the empirically verified pattern with a pattern predicted at the outset of the study. It is argued that if predicted and observed patterns coincide the findings have strong internal validity.
- *Explanation-building technique*. In this technique explanation is based on a series of iterations, which proceed in the following manner. An initial statement or proposition is made about the study object; the findings of the study are compared with this proposition, and if there is a discrepancy between proposition and findings, the proposition is revised according to the findings. The revised proposition is then compared with new findings and evidence; again, if discrepancies are recorded, the proposition is revised. The new revision is again compared with the findings for the third, fourth or fifth time, being revised each time as required. This process is repeated as often as necessary.
- *Time-series analysis*. In simple terms, in this technique trends over a certain period of time are compared with one theoretical proposition specified before the onset of the study, and with a rival proposition. This comparison indicates which proposition is correct.

    For example, it may be argued that the introduction of the De Facto Relationships Act has resulted in higher proportions of people entering *de facto* relationships (time-series pattern I); another proposition is that the introduction of the Act has not had any effect on the proportion of people living in such relationships (time-series pattern II – rival trend). Case-study research in this area employs time-series analysis to see whether the data support one model or the other, that is, whether the Act encouraged an increase in the proportion of people cohabiting or not. A comparison between the empirical data and each of the two propositions will show which time-series pattern matches the empirical data.
- *Making repeated observations*. This technique directs the analysis towards repeating observations at various levels, that is, over time, across sites and across embedded units. Examples of this technique are observing subjects in spring and autumn, observing units embedded in Case A, Case B and Case C, and observing units in various locations. Comparisons between these observations are considered in the context of analysis of the subject matter.
- *Case-study survey*. Here the survey is directed towards data that are already available, and it operates at a secondary level. This secondary analysis follows a strict procedure, such as development of a code book used for coding the material under consideration and studying the data on the basis of the codes and categories included in the book. The data resulting from this process are then analysed according to the preferences of the researcher or the requirements of the study object and the theoretical proposition that underlies the study.

3.4 Case studies in feminist research

Case studies, as a method of data collection or as a research model, are highly suitable for, and have been extensively used in, feminist research. This is due to their nature as a tool that focuses on specific units, regardless of whether they are representative or not, and to their interest in depth and detail. More specifically,

Box **9.6**

Case study research: techniques of data analysis

- *Pattern matching.* Compares empirical and hypothetical patterns.
- *Explanation-building technique.* Contrasts data with propositions set at the outset.
- *Time-series analysis.* Compares trends to theoretical propositions.
- *Repeated observations.* Compare observations made in different contexts.
- *Case study survey.* A secondary analysis of available data.

it is maintained (Pfeifer, 2000; Reinharz, 1992) that case studies are a tool of feminist research:

- used to document history and generate theory
- valued for its capacity to address specificity, exceptions and completeness, rather than generalisations
- suitable for giving voice to groups of women who do not fall within the ordinary or standard notion of women; and last but not least
- 'essential for putting women on the map of social life' (Reinharz, 1992: 174).

In particular, the sensitivity of the method to cases that fall outside representative social patterns and that do not lend themselves to generalisations make this research instrument highly suitable for feminist research that endeavours to give a voice to all women.

3.5 Strengths and weaknesses of case studies

Strengths

Case studies:

- allow in-depth research
- produce first-hand information, in that they work in natural settings
- employ methods that encourage familiarity and close contact with the informants
- allow the employment of a variety of interrelated methods and sources
- imply long-term contacts and personal experiences in the field
- focus on direct and verifiable life experiences
- produce information that covers the whole unit and not only small aspects of it.

Weaknesses

- Results relate to the unit of analysis only and allow no inductive generalisations.
- Findings entail personal impressions and biases; hence no assurance of objectivity, validity and reliability.
- Research cannot be replicated.

- There is limited access to the field and to the personal and subjective information that constitutes the basis of case studies.
- The interviewer effect may cause distortions; even the presence of the researcher in the field can be destructive.

There is no method that is free of problems, and case studies are no exception. They may have problems in meeting the requirements of objectivist methodologies, just as quantitative methods have problems in meeting the requirements of interpretivist designs. But overall, they are a most useful and popular method, as legitimate as any other method of social research.

MAIN POINTS

- Field research is a form of inquiry that takes place in the field and explores real-life situations as they unfold.
- There are several types of field studies; for example, exploratory studies, descriptive studies and hypothesis-testing studies.
- In principle, field study designs are similar to the standard research design explained earlier in this volume, but are less complex and more flexible than quantitative designs.
- A case study is 'an empirical inquiry that investigates a contemporary phenomenon within its real-life context when the boundaries between phenomenon and context are not clearly evident, and where multiple sources of evidence are used' (Yin, 1991: 23).
- In qualitative research, case studies are often employed as the main form of inquiry.
- In quantitative research, case studies are employed as a prelude to the main study, as a form of pre-test, or as a post-research explanation of the study.
- A case-study protocol contains an overview of the case-study project, field procedures, case-study questions and a guide for preparing the report.
- Ethnographic research originated in ethnography and social anthropology and is used in the social sciences in a number of areas, for example, by feminists.
- The main theoretical foundations of ethnographic research are culture, holism, in-depth studies and chronology.
- The methods employed in ethnographic research are descriptive or critical; they are similar to those employed in other areas but ethnographic fieldwork and ethno-historic research are more characteristic of this type of investigation.
- The value of ethnographic research depends on the underlying methodology being akin to positivistic and to critical research.

WHERE TO FROM HERE?

Before you leave this chapter, visit the companion website for the third edition of *Social Research* at http://www.palgrave.com/sociology/sarantakos to review the main concepts introduced in this chapter and to test yourself on the major issues discussed.

FURTHER READING

Atkinson, P. (1990) *The Ethnographic Imagination: Textual Construction of Society*. London: Routledge.

Carspecken, P. F. and Walford, G. (eds) (2001) *Critical Ethnography and Education*. London: Elsevier Science.

Coffee, A. (1999) *The Ethnographic Self: Fieldwork and the Representation of Reality*. London: Sage.

Davies, C. A. (1999) *Reflexive Ethnography: A Guide to Researching Selves and Others*. London: Routledge.

De Laine, M. (2000) *Fieldwork, Participation and Practice: Ethics and Dilemmas in Qualitative Research*. Thousand Oaks, Calif.: Sage.

Denzin, N. K. (1997) *Interpretive Ethnography: Ethnographic Practice for the Twenty-first Century*. London: Sage.

Hammersley, M. and Atkinson, P. (1995) *Ethnography: Principles in Practice* (2nd edn). London: Routledge.

Stake, R. E. (1995) *The Art of Case Study Research*. Thousand Oaks, Calif.: Sage.

Pink, S. (2001) *Doing Visual Ethnography: Images, Media, and Representation in Research*. London: Sage.

Taylor, S. (ed) (2001) *Ethnographic Research: A Reader*. London: Open University Press.

Warren, C. A. D. and Hackney, J. K. (2000) *Gender Issues in Ethnography* (2nd edn). London: Sage.

Observation

- offers an overview of observation as a method of social research
- delineates the types of observation in social research
- summarises the main steps of observation
- points to some problems of observation.

KEY HEADINGS

INTRODUCTION

Observation is one of the oldest methods of social research. It was initially employed by social anthropologists and ethnologists, with sociologists and other social scientists largely preferring surveys and other techniques. In time, however, observation became popular outside anthropology and ethnology, often using audio-visual support (Ellgring, 1991). Today, it is proclaimed as one of the central techniques of social research.

Observation entails gathering data through vision as its main source. It may be used as the only technique of data collection, or jointly with other techniques, such as intensive interviewing, documentary study or case studies. Although observation studies people, it focuses also on objects as products of human action or just as part of physical environments.

In this chapter we shall explore the nature, types and process of observation and examine its significance for social research.

1 TYPES OF OBSERVATION

Observation can study all observable social phenomena, as long as they are accessible; it is obviously not possible to observe personal, sensitive issues or causes and consequences of social phenomena, nor past and future events. Observation takes several forms which, although basically similar, differ in a number of ways (see Box 10.1), for instance, in the degree of the observer's participation in the field of observation, and in the extent to which it is structured and standardised. This distinction results in the basic types of observation listed below (see Benini, 2000; Lamnek, 1993; Pfeifer, 2000).

Participant and non-participant observation

In participant observation, researchers join the group they intend to study and observe it from the inside (Legewie, 1991); ideally it is not known that they are researchers. For instance, researchers who wish to study homosexual behaviour pretend to be (or are) gay, join homosexual groups and conduct their study from within. In a similar fashion, investigators who want to study the work conditions of factory labourers join them as labourers, working alongside them and observing them 'from the inside'. As members of these groups, they can study, among other things, their structure, process, problems and attitudes, both directly and as experienced by the members of the groups.

In non-participant observation, investigators study their subjects 'from the outside'. Their position is clearly defined and different from that of the subjects. Ideally, they are 'invisible', and remain unnoticed by the members of the group they observe. A typical example of non-participant observation is laboratory observation, where the subjects interact in a laboratory and the researcher observes them through a one-way mirror. Observing children in the school playground through a window is another example of non-participant observation. In both cases the observer does not actively participate in the group under study.

Box **10.1**

Types of observation

Factor	Type of observation
Structure	*Structured:* entails strict design and control
	Unstructured: entails a flexible design and no control
Observer's role	*Participant:* the observer is a part of the setting
	Non-participant: the observer is not a part of the setting
Observer	*Self observation:* observer observing self, e.g. using videos
	Other observation: observer observing others
Focus	*Human observation:* focuses on people and their activities
	Physical observation: focuses on objects, e.g. artefacts and physical remains
Setting	*Natural observation:* observation in natural settings
	Laboratory observation: observation in laboratories
Observer's commitment	*Active observation:* observer is committed to the cause of the study (i.e. is ideologically, and sometimes personally, involved in and supports the overall purpose of the study)
	Passive observation: observer is not committed to the cause of study
Depth of the study	*Naive observation:* simple, unstructured observation
	Scientific observation: systematic and highly structured
Observer's identity	*Open observation:* the observer's identity is known
	Hidden observation: the observer's identity is not known

Subjects are not always aware that they are being observed and the subject of a study in general. Subjects usually change their behaviour when they know that they are being observed, so researchers may take measures to prevent them realising that they are being studied, and hence eliminate the effects of reactivity. Where this is not important, the identity of the observer and the existence of the study are made known. The question that arises in this context is one of ethics; the researcher should have a very good reason choosing the appropriate type of observation.

Many types of observation lie somewhere between the two extremes of participant and non-participant studies. In certain cases investigators are more 'observers' than 'participants'; in others they are more 'participants' than 'observers'. Consequently, the difference between the various types often lies in the degree of participation/observation rather than in the nature of observation itself.

Structured and unstructured observation

As the terms indicate, these two types of observation differ in terms of the degree to which they are structured. Structured observation employs a formal and strictly organised procedure with a set of well-defined observation categories, and is subjected to high levels of control and standardisation. It is also organised and planned before the study begins. Here, the researcher specifies accurately what is to be observed and by what means, and how the results of observation will be recorded. Unstructured observation is loosely organised and the process of observation is largely left up to the observer.

Semi-structured observations lie somewhere between these two techniques; they may, for instance, be structured in their approach but unstructured in their setting. They are relatively common in social research and combine the advantages (and limitations) of both the structured and unstructured techniques of observation.

Box 10.2

Ten criteria of structured and unstructured observation

Structured observation

Employs a strict design
Is a non-participant observation
Employs high levels of standardisation
Focuses on aspects of the setting
Works in laboratory or natural settings
Mainly studies small groups
Is a formal observation
Is unobtrusive observation
Is direct observation
Employs mostly a quantitative design

Unstructured observation

Employs a flexible design
Is a participant observation
Employs low levels of standardisation
Focuses on the whole setting
Works in natural settings
Studies small and large groups
Is an informal observation
Is also unobtrusive observation
May be direct or indirect observation
Employs mostly a qualitative design

Other types of observation

- *Human and physical observation*. The former focuses on humans and human action; the latter focuses on objects.
- *Naive and scientific observation*. Naive observation refers to everyday, unstructured observation which people use when they interact with others in social situations. Observation becomes scientific when it is systematically planned and executed, when it is related to a certain goal, and when it is subjected to tests and controls.
- *Natural and laboratory observation*. The former takes place in natural settings, the latter in laboratories.
- *Open and hidden observation*. In open observation, the participants are aware of the identity of the researcher as an observer and the purpose of the study; in hidden observation, subjects are not aware that they are being observed.
- *Active and passive observation*. Active observation entails high involvement and commitment of the observer to the cause of the study; passive observation does

not. In the latter, the role of the observer is strictly professional, concerned with the recording of data. In this case, observation is a job to be done in an objective and neutral fashion.

- *Direct and indirect observation.* Direct observation studies people individually or in groups. Indirect observation studies people through the products of their action. In the latter, researchers may observe, assess and analyse artefacts and traces in general left behind by people who are no longer accessible and through this draw conclusions about their lives.
- *Self-observation and other-observation.* In other-observation the actor observes other people; in self-observation observers observe themselves, for example by focusing directly on how they react in particular circumstances, or indirectly by watching videos showing their interaction, such as the manner in which they handled critical aspects of observation (Rodriguez and Ryave, 2002).

These types of observation are not mutually exclusive. An observation can, for instance, be participant, active and open at the same time.

2 THE PROCESS OF OBSERVATION

2.1 The research model

Observation takes the same form as the general research model introduced earlier in this book. However, the content of each step includes elements that are more or less influenced by the nature of observation. The following is a brief summary of the basic steps of research as employed in the area of observation, mainly by quantitative researchers. Qualitative investigators may use the same steps but their content will have to be adjusted to the principles of the underlying theoretical framework.

Selection and formulation of the topic

At this stage the investigator will decide about the unit of observation. This is a necessary requirement in both structured and unstructured observation. Regardless of the methodological context, it is important that at this stage the object of observation is clearly stated. For example, it must be stated whether observation will focus on action, speech, attitudes or behaviour. Qualitative researchers may employ a rather general definition of the observation unit, but a specification of this unit will be given nonetheless. No researcher enters a field of study without a firm idea of what is to be studied. As well as identifying the unit of study, the researcher often outlines the logical and normative structure of the study.

In quantitative studies and structured observation, the topic is precisely defined so that the observers are well aware of the specific elements of the object to be observed. In addition, specific categories will be developed, which will help the observer to categorise the material (i.e. behaviour, relationships and so on). Categorisation can be based, for instance, on standards related to the purpose of the study, the degree of detail required, the interests of the researcher, the expected response of the observed and the nature of the situation. For instance, in a class observation, 'teacher centred', 'student centred', 'authoritarian', 'democratic', 'sexist' and 'non-sexist' are some of the categories that can be employed. These categories will finally be operationalised by identifying criteria that indicate their presence. Type of language, type of speech, tone of voice and facial expressions are a few examples.

These categories and indicators are developed after adequate exploratory work has been considered and before the observation has begun. Once these categories have been formulated and refined, they are employed in the same form throughout the study. This allows the researcher to categorise the units of analysis; it also allows comparisons to be made. Category construction will, finally, enable investigators to direct their attention to the elements close to the goal of the study, to collect valid and accurate data and, where multiple observers are employed, to produce more accurate, detailed and comparable findings.

In qualitative research, and where participant observation is employed, the approach is somewhat different. Certainly, the topic has to be chosen; the definitions, however, may not be very specific, and the categories – if employed – not explicit or deterministic. In most cases, categories will be developed during observation. The process of observation in this context is flexible and open in its approach (Lofland and Lofland, 1994).

As noted above, during this step of the research the investigator will choose the theoretical and methodological framework, and hence the type of observation: structured or unstructured, participant or non-participant and so on. With regard to the observation type, the investigator will also determine the role of the observer in the setting. In structured observation there is no flexibility in the role of the observer; here the observer will most likely be formal and detached.

In participant observation, there are many more options available. For example, complete participation (being a full participant), where observers are fully absorbed in the group under study; partial participation and observation (being partly participant and partly observer); and complete observation (being purely an observer).

Sampling procedures

Having established the details of the observation topic and unit, as well as the methodological parameters of the study, the researcher turns to the more practical aspects of the project. The next task to be completed is the choice of the subjects.

Where a strict quantitative design is employed, selection of the respondents is largely made by means of probability sampling. With respect to qualitative designs, for example where unstructured or participant observation is employed, the subjects are often chosen by means of purposive or theoretical sampling. In both contexts, sampling refers to more than just the selection of the subjects (see Mahr, 1995), as we shall see next.

Time

Observers have to decide when observation will be carried out. This is more significant in the case of participant observation, since certain times might offer different environments and experiences than others (days, weeks, months etc.). For this reason, choosing a definite time will have implications for the type, quality and quantity of information gathered. The structured observer does not necessarily need to comply with such requirements, since it is expected that observations will take place under controlled conditions (including time).

Duration

Having decided when observation will be conducted, the researcher will consider its duration. This entails firstly the length of each session (e.g. one hour during lunch time), and secondly the length of the study (e.g. every day for three months). Hence, the duration of the study is: one hour every day during lunch time, for three months. The commencement of the study will be determined when considering the 'time' (see above).

Place

Sampling refers also to the place in which observation will be conducted. If schools, hospitals or clubs are to be observed, for instance, one has to determine where in these systems observations will take place: that is, in which room, level or specific location.

Type of event

The type of event to be studied also has to be determined. Will the researcher observe everything, some events, routine events, unexpected events or special events?

Arrangements

As well as the sampling procedures, the investigator decides about the arrangements for entering the setting and recording the data. Entry into the setting is relevant for participant observers and is a very important aspect of observation. It chiefly involves getting permission to enter the environment in question, which is often no easy matter. While it may be relatively easy to observe children playing in a public playground, it is quite difficult to gain entry into a school, gaol, street gang, gay club or certain government committees. Arrangements have to be finalised before the process of observation can begin.

The observer

As in other research methods, so in observation, the researcher will decide on the person(s) who will collect the data. Apart from this, the investigator will assess the nature of observation and, alongside this, the attributes of the observers. Finally, this decision will also indicate whether the observer is expected to possess certain skills. Having addressed these issues fully, the researcher will proceed to the next point of the research mode.

Observer skills

The quality of the observer is often more significant in the context of observation than in other forms of data collection. This is because observation, particularly participant observation, relies very much on the attributes of the researcher to gather information in both quantity and quality. For this reason, observers must be chosen carefully. Their qualities may vary from case to case, particularly with reference to the type of observation chosen, but some qualities and skills are valued more highly than others (Pfeifer, 2000). Here are some examples of qualities required within the quantitative research paradigm:

- general personal ability in terms of perception and memory
- knowledge of the field of research and the surrounding (sub)culture
- specific knowledge of the topic
- previous experience of observation and other research
- ability to handle crisis situations
- flexibility and adaptability
- respect for the boundaries between the observer and the observed
- ability to feel the power of culture in everyday life
- ability to get along with others
- ability to follow instructions
- ability to control personal biases and ideologies
- honesty and trustworthiness
- awareness of and respect for ethical standards

Observer skills vary from case to case, depending particularly on the theoretical and methodological context of the project. Participant observers working within a quantitative context will be expected to be aware of its requirements and to possess skills that may be different from those needed within a qualitative context.

Observer training

In most cases the nature of observation makes it necessary for the investigator to carry it out alone, particularly in participant observation and in qualitative and case-study research. In other cases more than one observer may be employed. Multiple observers usually observe their groups separately and produce data, which are included in the final analysis. The use of multiple observers speeds up data collection but can also cause problems, especially with regard to inter-observer variability. Where more than one observer is employed, and where the observer is not the investigator, training becomes essential.

When training is required, it often concentrates on issues that are central to the study, possible sources of distortion, aspects of the study that require further explanation, and most of all on technical observation skills. Pilot studies will certainly show the way. However, focusing on the points listed in Box 10.3 is thought by many writers to be very useful (see, for example, Becker, 1989; Flick et al., 1991; Martin, 1988).

Even when only one observer will be involved in the study, training is important. What will be observed, when and how, are issues with which the observer must be very familiar. The extent of involvement is another issue. Also, becoming a genuine participant observer is a difficult task, and observers seldom reach that stage (Wolcott, 1992: 20). Training is always helpful.

Box **10.3**

Focus of observer training

Observer training focuses on:

- thorough understanding of the research topic
- knowledge of the peculiarities of the population
- understanding possible problem areas of the study
- familiarity with the categories (where appropriate) and their effective use
- introduction to ways of overcoming unexpected problems and conflicts
- ability to follow instructions accurately and adapt them without causing bias or distortion of the data
- adaptability and flexibility
- ability to observe several subjects and categories at the same time.

Collection of the data

During this stage the researcher executes all the instructions and employs all the techniques outlined in the research design. In practical terms, the observer approaches the subjects and collects the information. Only a few general points will be mentioned here.

Initiation

The initial duties of the observer are to prepare and introduce the appropriate setting, and to offer adequate instructions. More particularly, in structured observation the observer approaches the subjects and invites them to the laboratory, explaining their task in detail; this might involve offering a couple one hundred dollars and asking them to discuss how they would spend it. How much of the process of observation will be disclosed to them depends on the nature of the study.

If the structured observation takes place in natural settings the approach is similar. The subjects are, under normal circumstances, not informed of the fact that they are being observed, and no arrangements will be made regarding the setting. The observer visits the subjects and observes them, without them being aware of this. Recording will take place here or in laboratory observation in a manner determined by the investigator.

In qualitative observation, for example participant observation, the choice of the respondents and the initiation of the study are rather different. As stated above, no random sampling procedures are used here, and the participant is more than just an informant. The observer enters the field but aims to remain invisible and, most of all, not to affect the structure and functioning of the setting. In particular, the observer is expected to respect the observed, to be understanding and tolerant, and to be familiar with the lifestyle of the observed. The observer–observed relationship is close, based on cooperation, mutual understanding and mutual trust.

Data collection

In participant observation, data collection begins after entry to the setting is gained. Notes are taken in the way that best suits the circumstances. When the framework is qualitative, collection and analysis of data often take place simultaneously. Observation focuses on research units over a set period of time. In this sense data collection can relate to various time spans and therefore focuses on different time frames, generating different types of data collection. Below are a few examples.

- *Continuous observation*. In its most common form, observation is continuous; this means it records occurrences for the entire duration of the event. For instance, the observer will record the activity level of camping children for a period of four weeks.
- *Time-point observation*. Data collection can also focus on a specific point (time-point); here the observer is interested in what happens at a particular point in time; for example recording the place where elderly patients are at precisely 9.00 am. Are they still in bed sleeping, staring at the ceiling, reading, talking to others, walking around, helping others and so on? Time-point observation produces 'snap-shot' data, like a picture, separate from context or time frame.
- *Time-interval observation*. Between continuous and time-point observation is time-interval observation. Here, data collection is focused on what happens between two set times, say, between 9.00 am and 9.10 am. We assume that the observer has good reasons to collect data during that period and record everything that is significant.
- *Event observation*. This form of data collection relates to behaviours that occur as a result of other behaviours or events. The presence of an observation unit is conditional on the occurrence of another event. In our example, the activity levels of elderly patients in a geriatric ward are recorded after the doctor entered the ward. Here the observer is interested to see whether the patients are more/less active when the doctor is present than otherwise.

Recording

Recording of data is an issue that must be considered during the planning stage of the research; three issues are significant here: what will be recorded, when and how. This refers to the methods of recording, the events to be recorded, and the coding method.

Box **10.4**

Time focus of observation: four options

- Continuous observation focuses on activities over the entire period of the study.
- Time-point observation focuses on activities at a specific point in time.
- Time-interval observation focuses on activities during a specific time interval.
- Event observation focuses on the nature of specific events for as long as they occur.

Methods of recording

The method of recording varies from one type of observation to another. In quantitative research, recording of structured observation entails identifying the presence and frequency of occurrence of the various categories. This requires concentration so that all categories are recognised and adequately recorded. The process is rather technical and mechanical, and allows quantifiable responses. Recording varies according to the type of events studied, the density of information and the size of the group.

In qualitative research, the method of recording varies with the research topic and the observer's degree of familiarity with the available methods. In general, methods are constructed in a chronological or a systematic way. The most common methods of recording are: writing down information verbatim, in summary or in key words; tape recording conversations; video recording events; and taking photographs.

Note taking is the most common method, but is not always possible. For instance the information to be recorded may be too dense or there may be too many persons for notes to be taken, and the observer may not wish the subjects to be aware of the study. Apart from this, taking notes may divert the attention of the observers from the scene to the paper, causing them to miss part of what happens in the group. If circumstances do not allow note taking, the observer should write down key words or phrases as a guide, and complete the notes after observation, or leave the scene briefly to write up important notes.

Tape and video recordings are easier and certainly more efficient. The tapes can be listened to or viewed as many times as required, using more than one observer if desired, and this produces more accurate and more valid records. However, there are cases when recording is not possible or respondents object to it, and this limits its use. Apart from this, recording adds to the work of the observer – the task of writing up notes is merely postponed, and a lot of the recorded information is often of no use. The last of the methods we listed earlier, taking photographs, is of limited use.

Events

Recording is done within the context of a methodological framework. In quantitative studies observation is conducted on the basis of the observational categories developed by the investigator before the observation process. Such categories relate to items and subjects, indicating the existence of some characteristics, their content, trend and intensity. Observation may focus on the content of discussions, on feelings, facial expressions, aggression, patterns of communication and behaviour, or on general issues and items defined through the operationalisation process.

In qualitative studies observers may initially record whatever happens around them indiscriminately (that is, regardless of whether it seems at that point in time to be important or not), and keep accurate and detailed records and complete notes. Description of the setting, persons, discussions, relations and so on is the rule. Over the course of time, knowledge of the setting increases, and with it understanding of how relevant happenings are to the research topic. This leads to the establishment of screening mechanisms, which allow the observer to become more focused and more selective. Data collection and recording entail an element of analysis in their structure.

Coding

Where observation categories have been developed and the items of observation are clear, specific and known in advance, codes can be used to record the data. Codes serve as symbols, a shorthand recording, where actions and behaviours are replaced by numerals or keywords. This makes recording easier, particularly when there are many items to be recorded and many people to be observed. If categories are distinct and easily identifiable, mechanical devices can be used to record observation data. The interaction chronograph developed by Chapple, the audio-introspectometer developed by Thelen, and the interaction recorder developed by Bales and Gerbrauds are a few examples.

In quantitative research, codes are the result of careful operationalisation and accurate definition of the indicators. This process specifies accurately the aspects of behaviour that need to be observed in order for the object of study to be identified and assessed. Codes tell the observer what to look for and, in a way, what to ignore. They will tell observers what constitutes attention in primary school children and how to identify its indicators. While qualitative researchers will observe children at school in general, quantitative observers will focus on a specific aspect of school experience and will assess aspects of a child's behaviour.

Analysis and reporting

The way data are analysed and communicated to the public is an important aspect of the research process, and will be discussed in another chapter. At this stage it is important to note that in quantitative research, the frequencies of occurrence of the various categories identified during observation will offer the basis for a statistical measurement and analysis, employing appropriate statistical tests to establish relationships and allow explanations, comparisons and eventual predictions. In contrast, where qualitative research is employed, collection and analysis of the data are often interwoven and take place concurrently. This is the case in what we termed flexible qualitative design. The outcome of this analysis will help to generate the final report.

3 PARTICIPANT OBSERVATION

Participant observation is one of the central methods of observation in social research in general, and in qualitative research in particular. It is therefore important that a few additional comments are made on this method as employed within the qualitative paradigm. This is more relevant with regard to the major criteria that distinguish it from other forms of observation. The most important characteristics of this method (Benini, 2000: 36; Lamnek, 1993: 363) are shown in Box 10.5.

Box **10.5**

Main criteria of (qualitative) participant observation

Qualitative participant observation:

- Demonstrates a commitment to studying everyday events, which are studied in terms of the way they are experienced and understood by the participants.
- Is conducted in a natural environment. In this sense, observation remains natural and authentic.
- Observation is designed to study social events under all conditions, bringing data close to reality, the people living in it and the way they construct and experience it.
- Sets data collection within face-to-face interaction.
- Conducts data collection in an unstructured mode.
- Employs open and flexible methods.
- Perceives reality as constructed through the interaction and communication of the participants.
- Addresses reality in an interpretative manner.

More particularly, participant observation is characterised by the fact that it observes communication and interaction in an unstructured and natural manner, where the design is developed and modified while observation is carried out, in a face-to-face relationship, and in an open and flexible fashion.

4 PHYSICAL OBSERVATION

The discussion so far has related to various forms of observation of people designed to gather information about them and their relationships to other people and to their environment. It has given examples of 'human' observation. *Physical observation* focuses on objects, some of which are part of the physical environment, and others the product of human behaviour. There are two types of physical observation; the *observation of objects* used by the subjects or affecting subjects in some way, and the *study of physical traces* such as artefacts.

4.1 Observation of objects

This relates to observation of objects that have a significant impact on people's lives. They are useful in at least two ways: first, they disclose information about people's attitudes and behaviour; and second, they verify, falsify or amplify information otherwise offered to researchers. These types of observation may be employed as the only method of study or in addition to another method.

An example of the use of physical observation as the only method of study is one used to establish the marital status of two people who are known to be sharing the same apartment as tenants. Visiting their premises and employ- ing a structured method of observation, the researcher can establish some critical indicators of their actual relationship, as required by law, to show for example whether they are cohabiting. One such indicator may be the avail- ability of only one bed and one bedroom, with no other sleeping facilities in the apartment. Storage of personal items and underwear in the same cupboard may be another. The validity of these indicators, let alone the ethi- cality of the study, is irrelevant here. What is relevant is that physical obser- vation can provide sufficient data to draw conclusions about people without their assistance.

Physical observation is also employed in conjunction with other methods of data collection, such as interviewing. As noted above, in such cases, the informa- tion provided through observation can help to test the validity of information provided through other channels. For instance, a mother who is fighting to retain legal custody of her son, defending her case in an interview with a social worker at her home, may tell a convincing story but will find it difficult to win the case if the household environment reveals a different reality: a disorderly home, dirty surroundings, empty syringes next to her bed, empty whiskey bottles, evidence of heavy smoking and so on. Observation is here more informative and more convincing than the parent's statements.

4.2 Observation of physical traces

Physical traces are products of human activity that provide information about certain social trends, habits, behaviour patterns and cultural configurations of a group of people or a community. They can be studied in many ways, but particularly through observation. Here, observers focus their study on the 'traces' people left behind, and draw relevant conclusions about these people and their social and cultural life. There are two types of measures of traces. The one studies accretion, and the other is interested in erosion. The former deals with accumulation of residue, and the latter with deterioration or wear (Benini, 2000).

The concept of 'traces' has been used by researchers in two ways. In some cases, 'traces' are physical objects only, such as household garbage in public spaces. For instance, one can establish whether members of a household consume beer by searching their garbage. Similarly, smoking is indicated by the presence of cigarette butts on the ground or in ashtrays. This definition is the same as that employed to explain the study of objects introduced above. Objects here are seen as traces. In other cases, however, 'traces' are symbols, marks or drawings. Drawings in caves and graffiti in toilets, for example, are 'traces' that provide important information about the people who use(d) those environments.

More specifically, the study of physical traces can offer information about the culture and life of past communities, exemplified, for instance, in studies conducted initially by anthropologists or ethnologists. It can also provide infor- mation about the behaviour patterns and personal habits of population groups and individuals. Such studies provide unique information that other methods cannot produce, and may be employed as the sole method of investigation, or in addition to other methods.

There are several areas in which the study of physical traces can be very useful. For example, by observing the floor of a museum, one can draw some conclusions about the popularity of certain exhibits: if the floor in front of an exhibit is heavily worn or dirty, this indicates that more visitors are attracted to it. Hence, one may conclude that this exhibit is perhaps more popular than other exhibits.

Social researchers also use physical traces to infer the habits of certain population groups or individuals. In a recent study, for example, a researcher examined the household garbage bins of single mothers to ascertain the kind of food they eat, observing also the remains of other items of importance. In a similar project, the examination focused on drugs and alcohol, studying the number and type of bottles, used syringes, boxes that could have contained drugs and so on. Another project examined the garbage bins of wealthy homeowners and well-known personalities, to answer similar questions and to examine the kind of things these people throw away. Here the observer takes the role of an experienced detective who examines people's surroundings in order to learn about something that is hidden and unknown.

4.3 Research process

Data collection and analysis follow the general pattern of the research model, beginning with the identification of the research topic, followed by the collection and analysis. Both qualitative and the quantitative methodology can be applied depending on the type of physical observation. When studying physical traces, unstructured observation can be applied, or in some cases, structured observation will be possible. Interviewers can be given specific advice as to the kind of points to observe while interviewing, measuring their extent and quality as required by the research design. Physical observation is not as common in social research, and certainly not as prominent within observation, as human observation.

5 ETHICAL ISSUES

As in other methods of data collection, ethical issues are highly relevant and require due consideration. The nature of observation makes ethics a real issue, since observers have the opportunity to interfere directly with the personal life of the subjects, and since in many cases observation takes place without the subjects being aware of it. This becomes even more serious when the subjects do not know the identity of the observer, for example when the observer pretends to be a genuine member of the group under study.

For some writers ethics is not an important issue and should not hinder researchers from pursuing their research interests if they think that the investigation is carried out for a good purpose. They believe it is justifiable for them to conceal their identity if the research will eventually benefit society and perhaps the subjects. For most, however, ignoring ethical issues is not acceptable; observers should disclose their identity when entering the private domain of individuals, they should disclose their real intentions and the objectives of the research, and they should be honest about their intentions.

6 STRENGTHS AND WEAKNESSES OF OBSERVATION

Strengths (Mahr, 1995):

- Observation provides information when other methods are not effective.
- It employs a relatively less complicated and less time-consuming procedure of subject selection.
- It can offer data when respondents are unable and/or unwilling to offer information.
- It is conducted in a natural setting, and studies events as they evolve; this is particularly so in qualitative research.
- It offers first-hand information without relying on the reports of others.
- It allows the collection of a wide range of information, even when this information is thought to be irrelevant at the time of study. This is particularly true of participant observation.
- It is relatively inexpensive.

Weaknesses (e.g. Becker, 1989; Mahr, 1995)

- It cannot be employed when large groups or extensive events are studied.
- It cannot provide information about future or unpredictable events.
- It cannot offer data related to frequency of behaviour.
- It cannot study opinions or attitudes directly.
- It is inadequate when studying sensitive issues, such as sexual behaviour or family violence.
- It is relatively laborious and time-consuming.
- It is vulnerable to the observers' bias, and dependent on their selective perception and selective memory.
- In participant observation the observer is a part of the situation that is being observed.
- It offers no control measures to balance the bias, attitudes and opinions of the observer.
- It cannot offer inductive generalisations of the results.

Despite these limitations, observation is one of the most popular methods of data collection, employed by researchers of both the quantitative and qualitative domains.

7 PROBLEMS OF OBSERVATION

Observation is limited in its approach in many ways and can be affected by a number of problems. Some of these are caused by the observers, others by the nature and purpose of observation as well as by methodological arrangements. While a few of these problems have already been discussed, others are presented below as summarised by many writers (see Becker, 1989; Pfeifer, 2000).

7.1 Sources of errors

Errors are in practice associated with all aspects of observation if studies are not effectively prepared and designed. The purpose of observation can cause errors if the observers do not understand it correctly. Likewise, arrangements for observation may make recording cumbersome and at times impossible, leaving important information unrecorded. This is most obvious when codes are inadequate or inadequately defined. But most of all, the observer can be the source of many errors, a point that motivates researchers to take adequate preventive measures. A brief list of such errors is given below:

The observer as a source of errors

- *Lack of ability.* Errors may occur due to lack of ability, interest or willingness, as well as tiredness, boredom or attention problems.
- *Observer inconsistency.* Inconsistency occurs in two ways: first, when the observer is unable to perform observations in exactly the same way throughout the investigation; and second, when several observers are employed, and they do not operate uniformly.
- *Observers' non-verbal communication.* This may affect the attitude and expectation of the observed and influence their behaviour accordingly.
- *Observer bias.* This refers to observers' consistent tendency to perceive situations in terms of their personal ideology and bias, for example through selective choice of data and selective coding, producing a distorted reality.
- *Deviation.* The behaviour of the observer and his or her relation with the observed may deviate from the prescribed and expected behaviour.
- *Deception.* Observers might deceive the researcher; this is a problem that is difficult to detect and control, particularly in participant observation.
- *Lack of knowledge.* Some observers may lack knowledge of the subject matter, the context of observation, or the categories employed in the research.
- *Problems in recording and analysing data.* Facts may not be recorded accurately and the analysis might be non-systematic and subjective.
- *Lack of familiarity with the observed group.* The observer may not be familiar enough with the group to be observed.
- *Observer distortion.* The settings observed are distorted by the fact that the observer is added to the structure under study (participant observation), or that the respondents have to operate in an artificial environment (laboratory observation).
- *Expectations.* Expectations about responses can bias the outcome of observation.

7.2 How to prevent errors

The researcher should make a serious effort to prevent errors and, where these have occurred, to reduce their significance and eliminate their consequences. It is generally expected that the researcher should:

- Take the necessary steps to construct a design that will avoid errors as much as possible. Such steps could include making the study object and goals clear and the categories specific and easy to understand, providing effective tools for recording the data and, where possible, offering an environment that will have the least possible negative effect on the research process as well as on the quality and quantity of the data.

■ Choose observers and research assistants who have the ability and interest to work on the project, that is, who possess the personal qualities required for the project, have the capacity to learn and adjust to the research needs as required, and are willing to work under diverse and demanding conditions with people of diverse nature and origin.

■ Train observers adequately so that they have full knowledge of all aspects of the project, its goals and problems, and particularly the categories and their accurate and meaningful application.

■ Supervise observers so that
  – eventual deviations can be identified and controlled
  – advice can be given when questions arise
  – plans and categories can be improved through experience.

Errors occur in all types of research, and observation is no exception. Errors are a part of any investigation. It is the task of the researcher to make the necessary arrangements to prevent problems and, where errors are suspected, to adjust the analysis and interpretation of data accordingly.

MAIN POINTS

■ Observation is a method of data collection that employs vision as the only technique of collection.

■ There are several types of observation, including naive, scientific, participant, non-participant, structured, unstructured, natural, laboratory, open, hidden, active, passive, direct and indirect observation.

■ Quantitative researchers are more interested in structured observation; qualitative researchers prefer unstructured observational designs.

■ The steps of the research model employed in observation are similar to those of the standard model introduced earlier in this volume.

■ Sampling procedures in observation are similar to general procedures in this area.

■ Given the nature of the method, the observer is expected to be well qualified and have the required skills.

■ As a method of data collection, observation appears in a number of ways, including continuous, time-point, time-interval and event observation.

■ The study of objects and physical traces expands the scope of observation and strengthens its significance as a research method.

■ Observation is a unique method that can be employed in areas where other methods are unsuitable, and therefore offers several advantages.

■ Problems of observation can relate to a number of issues, for example, the observer, the purpose of observation, the tools used, the categories of observation and the expectations of the researcher.

WHERE TO FROM HERE?

Before you leave this chapter, visit the companion website for the third edition of *Social Research* at http://www.palgrave.com/sociology/sarantakos to review the main concepts introduced in this chapter and to test yourself on the major issues discussed.

FURTHER READING

Bakeman, R. and Gottman, J. M. (1997) *Observing Interaction: An Introduction to Sequential Analysis.* Cambridge: Cambridge University Press.

Humphreys, L. (1970) *Tearoom Trade: Impersonal Sex in Public Places.* Chicago: Aldine.

Janesick, V. J. (2004) *'Stretching' Exercises for Qualitative Researchers.* Thousand Oaks, Calif.: Sage.

Jorgensen, D. L. (1989) *Participant Observation: A Methodology for Human Studies.* Newbury Park, Calif.: Sage.

Rodriguez, N., and Ryave, A. (2002) *Systematic Self-observation.* Thousand Oaks, Calif.: Sage.

Sanger, J. (1996) *The Compleat Observer? A Field Research Guide to Observation.* Thousand Oaks, Calif.: Sage.

11 Surveys

Questionnaires

THIS CHAPTER

- presents questionnaires as methods of data collection
- points to the various types of questionnaires and their use
- demonstrates the construction of a questionnaire
- explains non-response in questionnaires.

KEY HEADINGS

INTRODUCTION

Surveys are the most commonly used method of data collection in the social sciences; so common, that they quite often are mistakenly taken to be *the* method of social research. This perception is strengthened by the fact that almost everyone has been surveyed at some time, by participating in census surveys, by completing a questionnaire at home or at work, or by filling out a questionnaire when applying for admission to a tertiary institution, for a bank loan or to become a member of a club. Everyone is familiar with what surveys are all about. Surveys are not only a common research tool, but also a part of a person's life experience (Bradburn and Sudman, 1988).

In general, surveys are methods of data collection in which information is gathered through oral or written questioning. Oral questioning is known as interviewing; written questioning is accomplished through questionnaires, which are administered to the respondents by mail or handed to them personally by the researcher in their homes, at work, at school or any other place; they are returned to the researcher after completion. These are also known as self-administered or self-completion questionnaires.

These are the methods we shall discuss next. In this chapter, we shall explore the central elements of questionnaires, such as their nature, structure, content, design and construction, their strengths and weaknesses, and the forms in which they are employed. Interviews, the other form of survey, will be discussed in the next chapter.

Since interviews also employ a form of questionnaire, in the format of an interview guide, and since such guides are quite often as rigid and as standardised as questionnaires, the discussion presented in this chapter is also pertinent to interviewing. Hence we will study questionnaires in a more general manner, concentrating primarily on questioning rather than strictly on questionnaires.

1 QUESTIONNAIRE STRUCTURE

Questionnaires are diverse; they vary according to the way they are administered as well as according to their nature. This diversity results in the following types of questionnaire.

- *Standardised questionnaires*. The structure of these questionnaires is highly rigid with a high degree of standardisation, allowing no flexibility in answering the questions. The answers are limited to those set in the questionnaire, and no other ideas, propositions or alternative answers are allowed. They are mostly employed in quantitative research.
- *Unstandardised questionnaires*. Generally, the structure of these questionnaires is less rigid, and the degree of standardisation fairly low. They are usually small and the questions well defined but open; hence the responses are unstructured, allowing respondents to formulate their answers the way they want. They are predominantly employed in qualitative and feminist research.

- *Semi-standardised questionnaires.* These questionnaires can logically be placed between the two other types, combining a moderate degree of structuration and standardisation. Their structure may include a combination of pre-structured and pre-standardised questions and of unstructured and unstandardised parts. The extent to which structure and standardisation are balanced varies from case to case, with some questionnaires being closer to the standardised model and others closer to unstandardised model. They are employed by both quantitative and qualitative/feminist researchers, although they seem to appeal more to the latter.

Questionnaires are either handed to the respondents personally, or are sent to them by mail. Regardless of whether the questionnaire is administered by the researcher or sent by mail, it has to be constructed according to certain standards and principles. One of these standards is that they must include three main parts; these are the cover letter, the instructions and the main body.

The cover letter

The aim of the cover letter is to introduce the respondents to the research topic and research team, to neutralise any doubt or mistrust respondents might have about the study, to motivate them to participate and answer the questions, and to ensure anonymity and confidentiality. More specifically, the minimum points it must cover are those shown in Box 11.1.

Box 11.1

The content of the cover letter

Cover letters should at least:

- describe the main objectives and social significance of the study
- identify the research team and its sponsors
- give reasons why the respondent should complete the questionnaire
- guarantee anonymity, privacy and confidentiality
- outline requirements for completion such as maximum time, conditions etc.
- give information about possible risks associated with the project
- cover issues related to ethics.

The cover letter has been recognised as one of the factors that influence the response rate: the way the questionnaire is presented and introduced and the type of assurances given to the respondents determine to a large extent the probability of their returning the questionnaire and of answering all the questions. Some writers (e.g. Benini, 2000; Mahr, 1995), for instance, suggest that the way the cover letter addresses the respondent (for example, Dear Sir; Dear Sir/Madam; Dear Mr Jones; Dear Householder) and even the colour of the paper used, the form of letterhead and the style and format of the letter are very significant, at least with regard to the response rate. Pilot studies and teams of experts are quite often employed to help prepare an effective cover letter.

Instructions

Instructions about how to fill in the questionnaire are mentioned only briefly in the cover letter (e.g. 'It shouldn't take more than 30 minutes of your time' or 'You only need to tick the box in front of the questions'). Instructions will be given on the questionnaire and/or on a separate sheet. As well as giving details as to how to state their answer or preference (e.g. in pre-coded questions) the instructions usually remind the respondents that they should not try to please the researcher, that there are no right or wrong answers and that all questions should be attempted, and instructs them about what to do with the completed questionnaire (for example, that it should be returned to the project director in the self-addressed envelop by a certain date). For obvious reasons the instructions are expected to offer as much information as possible and must be written in a simple language. Inadequate instructions are one of the major sources of non-responses and should be avoided.

The main body

The main body of the questionnaire includes the questions to be answered. In order to be effective, this part of the document must be worked out very carefully, especially with regard to content, structure, wording, flow, format and so on, and adhere to the basic rules of questionnaire construction (Foddy, 1993). This is the part of the questionnaire that will enable the researcher to collect the data required for the completion of the study, and will be discussed next.

2   QUESTIONNAIRE FORMAT

Questionnaire construction is a very demanding task which requires not only methodological competence but also extensive experience with research in general and questioning techniques in particular. This expertise provides the researchers with the necessary skills to cope with the major issues of this process, which relate to how the format of the questionnaire should be moulded, what types of questions should be considered and what they should contain, how long the questionnaire should be, and in general how it should be presented so that it is clear, easy to read and attractive to the respondent and, most importantly, so that it achieves its purpose.

The questionnaire format refers to the order in which questions are organised within the context of the questionnaire. A common requirement of all models is that the questions have to be listed in a logical order, allowing for transition and flow, that is, for a smooth passage from one topic to the next, and to avoid distortions and problems.

These criteria have been integrated by researchers into a number of questionnaire formats. The following six formats deserve to be mentioned:

- *Funnel format.* The questioning moves from general to specific, from impersonal to personal, and from non-sensitive to sensitive questions.

- *Inverted funnel format.* The questioning progresses from specific to general, from personal to impersonal, and from sensitive to non-sensitive.
- *Diamond format.* A combination of the inverted funnel format and the funnel format, where questions progress from specific to general and back to specific, from personal to impersonal and back to personal.
- *X-format.* The first part of the questionnaire employs a funnel format and the second part an inverted funnel format. The questions here change from general to specific and back to general, from impersonal to personal and again to impersonal and so on.
- *Box format.* Questions are uniform throughout the questionnaire, with all questions being kept at the same level.
- *Mixed format.* Here questions appear according to the logic of the project, shifting from general to specific and so on as required. Mixed format questionnaires may also contain sections, each adopting one of the above formats; for example, the first section may employ the funnel format, the second the box format, and the last the inverted funnel format.

The questionnaire format is chosen to suit the nature of the survey, the type of respondents, length of questionnaire, nature of administering the questionnaire, and the findings of a pilot study. It is important that the format serves the purpose of the study and not the personal preference of the researcher. Factors such as those controlling the soundness of questions must be taken into account when determining the format. It is also important that the questions are related to each other logically and are interesting and relevant to the topic; above all, the presentation and structure of the questionnaire should make the respondents feel at ease and appreciated, rather than the subject of a strict interrogation.

It should be borne in mind that an adequate format ensures a smooth completion of the questionnaire, allows the respondent to feel part of the research process, and helps to avoid fatigue and boredom, which can cause loss of interest and cooperation. If the questions are arranged according to the logic of the respondent, if they are adequately linked together, and if the respondent does not notice the passing of time and the intellectual effort required to answer the questions, a positive attitude to the study is maintained and the respondent is more likely to complete the questionnaire and return it to the researcher.

3 QUESTIONNAIRE SIZE

The size of the questionnaire depends on factors such as the research objective, the type of respondents, the methods of analysis and the availability of resources. The number of questions can range from only a few to several hundred. However, the golden rule with respect to questionnaire size is that one should include as many questions as necessary and as few as possible.

Some more specific guidelines will be introduced in the following sections. At this stage it should be noted that the questionnaire, regardless of whether it is offered to the respondent in a written form or as an interview, should be nothing more or less than a translation of the central elements of the research topic.

Whether a questionnaire will be long or short depends on the number of variables and indicators considered in the study, as well as the number of questions required to address the indicators fully. If, for instance, the research contained one variable only (e.g. social class), and the indicators of the variable were occupation, income and education, the questionnaire would include as many questions as is required to address the indicators.

Figure 11.1 shows where questions fit in the context of the study and the questionnaire. It shows, for instance, that the questionnaire may include questions about the occupation of the respondent (Q1), the occupation of the respondent's partner (Q2) and the occupation of the respondent's father (Q3). If information about the occupation of the respondent's mother, brother, sister, grandfather and so on is required, more questions will be included under the indicator 'occupation'. The number of questions related to the indicators 'income' and 'education' will be considered in the same context. The important point here is that there is a straight line between a question, an indicator and a variable. Questions without that link should not be included in the questionnaire unless there is a good reason for it (e.g. they may serve as secondary or tertiary questions; see below).

The size of the questionnaire also depends on the methodology used and the type of study. For instance, a Gallup poll might include only a few questions, but a census survey, or a detailed study of a social issue (e.g. a national family survey) would have many more.

4 TYPES OF QUESTIONS

The questions that are considered vary with respect to a number of criteria, especially regarding their purpose and relevance to the research topic, their structure and approach to the issue they address, their content and wording, and the type

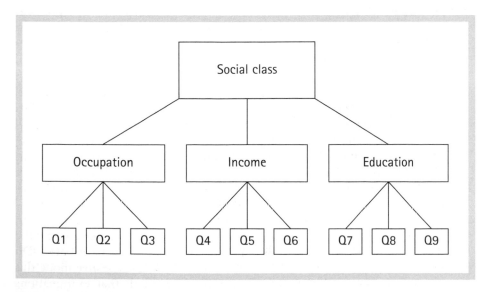

Figure 11.1 Diagrammatic presentation of question construction

of response they require (Converse and Presser, 1986). Some writers (Mahr, 1995) distinguish between essential questions (relating directly to the substance of the project), extra questions (set to check the reliability of the answers), and throw-away questions (used at the beginning to encourage rapport with the respondent); but there are many other types, as we shall see.

- *Primary questions.* Primary questions elicit information directly related to the research topic. Each question provides information about a specific aspect of the topic, that is, an indicator of a particular variable. In a study of marital power, the question 'Who controls the relationship?' may be a primary question.
- *Secondary questions.* Secondary questions are ones that do not relate directly to the research topic. They are of secondary importance in that they provide information on secondary issues such as consistency of opinions or the reliability of the instrument used. They do not add new information about the research topic, but they ensure methodological soundness, the integrity of the questionnaire or the truthfulness of the respondents.
- *Tertiary questions.* Tertiary questions have neither primary nor methodological significance. They help to establish a framework that allows convenient data collection and sufficient information without exhausting or biasing the respondent. Two examples are padding questions and probes.
- *Padding questions.* These questions are not central to the research but are of interest to the respondent. Acting as a 'breather', they are usually placed before or after sensitive questions.
- *Probes.* These questions are used in interviewing to encourage the respondent to complete, amplify or expand an answer, stimulating and guiding the discussion and establishing a friendly atmosphere, free of bias. There are several techniques of probing, with interviewers developing and applying them according to need; two techniques often referred to by writers are the summary technique and controlled non-directive probing (to be discussed later).
- *Direct and indirect questions.* Direct or personal questions ask the respondent to offer information about himself or herself. An example of a direct question is: 'Do you believe in God?' Indirect questions ask the respondent to offer information about other people, assuming that in this way the respondent will indirectly tell something about himself or herself. An example of an indirect question is: 'Do you think that people of your age believe in God nowadays?'

  Indirect questioning is mainly used when it is suspected that respondents will not feel comfortable about offering direct information on the research question; this is the case, for example, when the questions deal with sensitive, embarrassing or threatening issues, or when the topic of research is too difficult for the respondent to answer a direct question. In such cases, indirect questioning makes it easy for the respondent to answer the question. However, it raises ethical questions which deserve further consideration.
- *Suggestive questions.* Suggestive questions contain an implied attempt to tempt the respondent to confirm a view. For example, if we were to test the views of students to examinations, a direct question could have been: 'Do you think that examinations should be abolished?' In a suggestive mode this question could read as follows: 'Don't you also think that examinations

should be abolished?' Suggestive questions lead the respondent, and bias the direction of the findings.

■ *Filter and contingency questions.* Filter questions aim at eliciting, for the first time in the study, information related to a general aspect of the research topic, and are usually followed by another more specific question (i.e. a contingency question). An example of such a question is: 'Do you smoke?'

Contingency questions follow the filter question and aim to elicit additional and more specific information on an issue already addressed by a filter question. In our example, the contingency question may be: 'How many cigarettes do you smoke each day?' Asking contingency questions without filter questions is methodologically incorrect.

■ *Fixed-alternative (pre-coded) and open-ended questions.* According to their response format, questions can be divided into two categories: open-ended and closed (pre-coded or fixed-alternative) questions. These formats have a strong impact on the nature and usefulness of questionnaires, and are very common in social research (Geer, 1988). We shall discuss them in more detail below.

5 OPEN-ENDED AND PRE-CODED QUESTIONS

Open-ended (free-answer) questions allow respondents to state their answers in the way they see appropriate, in their own way and in their own words. Fixed-alternative questions (also known as pre-coded or closed questions) offer a set of responses from which the respondent has to choose.

For example, the question 'What do you think about the proposal of the student union to abolish examinations?' followed by an empty writing space, is an open-ended question. If the above question was followed by the response categories: 'Strongly agree (1); Agree (2); Not sure (3); Disagree (4); Strongly disagree (5)', it would be a fixed-alternative question. In this case the respondents are expected to indicate their response by placing a tick next to the relevant category or by circling the number that corresponds to their personal view, as instructed.

Whether to choose pre-coded and open-ended questions or not depends on a number of factors. In a discussion quite a few years ago (which, nevertheless, is still relevant today), Kahn and Cannell (1957) explained these factors as shown in Box 11.2.

In more general terms, whether to use open-ended questions or not depends on their strengths and weaknesses. Some central strengths and weaknesses of open-ended questions are shown below (Pfeifer, 2000).

Strengths

■ They allow freedom to express feelings and thoughts, especially when complex issues are being studied.
■ They offer more details than pre-coded questions, especially qualifications and justifications.
■ They offer information in areas that might not have been foreseen by the researcher.

Open-ended or pre-coded questions?

Open-ended questions are advisable if:

- the researcher is interested in ample information
- the attitudes, ability to communicate and motivation of the respondents are not known
- the respondents cannot communicate
- they are not well informed and have not yet structured an opinion.

Pre-coded questions can be employed if:

- the researcher is interested in classifying responses or respondents
- the situation of the respondents is known
- they can communicate
- they are well informed and have formed an opinion.

- They allow conclusions about the respondents' way of thinking and logic.
- They allow respondents to show creativity, self-expression and initiative.

Weaknesses

- They are not very suitable for sensitive questions.
- They produce large amounts of information which require extensive time and effort to code and/or evaluate.
- They are time consuming.
- They do not allow accurate comparisons.
- They can offer useless or irrelevant information.
- They are not suitable if the respondents have problems articulating well.
- They require additional processing if statistical analysis is intended.

The strengths and weaknesses of pre-coded questions are exactly the opposite of those listed above for open-ended questions. The strengths of the one are the weaknesses of the other. For instance, allowing freedom to researchers is a strength for open questions but a weakness for pre-coded questions. Hence there is no need to list their strengths and weaknesses separately.

6 RESPONSE FORMAT

6.1 Introduction

A characteristic of open-ended and fixed-alternative questions is that the former are easy to construct but difficult to process and the latter difficult to construct but easy to process. Constructing response sets for fixed-alternative questions is a complex and quite demanding task. In this section, we shall look at the options available for responses to pre-coded questions, leaving an examination of the factors affecting the choice of options to be discussed elsewhere (Benini, 2000).

It is a strict methodological requirement that response sets to fixed-alternative questions adhere to certain standards and principles, of which the most important is that response categories should be accurate, exhaustive, mutually exclusive and unidimensional. A brief description of such options is given below.

- *Accurate sets.* Response sets are expected to be accurate. In other words, they should, first, address the central point of the question; second, be relevant; and third, be related to the essence of the question. A response set developed to provide responses to the question 'How successful has your progress been on this course?' containing the response categories 'very satisfied', 'satisfied', 'unsatisfied' and 'very unsatisfied' is not accurate because it relates to satisfaction and not to success. These two issues may be interrelated but are nonetheless different: a business manager may be 'very satisfied' with the progress of a branch, but also rate its degree of success as 'moderate'.
- *Exhaustive sets.* Response sets must cover all possible options. When answering the question 'Number of children?', followed by '(A) 1 or 2 children; (B) 3 or more children', the set is obviously not exhaustive: it leaves out families with no children. In other cases, options such as 'other', 'no opinion', 'I don't know' must be considered in order for sets to be exhaustive. However, care must be taken that these responses do not become 'soft options', attracting large numbers of responses. In such cases, pre-tests must be employed to detect such cases and call for relevant action.
- *Mutually exclusive sets.* A set of categories is expected to include items that are clearly distinguishable from each other and mutually exclusive. The respondents should only be able to choose one true response, without confusion and ambiguity. The responses 'Single', 'Married', 'Living together', 'Divorced', 'Separated', 'Widowed' are (strictly speaking) not mutually exclusive, because the set allows a certain group of respondents to choose more than one option. For instance a divorced person who is cohabiting can equally tick the third or the fifth option.
- *Unidimensional sets.* This refers to the requirement that a set of categories should refer to and measure only one construct, in only one dimension. A response category that includes the items 'very reliable', 'reliable', 'unreliable', 'very unreliable' is unidimensional because it measures reliability. The response set 'very happy', 'happy', 'unsatisfied', 'very unsatisfied' is not unidimensional because it relates to two dimensions, namely happiness and satisfaction.

6.2 Response sets

The following are possible ways to form response sets in the context of questionnaires; while some are more common than others, all have been and are currently being used by social researchers.

Numerical responses

This response category includes a continuum, with two opposite adjectives at each end and a range of numbers in between, one of which must be circled or otherwise marked by the respondent.

> *Example A.* The response of the Prime Minister regarding maternal employment was: (Please circle the appropriate number.)
>
> Very satisfactory   5   4   3   2   1   Very unsatisfactory

Verbal scales

In many cases the expected response to a question is formulated in words. The respondent in such cases is expected to tick one of the words in the space provided for that purpose.

> *Example B.* The support provided by the Union was (please tick one):
>
> Very high   (. . .)
> High   (. . .)
> Moderate   (. . .)
> Low   (. . .)
> Very low   (. . .)

Scales of increasing strength

Some researchers opt for response categories indicated simply by a descriptor, and are followed by a set of numbers ranging from low to high, from which the respondent is expected to choose. The meaning of the numbers (e.g. 1 standing for very low and 10 for very high) will be explained in the general instructions for the questionnaire.

> *Example C.* In this country, the condition of women in the areas shown below can be characterised as: (Please circle the appropriate number.)
>
> | Human rights | 1 | 2 | 3 | 4 | 5 | 6 | 7 | 8 | 9 | 10 |
> | Employment | 1 | 2 | 3 | 4 | 5 | 6 | 7 | 8 | 9 | 10 |
> | Health | 1 | 2 | 3 | 4 | 5 | 6 | 7 | 8 | 9 | 10 |

Graphic responses

The use of graphic responses is not new in social research. In its simplest form, a response contains a continuum whose extremes are defined by two opposite descriptors connected by dots or a line. The respondent is expected to mark the line at a point that expresses the strength of his or her view. The researcher will then evaluate the answer according to the position of the mark by means of a standard pattern.

> *Example D.* Last Sunday's elections of the municipal officers were:
>
> fair … unfair

Graphic-numerical responses

A combination of graphic symbols and numerals is quite often used by social investigators. The direction of choice and evaluation is based on the selected position of the tick, which is not defined in words.

> *Example E.* My wife's reaction to last week's rise in taxes was: (please tick)
>
> (. . .)   +3
> (. . .)   +2
> (. . .)   +1
> (. . .)   −1
> (. . .)   −2
> (. . .)   −3

Thermometer scales

In these scales, the responses are set in the form of a thermometer, presenting a continuum that displays the reading range of a thermometer, the extremes of which are described by opposite adjectives, for example 'Very high', 'Very low'. The divisions given on the thermometer are used to reflect the respondent's level of response.

Face scales

Another graphic scale employed to record answers to pre-coded questions in a simple manner is the use of faces. Here, usually five to seven faces (or sets of faces) of equal size and structure are ordered on a line. The faces are identical, except for the shape of the mouth, which at one end is shaped in a U-form giving the impression of happiness, and progressively changes through a neutral position (straight line) to an inverted U at the other end describing unhappiness. There are no explaining adjectives here as it is assumed that the faces offer a clear indication of the implied feeling. The respondents are asked to indicate their feelings to the question by marking the appropriate face. A five-point response containing a combination of faces is shown below.

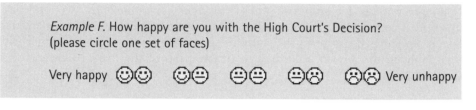

Example F. How happy are you with the High Court's Decision? (please circle one set of faces)

Very happy 😊😊 😊😐 😐😐 😐😟 😟😟 Very unhappy

Ladder scales

In a response set that employs a ladder scale, the responses are given on a ladder presenting a continuum of five or more steps, whose extremes are defined by two opposite adjectives (e.g. 'high', 'low' or 'strong', 'weak'). The question could be, for example, 'Whereabouts do you stand on the social ladder?', advising the respondents to place an X on the point of their choice.

Constant-sum scales

These scales ask respondents to score two or more objects or concepts so that they together add up to a given amount (e.g. 100). This relative measure is most suitable to ascertain, for instance, the psychological distance between stimuli. The respondents may be asked to allocate 100 points to the Labour Party or to the Communist Party, according to their handling of taxation issues. The rating may be 100 to 0 or vice versa, or 20 to 80, 60 to 40 and so on. Scores allocated by the respondents can be further computed and evaluated, for instance, by constructing relations of the pattern A/B = 60/40 = 6/4 = 1.5, or vice versa.

Likert-scale questions

Likert scales are widely used, particularly as a means for studying attitudes. The response categories range between two extreme positions divided into five points corresponding to a verbal-numerical scale.

Example G. The reaction of the nurses to the recent salary proposal is, in my opinion: (Please circle the number corresponding to your choice.)

Very positive   5
Positive   4
Neutral   3
Negative   2
Very negative   1

Ranking scales

Unlike many scales in which respondents are asked to tick one response only, ranking scales require that all responses be answered, for example by ranking them from highest to the lowest. In such cases there are as many ranks as there are items.

Example H. My ranking of the performance of the five political parties from 1 (very low) to 5 (very high) is as follows: (Please enter numbers in the brackets)

Democrats	. . . ( )
Labour Party	. . . ( )
Greens	. . . ( )
National Party	. . . ( )
Liberal Party	. . . ( )

Semantic differential scales

These scales are employed to evaluate social units such as teachers, parents, friends or politicians. They contain a set of opposites (up to 70) relating to three major dimensions; these are (a) *general impression*, (b) *power* or *potency* and (c) *activity*. The space between the opposites is graded from 0 expressing the lowest evaluation (e.g. very bad, very weak, very low) to 6, representing the highest evaluation (e.g. very good, very strong, very high). When these scales are employed, the respondents specify where exactly in that range, in their opinion, the person in question should be ranked. Examples of indicators for each of the three dimensions are given in Example I. The three groups of opposites correspond to the dimensions listed above.

Example I. How would you rate the role of your instructor in your class?

Good	6	5	4	3	2	1	0	Bad
Harmonious	6	5	4	3	2	1	0	Unharmonious
Sociable	6	5	4	3	2	1	0	Unsociable
Hard	6	5	4	3	2	1	0	Soft
Difficult	6	5	4	3	2	1	0	Easy
Unyielding	6	5	4	3	2	1	0	Lenient
Irritable	6	5	4	3	2	1	0	Calm
Active	6	5	4	3	2	1	0	Passive
Sharp	6	5	4	3	2	1	0	Dull

The structure, nature and size of the set of responses depend on many factors, but mainly on the nature of the study, the nature of the respondents and the extent to which statistical analysis will be used. For an accurate and effective construction of response categories of this kind, several techniques have been developed and are frequently used by researchers. Those introduced by Likert, Thurstone and Guttman are three examples.

7 QUESTION CONTENT

The content of the questions is obviously the most important element of a questionnaire or an interview guide. While form and order of questions may influence accessibility to information, the content of the questions will tease out the essence of the answer sought in the study. In order for the questionnaire to achieve its purpose, the content of questions must be organised according to the criteria listed below (see Becker, 1989; Mahr, 1995; Puris, 1995).

- *Focus*. Each question is expected to address one point only. Double-barrelled questions, where the question focuses on two points, should be avoided. For instance, the question 'Are your parents caring and supportive?' addresses more than one issue. First, it does not differentiate between father and mother (the mother may be caring and supportive while the father is not); it is not possible here for the respondent to describe the parents separately. Second, it asks about care *and* support. In such cases, one answer cannot express the respondent's response to the issues covered. Such questions should be avoided. If information for all these issues is required, separate questions should be asked.
- *Relevance*. The content of each question must be related to the research topic. Questions not directly related to the topic may be asked only if they are well justified and serve a specific purpose.
- *Symmetry*. The questions should address a specific element of the research topic and be symmetrical: there should not be many questions on one aspect and few on the others unless there are reasons for this. Unless there is good cause to treat the various parts of the questionnaire differently, each part should be given the same value and space.
- *Clarity and simplicity*. The content of the questions must be clear and simple in language and in content. Questions that are too general, ambiguous, vague or embarrassing should be avoided. Personal questions should be employed very carefully.
- *Language*. Questions should be formulated in the language of the respondent.
- *Attitude*. Questions should convey a positive attitude towards the respondent and the study, in general, should display friendliness and collegiality.
- *Presuming questions*. Questions that rest on presumptions or presuppositions should be avoided. It is also unethical to ask a student, for instance, 'When did you stop cheating in the examinations?' without first introducing a filter question about cheating.
- *Suggestive questioning*. 'Leading' or suggestive questions should be avoided. These are ones that encourage the respondent to give a certain answer (e.g. 'Don't you also think that examinations should be abolished?'), usually one preferred by the researcher.
- *Prestige bias*. This too should be avoided. It occurs when the respondent is encouraged to follow some generalised views of important people (e.g. 'Gerontologists believe that progressive age causes alienation and hostility among older males; what is your view on this issue?').

As we shall see later, the nature of questioning and of presenting questions to respondents varies. Qualitative researchers may disagree on a number of points made earlier in this section; however, there is little doubt as to the validity and acceptance of the points made above regarding question content.

8 RULES FOR QUESTIONNAIRE CONSTRUCTION

There are several rules for questionnaire construction. Some are more important than others, but a set of such rules should be considered during the construction of the questionnaires or interview schedules. The views of many writers on this point may be summed up as shown below (Mahr, 1995).

Rules for layout

- Questions must be easy to read and easy to follow.
- Questions and response categories must be easy to identify and distinguishable from other questions and response categories. Sufficient space should be provided between the questions.
- Clear instructions about how to answer the questions must be given; for example, 'Circle the appropriate number' or 'Tick the right box'. Nothing should be taken for granted.
- Sufficient space should be left for the respondent to make relevant remarks where required.

Rules for question content

- Every question must be relevant to one or more aspects of the study.
- Ambiguous, non-specific and hypothetical questions are to be avoided.
- Leading, double-barrelled and presuming questions should not be employed.
- Embarrassing, personal or threatening questions should be avoided.
- Vague words and academic jargon should not be used.
- The language of the respondent should be employed. If that is not possible, simple language should be used, without jargon, slang, double negatives or complicated expressions.
- The easy flow and logical progression in the questionnaire should be ensured.
- Each question should ask what it is supposed to ask.

Rules for questionnaire format

- The questionnaire must have a professional appearance and give the impression of a document that deserves respect and invokes feelings of responsibility.
- The questionnaire should be presented in a way that encourages the respondent to complete and return it.
- Writing on one side of the page only is preferable to writing on both sides.
- Print and colour of paper and ink must give the questionnaire an attractive appearance.
- The questionnaire should be presented as a complete document, with an inviting and reassuring introductory cover letter and a concluding note containing instructions about returning the questionnaire.

- The questionnaire size should be kept to a minimum, with as many questions as necessary, and as few as possible.
- Sufficient instructions and probes should be provided where necessary.
- Pre-coded questions should offer adequate response categories.
- All questions should be checked for possible bias and ethical adequacy.

These rules relate to the methodological, technical and practical aspects of surveys. Questionnaires are constructed within parameters that take into account professional standards and responsibilities. The respondents are also an important factor in this context. Well-constructed questionnaires with a friendly and inviting appearance encourage a high response rate, and this is a factor researchers have to consider very carefully.

9 STEPS IN QUESTIONNAIRE CONSTRUCTION

Questionnaires are constructed in a very focused and systematic manner. The process of construction goes through a number of interrelated steps, and offers a basis for the research stage to follow. The following are the most common steps in questionnaire construction (see Pfeifer, 2000; Puris, 1995):

Step 1: Preparation

The researcher first decides what the most suitable type of questionnaire is, and determines the way it will be administered. There should also be a search for relevant questionnaires, that might already have been developed by other investigators. If suitable questionnaires are found, they can either be adopted for the study or used as guides in preparing the new one. If the search is unsuccessful, the researcher will proceed with the construction of a new questionnaire.

Step 2: Constructing the first draft

The investigator formulates a number of questions, usually a few more than required, including questions of substance (directly related to aspects of the research topic), questions of method (those testing reliability and wording), and secondary as well as tertiary questions.

Step 3: Self-critique

The questions are tested for relevance, symmetry, clarity and simplicity, among other criteria, as well as for compliance with the basic rules of questionnaire construction presented above.

Step 4: External scrutiny

The first draft is then given to experts for scrutiny and suggestions. It is anticipated that some questions might be changed or eliminated, while new questions might be suggested.

Step 5: Re-examination and revision

The critique offered by the experts and group leaders will be considered and eventual changes implemented. If the revision is not significant, the investigator proceeds to the next step. If the revision is substantial, the questionnaire is presented again to experts and later re-examined and revised until it is considered satisfactory. The investigator then proceeds to the next step.

Step 6: Pre-test or pilot study

In most cases a pilot study or a pre-test is undertaken to check the suitability of the questionnaire as a whole (pilot study) or of some aspects of it (pre-test). A small sample is selected for this purpose, and the respondents are requested to respond to all or part of the questionnaire; the results are then analysed and interpreted.

Step 7: Revision

The pre-test and pilot study usually result in some minor or major changes. If the changes are relatively insignificant, the investigators will proceed to Step 8. If the changes are substantial they will return to Step 4.

Step 8: Second pre-test

The revised questionnaire may then be subjected to a second test, mainly with regard to the revised questions. This depends on the extent of revision and the complexity of the issue in question. Usually one pre-test is sufficient. The response is considered and adjustments and revisions follow.

Step 9: Formulation of the final draft

In this final step, apart from implementing the suggestions derived from the pre-tests, the investigator concentrates on editorial work: checking for spelling mistakes, legibility, instructions, layout, space for responses, pre-coding, scaling issues and the general presentation of the questionnaire. This copy will finally be sent to the printer.

10 PRE-TESTS AND PILOT STUDIES

Pre-tests and pilot studies are two instruments employed by quantitative researchers before the actual data collection commences. They are trial studies ('miniature preparatory studies') employed to ensure that the planning of the main study and its study tools are correct, suitable, reliable and valid. They serve similar purposes, but differ in certain ways, as we shall see.

10.1 Pre-tests

Pre-tests are small tests of single elements of a research instrument that are predominantly used to check its 'mechanical' structure. The response categories to a particular question might need to be tested, or the question might be found to be unclear or misleading. The response categories, for example, might not be sufficient to cover all possible options, and researchers need to avoid overloading the option 'Other, please specify'.

A questionnaire can be pre-tested, and the responses will demonstrate whether there is a need to re-arrange the response categories to a particular question. If the proportion of respondents opting for 'Other, please specify' is relatively small, the question will remain as it is. If, however, the number of the responses resorting to this item is relatively large, the response set will need to be adjusted.

A similar procedure will be employed if the researcher is doubtful about whether the subjects will in fact answer a sensitive question directly or opt for the neutral category 'Undecided', 'No opinion' or 'I don't know'.

10.2 Pilot studies

A pilot study is a small-scale replica and a rehearsal of the main study. While pre-tests help to solve isolated mechanical problems in an instrument, pilot studies are concerned with administrative and organisational problems related to the whole study and the respondents.

Pilot studies serve many goals, but those considered by most writers (e.g. Oppenheim, 1992; Sproull, 1988) to be the most important are shown in Box 11.3. To a certain degree, these points are relevant to both qualitative and quantitative research. In qualitative research, however, pilot studies aim to establish whether respondents are accessible, whether the site is convenient, whether the techniques of data collection generate enough information (neither too little nor too much), whether the plan is well constructed and whether any changes or adjustments are needed.

10.3 Evaluation

The results of the pre-tests and pilot studies will be evaluated in the context of the aims described above. The findings will offer straightforward answers to basic

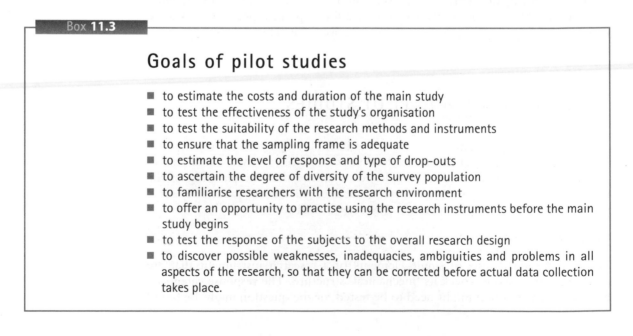

Box 11.3

Goals of pilot studies

- to estimate the costs and duration of the main study
- to test the effectiveness of the study's organisation
- to test the suitability of the research methods and instruments
- to ensure that the sampling frame is adequate
- to estimate the level of response and type of drop-outs
- to ascertain the degree of diversity of the survey population
- to familiarise researchers with the research environment
- to offer an opportunity to practise using the research instruments before the main study begins
- to test the response of the subjects to the overall research design
- to discover possible weaknesses, inadequacies, ambiguities and problems in all aspects of the research, so that they can be corrected before actual data collection takes place.

questions asked, and will indicate whether there are any problems that require attention. If, for instance, the researcher cannot establish the expected rapport with the respondents, if there are difficulties in convincing the majority of the respondents to take part in the study, if the respondents refuse to answer certain questions or give high proportions of 'I don't know' answers, if answers are given but with small notes or qualifications, and if the observed subjects tend unexpectedly to be distracted by the video camera or other environmental factors, then certain adjustments must be made (Becker, 1989). Pre-tests and pilot studies present a trial run of the study and offer an opportunity for adjustments and 'fine tuning' before the real work begins.

11   REVIEWING THE QUESTIONNAIRE

The questionnaire review often involves a large number of points, many of which relate to the nature of the particular research topic. However, many writers (Berger et al., 1989; Beninin, 2000; Puris, 1995; Selltiz et al., 1976) stress that the following points should be considered in the review:

- *Size of the questionnaire.* Is the questionnaire too large or too small? The rule here is that every question should have a specific purpose; if not, it has no place in the questionnaire.
- *Relevance of procedure.* Which point of the topic is the question related to? Is it strictly relevant? Does it ask what it is meant to ask? Questions must be tuned to one specific point in a clear and unambiguous way.
- *Necessity.* Is every question essential? Could some questions be omitted? Is there any repetition in the questions? Is more than one question needed for each item? Questions will be retained only if they have a certain purpose and are really necessary.
- *Clarity.* Are the questions easy to understand, clear and unambiguous?
- *Tone and content.* Is the tone of the questions acceptable? Are the questions unethical, threatening, insulting, patronising or otherwise biasing? Such questions must be changed or omitted.
- *Layout of the questionnaire.* Is sufficient space provided for recording answers given to open-ended questions? Are the layout of the questionnaire, the colour of the paper and the print size adequate and acceptable?
- *Pre-coded questions.* Are the response categories to pre-coded questions easy to understand, exhaustive, unidimensional and mutually exclusive? If not, they need to be restructured.
- *Adequacy.* Are all aspects of the topic adequately covered? If not, new questions should be added.
- *Instructions.* Are sufficient instructions given for filling out the questionnaire and for proper use of probes? Are these instructions adequate to guide the respondent through the questions?
- *Level of pitching.* Is the wording of the questions appropriate for the respondents' linguistic ability, education, interest and intellectual capacity?
- *Cover letter.* Is the cover letter constructed adequately? Does it offer the

required information? Are any points missing? Is it too long or too short? Are the respondents properly addressed in the cover letter?

■ *Pre-coding.* Is pre-coding (where required) recorded adequately and in accordance with the computer program used?

■ *Demographic data.* Are all demographic data of the respondent (age, education, occupation etc.) required? Are they sufficient? Are they positioned in the right place on the questionnaire?

■ *Principles.* Have the methodological principles regarding the questionnaire construction been adhered to?

■ *Legal responsibilities.* Are any questions likely to affect the rights of the respondents or third parties?

■ *Ethical considerations.* Is the questionnaire ethically sound?

■ *Overall impression.* Is the questionnaire easy to read and pleasant to follow overall?

This list concentrates on the most important issues. Individual projects will raise additional and more specific requirements that will need to be addressed by the investigator.

12 RELEVANCE OF THE QUESTIONNAIRE

As stated earlier, questions must be relevant to the research topic. Each question will concern one or more aspects of the topic, and all the questions together will cover all aspects of the topic. To ensure that questions are relevant to the topic and evenly distributed among the different aspects of the research question, and that no parts of the research issue are omitted from the questionnaire, researchers usually follow a number of steps. These were mentioned earlier in this chapter and are summarised below:

Step 1.   The concept(s) to be studied is (are) identified.
Step 2.   The dimensions of the concept(s) are ascertained.
Step 3.   Indicators are identified.
Step 4.   Indicators are translated into a number of questions.
Step 5.   These questions are put in a questionnaire following the procedures introduced above.

Thus, developing questions for a questionnaire is a process of translating research topics into variables, variables into indicators and indicators into questions. This process ensures that each question has a definite purpose and elicits information related to a specific aspect of the research object.

Let us see how this works in practice. Assume that we wished to study the 'Effects of religiousness on the scholastic achievement of teenagers'. Following the suggestion contained in Step 1 above we identify the concepts, which in this example are 'religiousness' and 'scholastic achievement'. In Step 2 we ascertain their dimensions (respectively, religious beliefs and practice, and attainment in maths, English, science and social studies). Following Step 3, we translate the dimensions into a number of indicators. For example, indicators for the first concept might be belief in God, church attendance, bible reading and participation in religious activities; for the second concept they might be grades in English, mathematics, science and social studies.

Box 11.4

The chain of translation

Concepts	Dimensions	Indicators	Questions
Religiousness	Beliefs	Belief in God	Do you believe in God?
		Belief in saints	Do you believe in saints?
	Activities	Church attendance	Do you go to church?
		Religious activities	Do you attend Sunday school?
Scholastic achievement	Maths	Grade	Your grade in maths?
	English	Grade	Your grade in English?
	Science	Grade	Your grade in science?
	Social studies	Grade	Your grade in social studies?

These indicators are then translated into questions (Step 4) such as whether the respondents believe in God; whether they attend church; whether they read the bible; whether they participate in religious activities; and what grades they achieved in English, in mathematics, science and social studies. While some indicators might be translated into one or two questions, others might require more. One might wish to know, for instance, about how often the respondents attend church, and also about their sibling(s), parent(s) or other relatives at the present time, last year or two years ago. The important point is that questions translate the meaning of a topic or variable and provide information for a particular aspect of the research topic.

If this chain of translation is followed carefully, all questions will be relevant to the research topic and the researcher will know exactly the purpose of every question in the questionnaire. As a result, every point of the research issue will have one or more corresponding questions, and every question will have one or more corresponding points in the research problem for which they provide information.

13 NON-RESPONSE IN MAIL QUESTIONNAIRES

13.1 Introduction

In survey research, particularly when mail questionnaires are employed, it is common that many people included in the sample will not take part in the research. More specifically, most of those who receive a questionnaire will not return it to the researcher by the due date. The most common reasons for this are thought to be those shown below (see Becker, 1989; Puris, 1995). For instance:

- They are *unwilling* to do so (for example, they disapprove of the research study, do not like the sponsor, do not like answering questionnaires, or the spouse disapproves of it).
- They are *unable* to take part in the study, due to physical, mental or linguistic problems (e.g. handicapped people or migrants).
- They are *not accessible* (e.g. have moved away, died or were not at home when visited).
- They *did not have time* to respond.
- They *did not receive* the questionnaire.
- They found the questionnaire *too complex.*

Given that this loss of respondents can often be very high, non-response is an issue that deserves serious attention. It is therefore understandable that investigators make a concerted effort to keep the non-response rate as low as possible.

This is accomplished through various measures, ranging from social, or psychological to economic measures, that fall into two main kinds. The first aims to prevent non-response in the first place, and employs techniques that encourage the return of the questionnaire. The other is to follow up non-responders and encourage them to return the questionnaire (see Box 11.5). In the latter approach, sending reminders to all those who did not return their questionnaire and urging them to do so is a standard procedure. Two reminders may be sufficient. After the second reminder, it is very unlikely that any further attempt will be successful. It is also tempting to offer incentives to respondents so they return the questionnaires. However, this can bias the sample by attracting particular people to the study.

13.2 Preventing non-response

In general, planning the study very carefully, taking appropriate measures and being vigilant can improve the response rate. There is also a lot more that can be done to deal with non-responses. The following suggestions (see Lamnek, 1993; Mahr, 1995; Puris, 1995; Selltiz et al., 1976) can be pointers in the right direction:

- *Approach.* The more serious, trustworthy and friendly the cover letter, the more likely it is that the questionnaire will be accepted and completed.
- *Explanation.* The more clearly the purpose, nature, usefulness and sponsorship of the study is explained, the more likely it is that the questionnaire will be completed.
- *Honesty.* The more honest, direct and concise the cover letter, the more likely it is that the questionnaire will be answered.
- *Length of cover letter.* The shorter the cover letter the better.
- *Principles.* The more convinced the respondent is of the anonymity and confidentiality of the study, the more likely he or she is to answer the questionnaire.

- *Reminders*. The more convinced the respondent is about the use of reminders and their relationship with anonymity, the more trust is generated and the more likely it is that the questionnaire will be answered.
- *Rationale*. The more convinced the respondent is of the rationale of the study and the reasons for taking part in it, the more likely it is that the questionnaire will be completed.
- *Time required*. The more specific the indication of the time required for the completion of the questionnaire, the more likely it is that the respondent will complete it.
- *Size*. The smaller the size of the questionnaire, the more likely it is to be completed.
- *Degree of difficulty*. The easier it is for the questionnaire to be completed, the more likely it is for the respondent to complete it.
- *Sensitivity*. The less sensitive the question content, the more likely it is that the questionnaire will be completed and returned.
- *Method of return*. The easier it is for the questionnaire to be returned(e.g. enclosing a self-addressed, pre-stamped envelope), the more likely it is that it will be returned.
- *Time of completion*. The more convenient the time for the respondent to complete the questionnaire, the more likely to be returned.
- *Administration*. The more friendly and personal the delivery of the questionnaire, the more likely it is to be returned by the set date.
- *Rewards*. The greater the rewards for returning the questionnaire, the more likely that it will be returned to the researcher.

Box **11.5**

Fifteen ways of improving response rate

- Make an effort to screen the sampling frame to eliminate drop-outs (e.g. people who have died or moved away).
- Make the return time not too short and not too long.
- Make the questionnaire brief; in general, long questionnaires are less likely to be returned.
- Make the questionnaire look good; appearance pays.
- Make it easy to read: e.g. good print, clear language, good instructions.
- Make it easy to answer: e.g. clear options, and tick boxes.
- Make it appear trustworthy: stress anonymity, confidentiality and ethical standards.
- Make it respectable and impressive, in terms of the envelope, cover letter etc.
- Make an effort to avoid being intrusive; do not offend the respondents.
- Make an appeal to morals or other principles, but be truthful and honest.
- Make the respondents feel important by addressing them appropriately.
- Make its status evident: highlight associations with sponsors, universities etc.
- Make it easy to respond: include a 'return paid' envelope.
- Make some promises, but be honest; don't overdo it; and don't beg!
- Make good use of one or two follow-ups, using honest and ethical standards.

- *Return dates.* The less appropriate the return date (too short or too long), the more likely it is that the questionnaire will not be returned.
- *Appeal.* The more appealing and attractive the cover letter, the more likely it is that the questionnaire will be completed and returned.
- *Layout and format.* The more appealing and attractive the layout and format of the questionnaire, and the more pleasant it is to answer the questions, the more likely it is that it will be completed and returned.
- *Appearance.* The more impressive the colour of paper, type of print and type of mailing, the more likely it is that the questionnaire will be completed.
- *Trust.* The more trustworthy the questionnaire in terms of confidentiality and adherence to clear standards, the more likely it is to be completed and returned.

14 QUESTIONNAIRES IN FEMINIST RESEARCH

It has often been argued that questionnaires are a research instrument of quantitative rather than qualitative investigators. This is particularly so for standardised questionnaires. Supporting this is the notion that questionnaires are mostly used by quantitative researchers and also that most criticisms of this instrument come from feminist and qualitative researchers.

Although it is correct that large-scale surveys employing standardised questionnaires are the monopoly of quantitative researchers, this does not mean that feminist and qualitative researchers abstain from using this research method. The latter employ unstandardised and unstructured questionnaires rather than standardised questionnaires, and use them more often than quantitative researchers do. Unstandardised and unstructured questionnaires, containing open-ended questions and allowing subjectivity and flexibility in the way questions are constructed and answered, are in accord not only with epistemological principles but also with common practice.

Feminist and qualitative researchers do not criticise questionnaires as such, but rather highly standardised formats and the objectivity and value neutrality which underpin their structure and presentation. Feminists and qualitative researchers in general propose ways of improving questionnaires but do not reject them out of hand. Finally, feminists are critical of the way in which researchers are set against the subjects, that is, of the hierarchy of roles and the distance that is systematically expected between them. According to these arguments, however, questionnaires are neither inconsistent with basic aspects of qualitative research, nor ignored by qualitative researchers.

This point is further supported by the fact that feminist empiricists consider questionnaires as important as quantitative researchers do. As with other feminist and qualitative researchers, so for empiricists the use of 'soft questionnaires' – ones that are brief and unstandardised, with open-ended questions and a close and an egalitarian relationship between the researcher and the researched – is an accepted method of data collection. Moreover, they show an interest in standardised questionnaires, and the implied compilation of data of a higher level of quantification and comparability, adequately adjusted to meet the specific requirements of their underlying paradigm.

Briefly, the distinction here for feminist and qualitative research is not associated with the research instrument per se but rather with the way in which it is conceptualised and applied in the various contexts; and as we already know, most methods – including questionnaires – leave a lot of scope for adjustment and negotiation.

15 STRENGTHS AND WEAKNESSES OF QUESTIONNAIRES

Questionnaires, as methods of data collection, have strengths and weaknesses, and hence advantages and limitations, that the researcher must be aware of. A list of both is given below.

Strengths

- Questionnaires are less expensive than other methods; in the words of Selltiz et al. (1976), 'questionnaires can be sent through the mail; interviewers cannot'.
- They produce quick results.
- They can be completed at the respondent's convenience.
- They offer greater assurance of anonymity.
- They offer less opportunity for bias or errors caused by the presence or attitudes of the interviewer.
- They are a stable, consistent and uniform measure, free of variation.
- They offer a considered and objective view of the issue, since respondents can consult their files and since many subjects prefer to write rather than talk about certain issues.
- The use of questionnaires allows a wider coverage, since researchers can approach respondents more easily than other methods.
- They are not affected by problems of 'non-contacts' (i.e. of respondents who are not available at the time of the study; a problem common in interviewing).

Weaknesses

- Questionnaires do not allow probing, prompting and clarification of questions.
- They do not provide opportunities for motivating the respondent to participate in the survey or to answer the questions.
- The identity of the respondent and the conditions under which the questionnaire is answered are not known. Researchers are not sure whether the right person has answered the questions.
- It is not possible to check whether the question order – where required – was followed.
- Questionnaires do not provide an opportunity to collect additional information (e.g. through observation) while they are being completed.
- Due to lack of supervision, partial response is quite possible.

In questionnaires, as in other methods in general, the focus of evaluation should be not only on the quality of the method but on its suitability. The nature of the research context should be given due attention: questionnaires may be very useful in one context but not in another.

16 QUESTIONNAIRES IN THE COMPUTER AGE

Due to their structure, questionnaires – especially those with a standardised structure – lend themselves to computer assistance. To a certain extent, the use of computers goes further than just assisting the researcher in data collection. In some cases the computer takes over questioning, and collection of data occurs between the computer and the respondent without the involvement of the researcher.

This is obvious in the area of interviewing, which will be discussed more extensively in the next section. The packages CAPI, CATI, CODSCI and CISUR allow interviews to be run through a computer, with the respondent reading and answering questions on the screen (following instructions from the computer). Interviews are administered like questionnaires; interviews become electronic questionnaires, often without an interviewer being present.

Apart from this, there are computer packages that take over the administration and completion of the questionnaires, replacing the traditional research assistant. The program 'Computerised self-administered questionnaire' (CSAQ) is one example. The respondent is given no questionnaires to fill in but is asked instead to sit in front of a computer terminal; the computer displays the questions on the screen, giving the necessary instructions and offering advice on technical aspects of the questionnaire when required. The respondent enters the responses in the computer and the computer saves the data in its memory and adds the responses to the research data, gradually preparing them for analysis.

Other programs operate in a similar way. The computer has, obviously, extended its function from its traditional role as assistant in statistical analysis to data preparation and collection, functions that were once performed predominantly by research assistants.

Beyond this, computers are the bridge to more advanced developments in the domain of electronic media, allowing the researcher easier and faster access not only to data but also to respondents. More specifically, the computer connects the researcher with the Internet, and through this to email and web pages, where researchers contact prospective respondents who may also fill in questionnaires. This opens the door to a significantly larger number of people and also to forms of questionnaire administration that almost eliminate the human factor on the side of the researcher.

As noted earlier, computers link researchers with the Internet, and so facilitate Internet sampling and surveys. Internet users may be attracted to the research, and those who finally agree to participate are guided to a site where the questionnaire is located. From then on, the procedure is the same as in other computer-assisted questionnaires. Questionnaires are completed and the results filed in databanks. Internet surveys have become popular, and many researchers as well as research organisations take advantage of them. An example of a systematic employment of Internet surveys is the construction of groups of volunteers who makes themselves available via the Internet to complete such surveys. (Set fees are in place for each member taking part.)

The Internet is also used in combination with other, more traditional methods. For instance, in order to control representativeness, researchers construct their samples using conventional methods, and respondents are then guided to Internet sites where they complete the questionnaires at their own convenience. This makes contact with researchers and travel to the research site unnecessary.

MAIN POINTS

- Questionnaires are a form of survey: a written survey.
- The main elements of a questionnaire are the cover letter, instructions and main body.
- The questionnaire format can be one of the following: funnel format, inverted funnel format, diamond format, X-format, box format and mixed format.
- A questionnaire usually contains primary, secondary and/or tertiary questions. They may be fixed-alternative or open questions.
- Response sets in fixed-alternative questions must be accurate, exhaustive and uni-dimensional, and must include mutually exclusive categories.
- Particular attention should be given to the question content, especially to composition, relevance, clarity and simplicity, level and type of language, and to the attitude conveyed through the questions.
- Questions are the last step in a series of translations, leading from the definition of the research topic to indicators and to question wording.
- Pre-tests are small tests of single elements of the research questionnaires, aiming to check their soundness and relevance.
- A pilot study is a small-scale replica of the main study involving a fraction of the sample.
- Pre-tests mainly address research instruments; pilot studies mainly address research process and outcomes.
- Non-response is a serious issue that requires serious consideration.

WHERE TO FROM HERE?

Before you leave this chapter, visit the companion website for the third edition of *Social Research* at http://www.palgrave.com/sociology/sarantakos to review the main concepts introduced in this chapter and to test yourself on the major issues discussed.

FURTHER READING

Arlek, P. L. and Settle, R. B. (1995) *The Survey Research Handbook: Guidelines and Strategies for Conducting a Survey*. New York: McGraw-Hill.

Couper, M. P. (2000) 'Web Surveys: A Review of Issues and Approaches.' *Public Opinion Quarterly*, 64: 464–94.

De Vaus, D. (ed.) (2002) *Surveys in Social Research*. London: Sage.

Dillman, D. (2000) *Mail and Internet Surveys: The Tailored Design Method*. Chichester: Wiley.

Foddy, W. H. (1992) *Constructing Questions for Interviews and Questionnaires*. Melbourne: Cambridge University Press.

Galavotti, M. C. (2003) *Observation and Experiment in the Natural and Social Sciences*. Boston: Kluwer Academic.

Mangione, T. W. (1995) *Mail Surveys: Improving the Quality*. Thousand Oaks, Calif.: Sage.

Sapsford, R. (1999) *Survey Research*. London: Sage.

Surveys 12

Interviews

THIS CHAPTER

- addresses interviews as methods of data collection
- defines the types of interviews and their use
- explains the process of interviewing
- stresses the strengths, weaknesses and problems of interviewing.

KEY HEADINGS

INTRODUCTION

Interviewing – verbal questioning – is one of the most common methods of data collection. Interviews and questionnaires together make up the survey method, which is one of the most popular techniques of social research. Interviews are employed as methods of data collection in most research designs, regardless of the underlying methodology. Quantitative researchers employ mostly standardised or semi-standardised interviews. Feminist and qualitative researchers employ mostly unstandardised forms, such as intensive and focused interviewing.

This form of data collection, in its richness and diversity, will be addressed in this chapter.

1   DIVERSITY IN INTERVIEWS

1.1 Types of interviews

As noted in the previous chapter interviews are, in a way, questionnaires that are presented verbally; they are 'talking questionnaires'. More importantly, questionnaires constitute the structure of interviews. This is relevant to our discussion in two ways. First, the discussion of questionnaires in the previous chapter applies here also, so there is no need to discuss them again in this chapter. Second, the diversity of questionnaires is reflected in the diversity of interviews: they are as diverse as the underlying questionnaires.

However, the questionnaire structure is only one of the sources of diversity in interviews. Interviews differ also in purpose, the role of the interviewer, sample size and presentation, as we shall see.

Structured and unstructured interviews

Structured interviews employ structured questionnaires which are verbally presented to respondents, with the answers recorded in the questionnaire by the interviewer. When conducting a structured interview, strict adherence to the order and wording of the questions and the instructions is required. The interviewer is expected to perform almost 'like a robot', acting in a neutral manner, keeping the same tone of voice across the interviews, offering a consistent impression to the respondents, using the same style, appearance, prompts, probes and so on, and showing no initiative, spontaneity or personal interest in the research topic. Response categories are fixed and prescriptive. This serves to reduce interviewer bias to a minimum and achieve the highest degree of objectivity and uniformity in procedure. This form of interview is employed in quantitative research.

Unstructured interviews employ unstructured questionnaires (interview schedules) containing a number of open-ended questions, whose wording and order can be changed at will. The interviewer acts freely in this context, on the basis of certain research points, (re)formulating questions as required and employing neutral probing. The structure of the interview is flexible and the restrictions minimal, in most cases taking the form of guides rather than rules. This type of interview is mostly used in qualitative and feminist research.

Semi-structured interviews lie somewhere between the structured and unstructured types. They contain elements of both, with some being closer to structured interviews, and others closer to unstructured ones. The degree to which interviews are structured depends on the research topic and purpose, resources, methodological standards and preferences, and the type of information sought, which of course is determined by the research objective. They are employed in qualitative, feminist or quantitative research.

Delphi interviews

This is a version of the ethnographic interview, employing a multi-stage ethnographic approach. The interviewer questions persons who are experts in the area of study. In a Delphi interview, respondents are asked to offer information, pass judgements on the issue in question, and make relevant predictions. The researcher summarises this information in a logical and sociological context and offers a written summary to the experts for comments and discussion. Eventual comments or identified deviations are discussed and considered again, and the new summary is again handed to the key informants for extra comments. This process is continued until the differences of opinion among the experts are reduced significantly.

Originally the Delphi technique (also known as the deface poll) was used in the 1940s in war situations and was used to predict future events, hence the name the 'Delphi' method. The Delphi principle can also be used via questionnaires, ensuring the anonymity of the experts.

Other types of interview

There are many other types of interview which cannot be accommodated in this discussion. A selection of these interview types is given below.

- *Analytic interviews.* These are designed to analyse concepts and theories following a specific paradigm.
- *Biographical interviews.* These record a person's life history; they are also known as narrative interviews.
- *Convergent interviews.* These include two interviewers taking notes independently and writing a report together.
- *Diagnostic interviews.* These aim to ascertain specific attributes of the respondents.
- *Dilemma interviews.* These evaluate the subject's response to a problem (dilemma) presented by the interviewer.
- *Elite interviews.* Respondents are well-known, prominent people.
- *Ethnographic interviews.* Respondents include key informants or experts aiming to study (sub-)cultures.
- *Group interviews.* Several respondents are interviewed at one time.
- *Guided interviews.* The interviewer takes a guiding not a dominating role.
- *'Hard' interviews.* These are based on strict procedures; the interviewer views the responses with doubt and scepticism, and the interview resembles an interrogation.
- *Individual interviews.* Only one respondent is interviewed at a time.
- *'Inquiring' interviews.* The interviewee is seen as an equal informing partner.

- *Neutral interviews*. The interviewer is neutral, factual, encouraging, friendly but also distanced and impersonal.
- *Open interviews*. These allow flexibility and change in their structure and process.
- *Panel interviews*. These are conducted more than once, employing the same sample.
- *Problem-centred interviews*. These are focused on a particular problem; they are open, and the interviewee's critical contribution is valued.
- *Receptive interviews*. The interviewee is the actor and the interviewer an active-supportive listener (Kleining, 1988).
- *'Soft' interviews*. The interviewer assumes a guiding role only.
- *Telephone interviews*. Interviews are conducted via the telephone.
- *Unique interviews*. These interviews are conducted only once.

1.2 Interviews in qualitative research

In qualitative research, the most common interviews are the semi-structured and unstructured ones, and more generally those that comply fully with the standards and principles of qualitative research. The methodological parameters and technical elements of qualitative interviewing (see Farber, 2001; Lamnek, 1993: 21–9; Pannas, 1996) are briefly listed below.

- *Reflexivity*. Qualitative interviewing employs methods and a process of analysis in which researchers reflect upon their subjective approach to the world, and take into consideration the implications of the knowledge they produce for social life.
- *Naturalism*. Qualitative interviews are directed towards studying reality as it really is, in its own terms, and as it is manifest in everyday life events.
- *Primacy of the respondent*. The respondents are experts who provide valuable information. They are as important as the researcher and not just a source of data.
- *Absence of standardisation*. Qualitative interviews are unstandardised interviews, allowing freedom to respondents to express their views without external limitations.
- *Openness*. Qualitative interviews do not use a strictly standardised approach. Rather, they employ a readiness to change, to correct and adjust the course of study as required by the research. Interviewers are expected to engage in open discussion with the respondent, and to maintain a stimulating, but not dominating, role.
- *Flexibility*. The qualitative researcher follows the course that emerges through the interview.
- *Life as process*. Qualitative interviews ascertain aspects of personal experience as displayed in everyday life.
- *Grounded theory*. Qualitative interviews in most cases aim at developing a grounded (data-based) theory.
- *Explication*. Findings emerge through the study and are interpreted during the process of interviewing.

These methodological and technical aspects show that qualitative interviews are far from being a soft methodological option or an easy form of research. On the contrary, they require more competence on the part of the interviewer and higher ability on the part of the respondent to verbalise views, opinions and ideas (see, for example, Lamnek, 1993; Pannas, 1996: 76–9).

1.3 Interviews in feminist research

Feminist researchers follow the standards and principles of qualitative research, but with an added element: they focus on women as researchers and researched. Like qualitative research, feminist research considers interviewing a very useful method, values it for its openness, qualitative nature and interviewee-guided mode, and employs it predominately to facilitate social reform. Reinharz argues that interviewing is 'particularly suited to female researchers' and feels that it 'draws on skills in the traditional female role' (1992: 20). She goes on to say that this method is very useful when conducted by a woman; for a woman to be understood it may be necessary for her to be interviewed by a woman (ibid.: 23).

The interviews employed in feminist research are those employed within other paradigms, adjusted to comply with the guidelines of feminist research. More specifically, feminist interviews are characterised by criteria similar to those shown in Box 12.1 (Pfeifer, 2000; Punch, 2000).

Although most feminists agree with this notion of interviewing, there are researchers from within this paradigm who disagree. Feminist empiricism, feminist

Table 12.1 Comparison of quantitative and qualitative/feminist interviews

Criteria	Quantitative research	Qualitative/feminist
Nature of questions	Mostly structured/semi-structured	Mostly open
Order of questions	Prescriptive	Not binding
Interviewing assumes	The primacy of the interviewer	The primacy of the respondent
Interviews are controlled	By the interviewer	By no one
Interviewers usually are	Distant from the subject; uninvolved, objective and ethical	Close to the subject; engaged, subjective and ethical
Probing/prompting	Controlled	Not controlled
Duration of interviews	Relatively brief	Relatively long
Details of interviewing	Are set at the outset	Are guided by the situation
Interviewees per study	Usually many	Usually few
Overall structure	Rigid	Flexible
Presentation of questions	Uniform across respondents	As required; flexible
Number of interviewers	Usually many	Usually one
Nature of interviewing	Question-answer	Discussion
Sample	Random; constructed before the study, and cannot be changed	Not random; flexible; expanded during the study

Box 12.1

Criteria of feminist interviewing

Feminism:

- rejects the androcentric principles of the male paradigm when constructing and conducting interviews
- employs female interviewers, and mostly female respondents
- rejects the notion of researchers being detached from the researched and advocates rapport and reciprocity
- avoids power relationship between researchers and researched, applying non-hierarchical relationship
- does not use structured questionnaires, allowing for flexibility
- adheres to the principles of sensitivity, emotional engagement and personal involvement in interviewing
- encourages the use of values, openness, self-disclosure and reciprocity.

postmodernism and poststructuralism are three branches that have developed their own impressions of interviewing and feminist research in general. This point emphasises the wide scope of the feminist paradigm, and the wealth of information which it can produce.

2 THE INTERVIEWER

Before the interviews begin, the researcher will make a number of important decisions that will facilitate a frictionless conduct of the research. A brief summary of the quantitative interviewer's tasks are summarised in the next section.

Additional tasks may be added, or some of those mentioned may be refined, when conducting research within a certain paradigm. For instance, in quantitative studies interviewers control the interviewing situation, are distant and uninvolved; in qualitative research they are expected to avoid controlling the interview situation, to be close to the subject and to be engaged.

2.1 The tasks of the interviewer

The role of interviewers in research varies significantly from one paradigm to another. There are some central tasks, however, which interviewers perform irrespective of the underlying paradigm. The most common of these are listed below.

- approaching the respondents and arranging the time and date of the interview
- conducting the interview
- controlling/guiding the interview, complying with the underlying paradigm
- ensuring they do not to influence the way the respondent answers the questions

- recording the answers accurately
- establishing and maintaining positive relations with the public
- observing ethical standards.

Box **12.2**

Administrative tasks in structured interviewing

- Advertise for interviewers and supervisors.
- Print interview schedules.
- Select interviewers, supervisors and personnel.
- Train interviewers.
- Arrange work conditions, payment and duration of employment.
- Arrange pre-interview meeting with respondents (where required).
- Deal with refusals to take part in pre-interview meetings.
- Choose the time and place of the interview.
- Initiate the conduct of interviews.
- Deal with refusals to take part in the study.
- Arrange field supervision.
- Ensure proper conduct of interviews and adherence to ethics.
- Arrange the return of completed interviews to the researcher.
- Phone respondents randomly to verify completion of interviews.
- Check interviews for completeness, and eventual faults and errors.

2.2 Interviewer selection

Because interviewers are so important to the research, investigators employ a very systematic process when selecting them. The criteria usually considered significant are (see Becker, 1989; Benini, 2000; Berger et al., 1989):

- honesty, trustworthiness and self-control
- intelligence, maturity and friendliness
- sociability and social acceptability
- carefulness, conscientiousness and ability to concentrate
- accuracy and dependability
- objectivity, and lack of bias or prejudice
- adaptability, independence and initiative
- verbal ability and ability to listen to others carefully
- interest in and familiarity with the research topic
- ability to work with others in a team of experts.

The qualities which interviewers are expected to possess may vary from case to case and will depend on the type of interview employed. Qualitative interviewers, for instance, will adhere to most of the criteria introduced above but would also be required to demonstrate the attributes included in Box 12.3.

Depending on the nature of the study, additional criteria may be considered, and a number of those listed above may be adjusted. Rigorous selection is often required to identify the most promising candidates.

Box 12.3

Attributes of qualitative interviewers

- personal qualities (e.g. sensitivity, friendliness)
- knowledge of the topic and its context
- processing ability that would assist with understanding and interpreting meanings and responding accordingly
- interest in and commitment to the research
- clarity in speech and thought
- adaptability, independence and initiative
- initiative in exploring the respondent's mind
- creativity in asking questions and devising tasks that would interest the respondent
- experience with leading qualitative interviews
- personal and professional maturity that encourage trust and respect.

2.3 Interviewer training

After selection, interviewers usually undergo training, the degree and intensity of which depend on their existing skills and experience, as well as on the nature of the research topic. Training aims to address two major issues; first, to reduce bias and error-producing factors, and second to familiarise the interviewer with the essence of research, encouraging accuracy, clarity and inter-interviewer consistency. With regard to the first point, errors and bias can be associated with the following factors, which are to be addressed in training (see Farber, 2001; Pannas, 1996: 89–91):

- *Lack of skills.* The interviewer can influence the results through lack of administrative and professional ability, sloppiness, or through contacting the wrong person, omitting or misreading questions, reading them out of order, recording the wrong answers, misunderstanding the respondent, and leaving questions unanswered.
- *Misconduct.* The interviewer may intentionally alter or omit answers, reword questions, replace respondents, or cheat by not contacting the respondent but answering the questions personally.
- *Presentation.* The interviewer's own presentation may cause distortion and influence the data. Appearance, tone of voice, attitude to the respondent and the research, and reactions to answers or comments made are some examples.
- *Expectations.* The expectations interviewers have of the respondents, for example as a result of their appearance or living conditions, may influence the process and outcome of interviewing.
- *Probing.* The research can also be influenced by the interviewer's use of probing, that is, whether probing is done, where and when, and also whether it was carried out as instructed. Improper probing is a definite source of distortion which should be avoided.

Knowledge of the nature and source of errors combined with effective interviewer training help to eliminate problems and errors, and to strengthen attributes that are required for a successful completion of the interviews. The training usually includes features such as those shown below (see Martin, 1988; Vlahos, 1984).

- Developing and practising interviewing skills, mainly through observation, practice and criticism. Observation includes watching filmed and video-taped examples of interviews, or even actual interviews conducted by the trainees, followed by general evaluation.
- Learning how to present oneself to the respondents, appropriate manners in relation to the lifestyle of the subjects, presentation and appearance (including clothing, grooming etc.) and how to enter the interview situation without affecting the environment to be studied.
- Learning essential techniques of persuasion to convince uncooperative respondents to participate in the study and/or to encourage respondents to feel free to answer the questions as required.
- Acquiring knowledge and skills related to obtaining relevant information and recording the responses accurately.
- Establishing standards of value neutrality, ethics, anonymity and confidentiality (for quantitative researchers).

These practices are employed almost exclusively in quantitative research, with qualitative researchers being less strict in these procedures (and conducting research without the assistance of interviewers). These strict procedures have been criticised by some writers as a form of conditioning that biases the interviewer and restricts views and perceptions by guiding sensitivity and approach to preconceived concepts and predetermined paths and experiences.

3 THE PROCESS OF INTERVIEWING

In quantitative research, interviewing is conducted in a number of stages, with each stage including certain tasks. The various types of interview are conducted in different ways, but some commonalities can be identified in all forms of interviewing.

3.1 Finding respondents

In most cases, the interviewers are supplied with a list of the names and addresses of prospective respondents to approach. They will need to familiarise respondents with aspects of the research such as its purpose and sponsor, assure them of anonymity and confidentiality, explain other details of the research (e.g. duration and possible effects of the interview), seek their cooperation, and either conduct the interview or arrange for it to be conducted at another time.

The interviewer must be prepared to cope with failures to meet the prospective respondent and/or with refusals. The person may not be at home, may have moved away or died, be incapable of communicating or refuse to cooperate. In the latter case, the interviewer should be prepared to gain the respondent's trust by providing relevant evidence (e.g. ID card, reference letters, brief publications of previous studies), stress the significance of the research findings, and demonstrate the significance of the respondent's participation in the study.

Box **12.4**

Why do respondents *refuse* to be interviewed?

Respondents may, for instance,

- not be interested in the research topic
- not agree with the research objective
- not find the interviewer friendly, serious, or polite
- not have time for the interview
- not be sure of the real intentions of the interview
- not feel at ease with the interviewer, be suspicious or fearful
- not find the research consistent with their professional work/commitment
- not have the consent of their spouse, who may be against it.

(Becker, 1989; Puris, 1995)

Interviewers are more likely to win the respondents' cooperation if they know the reasons for them refusing to be interviewed as well for agreeing to do so. Using these factors correctly, fairly and ethically helps to succeed in the search for respondents.

Box **12.5**

Why do respondents *agree* to be interviewed?

The reasons for agreeing to be interviewed may be:

- *Interest.* They may be interested in talking about contemporary issues.
- *Need to talk.* There can be emotional relief through talking about one's problems.
- *Feeling important.* They may feel honoured to be chosen to speak on important issues.
- *Altruism.* They may see the interview as a way of contributing to the well-being of the community.
- *Compassion.* They may see value in helping interviewers 'to do their job'.
- *Politeness.* They don't want to disappoint the interviewer.
- *Curiosity.* They are interested in the research topic and in the process of interviewing.
- *Boredom.* 'I didn't have anything better to do at that time'
- *Sense of obligation.* They feel indebted to the sponsor or research agency.

Another responsibility of the interviewer is to arrange the place and time of the interview, when respondents cannot be interviewed on the day of contact. The interviewer may need to find a place that is stimulating, comfortable and conducive to quiet, private and relaxed talk, although if the interview is brief and simple it can be performed on a street corner or in front of a supermarket. Time is another significant factor. The rule here is that the interview should be conducted at the time most suitable to the respondents, a time when they can have an unhurried talk without disturbance.

3.2 Conducting the interview

The conduct of the interview – the manner in which questions are to be asked – depends very much on the type of interview. In structured interviewing the questions are asked exactly as instructed. In general, the interviewer is expected to show interest in the research topic and in the respondent, and should avoid bias, leading questions and suggestive questioning.

Recording too takes place as laid down in the instructions. In many cases this means ticking or crossing boxes on the interview schedule; in other cases responses are recorded verbatim, or at least at length. Open-ended questions may be recorded verbatim or summarised, as the research requires. The use of audiovisual equipment makes the work easier, but the respondent must be asked for approval (which by the way is equally important when notes are taken). Some respondents object to the interviewer taking notes and/or to speaking in front of a microphone.

3.3 Ending the interview

Care should be taken to end the interaction between the interviewer and the respondent smoothly and in a friendly atmosphere, in a spirit of trust, cooperation and mutual respect, so that the respondent feels that the contribution made to the research and to society in general has been appreciated. In many cases, the researcher lays down the way of ending the interview by providing a sample format that the interviewer has to memorise and use at the end of the session.

3.4 Field supervision and checks

Despite the strong involvement of interviewers in data collection, or perhaps because of this, its administration is not left entirely up to them. Supervision and checking are essential, particularly when more than one interviewer is employed. Some interviewers may not be as thorough as they should be, and cheating is always a possibility. Usually, the researcher or supervisor checks the returned interviews for completeness, too much or too little probing, and inadequate recording of the data. Apart from this, the supervisor contacts respondents randomly to ensure, first of all, whether the intended interview has taken place, and then whether it was conducted as planned. Checks for bias, honesty, politeness, objectivity, ethics and interviewer–respondent relationships are part of this procedure.

4 INTERVIEWER–RESPONDENT RELATIONSHIP

The type of relationship that develops between the interviewer and the respondent depends on factors such as background methodology, the research topic and objective and the style of interviewing. However, some common features of the relationship involve criteria that should be adhered to in all situations.

Background and appearance

Interviewers are chosen to match the respondents in aspects that are thought to make the respondents feel comfortable and at ease; these include social background, gender, race, ethnicity, age and personality. A good example is taken here from the feminist paradigm, which stresses emphatically that women can only be effectively studied by women. As we already know, feminist research has been seen as research not only about women but also by women.

The logic behind this is that successful interviews are associated with positive and effective relationships, and these grow where interviewers and respondents come from a similar background. Background similarity makes the entry to the respondent's world easier; promotes trust, understanding and cooperation; and allows the development of a close and rewarding relationship between the interviewer and the respondent. Further women are equipped with the female 'lens' that allows a more effective study of women than the lens of men. Clothing and grooming are also significant. The interviewer is expected to be dressed neutrally, ideally in a way similar to that of the respondent, and unobtrusively, so that the centre of the interview is the research topic and not the interviewer.

Status of the parties

Interviewers should avoid patronising the respondents, showing disbelief in statements given, or judging the answers. They should not appear as wise judges but rather as interested researchers who wish to learn from the respondents. Neither should they encourage or discourage certain types of answers. They should be neutral, receptive and eager to know the respondents' views, which for the interviewer are interesting and valuable.

The neutral, distant role of the researcher is not accepted by qualitative and feminist researchers. In particular, the assumption that the interviewer is the 'knower', the 'expert', the one who asks questions 'from above', while the interviewee is the 'knowee' or 'ignorant' party has been criticised by feminist researchers, who argue that the relationship between the two parties must be more egalitarian and more humanised (Reinharz, 1992; Westkott, 1990).

5 PROMPTING AND PROBING

Prompts and probes are very common in interviewing, either to make it easier for respondents to answer questions, or to encourage them to continue with their response. More specifically, a prompt is a part of a question that offers a list of possible answers, from which the respondent is expected to select one or more. An example is the question 'Which religious activities have you attended during the past four weeks?' with the respondent being read or shown a list of such activities to choose from. This makes answers to certain questions easier and more accurate. Prompts are usually developed after careful pre-tests and pilot studies.

Probes are questions or neutral statements that encourage the respondents to extend or amplify a partial, irrelevant or inaccurate response, and/or to stimulate and assist them to answer a question, without affecting the direction of their thinking and without causing bias or distortion. Probes are employed in interviews where open discussion is allowed, such as intensive interviewing. There are at least two types of probe: *non-directive probing* and the *summary technique* (see Pfeifer, 2000). Examples of probes are:

Controlled non-directive probing entails a specific but non-directive comment or question. For instance, when the respondent gives an incomplete, inadequate or general answer, the interviewer may comment: 'That's interesting, tell me more about it!', or 'What do you mean by that?' or 'What would be an example of that?', or 'I see', or just remain silent. The summary technique encourages respondents to continue their comment by summarising the respondents last statement and waiting for them to add new information. An example would be when the interviewer following, for instance, the respondent's silence adds: 'OK, this was the first step. . .', followed by silence.

Probing and prompting is an issue that deserves consideration and calls for discussion and control only in quantitative research. In other research contexts interviewers are free to employ any tactics to encourage discussion without having to account for them. The nature of the paradigm, the perception of objectivity and the value of inter-interviewer reliability are some of the factors that generate this difference

6 NARRATIVE INTERVIEW (NI)

6.1 Introduction

The theoretical and methodological bases of narrative interviews were developed by Schütze (1977, 1979, 1981, 1982, 1983, 1987). Their principles come from phenomenology and the philosophical branch of the Chicago School, but the research has been influenced mostly by the School's sociology branch. The narrative interview is both an interview and an autobiographic method of data collection. It is therefore also referred to as the autobiographic narrative interview, or simply autobiographic interview. It entails content analysis, and this helps it to make use of the advantages of three methods. For some writers (e.g. Maindok, 1996: 97), the narrative interview is the most highly developed interview technique.

The main distinguishing characteristics of narrative interviews relate to the nature of the interview situation and the role of the interviewer (Hermanns, 1991). Narrative interviews tend to be closer to life and more natural than quantitative ones, and assign a relaxed and casual role to the interviewer. More specifically, narrative interviews are a form of communication with people, and in this sense communication refers to everyday life situations and experiences (Schütze, 1983: 434). Hence, the interview is constructed as a natural communication process (Maindok, 1996: 110; Benini, 2000), whereby the interviewer listens, encourages the interviewee to continue with the story, and does not interfere, interrupt, distract or disturb the interviewee in any way.

The NI places a strong emphasis on the narrative, which is seen as a language game that relates closely to experiences of the storyteller. The narrative is thought to reflect the teller's thinking processes, cultural patterns and determinants that guide or even dominate his/her life choices. The NI allows the interviewee full freedom of expression without limits posed by questions, the interviewer, time or set conditions. Not being 'guided' by the interviewer, the interviewee can express any views, opinions and ideas and can concentrate on any points of the topic at will.

6.2 Process of interviewing

The process of narrative interviews entails three elements (Maindok, 1996: 111–13): the main story, the narrative inquiry and the conclusion. A more detailed description of the process of narrative interviews, based on the work of Schütze and of other writers (especially Pfeifer, 2000: 62–79; Lamneck, 1993: 71–2), is presented below.

Stage 1: Introduction

- The interviewee is introduced to the interview situation, and is familiarised with the expectations and overall framework of the interview, including ethical standards, anonymity, confidentiality and so on.
- The topic is introduced, outlined, and its dimensions explained in detail.
- The interviewer introduces a question that motivates the interviewee to talk about his/her personal life and experiences.
- Arrangements for (audio-video) recording the interview are made.
- The interviewer does not ask direct questions about motives, reasons, causes and the like; instead (s)he leaves it up to the informant to refer to such issues if (s)he comes to it as a part of the narrative.

Stage 2: Narrative

- The interviewee is encouraged through a specific stimulus to talk freely about life experiences. The interviewer here does not interfere, but remains an 'interested listener'; only making remarks that encourage the teller to continue, indicating that the interviewer is listening carefully. This is shown in brief verbal expressions and simple gestures. The interviewee chooses the events (s)he considers most relevant, expands on topics considered relevant and important, stops whenever necessary, presents events in order of importance or as the memory dictates, and is free to decide the order of presentation, the events to talk about (e.g. childhood, adulthood, present time, or pre-war, wartime and post-war years).
- The interviewee is encouraged not only to describe personal and social experiences but also to compare them with other experiences and to explain these events as (s)he understands them. The NI motivates and enables the teller to transport past events to the present, to become aware of the experiences, to travel back to the old times and to relive them once again through telling.

Stage 3: Questions

- When the interviewee indicates the end of the story, the interviewer can ask for more information where gaps have emerged, or for an explanation when statements were unclear, ambiguous or incomplete. A characteristic of this stage is that questions are asked to gain information and not to criticise or pass judgment; the process continues to be a part of the narrative, where the story teller offers his/her wisdom to the researcher.

- If new points surface that require further story-telling, the interviewee is encouraged to begin again talking about this topic, bringing the NI back to Stage 2. Only when this stage is fully exhausted, do they proceed to 'questions' and then to 'explanation'.

Stage 4: Explanation

- At this stage, and after the basic information has been fully described to the satisfaction of the interviewee and the interviewer, more direct questions are asked. Here the interviewee is asked, first, to establish more general and abstract views of the situation and its regularities, identifying recurring events, and developing abstractions and systematic interconnections; second, to describe more general aspects of the issue in question, being given the opportunity to demonstrate his/her capacity in assessing this as well as to offer a more abstract explanation of the situation; third, to explain motives and intentions; and finally, to discuss with the interviewer the meaning of the story.
- If new points surface that require further story-telling, the interviewee is encouraged to begin talking about this topic again, bringing the NI back to Stage 2. Only when this stage is fully exhausted, does the researcher move to the next step.

Stage 5: Analysis

- The narrative as well as the debate that follows are transcribed. The methods of transcription employed for this purpose are similar to those employed in any other interview, including numbering the text lines and so on, although with a difference. Here, as Pfeifer (2000: 71) notes, emphasis is placed on 'sound', focusing on vocal emphasis and nuance rather than on written forms. The transcript is expected to reproduce the nature of the discussion as it happened, including pauses, hesitations, fluctuation in the tone of the voice, speed of talk, emotionality and similar features. As a rule, the transcript is prepared by the interviewer, who has a good knowledge of the nature of the interview and the speech in particular.
- The transcribed text is subjected to content analysis. This is known as 'conversation analysis', which is central to this method of data analysis.

The process of analysis is very complex and very demanding, perhaps more demanding than in a simple quantitative structured interview. A more detailed, but still summarised and restricted description of this analysis is given later in this volume. What is important here is that complexity, diversity and intensity in this research model result in a high quality of findings, which is the reason for employing narrative interviewing.

7   INTENSIVE INTERVIEWING

This is an unstructured interview technique employed by social researchers as either the sole method of research or in addition to other methods. The technique is also known as 'in-depth' interviews (Minichiello et al., 1990). It is a very sophisticated technique, requiring adequate knowledge of the research topic, extensive experience of interviewing, and an ability to communicate effectively so as to establish and maintain trust and rapport with the respondents.

The format of intensive interviewing is unstructured and flexible. There are no specific questions to be asked. The interviewer is expected to develop the questions when they are required and as they best fit into the interview situation. For this reason, the actual formulation and order of the questions might differ from interview to interview. Intensive interviews are usually long and may extend over two or more sessions. As a research instrument they have strengths and weaknesses that researchers must be aware of.

Strengths of intensive interviewing

- the rapport in the relationship between the interviewer and the respondent, which makes the respondent feel important
- the degree of commitment of the parties and their interest in the relationship and discussion
- the unstructured process of interviewing and the opportunity to cover issues not covered in the interview schedule
- the flexibility, continuity of thought, freedom of probing, and evaluation of behaviour during the interview
- the high quality of information obtained
- the ability of the interviewer to use listening and empathy as significant tools of interaction.

Weaknesses of intensive interviewing

- dependence on the skills, values, standards and ideology of the interviewer
- inability to generalise the findings
- inability to facilitate comparisons between cases studied since the elements of the interview may differ from case to case
- high demand on time and resources.

Intensive interviews are conducted like any other interview, so the general rules of interviewing introduced above also apply here. The lack of strict boundaries and the freedom of choice in the formulation of questions and the order of their presentation, as well as the primary focus on the interviewee, transform the general rules of interviewing accordingly, and also guide the process of interviewing to a path that leads closer to the world of the interviewee.

8 TELEPHONE INTERVIEWING

Telephone interviewing demonstrates the same structural characteristics as standard interviewing techniques, except that it is conducted by telephone. Although this difference might not appear to be very significant, it does have certain effects on some aspects of the research process (Frey, 1989). In the first instance, questions have to be constructed in a way that will allow a clear understanding of their content when presented over the telephone. Also, telephone interviews cannot be as lengthy as face-to-face ones. Finally, they have to be introduced in a manner that, on the one hand, will encourage the respondent to take part in the study and, on the other hand, will meet ethical standards. This in turn strengthens the chances of a prospective respondent agreeing to be interviewed. Such introductions contain information similar to that included in cover letters of mail questionnaires.

Telephone interviewing is employed when the interviews are simple and brief, when quick and inexpensive results are sought, when it is not necessary to approach the respondent face to face, and when sampling inaccuracies (e.g. non-subscribers and unlisted numbers) are not considered important. Where appropriate, this type of interviewing offers many advantages (e.g. Benini, 2000; Mahr, 1995), but also some limitations.

Advantages of telephone interviewing

- is less labour-intensive than other methods
- allows the study of relatively large samples
- is relatively economical
- produces quick results
- allows more open communication since the respondent is not confronted with the interviewer
- reduces bias since factors such as race, ethnicity, appearance and age do not influence the respondents
- offers more anonymity than other techniques, particularly when random-digit-dialling techniques are used.

Limitations of telephone interviewing

- high refusal rate
- inability to determine the identity of the respondent
- limited access to research topics
- relative inability to control the interview fully
- limited access to target population (people without a telephone or with unlisted numbers are not accessible).

Despite these problems, the advantages outweigh the weaknesses of this method, which is a very useful and popular technique of data collection.

9 THE INTERVIEW CONTEXT

Interviewing is not a straightforward process in which the interviewee freely surrenders information as required by the questions. Giving answers is a process that is affected by many situational factors, which can affect whether an answer is forthcoming as well as the truthfulness of the response. The nature of the topic, the interviewer and the interview situation are some of these factors. The latter may include aspects such as the way in which the question is presented, the environment in which interviewing takes place and the extent to which the questions allow comments and interpretation. For instance, an interview regarding drug use by teenagers will produce different results when conducted in the schoolyard, at home in the presence of parents, or in the police station.

One question that needs further elaboration is about the ways in which the interview situation can affect the probability of obtaining answers to interview questions, and the truthfulness of the answers. The intervening factors here may be related to the respondent's willingness and ability to give a truthful answer. Knowing these factors, the interviewer can achieve more, better and more accurate results. Writers on the subject (Pfeifer, 2000; Laatz, 1993) consider the following factors to be relevant.

- *Understanding the question*. The clearer the question, the more likely it is to receive an answer. Understanding can be hampered by factors associated with the interviewer, such as the tone of voice adopted, which may divert the respondent's attention, as well as conceptual factors, such as taking the question in general rather than in specific terms, and the respondent's capacity to understand its literal or conceptual content.
- *Cognitive processing*. Normally, messages are processed, connected with data held in the memory, and direct the respondent to the correct answer. Then the interviewees evaluate the suitability of the answer in terms of the accuracy of the response, as well as the expected assessment of the answer within attitudes, opinions, experiences, and facts. Finally, pieces of information will be put together to form a response. This process can be affected by the manner and context in which the question is presented, by the fact that they feel obliged to give an answer, and other similar factors.
- *Precision*. Questions requiring a high level of precision are more likely to produce inaccurate answers. This can be due to lack of knowledge and of access to relevant information required to answer the question. This, apart from anything else, may affect the self-esteem of the respondent, which in turn might have an impact on the remaining part of the interview.
- *Authority*. Respondents are least likely to offer truthful answers to sensitive questions when a person in authority (employer, parent, spouse, teacher, police officer etc.) is present. Neutral environments should be considered.
- *Social standards*. Respondents usually do not give answers that violate general social standards. They weigh the suitability of their answers against social expectations, and give an answer which will not transgress social or other standards and hence, in their view, will not receive negative social evaluation. Hence, there may be cases where the researcher receives socially desirable but not necessarily correct answers. It is therefore important that the interviewer and the researcher ensure that sensitive questions are formulated in a manner that neutralises external factors in interviewing. Three factors are of particular importance. These are: social desirability, relating to cultural norms and values; situational expectancy, relating to contextual requirements and expectations; and the role of the interviewee, relating to the perceived roles within the interview setting, such as the definition of the interviewer and interviewee and the implied boundaries.

- *Decision bias.* Respondents are confronted with a series of situations in which they have to make important decisions. These decisions direct performance in interviews and this can result in an unavoidable bias, such as conformity bias, preference bias, adjustment bias or incompleteness. The respondent answers correctly when the answer entails no bias and no high personal or social costs.

There are many more cases in which the interview situation can cause problems and distortions. Additional examples of such cases will be referred to later in this chapter. The rule in these and similar circumstances is that the interviewer and the researcher in general should construct the interview in such a way that it will avoid placing respondents in a situation that will compromise their position, and hence the truthfulness of their answers.

10 ADVANTAGES AND LIMITATIONS OF INTERVIEWING

Interviewing is so commonly used in the social sciences that it is quite often considered to be *the* method of social research. Despite criticisms (Reinharz, 1992), its popularity is often justified in terms of its various qualities, which give it an advantage over other methods of data collection. A brief list of its advantages and limitations is given below (see Pfeifer, 2000; Mahr, 1995; Roth, 1987):

Advantages

- *Flexibility.* Interviews can be adjusted to meet many diverse situations.
- *High response rate.* Interviewing attracts a relatively high response rate.
- *Easy administration.* Interviews do not require respondents to have the ability to read or to handle complex documents or long questionnaires.
- *Opportunity to observe non-verbal behaviour.* Such opportunities are obviously not available when questionnaires or indirect methods are used.
- *Less tedium.* Less patience and motivation is required than in other methods. Interviews need 'participation', not just 'response'. Participation involves another person with whom the respondent interacts to complete the task; hence interviewing is often perceived as a cooperative venture rather than a one-sided exercise.
- *Control over the environment.* Here the interviewer has an opportunity to control the conditions under which the questions are answered.
- *Capacity for correcting misunderstandings by respondents.* Such an option is very valuable and not available in other forms of data collection, such as questionnaires.
- *Control over the order of the questions.* Respondents have no opportunity to know what question comes next or to alter the order of the questions they answer. When the order of the questions is significant, an interview is much more useful than a questionnaire.

- *Opportunity to record spontaneous answers.* The respondent does not have as much time available to answer questions as when questionnaires are employed. When spontaneity is important, interviews offer a real advantage over other methods.
- *Control over the identity of the respondent.* When interviews are employed, the identity of the respondent is known; this is not so when other methods (e.g. questionnaires) are used.
- *Completeness.* The fact that the interviewer presents the questions guarantees that all questions will be attempted and the interview will be complete.
- *Control over the time, date and place of the interview.* Interviews can be conducted exactly as planned, regarding the time and date, and according to specified conditions. Such a guarantee cannot be given when questionnaires are used.
- *Ability to handle complexity.* More complex questions can be used because the presence of the interviewer can assist in answering them.
- *Length.* Greater length is possible in interviewing than when other methods (e.g. questionnaires) are used.

Limitations

- *Cost.* Interviews are more costly and time consuming than some other methods, such as questionnaires.
- *Bias.* Interviews are affected by the 'interviewer' factor and the possible bias associated with it.
- *Inconvenience.* Interviewing is less convenient than other methods, such as questionnaires.
- *Lack of anonymity.* It offers less anonymity than other methods since the interviewer knows the identity, residence, type of housing, family conditions and other personal details of the respondent.
- *Sensitivity.* It is less suitable than other methods when sensitive issues are discussed. For example, many people prefer to write about sensitive issues rather than to talk about them.

Apart from these limitations, interviewing is affected by factors common to other techniques of data collection, including deliberate misrepresentation of facts, genuine mistakes, unwillingness or inability to offer information and similar problems. It is easier to detect such problems when interviewing than when using other methods. A more detailed presentation of some important problems of interviewing are presented in the next section.

11   PROBLEMS AND ERRORS IN INTERVIEWING

Interviewing can be affected by many and diverse problems and errors. Problems associated with the nature of the method include data recording, evaluation errors and instruction errors. The following lists contain a few examples of such errors, as identified by Berger et al. (1989: 228–31).

Recording errors

- selective hearing or vision
- misunderstanding of the respondent
- too-early or too-late registration of the responses
- incomplete, faulty or illegible responses.

Evaluation errors

- *leniency effect*, when extremely negative responses are avoided
- *severity effect*, when extremely positive responses are avoided
- *projection effect*, when personal prejudice and stereotypes are projected onto the respondent, affecting perception and evaluation of responses
- *contact effect*, when loss of objectivity caused by knowing the respondent leads to a mild evaluation of responses
- *central tendency effect*, when the researcher tends to avoid recording extreme responses
- *reference-group effect*, when the researcher develops expectations related to the reference group of the respondent and judges the responses according to these expectations, examples being:
  - *the grandpa effect*, expecting too little from the respondent
  - *the authority effect*, feeling intimidated by the respondent's position of authority
  - *the Santa Claus effect*, expecting more or too much from the respondent (e.g. treating people thought to be more intelligent or sympathetic in a more forthcoming and understanding way etc.)
  - *the identification effect*, generating errors associated with the researcher's tendency to identify with the respondent and therefore treat him or her more mildly, and vice versa.

Instruction errors

- replacing non-responses with another person's responses
- withholding information collected
- introducing changes in procedure against the researcher's instructions , for example changing questions or the order of the questions
- forgery of parts of the data
- showing consent or rejection of responses while collecting data.

These shortcomings are by no means unique to interviews; they may occur in any other method. It is important that the researcher is able to recognise the areas in which such errors can arise, be aware that they may occur, and take appropriate measures to avoid them.

12 NON-RESPONSE IN INTERVIEWING

Unwillingness and/or inability to take part is a serious problem for all types of interviews, but more so for those used in quantitative research, where sampling is strict and deterministic, and where replacement of respondents is not permitted. It is true that approaching the respondents persistently until they relent is reported to be a relatively successful method of combating non-response. Offering rewards to 'difficult' respondents is another. On the whole, however, non-response remains a problem, and researchers employ a variety of techniques to prevent it or to restore full response. Many of the suggestions made with regard to questionnaires are also applicable in the context of interviews. In addition, when interviews are employed, it is suggested (e.g. Becker, 1989; Berger et al., 1989; Pfeifer, 2000; Puris, 1995) that consideration of issues such as the following may prove helpful:

- *Approach*. The more personal, honest, brief and pleasant the approach when visiting the respondent for the first time, the more likely it is that the respondent will participate in the study.
- *Explanation*. The clearer and fuller the explanation of the survey, including the sponsor, purpose, time required, anonymity and confidentiality, the more likely it is that the respondent will agree to take part in the study.
- *Appeal*. The more appealing and attractive the presentation of the study, and the more challenging and inviting the description of the topic, the more likely it is that the respondent will agree to be interviewed.
- *Honesty*. The more honest, polite, frank, reassuring and modest the researcher, the more likely it is that the respondent will take part in the study.
- *Respect*. The more respected the respondent feels in his or her role as an 'expert' to be consulted rather than as just a source of information, the more likely it is that the interview will take place.
- *Trust*. The more successful the researcher is in eliminating mistrust, insecurity, fears, confusion, doubts and ambiguity, the more likely the respondent is to agree to take part in the study.
- *Impression*. The more impressed the respondent is with the overall sincerity and appearance of the study, the more likely it is for the interview to take place.
- *Arrangements*. The more favourable and convenient the interview arrangements are for the respondent, and the more considerate the approach (e.g. phoning before visiting), the more likely it is for the interview to be completed.
- *Friendliness*. The more friendly and discreet the researcher, the more likely it is for the respondent to agree to be interviewed.
- *Sponsors*. Interviews conducted for the government, universities or other institutions are more likely to attract the cooperation of the respondent than interviews conducted for other sponsors or for the personal interest of the interviewer.
- *Purpose*. The more worthwhile the purpose of the interview, the more likely it is for the respondent to agree to be interviewed.

In brief, the most successful way of reducing the non-response rate is prevention. Knowing how respondents react to elements of the questionnaire or the survey helps researchers to plan its structure so that non-response can be significantly reduced.

13 INTERVIEWING IN THE COMPUTER AGE

New developments in the field of IT have had a positive impact on the practice of interviewing. Interviews can now be held between the interviewee and a computer, and where researchers are also present, their input is often restricted to giving instructions and to helping the respondent. The following are some examples of computer packages that are relevant to interviewing.

- *Computer-aided personal interview (CAPI)*. In CAPI, questioning and control of the responses is done through the computer. In this case, the interviewee, sitting in front of the computer, reads the questions appearing on the screen, and enters the responses as advised. The computer processes the responses automatically and prepares them for analysis. This program can be used by single interviewees or with a group of respondents. The researcher simply notes the identity of the respondents, leads them to the computer, and after completion of the computer entry, makes the usual closure of the session.
- *Computer-driven self-completion interview (CODSCI)*. This is a fully automated interviewing program in which there is no need for a human interviewer. The interview is carried out in a computer session in which the respondent reads the questions from the screen in direct communication with the computer; the computer 'asks' the questions, explains problems and provides help in answering the questions. After completion of the interview, the responses are saved automatically in the memory and added to previous interview data.
- *Computer-aided telephone interview (CATI)*. Here the computer is used by the interviewer, who reads the questions to the interviewee over the telephone as they appear on the screen and records the response in the computer. The computer can do more than just present the questions and receive the answers. It can draw the sample, choose the telephone number, dial the respondent through a self-dial system and 'connect' the interviewer with the interviewee.
- *Computer-integrated survey research (CISUR)*. This fully integrated computer program is more advanced than the previous ones in that it contains more functions in a wider area of the research process. This is another example of how computers are entering areas of research above and beyond the statistical analysis of data, gradually replacing the human element.
- *'The data collector'*. This program works on the same principles as the others and has similar goals and functions. Although a data collection device, it has additional features that make it a useful tool for social researchers. The program assists with the development of questionnaires and interview schedules, and provides measures for quantitative data analysis, such as descriptive statistics, frequency distributions, chi-square, analysis of variance, Mann-Whitney tests and correlations (r, rho and lagged correlations), as well as for qualitative analysis, for instance word counts, word/phrase searches and a variety of other options for searching text.

There are many more computer programs employed in this field. The few listed above are only examples of what computers can offer when interviewing is the method of data collection.

14 SURVEY METHODS IN COMPARISON

It has often been asked which survey method is the most appropriate. The correct answer is that all methods are effective and useful depending on the type of information required. They all are suitable for certain topics, certain respondents and certain types of information. Table 12.2 offers a brief overview of the characteristics of these survey methods.

Table 12.2 A Comparison of face-to-face, telephone and mail surveys

Major considerations	Types of surveys		
	Face-to-face	Telephone	Mail
Access to respondents	Limited only by hearing or speech impairment or disability	As in face-to-face plus no access to phone, or unlisted numbers	Limited by disability, or illiteracy
Length of questionnaire	Long	Medium	Short
Complexity of questionnaire	High	High	Low
Addressing sensitive topics	Fair	Good	Good
Response rate	Very high	High	Low
Completion time	High	Low	High
Interviewer bias	High	Moderate	Nil
Control over respondent's identity	Very high	Low	Very low
Allowed complexity of instrument	Very high	Moderate	Very high
Opportunity to probe	Very high	High	Nil
Asking sensitive questions	Least suitable	Just suitable	Most suitable
Costs	Very high	Moderate	Low
Inconvenience	High	Moderate	Low

MAIN POINTS

- Interviews are orally conducted surveys, are very common and appear in many and diverse forms.
- Interviews can be structured or unstructured, standardised or unstandardised.
- Interviews are conducted by an interviewer face-to-face with the respondent or by telephone.

- In qualitative research, interviews are single and personal, employ open-ended questions and are open and flexible.
- Choosing interviewers who are similar in background to the respondents not only makes entry into the respondents' world easier but also promotes trust, mutual understanding and cooperation and therefore reduces bias and distortion.
- Telephone interviewing produces quick results, can study large samples, is relatively economical, promotes open communication, reduces bias and guarantees more anonymity than face-to-face interviews.
- Errors in interviewing may be associated with inappropriate recording of data or evaluation of responses, or with failure to follow instructions given to interviewers.
- Interviews are employed in quantitative and qualitative research, although in different forms.
- Narrative interviews introduce a topic for discussion and encourage the respondent to offer as much information as possible. They are becoming increasingly popular and are mostly used by qualitative researchers.
- Intensive interviews are mostly unstructured and unstandardised, aiming at an in-depth exploration of the issues in question.

WHERE TO FROM HERE?

Before you leave this chapter, visit the companion website for the third edition of *Social Research* at http://www.palgrave.com/sociology/sarantakos to review the main concepts introduced in this chapter and to test yourself on the major issues discussed.

FURTHER READING

Adams, S. (2001) *Interviewing for Journalists*. London: Routledge.

De Vaus, D. (2002) *Surveys in Social Research*. London: Routledge.

Frey, J. H. and Oishi, S. M. (1995) *How to Conduct Interviews by Telephone and in Person*. Thousand Oaks, Calif.: Sage.

Gubrium, J. F. and Holstein, J. A. (eds) (2001) H*andbook of Interview Research: Context and Method*. Thousand Oaks, Calif.: Sage.

Keats, D. (1993) *Skilled Interviewing*. Hawthorn, Victoria: ACER.

Kvale, S. (1996) *InterViews: An Introduction to Qualitative Research Interviewing*. Thousand Oaks, Calif.: Sage.

Lavrakas, P. (1993) *Telephone Survey Methods: Sampling Selection and Supervision*. Beverley Hills: Sage.

Merton, R. K., Fiske, M. and Kendall, P. L. (1990). *The Focused Interview: A Manual of Problems and Procedures* (2nd edn). London: Collier MacMillan.

Rubin, H. J. and Rubin, I. S. (1995) *Qualitative Interviewing: The Art of Hearing Data*. Thousand Oaks, Calif.: Sage.

Riessman, C. K. (1993) *Narrative Analysis*. Newbury Park, Calif.: Sage.

13 The study of documents

Researchers study documents as much as – if not more than – people. They do so either in conjunction with or instead of studying people. More specifically, the study of documents takes the form of a literature review or a more in-depth study of the documents. In either case, this study deals with data produced by writers and researchers other than those studying the documents, and for a purpose that is possibly different from that of the original writer.

In this chapter we shall concentrate on document studies and content analysis, before we proceed further with text analysis, where discourse analysis, hermeneutics and postmodernism will be addressed.

INTRODUCTION

Documentary methods appear in a variety of forms, addressing the whole range of documents, from documents as the unit of analysis to texts. The following are the most common:

- *Document study*. Here the focus of analysis is on description, identification of trends, frequencies and interrelationships, and, sometimes, statistical analysis. Examples of document study are: basic analysis, producing mostly summaries of factual information; biographical research; and secondary analysis of a statistical nature, including also meta-analysis.
- *Content analysis*. This implies more complicated and sophisticated analysis. The research focuses on the manifest or latent content of documents, in a very detailed and analytical way, or on meanings. Both allow conclusions to be made on issues that are beyond the text and language. Although this method is conducted within a quantitative paradigm, it can also be used within a qualitative context.
- *Text analysis*. This approach sees text as a 'virtual reality' and the 'world as text', and, using methods such as semiotics, discourse analysis and hermeneutics, reaches the ultimate point of analysis, going far above the level other methods can reach.

The most common sources of data for secondary analysis are data archives and official statistics, which in most countries are also available electronically. Overall, the kind of documents used in this context are:

- public documents, namely census statistics, statistical year-books, court archives, prison records and literature (novels, poetry etc.)
- archival records, such as service records of hospitals, doctors and social workers, and records of organisations, as well as official statistics
- mass media outputs, such as printed media, films, and radio and television programmes (transcribed or live)
- personal documents, such as life histories, diaries, memoranda, confessions, autobiographies, suicide notes, letters, and visual objects
- administrative documents, such as proposals, memoranda, progress reports, agendas, minutes of meetings, announcements and other internal documents
- formal studies and reports.

There are at least three ways of gaining access to such sources (Cooper, 1998). First, there are informal channels, such as personal contact, personal solicitation and the World Wide Web. There are also formal channels, such as professional conference paper presentations, journal libraries, electronic journals and research report reference lists. Finally, secondary channels include texts such as research bibliographies, prospective research registers and reference databases. Particularly since the popularisation of electronic media and the Internet, and the spread of personal computers, access to documents has increased, linking the researcher with databases from all parts of the world. The introduction of freedom of information legislation has expanded the coverage of documents, which now extends to almost every aspect of social life. In addition, the unobtrusive and non-reactive nature of such documents (see Burgard and Lueck, 1991; Kellehear, 1993; Lee, 2000; Webb et al. 2000) adds to their popularity.

1 DOCUMENT STUDIES

1.1 Basic analysis

Before analysis can be conducted, the researcher must go through two steps. The first is the selection of the topic and the methodology. This entails a decision as to what is to be studied, and which methodology will guide the research. The other concerns sampling procedures. This refers to the choice of documents that will be considered in the analysis, such as books, journals, newspapers and diaries, as well as their location, time reference (e.g. *Time Magazine*, 1999 and 2000), and the method of selection.

The actual analysis of the documents varies according to the nature of the content as well as the purpose of the study. Within the confines of the document analysis, the researcher aims to capture predominantly surface impressions, sometimes with and sometimes without previous planning and preparation. The following are a few examples of the kind of approach that is employed in document analysis.

- *Descriptive analysis.* This is rather elementary and entails summarising data, identifying main trends and presenting descriptions. An example of a suitable topic is: 'How did the media respond to the recent amendment to the Freedom of Information Act?'
- *Categorical analysis.* This is a more systematic analysis, based on categories constructed before the commencement of the study. Its purpose is to identify and define diversity rather than to aid quantitative analysis. An example of a suitable topic is: 'How was power distributed between husbands and wives in the families of the 1950s?'
- *Exploratory analysis.* This searches for peculiarities, characteristic attributes and trends in the text that mark the identity of the message conveyed through the document. It involves identifying data, comparing them, weighing their relevance and significance, and recording them systematically. The integrated and interpreted image of the document will be presented in the conclusion. An example of a suitable topic is: 'How did women's magazines portray family life in the 1950s?'

- *Comparative analysis.* This compares social issues across times, countries and cultures. The analysis is very basic and emerges from reading the documents, often presenting the results separately for each point of comparison. Examples of suitable topics are: 'What were the attitudes of the students to gay marriage in England and Japan?' or 'What were the Sunday activities of mothers in the 1950s and 1990s in Australia?'

Researchers may use these methods to inquire about life styles, customs, trends, practices and so on of past times, thus establishing either a representation of life as lived at certain times in the past, or chronological or cultural comparisons. They can, however, be employed as a means of providing detailed information on a specific topic, before proceeding further with a study.

1.2 Biographical research

The biographical method refers to the study of personal and biographical documents that intentionally or unintentionally offer information about the structure, dynamics and function of the author's consciousness; in a way, it reconstructs the construction of life (Bude, 1984). Relevant documents are diaries, memoirs, autobiographies, letters, witness statements and other sources of a personal nature. As a systematic approach in the social sciences, this method was used for the first time by Thomas and Znaniecki (1958) in their famous study of Polish people, and by Shaw (1930) in his study of juvenile delinquency. Such studies opened the way for this form of research to become an established method of social inquiry (Fuchs, 1984).

As qualitative studies, biographical methods focus on two points (Friedrichs, 1987; Lamnek, 1993), namely:

- The author's definition of self and of social action, which reflects the way this person perceives and interprets the world in its totality. The point of analysis is not the individual but rather the biography (Fischer and Kohl, 1987: 26; Voges, 1987).
- The social regulation of individuality (Lamnek, 1993). This is based on the assumption that the way authors explain their subject reveals information about their lives; it also indicates the way in which they perceive reality, the relations between their opinions and their social environment, the influence reality has on their life and actions and, most importantly, the social origin of their individuality. It is proposed here that individual narrations are constructed by society (Hildebrand et al., 1984: 29; Kohli,1987; Kohli and Robert, 1984), and thus they allow an insight into the process of constructing individuality. In this sense, biographical methods facilitate the identification of determinants of individuality.

Biographical research employs a variety of methods. Examples of such methods are given below:

- *The holistic method.* A document is studied in its entirety with the aim of identifying elements relevant to the research objective. Analysis is based on the overall image of the document.

- *The particularistic method.* This concentrates on one or more specific aspects of the document.
- *The descriptive method.* This aims to establish associations between variables and test dependencies and relationships.
- *The comparative method.* Biographies are compared so as to identify similarities and differences.
- *The classification method.* This focuses on establishing and classifying categories.
- *Content analysis.* This is employed to analyse the manifest (clear and obvious) and/or latent content of the biographical documents. The former relates to the obvious, literary content of the document and the latter to hidden meanings, lying beneath the surface and 'requiring reading between the lines'.
- *Contextual analysis.* Here documents are studied in order to understand cultural and social contexts.

It goes without saying that since the biographical method belongs to the broader category of documentary studies, all methods employed in documentary analysis are suitable for biographical studies.

1.3 Secondary analysis

Secondary analysis deals with data gathered by researchers, public institutions or government authorities. Researchers produce data on specific issues that are of interest to other investigators, particularly for their content and possibilities for analysis, which the original researchers might have not attempted. This type of document study focuses primarily on archival data such as those maintained by various institutions holding survey data or census data. It employs primarily quantitative research and statistical analysis, but qualitative analysis is equally possible.

More attractive to researchers is the use of data collected, analysed and archived by public and government authorities, which not only cover extensive areas (and hence are relatively representative), but also lend themselves to comparisons and are longitudinal. In this sense, researchers can address questions relating to trends and developments in certain areas by focusing on such data.

Apart from these sources, researchers have access to archives of data produced by individual researchers, organised by various institutions, which make them available to interested persons on request (often for a fee). Over all, easy access to such sources, and in particular their accessibility via the Internet, makes secondary analysis easy, speedy, inexpensive and effective.

1.4 Meta-analysis

The term *meta-analysis* was coined by Gene Glass (1976) but Karl Pearson employed the procedure much earlier, when examining the effectiveness of vaccines against typhoid. Since then, meta-analysis became relatively popular among social researchers (Cook et al., 1992; Hunter, 1990; Mann, 1990; Wells and Rankin, 1991).

Meta-analysis is a type of secondary analysis of results relating to a specific topic. In effect, it converts the results of a number of studies to a common measure, so that their findings can be compared and integrated into a common

Box **13.1**

Criteria of secondary analysis

Secondary analysis:

- is concerned with analysing already collected data within another study
- implies that the previously collected data were fully processed and analysed
- studies existing data and produces new and more detailed information, and different conclusions than the original report
- addresses aspects of the issue that are different from those of the original author
- employs sophisticated methods that can reveal trends not accessible to common sense
- employs quantitative or qualitative methods
- focuses on 'private' or official sources of data
- is 'secondary' because it analyses data for the second time.

conclusion. It is like converting the average annual income of bus drivers in Austria, Japan, England, Peru and Israel, as given by the official census statistics of these countries (in their own currencies), into euros in order to be able to compare them. Without this conversion, a comparison is not possible. Meta-analysis guides researchers as to how to transform existing results given in different units so that they can 'speak the same language', and hence become more meaningful.

Let us consider another example. A researcher is interested in the effects of divorce on children. Although several studies have been conducted on this subject, and hence adequate results are available, the nature of the findings vary, and so do their measures. In their current format, they cannot identify a clear trend in this area. There is an obvious need to standardise the findings, so that they become comparable. Meta-analysis will convert the various figures produced by the previous studies to a common measure, and hence allow proper comparisons and conclusions about the research subject.

Like any other method, meta-analysis has its critics (Wachter, 1988), who are mainly concerned with the way conclusions are drawn from diverse and often incompatible methods, samples and environments. First of all, it is noted that meta-analysis is sensitive to the type of studies included in the sample and the way they are chosen. But apart from this, it is argued that the individuality of the sample studies is ignored and so are the conditions under which they were conducted (e.g. quality of samples, quality of research, quality of design). Often studies are not comparable. As a result, the units included in the individual studies can be different, and therefore a meta-analysis may relate to an artificially constructed sample of incompatible and different units, which cannot be drawn together in a logical context, and thus do not allow valid conclusions.

1.5 Strengths and weaknesses of document studies

A brief list of the most common advantages and limitations of documentary methods is given below (see Berger et al., 1989; Puris, 1995; Pfeifer, 2000).

Box **13.2**

What is meta-analysis?

Meta-analysis is a method that aims to integrate the findings of a number of studies of the same subject and to draw conclusions as to the direction of their findings. This is facilitated by standardising results expressed in different measures, and so facilitating comparisons and a collective analysis (Kulik and Kulik, 1992). In technical terms, meta-analysis transforms the different metrics of the various studies to a common measure 'such as Z's and one-tailed probability levels for significance and product-moment correlations, Fisher's Z's, and Cohen's ds for effect size' (Mullen and Miller, 1991: 429) allowing valid conclusions.

Strengths

- *Retrospectivity.* Documentary methods enable researchers to study past events and issues.
- *Quick and easy access.* Documentary research is free of the restrictions, difficulties and problems faced by other researchers who deal directly with people. Researchers do not encounter rejection, non response, bias, or any other respondent-based problems.
- *Spontaneity.* In most cases, documents are produced by the writers without being requested to do so by researchers. This reduces researcher bias significantly.
- *Convenience.* The researchers can study the research question at any time and for as long as they wish, and ask any kind of question they can think of, without the limitations and considerations that are evident in research contexts such as interviewing or observation.
- *Low cost.* Documentary research is more economical than most other types of research.
- *Less time consuming.* The research involves less time for data collection than other research models. The availability of documents electronically and through the Internet makes these tasks even easier.
- *Sole source.* Documents are often the only source of information (e.g. when studying past events).
- *High quality of information.* Dealing with first-hand original data allows the production of high quality findings.
- *Possibility of re-testing.* Given that documents are easily accessible, replication is possible.
- *Non-reactivity.* The method itself and the act of measurement do not affect the results.

Weaknesses

- *Lack of representativeness.* Documents are not necessarily representative of their kind and thus do not allow generalisations
- *Lack of accessibility.* Some documents are not easily accessible (private letters, diaries etc.).

- *Incomplete data.* Some documents are not complete or up to date.
- *Reliability.* The reliability of some documents is questionable.
- *Comparability.* Comparisons between documents are not always possible.
- *Methodological questions.* They demonstrate methodological problems, such as coding problems and state of presentation.
- *Personal bias.* Documents may be biased, since they represent the view of their authors.

Despite their limitations, documentary methods are a very useful tool of social research and an indispensable one, particularly when the research is focused on past events. In such cases documentary methods are the only way of collecting data on this issue.

2 CONTENT ANALYSIS

2.1 Introduction

As a method of social research, content analysis is a documentary method that aims at a quantitative and/or qualitative analysis of the content of texts, pictures, films and other forms of verbal, visual or written communication. This analysis may be related to forms of communication, intentions of the communicator, techniques of persuasion, text style, the audience and motives, attitudes or values. Feminists, for instance, have investigated women's issues by focusing on documents such as children's books, fairytales, billboards, feminist fiction and non-fiction, children's artwork, fashion, girl scout handbooks, works of fine art, newspaper rhetoric,

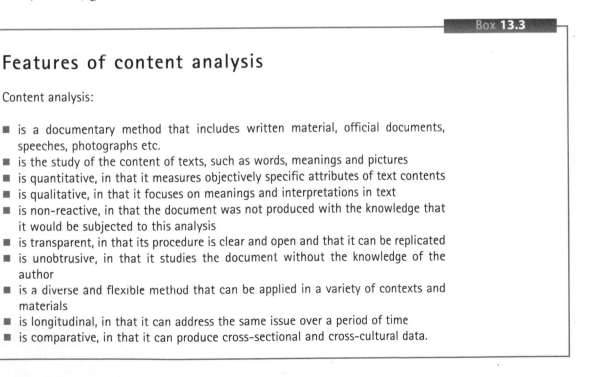

Box **13.3**

Features of content analysis

Content analysis:

- is a documentary method that includes written material, official documents, speeches, photographs etc.
- is the study of the content of texts, such as words, meanings and pictures
- is quantitative, in that it measures objectively specific attributes of text contents
- is qualitative, in that it focuses on meanings and interpretations in text
- is non-reactive, in that the document was not produced with the knowledge that it would be subjected to this analysis
- is transparent, in that its procedure is clear and open and that it can be replicated
- is unobtrusive, in that it studies the document without the knowledge of the author
- is a diverse and flexible method that can be applied in a variety of contexts and materials
- is longitudinal, in that it can address the same issue over a period of time
- is comparative, in that it can produce cross-sectional and cross-cultural data.

clinical records, research publications, introductory sociology textbooks and citations (Reinharz, 1992: 147).

As a quantitative method it is employed when determining the time, frequency or duration of an event; when investigating the thematic content of communication that aims to make inferences about individual or group values, sentiments, intentions or ideologies – as expressed in the content of communication; and when assessing the effects of communication on the audiences reached (Mahr, 1995).

This discussion indicates that the focus of content analysis is on the manifest and the latent content of documents. The *manifest content* refers to the visible, surface text, the actual parts of the text manifested in the document: the words, sentences, paragraphs and so on. Here analysis relates to the straightforward and obvious, the visible content of the document, and involves counting frequencies of appearance of the research unit.

The *latent content* is the underlying meaning conveyed through the document. Here the researchers read between the lines and register the messages; they also identify the hidden meanings that are inherent in the messages. They delve into the purpose of communication, and the underlying cultural patterns, attitudes, prejudices, norms and standards that are encoded in the message. They search for ways of decoding the meanings and symbols that are inferred or hidden and that ultimately guide people's behaviour. The task of content analysis dealing with latent contents is to deconstruct and reconstruct such messages, to identify their real meaning and the impact the context has on the construction of meanings and their underlying justification.

As noted earlier, latent content is usually the focus of more detailed analyses, particularly those dealing with text analysis. Nonetheless, they are equally forms of content analysis, and they are often referred to as such in the professional literature.

2.2 Types of content analysis

It has already been indicated that content analysis is by no means a uniform research tool. There are at least four major types of content analysis: descriptive, contextual, comparative and processual or particularistic content analysis.

- *Descriptive content analysis.* This type of analysis aims at identifying and describing the main content of data, chronologically, thematically or otherwise. It uses narratives to make description vivid and to bring its content close to the natural setting. Description can be either subject-focused or researcher-focused, and involves counting, listing, operationalising and categorising, as well as some evaluation and interpretation.
- *Contextual analysis.* This studies the research object in context and aims to understand the context through the meaningful statements of the authors found in the texts.
- *Comparative content analysis.* This entails comparing texts of different media/authors, for example to identify ideological or other differences in the presentation of information, and examines the validity, reliability, and credibility of media.
- *Processual or particularistic content analysis.* This studies elements or aspects of the whole process, such as the sender, the receiver, the medium, or the

message. It studies, for instance: 'Why was the message communicated?' or 'What was the intent/expected outcome of the message?'

Some models of content analysis employ more specific and detailed techniques, which allow a more complex and more critical appreciation of contents and contexts. Some of these methods will be discussed later.

2.3 Doing content analysis

The general pattern of the research model applied in content analysis is identical to the general model of social research described earlier in this book. The only difference lies in the content of each step, which should obviously be directly related to the nature of the technique as well as to the area of study. The research model of content analysis involves the following steps:

Step 1. Selection of the research topic and methodology. This step will determine what will be studied and in which context. The topic may be words (e.g. sexist expressions), phenomena, themes, attitude, outlook or other elements. The methodology can be quantitative or qualitative, employed within a conservative or critical-emancipatory paradigm.

Step 2. Methodological construction of the research topic. This involves the process of defining, exploring and operationalising the topic, for example determining the unit of analysis (words, phrases, pictures, idioms, meanings etc.), formulating hypotheses where necessary, and finally, constructing categories. Where required, pre-testing the procedure follows. Within a qualitative paradigm, the topic will be defined in more general terms, allowing for flexibility and further refinements while the topic is studied; also, there will be no need for operationalisation.

Step 3. Sampling. In this step, it is decided what documents will be studied and which sampling methods will be employed. More specifically, the following points may be considered:
- selection of the sampling strategy for choosing the proper medium
- selection of the medium (e.g. newspaper, journal, periodical, book series)
- selection of date of publication (e.g. between 1 June and 31 December)
- selection of the part(s) of the medium to be studied (e.g. editorial, business section, employment section).

Step 4. Collection of data. This step first involves the selection of the methods of data collection, as well as deciding about what assistance is needed for data collection. Following this, the researcher will begin identifying and counting the frequencies, prominence, direction and intensity of the research units. This process is known as coding (see below). More specifically, it is generally accepted (see Martin, 1988) that data collection will address the following aspects, among others:
- The appearance of research units, namely whether or not the chosen units appear in the text. For example, whether 'previous experience' is included in advertisements for academic positions in tertiary institutions.

- The frequency of appearance of the units in the text studied. For instance, 'previous experience' as a requirement for an academic position may appear in 85 per cent of the advertisements.
- The significance or prominence of the units that appear in the document, for instance whether 'previous experience' is stated before or after qualifications, publications and the like; its prominence might be defined in terms of the emphasis and space given to it in the text.
- The evaluation of the unit, that is, whether it is positive, neutral or negative. In our example the advertisement may state that 'previous experience is an advantage' or that 'previous experience is not essential'.
- The intensity of the statement regarding the research unit. In our example, it will be recorded whether 'previous experience' was not stressed at all, was stressed somewhat, strongly or very strongly.
- The context in which the chosen unit appears in the text. The researcher will attempt in this case to identify whether the unit appears alone or in conjunction with other criteria or conditions. Using the same example referred to earlier, data will be sought as to whether 'previous experience' appears on its own or together with other categories, such as those concerning place, length, or level of experience. Such statements may take the form of: 'previous overseas experience', 'previous experience for at least three years', or 'previous experience at the advertised level'.

Step 5. Analysis and interpretation of the data. Depending on the orientation of the researcher and the objective of the study, the collected data will be analysed. More particularly, the following specific methods can be employed:
- computation of frequencies of symbols and indicators
- analysis of symbols and indicators collected in the study
- analysis of values derived from the analysis of symbols and indicators
- analysis of the form, direction and quality of evaluation identified in the study (evaluation analysis)
- analysis of contextual references.

The results will then be reported in some way and form, depending on the nature of the study and the type of audience.

Constructing categories

Selection and definition of categories

One way of addressing contents is the construction of categories. A category is a set of criteria that are integrated around a theme or value. For instance, in a study of the criteria used by young people to choose their marital partner, the researcher may be interested in two types of criteria: those related to love, attraction, affection and so on, and those related to employment status, assets and economic security, education and the like. The researcher can employ two categories when studying the texts; the one is emotionality, corresponding to the first group of criteria, and the other rationality, corresponding to the second type of criteria. During the analysis, the information will be classified under these two categories. In this way it will be possible to establish which of the two categories was more prevalent at the time that the documents were published.

Some of these categories will be more central to the analysis than others (primary categories), some will be of secondary importance (secondary categories), and others may address important but peripheral aspects (tertiary categories). In general all categories must have the attributes listed in Box 13.4.

Box **13.4**

Criteria of categories

Categories are expected:

- to be clearly defined and unambiguous
- to relate exclusively to the research topic
- to focus on a specific part of the research topic
- to be exhaustive, that is in combination to cover the whole topic
- to be accurate, unidimensional and mutually exclusive
- to be independent from each other.

In a study developed within a qualitative paradigm, categories are equally important. The only difference is that they are not chosen and accurately defined before the study begins; rather, categories are expected to emerge through the collection and analysis of the data.

Selection of the units of analysis and coding

In general, units of analysis are words, symbols, items, sentences, characters and themes, as well as messages, meanings and symbols, which indicate the presence of one of the categories. The context in which the unit of analysis will be sought must also be chosen. This might be a sentence, a paragraph or a chapter. More specifically, the type of unit of analysis depends on the type of content the study aims to analyse, namely a manifest or a latent content.

Following this, the researcher will commence coding, that is, recording the presence, frequency, intensity and so on of the units in the document. These units may be manifest or latent; hence there are two types of coding: manifest and latent coding. Manifest coding deals with parts of the text. Latent coding deals with meanings, as they become evident through more general reading.

When the study is conducted within a qualitative design, emphasis will be placed not on counting but rather on identifying meanings and indicators of categories that would explain aspects of the research topic. However, there are qualitative studies which make use of presence and intensity of certain aspects of the research topic.

Testing categories

After the categories, units and contexts have been chosen and defined, they are tested. Statistical procedures are one way of conducting the tests. Another approach is to use the expertise of other researchers; for instance, experts are given samples of relevant texts and asked to define the categories, and to select the recording units independently. If there is substantial agreement between the categories identified by the experts and those of the research director (say, about 80 per cent) the reliability test is satisfactory. Otherwise, the researcher must refine and redefine categories and units of analysis.

The meaning of data

Content analysis provides data, like any other method of data collection. Irrespective of whether the approach is qualitative or quantitative, the data will offer some evidence about the dominant category. If quantitative methods are being employed, the data will be presented in the form of proportions, graphs, tables or diagrams, supported by statistical tests, such as tests of significance. If qualitative methods are used, data will most likely be presented in the form of words, graphs or matrices, without statistical analysis presentations.

Box 13.5

Content analysis: an example

A researcher wishes to study the status of pre-Second World War women in the media. She may proceed as follows:

a. The topic may be women's presence in the media, to be studied within a feminist paradigm.
b. Presence will include two aspects, namely the 'extent' of inclusion in mass media, and the 'nature' of presence (i.e. how women appeared in the media; in what roles; and how was this justified).
c. Information will be extracted from the five 1938 newspapers of the region, chosen according to their popularity.
d. The researcher will identify and record the frequency of references to women, the nature of roles they were presented in, the meanings reflected in the references, and contextual indicators referring to women. Numerical frequencies and descriptions will be recorded.
e. Analysis of the collected data will proceed following qualitative standards, to show what the figures and explanations show about women's place in the society.
f. Interpretation will address eventual taken-for-granted rules based on cultural prescriptions, which may explain historical aspects of the status of women in societies, and their significance for the life of modern women.

Coding

In general terms, the type of coding employed in content analysis depends on a number of factors, particularly the study content and the underlying methodology.

Coding means the assignment of codes to units identified in the study. Codes can be numbers, words or symbols. If the research relates to manifest content, then manifest coding is employed. Likewise, if it relates to latent content, the investigator will use latent coding.

Manifest coding implies identification of the presence and frequency of visible, surface text elements such as words, sentences or symbols; in more general terms, the analysis will relate to the manifest units which were chosen for analysis.

Latent coding implies identification of the presence and frequency of semantic units, that is, those related to meanings, as defined in the early stages of the study. Here the researcher will read the text and assign it a label indicating the criteria considered in the study, preparing it for counting and analysis. This form of coding is more complex and time consuming than manifest coding.

Both types of coding are employed in content analysis, either separately or together in the same study. Given that manifest coding deals with concrete units that involve no interpretation and personal judgement, it is often thought to be by nature more reliable than latent coding. Codes and coding are most relevant in qualitative studies, although the manner in which coding is conducted may vary.

2.4　Methods of data analysis

Quantitative analysis

The methods and techniques of analysis employed by quantitative researchers to analyse data collected through content analysis are many and varied. Examples of some common methods of analysis are given below (see Pannas, 1996; Sofos, 1990):

- *Descriptive analysis*. Here, analysis means counting the frequency of appearance of certain elements of the research question and comparing this with other elements.
- *Categorical analysis*. Here, analysis involves a study of the documents by means of a set of categories, producing nominal as well as ordinal and interval data, which are then processed statistically.
- *Valence and intensity analysis*. In this form of analysis, data are processed by means of multi-step scales based on theoretical criteria. In valence analysis the scales have no discrete criteria but have polar values, such as 'in favour of' or 'against'. Intensity analysis employs scales with multiple steps (Lamnek, 1993).
- *Contingency analysis*. This analysis is basically a semantic communication analysis, usually employed to make an inference from the text about the personality of the author (Merten, 1983).
- *Contextual analysis*. Here the sequence in which certain concepts appear together in set texts is examined. The systematic co-appearance of certain concepts is not considered to be accidental but is taken to express an author's thinking patterns or to correspond with a speaker's communicative intentions. Such occurrences are thought to signify 'cognitive representations of social reality'.

Qualitative analysis

The type of content analysis employed in qualitative research is fundamentally different from that of quantitative studies. The differences relate to theoretical and methodological standards and principles of qualitative analysis, such as openness, communicativity, naturalism and interpretation. Briefly, qualitative data will be analysed as follows: after the units of analysis have been ascertained (e.g. texts of books, transcripts of interviews, or other forms of verbal or visual communication), the researcher will identify and evaluate the items that appear to be theoretically important and meaningful and relate them to the central question of the study. The core of qualitative analysis is in the reconstruction of single cases and the identification of typical structures.

In some cases, the researcher will study the text semantically and syntactically, employ the rules of logic, relate the meaning of parts of the text to the whole document and the general thinking of the author, and develop relevant hypotheses (Danner, 1979; Sofos, 1990). In other cases, the processes of collection and analysis of data are seen as an attempt to identify criteria in the text that may refer to actions, effects of expressions and principles that will allow statements about the emotional and cognitive background, as well as about the behaviour of the communicators. More particularly, Mayring (1983, 1985, 1988, 1991, 2000) proposes that the analysis here will proceed in one of the following ways:

- *Summative content analysis.* In this approach data are reduced, so that the text is integrated, important elements are retained and text becomes clear and transparent.
- *Inductive category construction.* Here, summarising is taken further, to gradually develop categories from the data. Further analysis of and work with categories allow the construction of overarching categories, and further analysis and research produce the desired answers.
- *Explicating content analysis.* This aims at explaining unclear parts of the text (e.g. concepts or sentences). It entails systematic and controlled gathering of extra information. This can be done in two ways, using either information from the same protocol (narrow context analysis), or sources outside the protocol (wide context analysis). The important characteristic of explication is its reference to the context; analysis here is explaining through the context (in other words, a context analysis).
- *Structuring context analysis.* This involves developing structures by putting the material in some kind of order, for example by means of previously defined criteria (Mayring, 1988: 75). Such structuration may be related to formal criteria (formal structuration), content criteria (content structuration), type or dimension criteria (type structuration), or criteria related to dimensions of scales (scaling structuration). This eventually leads to the development of dimensions of structuration that can be divided in single categories. This assists with the development of definitions, identification of typical examples and a coding guide, which make the process of structuration more precise.
- *Objective hermeneutics.* This is a method of content analysis as well as a complete research method (see next chapter). It aims to uncover latent struc-

tures of meaning, which lie behind single forms of action and which guide individual action. It is interested in objective and subjective interpretations of social situations, and in the way subjective meanings contrast with the latent structures of meaning (objective interpretations).

Historically, a shift has been evident in the methods of content analysis from quantitative to qualitative forms. Although both methods are employed, there are more qualitative approaches to content analysis now than before.

2.5 Content analysis in the computer age

The nature of content analysis lends itself easily to computerised operations. The fact that this method deals to a large extent with words and symbols of some kind makes it easy to employ electronic devices, which assist not only in reading text and identifying the occurrence and frequency of units and categories, but also in the actual analysis of the findings. There are already computer programs available to assist with these tasks: 'The general inquirer' and 'Oxford concordance program' are two examples.

'The general inquirer' is used to list and compare various indices. Using programs such as KWIC (Key-word-in-context) and KWOC (Key-word-out-of-context), INTEXT, MAX, ATLAS.ti, the computer can identify important concepts in text automatically, compute their frequency, present the findings in graphs, arrange them into systems of categories and compute some basic statistical tests. A comprehensive reference to computer programs employed in content analysis (and social research in general) will be presented in another section of this volume. Here only two examples of such programs will be given.

TEXTPACK is a program developed for use in content analysis. It offers routines for text processing, text exploration and text coding. TEXTPACK is equipped with an automatic coding of text, guided by a dictionary set up by the user, which contains codes. Description and presentation of numerical data regarding frequencies and other aspects is available in TEXTPACK, which is also compatible with statistical programs such as SPSS and SAS.

AQUAD is an equally versatile and useful program. Content analysis using AQUAD progresses from text reduction, to reconstruction and to comparisons. During reduction, the tests are reduced and interpreted as meaningful units, and also arranged according to the categories that are set at the beginning of the process by the researcher. In the second and third stages, the program raises the analysis to higher and more complex levels. Data can be presented in tables, such as text-matrix and code-matrix.

2.6 Strengths and weaknesses of content analysis

As a documentary method, content analysis demonstrates all the strengths and weaknesses of the documentary methods presented above. Here reference will be made to only a few points.

Strengths

- Content analysis is unobtrusive and therefore has no effects on the respondent.

- Content analysis can be used when access to the research topic or research units is not possible. In some cases the research topic might not be currently accessible and cannot be approached through other methods. Content analysis is the only way of data generation.
- Content analysis does not require respondents, and so avoids the various problems often associated with them.
- The fact that content analysis involves already completed material and no respondents eliminates researcher bias.
- Accessibility of the research material is a significant advantage. Texts are readily available for testing and re-testing. This is not possible when the human factor is involved in research.
- Content analysis is a low-cost method compared with other methods, such as surveys.
- Content analysis entails less bias than other methods, given that text offers information in a neutral form, ready to be researched by the investigator.

Weaknesses

- Some documents may not be accessible to the researcher; personal letters and diaries, for instance, might be difficult to obtain.
- Documents often contain information related to a small proportion of people, and are therefore not representative.
- Content analysis cannot study unrecorded events: it is therefore restricted to what has been documented.
- Documents often are not complete; the information may therefore be biased and often unreliable.
- Content analysis is less suitable for making comparisons than other methods.
- Content analysis is susceptible to coder bias.

It should be noted that content analysis is a diverse method, and hence the main points listed above may not pertain to all its branches. Apart from this, what are advantages in some contexts (e.g. quantitative models) may be disadvantages in others (e.g. qualitative models), and vice versa.

3   TEXT ANALYSIS

As noted earlier, the study of documents is employed at different levels, in diverse contexts and within diverse paradigms and epistemologies. In some cases it serves as a method of data collection, in other cases it presents research models that entail complex epistemological principles and construct ways of thinking and perception, departing significantly from the kind of method that was presented in the previous section. Its distinguishing characteristic is its focus on and perception of text. In general terms, this approach to documentary analysis is referred to as *text analysis*, where in certain cases the world is seen as text.

In this section we shall address three forms of text analysis: discourse analysis, hermeneutics and postmodernism.

3.1 Discourse analysis

What is discourse analysis?

Discourse analysis is a precise application of content analysis in a qualitative context. It deals with communication, text, language, talk and conversation, but also with the ways of seeing, categorising and reacting to the social world in everyday practices (Atkinson and Heritage, 1984; Jupp, 1996: 300; Marshall, 1995). Language is studied as it appears in social texts, that is, wherever it appears as a social product, in written or spoken form. Put simply, discourse analysis deals with group discussions, interview transcripts, and policy documents.

Box **13.6**

What is discourse analysis?

Discourse analysis deals with discourses. These are socially constructed frameworks of meanings that act upon people like rules, norms or conventions. Discourse analysis deals primarily with language, but especially with its constructive and action-oriented nature; language and discourse are more than words and sentences. They are ways in which individuals present themselves. In discourse analysis, language has a value in itself; it is the study object where one learns its structure and traits, regularities and recurring patterns. Discourse analysis attempts to capture the ways in which such variations occur, and the reasons for these variations.

Focus of discourse analysis

The focus of this paradigm is on discourses, which are defined as socially constructed frameworks of meanings which serve as guiding rules, norms or conventions. They are expressed in statements which contain information about what is appropriate or inappropriate, allowed or not allowed, acceptable or not acceptable, valued or not valued. Hence, people know them, apply them unconsciously in their everyday life, and take them for granted. More specifically, discourses:

- are socially and culturally constructed, and reflect aspects of their socio-cultural context
- depend on social structures, the speakers and the audience (meanings vary accordingly)
- are connected with and the result of power
- reflect the social context and are a part of this context (see Marshall, 1995).

Discourses not only entail the standards of social life; they also produce the 'versions of the world, of society, events and inner psychological worlds' (Potter, 1997: 146). Discourse is also seen as evidence, and as a mediator of social, political and economic processes and outcomes.

Box **13.7**

What are linguistic repertoires?

Linguistic repertoires are clusters of terms, descriptions and figures of speech; they are the building blocks used to make constructions or versions of cognitive processes, actions, policies and other phenomena. Studying the linguistic constructions and interpretative repertoires (i.e. the linguistic repertoires) that are evident in social texts offers an insight into the speaker's background rules and principles. Linguistic repertoires are at the centre of discourse analysis.

Purpose of discourse analysis

The purpose of discourse analysis is to examine the way in which meanings of social phenomena, as they are employed by people to make sense of their lives, are constructed. Given that meanings are culturally transmitted and shared, individual accounts display more than personal views and opinions. More specifically, discourse analysis is often described (e.g. by Potter and Wetherell, 1994: 48) as primarily concerned with:

- human experiences embedded in the discourse or influenced by it
- 'talk, text and social practices' and 'linguistic content' (meanings and topics)
- linguistic structure (grammar and cohesion)
- action, construction and variability
- rhetorical or argumentative organisation

Discourse analysis deals primarily with language, especially with its constructive and action-oriented nature; language and discourse are more than words and sentences. In this sense, the questions discourse analysis pursues are: how speech and word are used, and how accounts are associated with power (Pfeifer, 2000). Its emphasis is on how discourse is organised and structured, and on the impact of certain forms of discourse on the readers.

The search here is for linguistic constructions that reveal interpretative repertoires used by people to make sense of their lives. Linguistic repertoires are clusters of terms, descriptions and figures of speech; they are the building blocks used to make constructions or versions of cognitive processes, actions, policies and other phenomena (Wetherell and Potter, 1992).

Such linguistic constructions vary, and with a particular purpose. Hence, discourse analysis attempts to capture the ways in which variations occur, and the reasons for them. Studying the linguistic constructions and interpretative repertoires that are evident in social texts offers an insight into the speaker's background rules and principles. Hence, knowledge of the speaker's accounts can enable the researcher to gain an insight into the guiding principles and parameters of life that shape the lives of ordinary people.

Doing discourse analysis

The object of analysis here is text and language. More specifically, as many writers have noted (Jupp, 1996; Marshall, 1995; Pfeifer, 2000; Wetherell and Potter,

1992) the essence of discourse analysis lies in the way it deals with language as its unit of analysis. Language and discourse are ways in which individuals present themselves. In discourse analysis, language has a value in itself; it is the study object where one learns its structure and traits, regularities and recurring patterns.

The research model of discourse analysis draws heavily from a number of qualitative research paradigms, of which constructionism and interpretivism are the most important. To these is to be added the critical paradigm. Following this, discourse analysis conducts its research within the qualitative methodology, in the same way as qualitative content analysis. The difference lies in the centrality of discourse and the emphasis placed on text, language and linguistic repertoires. In a rather simplistic way, in discourse analysis the research model can be as shown below.

Doing discourse analysis: an example

1. *Choose the topic.*
   For example, social status of ethnics.
   Choose the research model.
   For example, discourse analysis.
2. *Define the research unit.*
   For example, the interpretative repertoires, available to and used by subjects.
3. *Choose a sample.*
   For example, 15 respondents chosen freely.
   Choose the method.
   For example, unstructured interviews.
4. *Data collection.*
   Choose the method of data collection (e.g. interviews).
   Interviews are conducted, recorded and transcribed.
   Interviews are practised as interaction – identifying interpretive repertoires, discursive practice; producing 'social texts'.
5. *Data analysis.*
   ■ Reading texts thoroughly; re-reading.
   ■ Identifying interpretive repertoires, that is, recurrent patterns in the organisation and content of texts.
   ■ Identifying the context of repertoires.
   ■ Isolating examples showing similarities in what is being said, differences or variations.
   ■ Taking out extracts denoting one particular repertoire; repeating this; placing them under a heading. Consistency within/between interviews is seen as a pointer that a repertoire is used.
   ■ Examining variations to see how many repertoires are used by participants; examining all extracts to see how they have been used.
   ■ Ascertaining possible consequences of the use of the various repertoires.
   ■ Examining the relationship between repertoires. Are they related? Do they complement or undermine each other?
6. *Reporting*
   Report writing follows the guidelines of qualitative research.

Interpretation of the findings follows the general rules of content analysis, although within a qualitative critical paradigm. Further modes of interpretation are also adopted from other theoretical paradigms, presented later in this chapter. It goes without saying that discourse analysis can work with previously collected data presented in media outlets of some kind. Wherever there is text, discourse can be a useful method of analysis.

Box 13.8

What is hermeneutics?

Hermeneutics is a special technique of text interpretation. The central point of this approach is *Verstehen*, that is, understanding. The focus is not on *what* to understand but on *how*. It is about understanding how we understand the world, about the process, the rules, the pattern, the implicit conditions, and the ways in which explanation and understanding are transmitted to people from generation to generation.

3.2 The hermeneutic tradition

Introduction

Hermeneutics focuses on text interpretation; this includes both grammatical as well as psychological interpretation. In its original meaning (the Greek Ερμηνευω) it denotes the art of translating texts (biblical exegesis, interpretation of scriptures), and constitutes an approach to texts and fixed expressions of human life with the purpose of understanding and interpreting them as well as their creators. The central point of this approach is *Verstehen*, particularly of how understanding is achieved rather than of what understanding entails. It is about the process, the rules, the pattern and implicit conditions, and about the ways in which explanation and *Verstehen* are transmitted to people through socialisation (Farber, 2001; Gadamer, 1975; Honer, 1999; Söffner, 2000: 164).

The purpose of this is to extract the author's intentions and meanings. This means going back to the time, place and context of the author and attempting to understand the author's meaning as well as the context. Understanding becomes a very complex process, leading researchers and theorists to various levels of human life, and takes various forms. Critical hermeneutics and dialogic hermeneutics (Scheele, 1991) are two types of hermeneutics; objective hermeneutics is another (Lenssen and Aufenanger, 1986). The latter will be described in more detail below.

Objective hermeneutics

Objective hermeneutics (OH) was introduced by Övermann (Övermann et al., 1979, 1983) and deals with interactions imbedded in text and with the reconstruction of objective structures of meaning in texts (Reichertz, 2000: 514; 1991). Briefly, OH is based on the following assumptions (Aufenanger and Lenssen, 1986; Bohnsack, 1993, 1999; Heinze, 1987: 77; Övermann et al., 1979, 1983):

- Behind individual actions there are latent structures of meaning.
- Latent structures of meaning exist independently, and ultimately become autonomous forms of reality for the interacting people, guiding their action, regardless of whether they are aware of their existence.
- Individual actions are expressions of latent, objective structures.

The purpose of OH is to work out these latent structures of meaning, and to contrast them with the meanings employed by individuals. This contrast allows judgements as to the status of individual meaning and action. Analysis in this context is conducted by means of a series of complex procedures. There are three methods, strategies or variants of text interpretation available to the researcher (Reichertz, 2000: 517; Lamneck, 1993; Övermann et al., 1979, 1983). These are fine analysis, sequence analysis and structural analysis.

Objective hermeneutics is most suitable for analysing single cases. Larger samples based on standardised sampling procedures are methodologically unsuitable. As often noted, 'only non-standardised sample data and their objective-hermeneutic interpretation can guarantee valid results' (Reichertz, 2000: 517)

The central element of this analysis is a constant comparison of the meanings of individual texts with those of the relevant life-worlds. This is seen as a spiral, the hermeneutic spiral, which rests on the belief that the 'understanding of texts evolves upwards through a spiral of understanding: Analysing the meaning of individual texts, relating this to the totality of the life-worlds in which they originated, and then re-interpreting the separate texts anew' (Foster, 1995: 150).

Box **13.9**

What is hermeneutic spiral?

Hermeneutic spiral is a technique employed to link the unknown whole with the known parts and to arrive at a full understanding. This is based on the assumption that the whole and the parts are interdependent; the context supplies the rules that guide the structure and action of its parts. In turn, the parts carry the 'stamp of the context' on them, and knowing the parts enables understanding of the whole, and vice versa. Understanding is circular. Hence, the meaning of the sentence is understood when the words are known, and the meaning of the words depends on the context, that is, on the sentence.

A brief description of this process, presenting at the same time an example of how objective hermeneutics operates in real situations, is given in Box 13.10 (Reichertz, 2000; Foster, 1995).

Objective hermeneutics is a useful research method for conducting textual analysis, and is employed in a variety of fields. An example is the study of media advertisements for personal contacts (Nagler and Reichertz, 1986), but the fields of psychiatry and socialisation are most receptive to this method. In Germany, Austria and Switzerland, objective hermeneutics is one of the most prominent theoretical perspectives and one that contributes strongly to qualitative research (Bohnsack, 1999; Hitzler and Honer, 1997).

Box **13.10**

The hermeneutic spiral

Steps	*Tasks*
Step 1: Eliciting and understanding the meanings of individual texts	■ Read texts; search for **themes** first in one text then within clusters of documents ■ Become **empathetically immersed** in the available textual descriptions ■ Keep eliciting - focusing on **meanings** (not analysis) ■ Identify 'taken-for-granted' **assumptions and viewpoints** of the author(s) ■ Enhance **understanding** of themes and sub-themes ■ Ascertain the **frequency** of occurrence of such meanings to assess their importance ■ **Scrutinise meanings**, their nature and significance within the wider context ■ **Triangulate** with our understanding of other contexts, and in the individual texts ■ Ascertain how **contexts are linked** and eventual **contradictions** between them
Step 2: Identifying themes and sub-themes	■ **Link themes** with each other ■ **Searching for a central theme** that provides a higher-order understanding of contradictory sub-themes
Step 3: Identifying thematic clusters	■ Ascertain **groupings of text** "which have an inner unity and commonality of meanings" ■ **Cluster documents** according to their own inner cohesion and logic
Step 4: Triangulating documentary data	■ **Contrast** them with other texts of the author or other authors of different interpretations of the issues discussed ■ **Make reference** to other texts and forms of data, to evaluate the true meaning of individual text segments
Step 5: Checking validity and reliability	■ Ask other researchers to **check the rigour** of the study ■ Ask to check whether the textual **extracts are representative** for the documents of which they are a part, and for the text clusters ■ Check whether the researchers **have controlled** their own presuppositions and subjective viewpoints ■ Check whether the researcher **has been rigorous** in the application of the hermeneutic spiral.
Step 6: (Re)con-textualising documentary data	■ **Contrast the data** again with the context of which they are a part ■ **Contrast the data** with findings of the same level produced by other studies to check their status.
Step 7: Selecting representative material	■ **Select a set of documents** that would be used for presentation in publications.

3.3 Postmodernism

General characteristics

Postmodernism emerged after the Second World War, initially being associated with 'armchair radicals' (Thomas, 1993: 25) who espoused anarchist, existentialist and nihilist philosophies, and especially philosophers like Heidegger, Nietzsche and Wittgenstein; it has become what is often referred to as an elitist and fashionable school of thought. Overall it represents a different direction in academic thinking and action, and takes a critical view of everything that makes up modern thinking, science and the world (Denzin, 1991; Harding, 1990; Kellner, 1988, 1992).

We are primarily interested here, of course, in the way postmodernists conduct research; however, we already know that the research parameters of any research model are informed by the principles and standards of its philosophical underpinnings. In simple terms, postmodernists construct their research according to the way they define reality, knowledge and science. Hence, there is a need to explore these parameters before we address postmodernist research.

Postmodernists are critical of the very basis of methodology, including ontology, epistemology and, to a certain extent, the methods of inquiry. This includes the notion of collecting knowledge about the world in a 'scientific' manner, as well as the possibility of arriving at any totalising or exhaustive explanations or theories (Gubrium and Holstein, 1997: 75). There are two types of postmodernism: radical (or sceptical) postmodernism, and moderate (or affirmative) postmodernism.

Radical postmodernism expresses a strong disbelief not only in the ontological foundations of the social sciences but also in their epistemological principles, and hence the notion of empirical reality. It follows a strict anti-positivist direction regarding both methodology and perception of reality.

Moderate postmodernism does not dismiss modernism and modern paradigms, but takes a constructive view of their theoretical foundations, goals and principles, and proposes ways to reconstruct them so that they can be more effective in reaching their goals. Moderate postmodernists, while still critical of positivism, employ a moderate approach to reality and to research, in contrast to radical postmodernists.

In very general terms, integrating the main views on this issue (see, for example, Crotty, 1998; Gubrium and Holstein, 1997; Richardson, 1992; Rosenau, 1992; Usher et al. 1997), the methodological foundations of this school of thought can be described as shown below.

Reality. What do postmodernists study?

Radical postmodernists are doing away with the notion of reality altogether; for them, there is no 'real reality' to refer to; there are no real-world referents; the meanings of descriptions are simple representations (Baudrillard, 1983: 19). Some doubt even the need for a conception of reality (Rosenau, 1992). Hence, research of the kind we know has no place in this paradigm, and similarly there is no place for this paradigm in our discussion.

Moderate postmodernists see reality not as objectively given but as being created, interpreted, and maintained in interaction. They also reject the modernist notion that the world is unitary, uniform, homogeneous and self-evident; they rather see it as pluralistic and split. Hence, the world does not contain fixed or singular meanings for researchers to collect and analyse, but plural, multiple and ever changing meanings. Following this, modernist research cannot address the world but only parts of it. As often noted by writers on the subject, the world 'does not come in well organised components' to be captured, measured and evaluated.

More importantly, for moderate postmodernists, social and cultural processes construct hierarchies within the social system and generate power systems that subject people to control and domination. This relates not only to status, material advantages and privileges, but also to the way in which the world is perceived, interpreted and constructed, to the way people communicate with each other, the nature and structure of meanings, to systems of language, and to human creation in general.

Hence, 'postmodernism suspects all truth claims of masking and serving particular interests in local, cultural and political struggles' (Richardson, 1994: 517). This means that what the world researchers want to investigate is not only diverse and pluralistic but also controlled by power systems that determine 'what is', and 'how' to perceive and address it. Hence, this perception of power and of the world determines what knowledge is and how to perceive it.

Knowledge

What kind of knowledge do postmodernists aim to gather? Unlike modernists, who, we are told, believe that knowledge is invariant, universal, singular (one truth, one certainty!), superordinate, secure and disinterested, moderate postmodernists believe that knowledge is pluralistic and dominated by an inherent diversity, ephemeracy, fragmentation and ambiguity; depends on social and cultural conditions, discourses, belief systems, interpretive models, language systems and power systems (e.g. class, race, gender and families); and is socially constructed.

The parameters of learning and knowledge – what people are to know, and how to search for knowledge – are controlled by the system. The language that people unconsciously acquire during socialisation is not just a mediator of thoughts, feelings and commands but also a formative tool that creates their frame of thinking and their epistemological codes. Hence, meanings that constitute language and the tools of research are by no means uniform and self-evident, but part of the system in which people live. Even the researcher and the research enterprise are socially constructed; the system makes sure that researchers have the 'right' skills, the 'right' ethical standards and the 'right' tools of research.

Hence, knowledge is socially constructed, conditional, created by and bound to power, not invariant but constantly changing.

What is the postmodernist vision of science?

Science has no particular monopoly on truth, which is relative, and even impossible to attain. Hence, scientific outcomes are no more valuable than any other accounts. Postmodernists distrust science, first, because they see no inherent value in it; and second, because they believe science serves the powerful. Equally

Box **13.11**

Foundations of (moderate) postmodernism

- Reality is interpreted and reinterpreted and hence, created and maintained.
- Knowledge is constantly changing, partial, fragmented; there are many truths.
- Knowledge is produced through discourse; constructed; bound to power!
- Many truths, many certainties: ' the only certainty is uncertainty'.
- Science has no inherent value; it serves the powerful.
- Objectivity is not possible or valuable; it is relative to time and space.
- Moderate postmodernism accepts conventional methods, but also questions and distrusts them.
- Methods are 'unfolding': they are adopted–modified–criticised–remodified and so on.
- The research process is not fixed but open to new questions, new ways of knowing.
- The researcher is involved, creative, learning, interpreting, creating knowledge, possessing no superior skills, knowledge or value.
- Results are reported and communicated in a down-to-earth and flexible manner; taking the most 'suitable' form, ranging from ordinary reports to poem, music or drama.

rejected is the idea that modernisation is synonymous with progress.

Rosenau (1992: 8) notes that the postmodernist perspective of social science becomes a more subjective and humble enterprise as truth gives way to tentativeness. Confidence in emotion replaces efforts at impartial observation. 'Relativism is preferred to objectivity, fragmentation to totalisation'.

Postmodernism proposes that there are no standards to judge truth and falsity, or to claim validity. Here objectivity is displaced by relativity; hence science, truth and justice are concepts relative to time and place. Postmodernism questions the belief in progress and emancipation (Usher et al., 1997), and that these can be reached through rationality and science; it rather endorses a crisis of confidence in Western conceptual systems. Science cannot predict the future, or provide guidance in shaping effective policies: the world will never improve (Pfeifer, 2000).

Research parameters

The position of postmodernists on methodology, research and methods is diverse. Some writers note, for instance, that the emphasis placed by postmodernists on signs, cinema and television, as well as on the notion of hyper-reality, support the view that postmodern research is nothing more or less than a 'cinematic ethnography'. Others are convinced that postmodernists reject quantitative methods and employ a qualitative inquiry instead. In a third view, the possibility even of a qualitative inquiry is disputed. Gubrium and Holstein, for instance, state that indeed 'the challenge comes in crisis proportions, taking inquiry away from, and beyond empirically grounded what and how questions. The crisis is about representation itself, with radical postmodernism completely displacing reality with representation' (1997: 76).

More specifically, Rosenau contends that postmodernists define everything as text, seek to 'locate' meaning rather than to 'discover' it; and offer 'readings', not 'observations', 'interpretations' or 'findings'.

> They never test because testing requires 'evidence', a meaningless concept within a postmodern frame of reference. . . . They look to the unique rather than to the general, to inter-textual relations rather than causality, and to the unrepeatable rather than the re-occurring, the habitual, or the routine.
>
> (Rosenau, 1992: 8)

As noted earlier, the extremist position of radical postmodernists makes it impossible to accommodate it in any systematic research model, even that employed by moderate postmodernists. In this discussion, therefore, we shall concentrate mainly on moderate postmodernists.

How, then, is modern postmodern research conducted and what are the main principles of this type of research? Most moderate postmodernists are reported (Benini, 2000; Pfeifer, 2000; Richardson, 1994; Usher et al. 1997) to subscribe to a number of principles, the most important of which are shown below.

Research paradigm. In postmodernism, research is conducted in a critical context toward the practice of sense-making and sense-taking. Postmodernism shares with critical theorists the notion that there is appearance and reality, and sees its goal as getting through appearance to uncover reality, hidden structures, power systems and forms of oppression. It differs from conventional research, which is seen as a tool of oppression that entails power over the researched by holding a monopoly of meanings, data collection and data meaning. The orthodox consensus about how to do research scientifically has been displaced (Pfeifer, 2000).

As Usher and associates (1997: 211) report, postmodernism studies 'not the world which is constructed and investigated by research but the way in which that world is written in the research text'. Postmodernist research adopts the interpretivist notion of reality as being not fixed and objective but diverse and constructed; yet, it focuses not on 'the world, which is constructed and investigated by research but on the way in which that world is written in the research text' (Usher et al 1997: 211).

Research design. As shown above, postmodernism follows the research principles of constructionism and interpretivism, developed within a critical paradigm. Hence, postmodernist research is conducted within a qualitative methodology, without marked deviations from the model discussed earlier in this text. Research methods are qualitative, with an added portion of doubt and scepticism regarding their monopoly of the power to extract truths and knowledge. Methods unfold, are refined, modified and further applied in their new form. In general, postmodernism accepts the conventional methods of knowing, but not as religiously as other researchers! Objectivity and validity are greeted in a critical qualitative context and so is the role of the researcher in the research process.

Reporting. Postmodernists report their findings in a rather distinctive manner, which deserves special mention. They use their intuition or emotions, and share their descriptions with others in a down-to-earth and non-systematic manner; The report may take the form of poetry, music, dance or drama. Richardson (1992), in a study of single mothers, presented her report on the lived experiences of one of her subjects in the form of a poem. Beyond this, she included in her report aspects of her own experiences, so presenting a mix of her own and the subject's lived experiences. In her view, this is an advantage since it implicates the author, the subject and the reader. Richardson (1992: 136) notes on this: 'Representing the sociological as poetry is one way of decentring the unreflexive "self" to create a position for experiencing the self as a sociological knower/ constructor – not just talking about it, but doing it. In writing the other, we can (re)write the Self. That is the moral of this story.'

The status of postmodern research is not as solid as that of other research models. The extremist position of radical postmodernists takes the whole paradigm to a rather critical position. Overall, apart from its critical stance towards the social order, its epistemological outlook – including its perception of reality, knowledge, truths and research – motivates many researchers and writers alike to set postmodern research outside the perimeter of social research.

MAIN POINTS

- Documentary methods are 'indirect', in that they help gather data without the direct participation of the respondents. They are also called 'unobtrusive methods'.
- They include document studies, content analysis and text analysis.
- They examine documents to inquire about the behaviours and attitudes of people reported in the content of the documents.
- Document studies focus on public documents, archival records, personal documents, administrative documents, formal studies and reports.
- Documentary methods are valued for their retrospectivity, accessibility, spontaneity, low costs, high quality, possibility of re-testing and non-reactivity.
- The biographical method entails the study of personal and biographical documents.
- Content analysis is a documentary method that examines the (manifest or latent) content of documents.
- In content analysis, data collection concentrates on the presence, frequency, prominence, direction and intensity of the research units.
- Documentary methods also include text analysis, which employs discourse analysis, hermeneutics and postmodernist principles.
- Documentary methods may be employed as the only methods of study or in conjunction with other methods.

WHERE TO FROM HERE?

Before you leave this chapter, visit the companion website for the third edition of *Social Research* at http://www.palgrave.com/sociology/sarantakos to review the main concepts introduced in this chapter and to test yourself on the major issues discussed.

FURTHER READING

Coulthard, M. (1994) *Advances in Written Text Analysis*. London: Routledge.

Cheek, J. (2000) *Postmodern and Poststructural Approaches to Nursing Research*. Thousand Oaks, Calif.: Sage.

Fawcett, B. (ed.) (2000) *Practice and Research in Social Work: Postmodern Feminist Perspectives*. New York: Routledge.

Hunston, S. and Thompson, G. (2000) *Evaluation in Text: Authorial Stance and the Construction of Discourse*. Oxford: Oxford University Press.

Lather, D. (1991) *Getting Smart: Feminist Research and Pedagogy with/in the Postmodern*. New York: Routledge.

Lee, R. M. (2000) *Unobtrusive Measures in Social Research*. Buckingham: Open University Press.

Neuendorf, K. A. (2002) *The Content Analysis Guidebook*. Thousand Oaks, Calif.: Sage.

Potter, J. (1996) *Representing Reality: Discourse, Rhetoric and Social Construction*. London: Sage.

Reed, M. (2000) 'The Limits of Discourse Analysis in Organisational Analysis.' *Organisation*, 7: 524–30.

Riffe, D., Lacy, F. and Fico, F. G. (1998) *Analyzing Media Messages: Using Quantitative Content Analysis in Research*. Mahwah, N.J.: Lawrence Erlbaum.

Roberts, C. W. (ed.) (1997) *Text Analysis for the Social Sciences: Methods for Drawing Statistical Inferences from Texts and Transcripts*. Hove: Laurence Erlbaum.

Robinson, E. and Robinson, S. (2003) *What does it Mean? Discourse, Text, Culture: An Introduction*. Sydney: McGraw-Hill.

Rolfe, G. (2000) *Research, Truth, and Authority: Postmodern Perspectives on Nursing*. Basingstoke: Macmillan.

Saulwick, W. (1987) *Sex Role Portrayal of Women in Advertisements: A Content Analysis*. Canberra: Office of the Status of Women.

Scheurich, J. J. (1997) *Research Method in the Postmodern*. London: Falmer.

Silverman, D. (2001) *Interpreting Qualitative Data in Methods for Analysing Talk, Text and Interaction*. London: Sage.

Webb, E. J., Campbell, D. T., Schwartz, R. D. and Sechrest, L. (2000) *Unobtrusive Measures*. Thousand Oaks, Calif.: Sage.

Weber, R. P. (1990) *Basic Content Analysis*. Newbury Park, Calif.: Sage.

Wood, L. A. and Kroger, R. O. (2000) *Doing Discourse Analysis: Methods for Studying Action in Talk and Text*. Thousand Oaks, Calif.: Sage.

Applied research

INTRODUCTION

Applied research focuses on 'application'; in other words, it addresses real life situations that require immediate attention. Unlike basic research, which aims primarily to gain new knowledge and to promote the scientific understanding of the world, applied research is primarily interested in identifying problem areas, searching for relevant solutions, and producing direct answers (see Walker, 1985). While basic research may study the causes and effects of HIV, applied research may investigate a particular community, identify its needs for HIV-related services, and make specific recommendations as to how to address this community issue.

There are many types of applied research. The most commonly cited (Pfeifer, 2000) and widely practised are epidemiological, feasibility and evaluation research. *Epidemiological research* focuses primarily on health and is employed to ascertain the extent to which certain population attributes occur. It employs quantitative research, including representative samples, and most commonly survey methods. *Feasibility studies* are commonly used to estimate whether the expected costs and benefits of a proposed programme justify its introduction. It is usual for government departments, before introducing costly programmes, to begin with a feasibility study, and proceed only if this study produces positive results. *Evaluation research* is employed to assess the status of a programme, for example, whether its performance justifies continued support. This is very popular, particularly in the areas of social work, social welfare and social policy.

Given that all three types of applied research entail a strong element of evaluation, and employ the same or similar designs, many writers address them together under the heading of evaluation research. These methods, as well as participatory and demystification research, are reported to be employed by other researchers and to be consistent with and employed by feminist researchers (Reinharz, 1992: 180–94). In this sense, feminist research is presented as applied research that employs feminist and other methods to emancipate people and to bring about change in specific areas of social life.

In this chapter we shall discuss three of these methods: evaluation research, needs analysis and action research. In this discussion, their applied, emancipatory and political nature will become evident.

1   EVALUATION RESEARCH

1.1 Introduction

Evaluation research is a type of inquiry employed to assess the merit of programmes, policies, services or interventions. It is usually employed by social workers, psychologists, counsellors, welfare officers and economists. More specifically, its main purpose is to provide information about various aspects of programmes, such as whether proposed programmes, policies, services or interventions are worth pursuing, supporting or continuing (Clarke, 1999: 3; Greene, 1994; Sanders, 1999). Evaluation research is associated with the ongoing demand for accountability, which requires programmes to be validated by means of research evidence.

Evaluation research is expected to be systematic and precise in its operations, and this requires a clear plan, programme or design. It emphasises the provision of practical knowledge to aid the decision-making process; hence, it is a form of policy research with a practical orientation and a policy focus; it entails a political element (Rossi and Freeman, 1993). In methodological terms, evaluation research uses as respondents individuals and/or groups who have vested interests in the research topic, and employs quantitative methods as its primary tools. Despite claims to the contrary, evaluation research also employs qualitative methods (see Judd et al., 1991: 329). The main characteristics of evaluation research can be summarised as shown in Box 14.1 (see Lincoln and Guba, 1986; Patton, 1986; Rossi and Freeman, 1993).

Box **14.1**

Characteristics of evaluation research

Evaluation research is:

- Applied research, not an 'audit': it applies research findings in specific areas.
- A type of policy research aiming to help policy formation or re-formation.
- A disciplined inquiry, in that it employs conventional research designs and procedures.
- Systematic collection of information, employing qualitative or quantitative designs.
- Systematic application of research procedures following a research design.
- Practical, in that it has a practical orientation and a goal-oriented focus.
- Action oriented, taking steps to convince the power holders to take action.
- Political, in that it engages the researcher politically, engages the community, and employs political means to achieve its goals.

The nature and objectives of evaluation research direct its focus and interests towards certain aspects of social reality, which may not be at the centre of the research activity of other types of research. Hence, evaluation research is generally considered to be about issues such as those listed in Box 14.2 (Chelimsky and Shadish, 1997; Clarke, 1999; House, 1993; Patton, 1986; Rossi and Freeman, 1993).

1.2 Types of evaluation research

Evaluation research appears in many forms, depending on the nature, structure, purpose, and design of the research. The following are the most popular.

- *Informal and formal evaluation.* Informal evaluation is based on informal practices and, although it can provide 'hints' as to the way programmes can go, it is not used as the only source of information for serious deliberations regarding the fate of programmes. Formal evaluation employs scientific

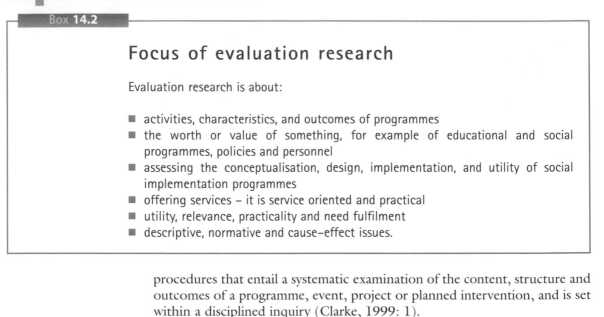

Box **14.2**

Focus of evaluation research

Evaluation research is about:

- activities, characteristics, and outcomes of programmes
- the worth or value of something, for example of educational and social programmes, policies and personnel
- assessing the conceptualisation, design, implementation, and utility of social implementation programmes
- offering services – it is service oriented and practical
- utility, relevance, practicality and need fulfilment
- descriptive, normative and cause–effect issues.

procedures that entail a systematic examination of the content, structure and outcomes of a programme, event, project or planned intervention, and is set within a disciplined inquiry (Clarke, 1999: 1).

- *Formative and summative evaluation.* Formative evaluation aims to identify the strengths and weaknesses of the programme in question, always with the intent to make it as workable as possible (e.g. Judd et al., 1991: 329). Summative evaluation is a form of passing judgment on the fate of a programme, based on previous performance and community needs. While formative evaluation asks 'What can be done to make this programme work', summative evaluation asks 'Is the programme good enough to continue?'

Box **14.3**

Formative and summative evaluation: a comparison

Formative evaluation	*Summative evaluation*
1 Asks: How can the program be improved?	1 Asks: Should the program be continued or terminated?
2 Is done by participants, managers, and other interested people.	2 Is done by policy planners and/or fund providers.
3 Involves both process and outcome evaluation.	3 Involves both process as well as outcome evaluation.
4 Offers feedback aimed at improving the program.	4 Assesses overall effectiveness of the program in question.
5 Uses quantitative and/or qualitative methods.	5 Uses quantitative methods and produces data that facilitate detailed assessment.
6 Researchers are involved, interactive and compassionate.	6 Researchers are passive, independent, uninvolved.

- *Cost–benefit analysis.* This aims to gather information which will assist policy makers and other customers to assess the economic implications of a new programme. It is usually conducted just before policy action is undertaken, to ensure that this action is viable and worth introducing. Cost–benefit analysis produces data about the actual costs of the action in question and the benefits it will bring to the community. Having access to these data, policy makers will be in a position to decide whether to accept or to reject the proposed programme.

- *Needs analysis.* This operates within the same parameters of policy development. In simple terms, it assesses the status of a community, looking at the kind of needs that require attention, as well as which of them must be addressed first. Presence and priority of needs are the two most important points that a needs analysis will address.

- *Process analysis.* This is employed when the running of a programme is to be evaluated. In doing this the researcher will ask whether the programme, service or intervention is actually doing what it is supposed to be doing, and if not, how distant it is from the intended target.

- *Outcome analysis.* Here the focus is on the type of results of the programme and on whether it achieves the outcomes it was intended to achieve. The question here is about the extent to which the 'real' outcomes of the programme deviate from the targeted outcomes, allowing policy makers to make an informed decision about the future of the programme.

- *Impact assessment.* This is similar to outcome analysis, with the difference that while the latter asks whether programmes, services and the like are doing what they were expected to do, impact assessment asks how the programme affects the community. Given that programmes, services and interventions are intended to assist people in the community, impact studies are very useful, as they are the only studies that can satisfactorily answer questions about the usefulness of the programmes.

- *Quantitative and qualitative evaluation research.* These types of evaluation research emerge when methodology is taken as the criterion of distinction (Kardorff, 2000). They employ, respectively, a quantitative and a qualitative paradigm (see Shaw, 1999). The choice of type depends on many factors, such as the evaluation topic, the data required, the purpose of evaluation and the theoretical paradigm that guides evaluation. It is important to note that all types of evaluation can be conducted within either of these options.

  Quantitative evaluation research entails a variety of models, all depending on the nature of research they employ and hence on the type of data they produce. One such model is, for instance, descriptive evaluation research, which concentrates on collecting descriptive information, for example about the number of people using the programme, the proportion of those making suggestions for improvement or the costs associated with the programme. Another type of quantitative evaluation research is a cause–effect evaluation, which is interested in the extent to which resources employed in the programmes produced the expected outcomes.

  In *qualitative* evaluation research the variety is equally large and diverse. Descriptive evaluation, for instance, can be equally employed within a qualitative paradigm, although the kinds of description produced might differ from those of the quantitative model. The context of evaluation will determine which model will be most suitable for the study. What is more related to qualitative than to quantitative evaluation research is *normative evaluation research*, which focuses on what is right or wrong with the programme, including legal, moral and religious issues, and passing value judgments on the nature and outcomes of the programme.

■ *Clinical and non-clinical evaluation research.* Clinical evaluation research is concerned with evaluations relating to people who ask for assistance voluntarily or are advised to do so by social workers or other professionals. It usually deals with single (or a limited number of) cases at a time. Social workers, for instance may advise a couple experiencing violence at home to follow certain procedures that are expected to normalise their relationship. Evaluation will in this case show the outcome of the treatment. Similarly, a 'difficult' child may be treated medically to control his or her behaviour, and clinical evaluation will demonstrate whether the outcome is as expected. The methods employed in this context are before–after experiments without control groups. Non-clinical evaluation covers everything else; it is what we know as programme evaluation and is directed to public programmes affecting large social groups. The studies are conducted by means of quasi-experimental designs.

■ *Quality of life analysis.* This is another type of evaluation research that is employed in many countries to establish whether the living standards in a particular context are high, moderate or low, whether they have changed over time, and how they compare to those of other contexts. The quality of life is measured in terms of social indicators containing a set of criteria that are considered important. Using these indicators, social researchers can describe accurately whether workers are better off now than 30 years ago, whether the living conditions of students have improved over the last ten years, or the quality of life of women is now significantly better than in the 1970s.

The indicators employed by researchers to measure quality of life are either objectively defined by the researchers or constructed on the basis of consultation with the groups studied. In the first case, researchers employ generally accepted and approved standards – social indicators – to operationalise quality of life. Here the government and the researchers decide what is a high or low quality of life. They decide when people are assumed to feel happy with their life and when not. The other mode of defining quality of life is when the people concerned, old people, say, decide what they see as good or bad, rather than the authorities and the researchers. In such cases, scales that measure the quality of life of old people should be constructed in consultation with those people, and not by experts alone. Simply, what is considered to be good by the experts may not be so perceived by the elderly.

As a rule, quality of life is studied within a quantitative research model, leading to results that are not only accurate and precise but also generalisable and comparable. However, qualitative research can also be applied in this context, although using different measures and producing different impressions of the concept. Qualitative evaluation produces more personal impressions of quality of life, reflecting individual views, and offers limited generalisability.

1.3 The purpose of evaluation research

The discussion so far has explained indirectly the reasons for using evaluation research as well as the expected outcomes of this procedure. Practical applications and policy issues are at the heart of this type of research. More specifically, evaluation is expected to assess the impact of social interventions and so 'to reduce uncertainties, improve effectiveness, and make decisions with regard to what those programmes are doing and affecting' (Patton, 1986).

For instance, in the areas of psychology, psychotherapy and social work, evaluation research can look at clinical programmes and interventions for individuals with mental illnesses or interpersonal difficulties (family conflicts and violence) (Ellis, 1994). Although goals vary from one type of evaluation to another, there are certain goals that are broadly shared by most types of evaluation. The most commonly cited (see Bauer, 1994; Chelimsky and Shadish, 1977; Ellis, 1994; Kardorff, 2000: 239; Torres et al., 1996; Weiss, 1997, 1998) goals of evaluation research are shown in Box 14.4.

Box **14.4**

Goals of evaluation research

- to assess the quality, effectiveness, efficiency and goal achievement of political, social and ecological measures, models or laws of all kinds
- to stimulate, document and accompany social and organisational changes and learning processes
- to contribute through new research findings to a deeper understanding of the areas in question
- to identify the need for programmes, and ways of improving the effectiveness of existing ones
- to improve knowledge, programming and policy making
- to discover gaps in services and to investigate the alternatives employed to meet the unmet needs
- to offer systematic evidence that informs experience and judgment
- to predict whether a planned programme will be successful
- to establish whether a programme is cost effective, and whether benefits outweigh costs
- to offer assistance with decision making and planning from the perspective of the contractor so as to achieve better guidance, higher rationality and improved quality of offers, as well as arguments for legitimate enforcement of goals and interests.

1.4 The steps of evaluation research

When considering the way in which evaluation research of any kind will be conducted, we must bear in mind two major points. The first is that evaluation research is not about new research methods but rather an application of the research methods discussed earlier in this text. The second point is that evaluation research can be developed within either a quantitative or a qualitative methodology (Cook and Reinhardt, 1979). Following this, the steps of evaluation research will be those of either the quantitative fixed design, the fixed qualitative design or the flexible qualitative design. In most cases, however, the quantitative design is employed.

Example of steps

To better understand the design, let us take an example. In a country town, the council was under pressure from a number of community groups to reduce teenage vandalism and rowdiness in the evening in certain parts of the town. On the advice of the social worker, the council decided to open a youth centre for teenagers, where they could meet with their friends, play games and have drinks, listen to their music and find a congenial social environment. The evaluation study is to assess the effectiveness of the programme after one year of running.

Step 1. Topic and methodology

The first point to be determined clearly here is *what* is to be studied and in what context. Is the study a formative or a summative evaluation? Finally, which methodology will be employed, a quantitative or a qualitative one?

Step 2. Methodological construction of the topic

At this stage, it is important that the points of study are clearly specified. The most important point that needs to be clearly specified is the specific purpose of the evaluation. In our example and in a quantitative design, the research question will focus on two variables: the independent variable, which is the youth centre, and the dependent variable which is 'community peace', or community trouble. The logical question is whether, after the youth centre has been open for a year, the situation has changed in some way

Following this, the researcher will have to demonstrate how 'community trouble' and 'youth centre' will be defined. More particularly, the behaviour of the young people needs accurate measurement and operationalisation, using indicators such as 'noise', 'vandalism' or 'running in the street'. The youth centre will be considered in a similar manner. This indicates that clear and accurate definitions will be given of what is to be evaluated and measured, and also how this measurement is to be facilitated.

More demanding is the operationalisation of the independent variable (the youth centre). In the first place how can one 'measure' the concept 'youth centre' so that it makes methodological sense? And then, how would one know whether changes in the life of the community (e.g. less noise and fewer acts of vandalism) were associated with the opening of the centre?

These are questions that need to be specified very clearly at this stage of the research. The basic question that requires special consideration is whether the initial situation has changed in any way.

Step 3. Sampling

The samples may include: people who have knowledge of the programme and its effects on the community; people responsible for its development and/or introduction; those working with the programme or who are responsible for the services it provides; stakeholders; experts; government authorities; and community groups. The choice of respondents will be accomplished through methods relevant to the methodology chosen for the study. They may include only the people who were initially affected by the noise and acts of vandalism, who could say whether they are now affected by these acts as much as before the youth centre opened. The survey may also include young people who know about night life in the community, who could tell whether there have been any changes and if so why and how.

Step 4. Data collection

The methods of data collection employed within this research design are the same as those employed in other types of research; the differences – where present – relate to the objectives, not to the nature of the methods (Babbie, 1995; Berk, 1995; Rossi and Freeman, 1993). In our example, a survey of members of the community, as described above, can be very helpful. Surveys will cover all relevant aspects of the issue, especially the two major variables. In addition, information can be collected by other methods, such as Delphi interviews and focus groups including members of a variety of groups, whereby issues relating to community troubles and youth groups can be addressed very effectively.

Step 5. Data analysis

Data analysis is mostly quantitative but can also be qualitative. In our example quantitative analysis is most appropriate. The survey will show whether those residents who were complaining about the young people in the past have noticed any difference since the opening of the centre. Similarly, council records will show whether the number and seriousness of acts of vandalism have changed during the period in question. Finally, police records can shown whether those who committed offences before the establishment of the centre are still involved in crime, and whether those who committed offences recently have used the centre. The results of this analysis will then indicate the extent to which the programme achieved its purpose or not. Depending on whether the evaluation is summative or formative, the researcher will be able to recommend that the programme be continued or stopped, or whether it requires the attention and support of the council.

Step 6. Reporting

The findings of a study are usually communicated through a variety of channels. The most common is an internal report submitted to the authority that requested the evaluation. Conference presentation is another way of communicating the findings, provided that this is permitted by the sponsor. Under the same conditions, the findings can be published in journals, as monographs and/or government publications. In our example, the findings of the study will be presented in a report to be submitted to the council, with relevant recommendations.

1.5 Putting it together

Evaluation research entails a variety of elements that make it challenging but also difficult to put in practice. The combination of quantitative and qualitative paradigms and its inherent association with community politics and action research make it both interesting and demanding. Nonetheless, its research path is not different from other, more straightforward research models. This goes to show that, regardless of the nature and type of research, the six steps of the research process constitute the universal path of the process of social research.

A final point to make here is that in any case, before research action can be considered, one must be aware of the theoretical and structural parameters of research and research context. This is why, in discussing research designs in evaluation research, proper reference to its nature, structure, and purpose was made. We need to know as much as possible, before research is put into practice

2 NEEDS ASSESSMENT

Needs assessment is a type of evaluation research that is employed to ascertain, first, the needs of the community that require attention, and second, which of these needs require immediate attention. This type of research evaluates the state of community life by using standard methods of social research, gathering valid estimations from experts and survey data. It identifies the 'sore points' of the community, ranking them in terms of priority. Such information is used to inform policy makers so that they can address community problems constructively, effectively and, in many cases, before they become problematic.

As a type of evaluation research, needs analysis follows the same steps and procedures introduced in evaluation research. Hence, there is no need for these to be discussed again. However, there are a few points that require further consideration. The choice of the topic is one such example.

The choice of the topic refers to three areas. The first is the type of needs that the study will address. Will it assess general needs, or specific needs, such as a lack of economic services, legal services and so on? The second point is the reference point of needs. Will the study address objective needs (needs as seen by the experts), subjective or felt needs (as perceived by the stakeholders), or observed

---

Box **14.5**

Goals of needs assessment

The goals of needs assessment are:

- to identify community needs, e.g. the type of services required
- to analyse needs and determine which require priority treatment
- to assist the government with policy formulation
- to facilitate a rational allocation of resources
- to emancipate people and make them aware of the state of affairs in the community
- to empower stakeholders to work for change
- to establish an action plan for future intervention programmes
- to compare communities within a region and between regions
- to assess the efficacy of policies and programmes of a particular agency
- to facilitate further evaluation research by delivering necessary information.

needs (as described by those who know more about the people concerned, such as key informants and counsellors)? The third point refers to the context within which the needs will be identified and analysed. Such contexts may be a small rural community, a city suburb, a city or even larger contexts.

In real situations, needs are defined in any of these three ways, although they are assessed within reasonable standards. The choice in such cases must be made with caution. Objective definitions may be alienated from the real world of needs. Equally questionable are definitions based on the personal needs of those concerned. Even if they come 'from the heart' of the people in need, they may not be of great value. Defining the need of drug users for free availability of drugs at will and without control is extremely questionable on many grounds.

The nature of needs must be further defined and formulated in order for the researcher to be able to assess and analyse them in detail, and in a way that would permit accurate evaluations and comparisons. How will needs be defined and identified? What will the researcher be looking for? Where will the researcher search to identify and assess needs? These are additional questions that will help the researcher proceed with the study effectively.

Box **14.6**

Who uses needs analysis?

Needs assessment is used by:

- government departments, for instance to identify areas of social life that require intervention and to guide policy action
- private business, to ascertain whether the establishment of relevant services is justified
- researchers and academics, to gain new knowledge on a subject and inform interest groups and government authorities directly
- social workers, to allocate community resources effectively
- interest groups, to emancipate and empower stakeholders and to introduce changes.

A final point that requires the researcher's attention at the first stage of the design is the choice of research methodology. This will be decided according to the purpose of the analysis, the nature of needs and the nature of the data required. As noted above, it is very common for quantitative methods to be employed, although qualitative methods are equally legitimate. If a quantitative methodology is applied, which is usually the case, a rigid design will be employed. If the researcher opts for a qualitative methodology, the design may be either fixed or flexible.

The manner in which the research will be conducted depends on the choice of methodology and the nature of data to be collected. Put simply, the researchers will follow the steps of the design they consider suitable. What distinguishes a study is the choice of specific instruments, and particularly those that are most suitable for studying community needs.

The choice of the methods employed to identify and assess needs depends, among other things, on how needs are defined; in other words, whether the researcher focuses on objective, subjective or observed needs. When needs are studied in objective terms, the use of social indicators may be a useful and appropriate method. Social indicators are easily accessible and offer sufficient information to allow valid and accurate judgements as to the presence and extent of needs in the community.

When needs are addressed as they are experienced or felt by the people concerned, the most proper design will be a quantitative one that employs surveys as a method. In such cases, representative community surveys will be the most appropriate means of data collection and analysis. Their results will demonstrate the presence or absence of any needs in the community that need attention; if various needs are present, it will list them, and finally it will specify which are thought to require most immediate attention. The survey will also provide information about the extent to which existing services are used, and about the reasons for people using or not using them.

When needs are seen as perceived by those who know most about the people concerned (experts, key informants, service providers etc.) the methods can be small surveys, Delphi panels, focus groups and the like. The purpose of these methods is to get together people who are well informed about community needs, and about how clients respond to community services, and to encourage them to talk about needs, to identify the ones that require attention, and finally to decide which require immediate action.

3 ACTION RESEARCH: RESEARCH IN ACTION

3.1 Introduction

As stated previously, some investigators consider that political interests and research should be kept apart. Researchers are not politicians. Their task is to create knowledge and explain social phenomena, not to reorganise society. Certainly, new knowledge can lead to social reconstruction; however, this should be the outcome of political action, not of research action.

This is one view. Another is that research can take dimensions which can involve political action, involving respondents in the process of research and through this in political action as a part of the research process. This combines research practice with political action, in the form of action research. In this sense, political interests are not the monopoly or privilege of politicians and interests groups, but also of the researcher. Researchers become the source of direct and/or indirect influence on the investigation through the decisions they make, the methods they choose and the extent to which they accept the demands of their sponsors (Greenwood, 1994).

But politics goes even deeper than that. There are cases where the researchers identify themselves fully with political ideologies and programmes, and take positive (or negative) action in an attempt to put their views and opinions into practice (Schensul and Schensul, 1992). Research becomes for them a political instrument and a tool for social change and reconstruction; in this sense it is often used to promote the interests and convictions of disadvantaged groups. Action research is the best example of this and represents a research type that has been employed since the 1920s (Whyte, 1991) in almost all areas of social research (Reason and Bradbury, 2001; Thomas, 1993).

3.2 What is action research?

We understand action research to be 'the application of fact finding to practical problem solving in a social situation with a view to improving the quality of action within it, involving the collaboration and cooperation of researchers, practitioners and laymen' (Burns, 1990: 252; Oja and Smulyan, 1989). This type of research is characterised by a number of criteria (Burns, 1990; Benini, 2000), as shown in Box 14.7.

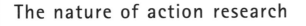

Box **14.7**

The nature of action research

Action research is:

- *Applied.* It addresses specific problems and proposes immediate solutions.
- *Situational.* It diagnoses a problem and attempts to solve it.
- *Topical.* It focuses on topical issues of social and political currency.
- *Collaborative.* It requires the efforts of researchers and practitioners.
- *Participatory.* Researchers take part in the implementation of the findings.
- *Political.* It employs a political stance and direction in its orientation.
- *Emancipatory.* It attempts to actively involve people in the process of change.
- *Self-evaluative.* It involves a constant evaluation of its process and modifications to adjust research and practice.

Briefly, action research criticises the theoretical and methodological basis of conventional social research, both by its challenges and by its claims. As Winter (1987: 2) puts it, 'it challenges a scientific method of inquiry based on the authority of the "outside" observer and the "independent" experimenter, and it claims to reconstruct both practical expertise and theoretical insight on the different basis of its own inquiry procedures'. Further, action research is applied research, and hence employs the same type of research design as other research types, with some modifications regarding the role of the respondent and the manner in which data collection is conducted. To a large extent, action research employs the same research design as evaluation research does.

3.3 The essence of action research

The elements that characterise action research are the personal involvement of the researcher, the emancipatory nature of the research, the active involvement of the researched, and its opposition to certain established policies and practices. This will set action research within the parameters of the critical perspective explained in Chapter 2. The researcher here takes the side of the respondents, helps them understand their real situation (in terms of discrimination, disadvantage etc.), explains to them the reasons for this, and shows them ways of change and 'liberation'. The researcher and the respondents work together towards change. Research becomes the vehicle of change and reconstruction. For instance, the respondents are shown how social order is shaped, how they came to be what they are in the community and their personal life, who benefits from it and what can be done to improve their life.

In certain cases, the background motives are related to deep-seated beliefs, convictions and theories that demand a radical reconstruction of the social order; Marxism is an example of this. In other cases, the motivating theory is less radical but equally influential. Feminism, for instance, influenced research activity that implied a strong element of participation, action and emancipation. Finally, action research is undertaken by researchers who wish to change conditions in ways which, although not as fundamental as the previous two, are still socially significant.

Box 14.8

Basic principles of action research

- *Commitment* to the cause of the study: research is not a task but a duty.
- *Emancipatory nature*: explaining social structures and pointing to the causes of problems.
- *Active involvement* of the respondents in the study, working together with the researcher.
- *Opposition* to established systems, policies and practices.
- *Political nature* of the study, its cause and consequences.
- *Applied nature* of the underlying research; it focuses on solving problems.
- Commitment to a *critical paradigm*, which drives the research and its political basis.
- *Empowerment* of participants to effect change in their own environment.
- Commitment to *change and reconstruction* of the social order.
- *Value-laden* procedures and operations.

In all cases, action research is based on the researcher's political convictions, initiates action-loaded investigation of social conditions, involves people, mobilises their forces, guides them to set goals, produces findings and follows them through until they are implemented. The researcher carries the work through, and makes sure that the findings are given the attention they deserve. In this sense, the researcher is not just an investigator but a collaborator and a facilitator: the political nature, the participatory character, the emancipatory elements and the direct, committing and personal involvement of the researcher are at the forefront of the research activity. Ultimately, action research helps to empower participants and to develop the skills and knowledge they need to effect change in their own environment (McNiff, 1992).

Political interests, priorities, values and ideologies affect the nature, type and extent of research, and the nature and application of its findings. In a similar fashion, research affects social and political life. It is this that motivates politicians and policy makers to be cautious about what type of research to support and what types of findings to make public. It is this interrelationship that social researchers must be aware of, and hence they must make their decisions according to ethical standards and principles (Kimmel, 1988).

3.4 The research design

The design employed by action researchers follows the same steps as in other types of research. It will begin with the arrangements entailed in the preparation step, and proceed through research design, data collection and analysis and finally to the step of publication of the findings. Below is an example of this.

Step 1. Preparation

In the first instance the researcher will begin with the choice and definition of the topic. Like every other researcher, the action researcher will identify an issue that needs investigation and define it to make it clear and specific, identifying the discrepancies and injustices, and naming the problem (Wadsworth, 1991: 5). Action research differs from other approaches in that the researcher is more likely to opt for a topic that is controversial, relates to problems, neglect and oppression and so on. However, this is not an element of the research design but rather of the type of theoretical perspective chosen: action research is more likely to be guided by critical, Marxist or feminist principles than by positivist principles and standards.

Step 2. Methodological construction of the topic

Here the main concepts will be defined and/or clarified. An example of this may be a study of oppression of homosexuals in a small country town. Here the researcher will have to clarify what types of homosexuals are referred to (e.g. gays, lesbians, single, committed, with/without children), the types of oppression that need to be investigated and the specific suburbs that will be considered in the study, unless the research is imbedded within a qualitative design.

Operationalisation of the topic will be as much a part of action research as it is in any other research type. If the issues to be explored need refinement and processing before they are taken to the respondents, operationalisation is an essential element. In the example introduced above, oppression will definitely have to be clarified and specified and above all prepared for measurement, that is, if measurement is a part of the study. If this is not the case, oppression will be addressed as in any other qualitative study. The same may be said about hypotheses.

Step 3. Sampling

The sampling procedures employed by action researchers are the same as those employed by other researchers. They may use probability or non-probability samples, and may include a few or many respondents. Such studies will probably employ snowball sampling and/or recruitment techniques via gay organisations, where access to respondents is likely to be gained.

Step 4. Data collection

The methods employed by action researchers are the same as those employed by other investigators. The most likely method here will be intensive interviews and focus groups. For the most part, data collection in action research is the same as that in other types of research. This is true with regard to the technical aspects of getting to the respondents and collecting the required information. However, there are some differences here.

Action research supports a higher degree of respondent participation in the work. Some members of the units under study are expected and indeed encouraged to participate actively with the researcher throughout the study. This participation may begin with the initial identification of the research topic and design and may continue up to the publication of the findings (Whyte, 1991). Homosexual groups will be consulted and researched, but also guided as to how to approach the authorities more effectively, with the assistance of the research team and their supporters.

Step 5. Data analysis

Analysis and interpretation of the findings are conducted within the parameters of the underlying research methodology. As in any other type of research, action researchers will use appropriate methods to identify trends and to justify conclusions pertinent to the research question. Quantitative methods may be employed, but the results of intensive interviewing and focus group discussions may lend themselves more readily to qualitative analysis.

Step 6. Reporting

As in previous steps, so here reporting will basically follow the path of other types of research. However, the nature of the research implies a more proactive perception of the findings, with the researcher and the researched making a concerted effort to give the findings the attention they deserve.

Step 7. Further action

While other researchers will be content to see their findings published in a professional journal or report of some kind, action researchers see it as a part of the study to bring the recommendations to the attention of the authorities and ensure that they are implemented. This may even require that additional pressure be put upon the relevant authorities, such as interest groups, visiting relevant authorities together with the researcher so that the right decisions are made, approaching the local member of parliament to take relevant action, employing media campaigns to publicise their findings so as to win public support, and even demonstrating in the front of parliament and elsewhere to make their point and intention clear to those concerned.

We have deliberately left the factor of theoretical perspective out of the design presented here. This is because the perspective permeates the whole process of research and offers guidance and direction; such guidance and direction are the determinants of action research and of any research in general. This means that if one takes away the theoretical and methodological bias, the technical aspects of action research are not very different from those of other types of research. Consequently, the factor that makes the difference here is politics, as entailed in the theoretical framework of action research.

3.5 Strengths and weaknesses of action research

Action research has been employed very successfully in the past and is becoming increasingly popular. The particular emphasis put upon this type of research by many critical researchers, Marxists and particularly feminists, give it a most fertile ground to grow and thrive. The reasons for this lie in its many strengths and the few (and less significant) weaknesses, as shown in Box 14.9.

The weaknesses referred to in this context relate to criticisms of the kind of action research that is based on qualitative research; in effect they relate to qualitative research in general and less to action research as a model of investigation. Where action research is based on a quantitative paradigm, most of these criticisms are irrelevant. Be that as it may, action research has a lot to offer, and many of its great advantages outweigh the alleged problems. However, it must be noted that what makes this research important and useful is not its design or methods but rather the 'action' that guides its process. It relates, first, to the way it uses and adjusts existing methods to enhance its impetus, and second, to the political engagement and commitment of the researchers and respondents.

Box **14.9**

Strengths and weaknesses of action research

STRENGTHS of action research

It encourages public participation
It encourages stakeholders to take active responsibility in the project
It furthers emancipation

It serves the public interest

It is set to promote change

It makes social and political processes transparent to the public

WEAKNESSES of action research

It allows no replication
It may verify preconceived ideas of the researcher
It is biased towards the interests of certain groups
It cannot assure representativeness, objectivity and generalisability
Low credibility due to the involvement of non-professionals in the project
No control of the nature of the findings and quality of research design

---

This is not to say that this research is therefore less interesting. On the contrary, it is an approach that entails a balanced combination of methodology and politics that makes it 'full' and extremely useful. The point to consider here is that, as far as design is concerned, this type of research borrows from quantitative or qualitative research and is as valid as qualitative and quantitative designs are.

MAIN POINTS

- Basic research focuses purely on gaining new knowledge and promoting the scientific understanding of certain aspects of the world.
- Applied research addresses specific problems and searches for solutions. The motivation here is not scientific knowledge per se but rather application, solution of problems and change.
- The three most common types of applied research are epidemiological, feasibility and evaluation research.
- These forms of research are widely employed by social workers and the caring professions in general, and constitute the most popular tools of feminist research.
- Evaluation research is a unique form of social inquiry that is employed to assess the merit, worth or value of an established policy or planned intervention
- Evaluation research appears in many forms: summative and formative evaluation, needs analysis, impact analysis, and process analysis are a few examples.
- Needs assessment is valued for its diagnostic outcomes, which inform public policy and community intervention.
- Action research combines standard methodology with a political drive and the active participation of stakeholders. Apart from working more closely with respondents, it entails an element of emancipation and change.
- Action research fits very well within the feminist research paradigm and has been extensively used by feminist researchers.
- The value of these research designs lies in their 'application' and purpose rather than in the nature of their methods.

WHERE TO FROM HERE?

Before you leave this chapter, visit the companion website for the third edition of *Social Research* at http://www.palgrave.com/sociology/sarantakos to review the main concepts introduced in this chapter and to test yourself on the major issues discussed.

FURTHER READING

Boruch, R. (1997) *Randomized Experiments for Planning and Evaluation: A Practical Guide*. Thousand Oaks, Calif.: Sage.

Cunningham, J. B. (1993). *Action Research and Organisational Development*. London: Praeger.

Hawe, P., Degeling, D. and Hall. J. (1993) *Evaluating Health Promotion: A Health Workers Guide*. Sydney: Mclennan and Petty.

Hicks, C. and Hennessy, D. (1997) 'The Use of Customised Training Needs Analysis Tool for Nurse Practitioner Development.' *Journal of Advanced Nursing*, 26: 389–98.

Hicks, C., Hennessy, D. and Bawell, F. (1996) 'Development of a Psychometrically Valid Framing Needs Analysis Instrument for Use with Primary Health Care Teams.' *Health Services Management Research*, 9: 262–72.

Pawson, R. and Tilley, N. (1997) *Realistic Evaluation*. London: Sage.

Posovac, E. J. and Carey, R. G. (1997) *Program Evaluation: Methods and Case Studies*. Upper Saddle River, N.J: Prentice-Hall.

Reason, P. and Bradbury, H. (2001) *Handbook of Action Research: Participative Inquiry and Practice*. London: Sage.

Robson, C. (2000) *Small-Scale Evaluation: Principles and Practice*. London: Sage.

Selener, D. (1997) *Participatory Action Research and Social Change*. Ithaca, N.Y.: Cornell University.

Shepherd, J. C. (1994) 'Training Needs Analysis: Necessity or Luxury?' *Journal of Nursing Management*, 3: 319–22.

South Australian Community Health Research Unit (1991) *Planning Healthy Communities: A Guide to doing Community Needs Assessment*. Adelaide: Flinders Press 1991.

Weiss, C. H. (1997) *Evaluation: Methods for Studying Programs and Policies*. Upper Saddle River, N.J.: Prentice-Hall.

Data analysis

PART

IV

Qualitative
analysis

- highlights the nature and idiosyncrasies of qualitative analysis

- introduces data presentation in qualitative research

- depicts grounded theory and analytic induction

- discusses narrative interviews

- offers a basis for comparisons between qualitative and quantitative analysis.

INTRODUCTION

The characteristic of qualitative analysis is that it deals with data presented in words; that it contains a minimum of quantitative measurement, standardisation and statistical techniques (Engel and Weggenig, 1991), and that it aims to transform and interpret qualitative data in a rigorous and scholarly manner (Coffey and Atkinson, 1996: 3). Beyond this there is simply no consensus as to how qualitative analysis should proceed, or what makes an acceptable analysis. Writers on the subject (e.g. Farber, 2001; Jankowski and Wester, 1991) note that the process of analysis is deeper, more focused and more detailed than in quantitative research, and takes one of two options. These are *analytic induction* and *grounded theory*. But the list of options for qualitative analysis does not stop here.

Other writers describe further discursive approaches, based mainly on discourse analysis, deconstructionism, conversation analysis, dramaturgical analysis, hermeneutic analysis, postmodernist analysis, narrative analysis, semiotics, structuralism and poststructuralism; in brief, qualitative analysis embraces many methods, has many uses, many audiences and many sponsors (Fielding and Lee, 1998). Wolcott (1992; 1994) lists more than 20 research strategies or methods, while Tesch (1990) raises that number to 27. The common elements of these analytic methods are their affiliation with interpretive or hermeneutic paradigms, their understanding of the world as being socially constructed through language, and the notion that analysis deals with the presentation of cultural representations treated as texts (Benini, 2000; Farber, 2001).

In this chapter we shall introduce the most common methods of qualitative analysis and explain their timing and nature in more detail.

1 THE TIMING OF QUALITATIVE ANALYSIS

Unlike quantitative research, where analysis is conducted after data collection, in qualitative research the timing of analysis varies. In some cases it follows the same path as in quantitative research, but in most cases it is conducted during data collection. A combination of both models is also possible.

1.1 Analysis during data collection

Analysis during data collection is the most common practice, and the one that is most consistent with the principles of qualitative research. In this case, data are collected, coded, conceptually organised, interrelated, analysed, evaluated and then used as a spring-board for further sampling, data collection, processing and analysis, until saturation is achieved. Data collection is thus merged with data analysis.

For instance, field researchers scrutinise the collected data thoroughly, and may even meet with colleagues to discuss their findings, compare notes, check consistency, conduct data analysis and draw conclusions before continuing with further data collection. This process takes the form of a spiral that goes from data analysis and reduction to data organisation and to interpretation of the data, and then back to data collection, analysis, reduction, organisation and interpretation, until saturation has been achieved.

During this process, researchers refine, confirm and test the validity of the conclusions drawn so far, establish commonalities and eliminate negative cases, leading to a degree of consistency and to small-scale generalisations. They further link generalisations together, testing and re-testing, contrasting, and comparing constantly, leading to typologies and eventually to theories (see Box 15.1).

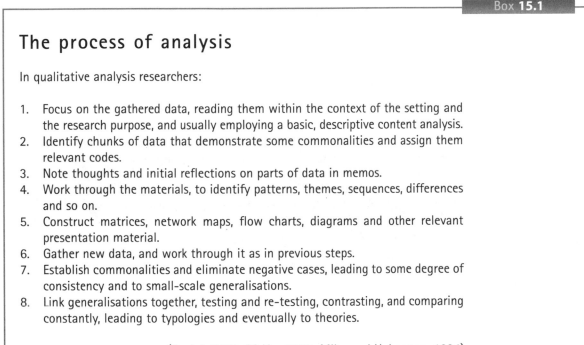

Box **15.1**

The process of analysis

In qualitative analysis researchers:

1. Focus on the gathered data, reading them within the context of the setting and the research purpose, and usually employing a basic, descriptive content analysis.
2. Identify chunks of data that demonstrate some commonalities and assign them relevant codes.
3. Note thoughts and initial reflections on parts of data in memos.
4. Work through the materials, to identify patterns, themes, sequences, differences and so on.
5. Construct matrices, network maps, flow charts, diagrams and other relevant presentation material.
6. Gather new data, and work through it as in previous steps.
7. Establish commonalities and eliminate negative cases, leading to some degree of consistency and to small-scale generalisations.
8. Link generalisations together, testing and re-testing, contrasting, and comparing constantly, leading to typologies and eventually to theories.

(Benini, 2000; Pfeifer, 2000; Miles and Huberman, 1994)

1.2 Analysis after data collection

In a number of cases, regardless of the nature of the research paradigm, there is some work left for analysis after completion of data collection. There are even cases where qualitative analysis is wholly conducted after data collection. This is, for instance, the case when the recording of data is facilitated electronically, for example on video and audio tapes. In this case, the main analysis is conducted after data collection, when the videos are viewed. The type of analysis varies according to the nature of the study.

1.3 Analysis during and after data collection

It goes without saying that a combination of both methods is not only possible but also frequently used. It is common, for instance, that while collecting data, researchers conduct some basic analysis, record the data and then intensify their analysis when the study is completed by focusing on more specific aspects of the research question as shown in the transcripts. In a number of cases, analysis during data collection serves to guide research in the right direction, and to facilitate a more effective treatment and coverage of the research topic. The actual analysis is conducted after data gathering is completed.

In other cases, the final analysis after data collection serves to refine and verify early analysis. This is the case for instance when conclusions drawn during later stages of data collection are tested against final notes or electronically recorded data (audio or video tapes). Here additional information helps reinforce, and in some cases correct, initial conclusions. The researcher may, in fact, ask colleagues to listen to audio recordings or view video tapes together and use their advice to clarify trends and verify initial interpretations.

2 VARIETIES OF QUALITATIVE ANALYSIS

The discussion above, apart from explaining where in the qualitative research design analysis is placed, also describes how this analysis is conducted. This description was rather brief, but nevertheless it pointed to the main characteristics of this analysis when it occurs after, or during, or during and after data collection.

Qualitative analysis entails a lot more than what was introduced above, however. More specifically, the process of analysis can be categorised in three distinct groups. These are the fixed, the iterative and the subjectivist models of analysis. Briefly, the fixed model is employed when data analysis occurs after collection, and the iterative model is employed when analysis is conducted while collecting data. The subjectivist model follows few – if any – rules, and hence one can say little about it (see Box 15.2)

Box **15.2**

Main types of qualitative analysis

- *Iterative qualitative analysis.* This analytic method employs two major strategies. These are *grounded theory* and *analytic induction.* They are characterised by the fact that their analytic process involves repeated use of data collection and analysis.
- *Fixed qualitative analysis.* This method of analysis is employed mainly when research followed a fixed research design. In this case, data analysis is conducted after data collection, and chiefly entails a method of content analysis or text analysis. The type of method depends on the nature of the data, the purpose of analysis and the nature of the underlying paradigm.
- *Subjectivist qualitative analysis.* This type of qualitative analysis in effect covers whatever cannot fit into the other two types of analysis. All these types share their relative aversion to structured research and analysis, and a mistrust of strict techniques and methods. In a number of cases, the disbelief in objective truth, as well as in the ability of standard methods to extract knowledge, leads to a subjective choice of methods that do not rely on general rules and principles.

The *fixed model* of qualitative analysis deals primarily with written records, that is, with documents. It deals with transcripts which the researcher must read and analyse. In this sense, the methods of analysis are those employed when studying documents: document study, content analysis or text analysis. As these have already been considered, we shall not discuss the fixed model of qualitative analysis in this chapter.

The *subjective model of qualitative analysis* is diverse and in practice covers whatever does not fit into the other two types of analysis. All these types, however, share a rejection of structured and disciplined modes of inquiry, of belief in an ordered world, objective truth or knowledge, and of the assumption that methods are capable of gathering knowledge that can be shared by all academics. Personal choice, decisions and preferences as well as subjective views about truths and knowledge are the basis of this school of thought. Radical postmodernism is an example.

Given that the parameters of subjective analysis follow no common standards like those of other models, and that in certain cases researchers borrow relevant procedures from other models, there is no need to discuss this model further. Hence, in the remainder of this chapter we shall discuss the analytic procedures that fall within the iterative model: namely, grounded theory, analytic induction and construction and reconstruction.

3   GROUNDED THEORY

3.1 Introduction

As noted above, the context in which qualitative analysis usually takes place is the flexible model, which is informed by grounded theory. Hence, in discussing the nature of qualitative analysis – and without ignoring the inherent diversity of this research paradigm – it is logical and legitimate to refer to grounded theory, and to give it the attention it deserves. Summarising the description of the process of analysis of this research model, we can say that data analysis is here a dynamic process which incorporates several elements of the research process, and is certainly not deferred until after data collection is fully completed. In the words of the experts (Strauss, 1987, 1990/1991: 51; Glaser, 1992), data analysis entails the procedures listed in Box 15.3.

We shall see later in this section exactly how this process takes place. At this stage, there is a need to define and explain some basic concepts and practices of grounded theory, such as categories, theoretical sampling, theoretical saturation and coding.

3.2 Instruments of analysis

Concepts and indicators

Indicators are concrete data, such as behaviour patterns and social events, which are observed or described in documents or interview texts. They indicate the presence of a concept which the researcher develops, at first provisionally and then with more confidence. Such concepts occupy a central position in the context of grounded theory.

Box 15.3

Aspects of grounded analysis

1. Identifying indicators of a concept.
2. Studying indicators and comparing them with each other.
3. Coding indicators, looking for answers and formulating hypotheses.
4. Categorising similar indicators as a class.
5. Naming the class and perceiving it as a coded category, which reflects the indicators' similarities, and the smallest common denominator. This is the conceptual code, the concept.
6. Comparing indicators with concepts and with other indicators; this helps to refine them and relate them optimally to the data.
7. Working through more attributes of the categories, refining them and getting additional information until the codes are tested and saturated. The more similar the indicators regarding the concept in question, the higher the degree of saturation of the attributes of the concept.
8. Developing and saturating more categories through the process of constant comparisons.
9. Including in the theory concepts and their attributes developed as described.
10. Further testing, contrasting and comparing of theories, and perhaps refining and changing them.

Categories

A category is a unit of information that entails events, happenings, and instances (Benini, 2000: 65; Böhm, 2000). Categories that are adequately processed lead to the identification of key categories which assist with theoretical sampling and data collection. A key category is one that possesses the power required to explain the largest degree of variance in behaviour; it also helps to integrate, tighten and saturate a theory. In the words of the founder of this research model (Strauss, 1991: 67–8), a key category must meet the following criteria. It

- must be neutral
- must appear frequently in the data
- should allow easy reference to other categories
- should possess clear implications for the formal theory.

Most significant is the core category, which is what this research model aims to establish, namely the grounded theory.

Theoretical sampling

Unlike quantitative research and many qualitative models, where sampling procedures are finalised before the research has commenced, in grounded theory the subjects, settings and events are selected predominantly during the process of data collection and analysis. Here sampling begins with a guided selection of the first unit. The information collected from the first respondent guides the researcher as to who the next respondent will be. The information that emerges through the study of the two respondents will lead to the selection of the third respondent and so on. More specifically, the emerging theory controls the choice of the respondents (Strauss, 1991: 70); this is why it is called theoretical sampling.

Theoretical saturation

Saturation indicates the stage in the research process at which no new or relevant data emerge, the category is well developed, and 'the relationships among categories are well established and validated' (Strauss and Corbin, 1998: 212).

Coding

Coding is one of the most central elements of grounded theory, and is equally diverse and complex. For this reason it will now be discussed in more detail.

3.3 Coding

Within grounded theory, coding is the central pathway to theory construction; hence it is important that it is performed in an accurate and disciplined manner. In the words of the founder of grounded theory (Strauss, 1991: 122–3), researchers should take the precautions listed in Box 15.4 when coding.

Within these parameters, coding appears in three forms: open, axial and selective coding. Each type proceeds in a particular manner, and aims at certain goals within the process of theory construction, as we shall see.

Box **15.4**

Be cautious with coding

- ■ Do not paraphrase sentences but discover and name genuine categories.
- ■ Set categories as directed by the coding paradigm (i.e. in reference to conditions, strategies, consequences etc.).
- ■ Set categories in relationship with subcategories, one by one.
- ■ Relate categories to data and refer to them adequately.
- ■ Stress the factors that make sorting easier.
- ■ Interrelate categories and subcategories.
- ■ Relate or eliminate unrelated categories.

Open coding

The purpose of open coding is to identify first-order concepts and substantive codes. In this process, the researcher begins by opening up the data: breaking it down and looking for empirical indicators of concepts. This implies taking notes constantly, sorting them out, looking for meanings, and comparing notes. Following this, the researcher labels the data, and while working through them, changes the labels as required in order to 'conceptualise' the data, looking for conceptual patterns, for what is central, while labelling. This leads to the emergence of concepts that eventually become the basis of a theoretical model (Böhm, 2000). The newly developed conceptual categories are tested within the data to see whether they have the explanatory power they are supposed to have. They are therefore applied first in a small area, then in a larger one, and finally right through the whole text. Knowledge of the context is most useful in this process. New categories are compared to others, and this offers hints of possible variations of their aspects. Finally, comparing and setting concepts against each other shows which ones are important and deserve further analysis, and which will be dropped.

Axial coding

Axial coding (also known as theoretical coding) is a more advanced level of coding and aims to interconnect substantive codes and first-order concepts to construct higher-order concepts. In this form of coding, the researcher puts an 'axis' through the data to connect the concepts. While open coding 'opens' data to theoretical possibilities, axial coding 'puts together' concepts, and interrelates them to reach a higher level of abstraction. This eventually leads to the construction of 'theoretical codes' and produces categories: refinement and differentiation of the new concepts 'bestows upon them the status of categories' (Böhm, 2000). Central categories are further tested by applying them in small and large texts and in the whole text, relating them to each other and to concepts in terms of content and form, and studying them with regard to space, time, cause–effect relationships and means–end argumentation. Hypothetical relationships between them are tested using new material, and further tested through coding, eventually leading to conditional propositions.

Selective coding

Analysis enters higher levels of abstraction in this step. The researcher works towards identifying 'the higher-order core category'. This means that from the categories identified so far, one has to be chosen which meets the demands of the tests. Here the analysis is directed towards a central focus. The process of analysis goes through paths that are similar to those employed in the previous steps. This means working through notes, diagrams and categories, searching for the central phenomenon and the central category. The attributes and dimensions of possible core categories are related to those of other categories, looking for regularities, generalisations, level of abstraction etc. that are outstanding and have high explanatory power. The higher the abstract level of the categories, the wider the applicability of the theory (Böhm, 2000). Principles of the theory are converted to hypotheses and contrasted again with reality. This process is continued until a theoretical saturation is reached: that is, when no more aspects to the theory can be added. This denotes the end of the analysis.

Overall, this research design has all the strengths and weaknesses of other types of qualitative research. A few added questions relate to some major aspects of application, most of which stress the extreme subjectivity and high level of arbitrary decisions made by the researcher (Flick, 1995: 205) – for example the decision to shift from one step to the next or the conclusion as to when saturation has been reached – given the small research sample, and the few theoretical parameters set at the outset.

4 ANALYTIC INDUCTION

Analytic induction is a procedure employed to conduct an analysis of qualitative data (see Bühler-Niederberger, 1985; Manning, 1982). It was introduced by Florian Znaniecki in the 1930s, and since that time has become increasingly popular among qualitative researchers. In simple terms, analytic induction aims to produce complete and universal statements about social phenomena (Fielding and Lee, 1998: 22). Induction means proceeding from the specific to the general, that is, constructing abstract concepts from a study of specific data. This is the opposite of deduction, which proceeds from the general to the specific, verifying abstract concepts by testing whether they are supported by data. In a way, analytic induction entails both induction and deduction (Hammersley and Atkinson, 1995: 234–5). As an 'induction' it studies data obtained through qualitative research and attempts to establish regularities and commonalities that could support the formulation of hypotheses. As a 'deduction' it tests the validity of these hypotheses by contrasting them to research data, and examines whether they are still applicable and valid. This is commonly referred to as the analytic spiral.

How is analytic induction conducted? Basically, the path of analysis follows the process of analytic spiral introduced above. This process sees the analysis as moving between the general and the specific, a hypothesis and research data, until an agreement is reached. This process can be summarised as shown in Box 15.5 (Farber, 2001; Fielding and Lee, 1998: 22; Jankowski and Wester, 1991).

The purpose of analytic induction varies from case to case according to a number of criteria. There are writers (Manning, 1982: 280) who see this method as an exhaustive examination of cases with the purpose of proving universal,

Box **15.5**

Using analytic induction

1. Define and describe the topic.
2. Examine raw data produced through the study.
3. Formulate a working hypothesis as to the nature of the characteristics which the researcher initially assumes are the most important.
4. Examine a specific case to establish whether the hypothesis regarding the assumed characteristics applies.
5. If the case confirms the hypothesis, continue the comparison by considering new data, until saturation is achieved. The hypothesis is then accepted, and its validity confirmed.
6. If the case does not confirm the hypothesis, either exclude the case and redefine the phenomenon, or reformulate the hypothesis, changing the originally hypothesised characteristics so that the case may become part of the phenomenon under study.
7. Continue contrasting with new cases until analysis leads to a theory that would explain the phenomenon within a particular context.

causal generalisations. Others are hesitant to assign analytic induction to such difficult tasks. Instead they argue that this procedure is not able to establish causality, to predict events, or to produce universal statements. They see analytic induction as being suitable for examining cases that might be related to a concept in development (Jankowski and Wester, 1991).

5 CONSTRUCTION AND DECONSTRUCTION

Construction and deconstruction are parts of an analytical mechanism that is most closely associated with interpretivism and the notion that the world is constructed; this was introduced earlier in this text. Since this mechanism is very frequently used within qualitative analysis, a brief description of its process deserves our attention. Lueger (2000: 76–80) describes the following four components of this mechanism.

- *Deconstruction*. In order to achieve a deep understanding of phenomena, it is necessary to separate oneself from everyday occurrences, explanations and typicalities. One must go beyond the 'known'. In this sense, the capacity of interpretation must be widened, hasty identifications of phenomena avoided, and new structuration of knowledge achieved. For this to happen, materials must be cut into the smallest pieces and de-contextualised, to the extent that their original context can no longer be recognised. In this way, texts are converted to small units of meanings, free from previous meaningful connections, to other units and to contexts, and free from overarching, general assumptions.
- *Comparative differentiation*. The resulting de-contextualised parts are then integrated into new constructs, which are then compared to other possible alternative options. This is done so that the researcher can widen the understanding of the whole process of the object under investigation.
- *Contextual construction of meaning*. This entails an analysis of the reconstructed materials within a material and a social context.
- *Extensive interpretation of meanings*. The researcher speculates here as to various possible meanings, and analyses such possibilities as if they were factually effective. This is intended to allow the researcher to achieve possible information about the whole context of the phenomenon.
- *Testing of results*. Testing of the outcomes of this process is continued further, until the validity of the resulting constructs is established.

This brief discussion demonstrates that analysis and interpretation in qualitative research are neither simple nor uniform. The diversity in this area is so important and so well founded that it is almost impossible to integrate it into one model, pattern or template. Unlike quantitative research, in qualitative research analysis and interpretation are pluralistic, as pluralistic as the methods used and (even more so) as pluralistic as the underlying paradigms.

6 DATA ANALYSIS IN NARRATIVE INTERVIEWS

In narrative interviews, analysis begins when narration, debate and transcription have been completed. In this sense, analysis means analysis of transcripts, content analysis or textual analysis. It is characteristic of this form of interview that the focus of analysis is primarily not on the interview itself but on the text that is produced while documenting the story presented during the interview (Lamnek, 1993: 34; Hermans, Tkocz and Winkler, 1984).

For instance, attention is given here to the analysis of conversation (it is therefore referred to as conversation analysis; see, for instance, Bergmann, 1991), with particular emphasis on the structure of conversation, such as the fluctuations in story-telling, patterns of presentation of the story, the ranking of experiences, hesitation in the flow of narration, fluctuations in the degree of detail in story-telling, inconsistencies or contradictions in information content and so on. The presence of such gaps, inconsistencies and contradictions in the narrative are taken into consideration when drawing conclusions about structures and processes. It should be noted, though, that such aspects of the narrative do not necessarily relate to problems in the interviewee's construction of reality but can be characteristics of the reality itself.

The process of analysis of the transcripts of narrative interviews can be broadly summarised in six points. Following the central lines of Schütze's work, as presented in his writings as well as in reviews of other writers (especially Benini, 2000: 913; Pfeifer, 2000: 62–79, 132–46; Heinze, 1995: 70–6; Bohnsack, 1993: 91–107), these steps can be described as shown below:

1. *Formal textual analysis.* The first step of analysis includes cleaning the text of non-narrative material and preparing the text for analysis. This includes the identification of sequences in the text, the search for the presence of types of information presented by the interviewee in different levels of significance (that is, whether the interviewee sets some events as more important or of a higher priority, and others as less important or of lower priority). In this way the text is divided into sequences that demonstrate the way in which the respondent perceives, describes and assesses the events in question. Analysis then follows within the context of the sequenced text.

2. *Structural description of the content.* Here emphasis is placed on the overall structure of the text and on its composition. To achieve this, the text is searched for indicators of connectors between individual presentations of events (such as 'because', 'then', 'after', 'already' etc.) as well as of deficient plausibility shown in the tone of the voice, structure of language, self-corrections and the like (Heinze, 1995: 72). The purpose of this is to demonstrate which parts of the statements have a limited and which a more general significance.

3. *Analytic abstraction.* At this point of analysis, the results allow a perception of the situation which is less bound to single statements or descriptions of single events and more to general and abstract expressions. Such abstract statements are contrasted with statements relating to specific life sequences, and their validity is tested. This is expected to lead to an identification of the basic and dominant experiential frequency that best describes the life events.

4. *Knowledge analysis.* Analytical abstraction prepares the scene for a more realistic and convincing interpretation of the life processes of the informant, extending to levels of knowledge, and an analysis of the ways in which knowledge is employed to respond to social demands.

5. *Comparisons.* At this stage comparisons between more text parts are undertaken to allow relative generalisations. This eventually leads to the construction of elementary categories.

6. *Construction of a theoretical model.* The final aim of this analysis is to construct a theoretical model whose elements are sequentially contrasted to statements presented in the text. Those consistent with the text are maintained; others are eliminated. This contrast of the whole with the parts and vice versa is critically important for the construction of the model.

The researcher is here interested not simply in detailed uninterpreted descriptions of social conditions, but in the story. Descriptions are reports of happenings as recalled by the teller. Stories are characterised by the fact that they not only bring the listener to the scene of the happening, including space and time, but entail also a sequential presentation of the event, and most of all a retrospective interpretation and a concluding summary of the story. Basically the NI focuses on a reconstruction of the orientation of patterns of action. The two most important characteristics (and advantages) of NIs are the retrospective interpretation and the closeness of detailed stories to reality.

The theoretical basis of the analytical interpretation employed in the NI is the homology of narrative and experience, namely that narratives and experiences are identical (a point that has been criticised by other researchers). This means that stories about the personal life of the interviewee truthfully reflect life experiences which contain information about basic structures and mechanisms of social life that are pertinent to other people. Following this, the NI is thought to have the capacity to focus not only on life stories of the interviewee but also on stories about collective experiences with social structures and processes, historical events, community experiences and reactions and other community responses to social events of the time.

The process of analysis of transcripts of narrative interviews bears a strong resemblance to the general pattern of qualitative analysis introduced earlier in this chapter. The imminent contrast of abstractions to raw data and the constant validation, as presented in the analytic induction, is more than evident also in this analysis.

7 DATA PRESENTATION IN QUALITATIVE RESEARCH

7.1 Introduction

Qualitative researchers employ various methods to present their data visually. While some employ methods of presentation used by quantitative researchers, in their original or in a modified form, in other cases different forms of presentation are used. Certainly, tables and graphs are useful tools of presentation in qualitative research, but the structure of presentation does not seem to adhere to any strict rules and procedures, given that graphs and tables in qualitative research are always tailored to serve the needs of the particular study.

The methods seem to be developed by researchers for a particular study to meet their personal styles, but those that prove useful are taken up by other researchers and after some time they become an element of qualitative research. Miles and Huberman, for instance, presented some of the methods used in their studies in a widely-read publication (1994); many of these are very interesting and are used widely by other qualitative researchers. In the following sections we shall report on some of their techniques, as presented and justified theoretically and methodologically by these writers, giving a few examples of the types of displays that they report.

7.2 Matrices in qualitative research

A matrix is a form of data presentation that, to a large extent, resembles and is equivalent to a table. It has a title, a heading, cells, and other forms of information similar to those of the tables typical of quantitative research, but it differs in its purpose and nature.

Matrices are a form of summary table. They contain verbal information, quotes, summarised text, extracts from notes, memos, standardised responses and, in general, data integrated around a point or research theme that makes sense. In the main, matrices contain information about and explain aspects of research, and allow the researcher to get a quick overview of data related to a certain point. In this sense they serve a similar purpose to that of tables employed in quantitative research.

Matrices can become very complex and also serve many diverse goals. In one form (*checklist matrix*) they present integrated data on a summative index or scale, organising in that way several components of a single, coherent variable (Miles and Huberman, 1994). In another form they contain information ordered by time (*time-ordered matrix*) or according to roles (*role-ordered matrix*). The former can be thought of as a table in which the columns are arranged in a time sequence, demonstrating what happened and when as the research progressed from one point of time to the next. In a role-ordered matrix, the table rows contain verbal information about the views of role occupants on a specific issue of the project. A combination of the elements of matrices is also possible (e.g. role by time or role by group matrix).

Matrices can be ordered according to a central theme (*conceptually clustered matrices*), or according to outcomes and dependent variables (*effects matrices*), or present forces that are at work in particular contexts showing processes and outcomes (*site dynamics matrices*); they can present series of events displayed in any possible order (*event listing*), or in the form of a *causal network*. In the latter case, the matrix presents a field of interrelationships between dependent and independent variables describing causal connections between them.

It must be noted that models such as those described above, although of a qualitative nature, have some strong quantitative overtones, which might not be accepted by traditionally orientated qualitative researchers. Terms such as variables, for instance, defined as dependent and independent, especially when a notion of causation is attached to them, are elements that many researchers may find incompatible with qualitative analysis. This illustrates how diverse the field of qualitative research is.

Building matrices

Constructing a matrix is a process that relates more to the personal ingenuity, competence and creativity of the researcher than to rules and principles. Miles and Huberman (1994: 240–1) admit that there are no fixed canons for constructing a matrix, and that there are no 'correct' matrices, but rather, functional ones. They nevertheless recommend that researchers follow some 'rules of thumb' when working with matrices. Such 'rules' suggest that matrices should be kept to one-page displays; should include between 15 and 20 variables in rows and columns; be constructed while keeping in mind that they can and will be changed, regrouped and modified by adding new rows and columns; that rows and columns be kept fine-grained so that adequate differentiation is possible; and that new matrices may evolve out of other matrices as the research unfolds.

7.3 Figures in qualitative research

Figures are as useful in qualitative research as matrices. They combine lines and curves with verbal comments and indicators. However, there is no set format of organisation and construction; how a figure will be constructed and what format it will take depend on the complexity of data and on the ability and imagination of the field worker (Miles and Huberman, 1994).

7.4 Charts in qualitative research

Miles and Huberman (1994) describe a form of chart that they call a *context chart*. This presents in graphic form the interrelationship that exists between elements of the environment, for example roles and groups that make up the context in which behaviour develops. Context is a significant factor in the understanding of behaviour. Context charts offer a visual presentation of behaviour in context.

7.5 Displays in qualitative research

Displays are employed in qualitative research for many and diverse purposes. To a certain extent, displays substitute for the work accomplished by means of statistics. In this sense, charts, matrices and figures provide the information that mathematical figures and coefficients provide in quantitative research. They present visual information which allows the researcher to make sense of the collected information and so to draw relevant conclusions. There are several types of displays, each of which differs in type and complexity and serves a different purpose. Miles and Huberman (1994) offer a very detailed discussion of these types of displays; a brief list is given below.

Within case displays

The first group of displays comprises the Within-Case displays, which have the purpose of exploring and describing conclusions related to a single case study. The types of displays used in this context are: partially ordered displays (including context charts, check-list matrices and transcript-as-poem displays); time ordered displays (such as event listing, critical incident charts, event-state networks and activity records); role-ordered displays (e.g. role-ordered matrices and role-by-time matrices); and conceptually ordered displays (such as conceptually clustered matrices, thematic conceptual matrices, fork taxonomies, cognitive maps, and effects matrices).

In the same group belong also types of displays which are intended not only to describe but also to provide explanations and predictions. Such displays include the case dynamic matrix, which displays 'a set of forces for change and traces the conceptual processes and outcomes' (Miles and Huberman, 1994: 148) and the causal network which displays the various variables and their interconnections.

Cross-case displays

The second group of displays involves more than one case. Some of these displays aim to explore and describe conclusions, others to order and explain findings. Some are partially ordered displays, others are case-ordered and time-ordered displays. Many of these displays are matrices, graphs and tables. But other types of displays are also used; the scatterplot is an example. Here a relative affinity to quantitative research is evident. This is more so when we explore the second part of this group, which relates to ordering and explaining. Here a strong emphasis is placed on predicting and variable analysis as well as on causal analysis (causal chains and causal networks), which for many qualitative researchers do not belong to the qualitative methodology.

8 COMPUTER-AIDED DATA ANALYSIS (CADA)

Computers can be, and are being, used in qualitative research in the context of both pure qualitative research, where analysis is done the traditional way, and the so-called 'enriched' qualitative research (Contrad and Reinharz, 1984; Fielding and Lee, 1998; Fisher, 1997; Richards, 1986; Richards and Richards, 1987, 1994; Weitzman and Miles, 1994). Computer-aided data analysis (CADA) is used in many forms and allows the qualitative researcher to process data in a way parallel to that in quantitative research (Huber, 1991; Madron, Tate and Brookshire, 1987; Ragin, 1987).

There are now more than 24 programs currently in use in qualitative research (Fielding and Lee, 1998; Weitzman and Miles, 1994). Apart from basic word-processing programs, which are used in low-level analysis of qualitative data, there are programs devised specifically for research purposes. Each program is specialised in a particular area of research, for example text retrievers that code and retrieve information, text managers that manage text, conceptual network builders that draw diagrams, or code-based theory building programs that test hypotheses, and develop theories.

Some of the most common programs are (see Flick et al., 1991; Kelle and Erzberger, 1999; Richards and Richards, 1987, 1994; Weitzman and Miles, 1993, 1994):

AQUAD	HyperSoft	MECA	TextBase Alpha
AskSam	Info Select	Metamorph	The Ethnograph
ATLAS.ti	Kwalitan	Nud*ist	The TextCollector
HyperQual	Martin	NVivo	The WordCruncher
HyperRESEARCH	MAX	Qualpro	ZyINDEX

The extent to which CADA is used by qualitative researchers depends on the nature of the study, type of analysis and underlying paradigm. Briefly the types of functions offered by computer programs are shown in Box 15.6.

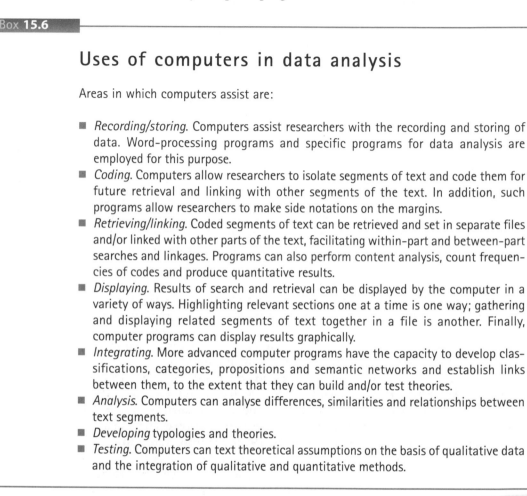

Uses of computers in data analysis

Areas in which computers assist are:

- *Recording/storing.* Computers assist researchers with the recording and storing of data. Word-processing programs and specific programs for data analysis are employed for this purpose.
- *Coding.* Computers allow researchers to isolate segments of text and code them for future retrieval and linking with other segments of the text. In addition, such programs allow researchers to make side notations on the margins.
- *Retrieving/linking.* Coded segments of text can be retrieved and set in separate files and/or linked with other parts of the text, facilitating within-part and between-part searches and linkages. Programs can also perform content analysis, count frequencies of codes and produce quantitative results.
- *Displaying.* Results of search and retrieval can be displayed by the computer in a variety of ways. Highlighting relevant sections one at a time is one way; gathering and displaying related segments of text together in a file is another. Finally, computer programs can display results graphically.
- *Integrating.* More advanced computer programs have the capacity to develop classifications, categories, propositions and semantic networks and establish links between them, to the extent that they can build and/or test theories.
- *Analysis.* Computers can analyse differences, similarities and relationships between text segments.
- *Developing* typologies and theories.
- *Testing.* Computers can text theoretical assumptions on the basis of qualitative data and the integration of qualitative and quantitative methods.

Although most computer programs employed for qualitative analysis contain modules for recording, coding and retrieving data, higher-level functions such as linking, displaying and integrating are available in a few programs only. ATLAS.ti, HyperRESEARCH, MECA, MetaDesign, Nud*ist and QCA are a few examples of programs with advanced capabilities. Overall, the strengths and weaknesses of CADA those listed below (Ragin and Becker, 1989; Tesch, 1989, 1990).

Strengths of CADA

- *Saves time.* Computers are faster than researchers in almost all analytic tasks. Even when taking into account the time required to program the computer to complete tasks, computers are faster. Given also that most instructions are systematised and packaged, ready made for the user, computer advantage is more than obvious.

- *Saves work.* Many tasks are not integrated and a lot of work that was once necessary is no longer required. Relieving researchers from a large part of the menial work allows them more time to concentrate on more important aspects of analysis.
- *Produces quick results.* Operations are completed in a fraction of the time required for assistants to complete them.
- *Is convenient.* Researchers can use computers at any time and place (e.g. late at night, during holidays, in an airplane).
- *Reduces the need for personnel.* Computers perform the work of several people, reducing the number of assistants required.
- *Offers a more efficient analysis.* Computers make no mistakes in recognising or counting codes.
- *Offers easier access to texts and codes.* This is particularly the case when data is stored electronically.
- *Offers easier text reproduction and sharing.* Copying parts of the text, identifying similar codes and integrating them into a common file, sending files to other researchers and similar tasks are conducted more easily with the aid of computers than manually.
- *Is accurate.* It is more accurate than manual processing.
- *Is reliable.* It is more reliable than manual processing.
- *Is flexible.* It allows flexibility in the analysis.
- *Is powerful.* It allows the processing of larger amounts of data than manual processing.

Weaknesses of CADA

- *Costs.* CADA requires an infrastructure that adds to the costs of the project budget, for computers and programs.
- *Artificial treatment.* It is often argued that the essence of data is not accessible to 'machines', regardless of how intelligent the programs may be.
- *Theoretical inconsistency.* Qualitative methods offer in essence a path away from structured thinking and operations, such as quantification and researcher distance from the researched. The use of computers in qualitative research works against this principle, and makes it no different from the models it is intended to overcome and avoid.
- *Inadequacy of programs.* There is often no consistency between computer methodological principles and the assumptions of the theory that underlies the research. This is clearly shown by in the fact that one computer program can serve so many and diverse qualitative theories. The increase in the number of computer programs and their growing diversity may rectify this weakness.
- *Emphasis.* The use of computers often displaces the weight of the analysis from theory development to coding, and to technical aspects of analysis.

On balance, CADA brings more advantages to researchers than manual processing. It is a matter of time and training to correct weaknesses, to make researchers aware of the dangers of computerised analysis, and to adjust computer programs so that they accurately meet the needs of the researchers and the academic community in general. Computers are an indispensable tool of research, and as technology advances will become even more useful, even indispensable, in the future.

- In most cases, qualitative analysis is conducted either during data collection, or during and after data collection.
- Overall, qualitative analysis is not as fixed or as uniform as quantitative analysis.
- There are also cases where qualitative analysis follows the straight line of a fixed design, where it begins after recording, transcription, checking and editing have been completed, followed by interpretation, and generalisations.
- Most qualitative researchers do not employ mathematical/statistical methods in data analysis.
- Qualitative researchers use computers extensively in data analysis. Several computer programs have been developed to aid with qualitative data analysis. They are used for recording and storing, coding, retrieving and linking data, and displaying and integrating data.
- Overall, data analysis in qualitative research is not as clear or as uniform as it is in quantitative research.
- In qualitative interviews one possible way of data analysis entails transcription, checking and editing, analysis and interpretation, generalisations and verifications.
- Qualitative analysis is more advanced and more complex when it entails analytic induction, construction and deconstruction, and grounded theory.
- In case-study research, data analysis can be accomplished by one or more of the following methods: pattern-matching, explanation-building techniques, time-series analysis, making repeated observations and secondary analysis.
- Computers are used in qualitative research for recording and storing, coding, retrieving and linking data, and displaying and integrating data.
- Graphs are common in qualitative research. Examples are matrices, figures and charts.

Before you leave this chapter, visit the companion website for the third edition of *Social Research* at http://www.palgrave.com/sociology/sarantakos to review the main concepts introduced in this chapter and to test yourself on the major issues discussed.

De Vaus, D. (2002) *Analyzing Social Science Data*. London: Sage.

Ezzy, D. (2002) *Qualitative Analysis: Practice and Innovation*. Crows Nest, N.S.W.: Allen and Unwin; London: Routledge.

Boyatzis, R. E. (1998) *Transforming Qualitative Information: Thematic Analysis and Code Development*. Thousand Oaks, Calif.: Sage.

Hayes, N. (1997) *Doing Qualitative Analysis in Psychology*. Hore, UK: Psychology Press.

Altheide, D. L. (1996) *Qualitative Media Analysis*. Thousand Oaks, Calif.: Sage.

Gibbs, B. (2001) *Qualitative Data Analysis: Explorations with Nvivo*. Buckingham: Open University Press.

Hodson, L. (1999) *Analysing Documentary Accounts*. Thousand Oaks, Calif.: Sage.

Lofland, J. and Lofland, L. H. (1995) *Analysing Social Settings: A Guide to Qualitative Observation and Analysis*. Belmont, Calif.: Wadsworth.

Silverman, D. (2001) *Interpreting Qualitative Data: Methods for Analysing Talk, Text and Interaction*. London: Sage.

16 Quantitative analysis

INTRODUCTION

Quantitative analysis is a diverse and complex process. In the first instance, it entails a primary analysis (dealing with raw data freshly produced by a study), a secondary analysis (involving previously analysed data), or a meta-analysis. Apart from this, it contains statistical techniques of a varying degree. Statistical processing can be conducted manually or electronically (Rassenberger, 1989; Reid, 1987). Easy access to computers and the many advantages of electronic processing have made this a standard procedure of quantitative analysis. Examples of such advantages are

- fast data processing and analysis of huge amounts of data
- relatively inexpensive data processing and analysis
- high reliability
- accuracy of computations
- accessibility of sophisticated statistical tests to non-statisticians.

The diverse and complex nature of quantitative analysis will be addressed in this chapter in a manner that not only simplifies its diversity without neglecting its quality but also avoids entanglement in the problems of its mathematical nature. In essence, this chapter will introduce statistics, in a student-friendly manner, where no mathematics, no formulae, no manual computations, and no old-fashioned statistical methods will be employed. The focus of data analysis will be mainly on what quantitative analysis entails; when, and under what conditions statistical procedures are used; how computers are instructed to conduct the tests for you, and how the test results are interpreted within the study.

You will see that one can conduct effective statistical analysis without statistical formulae and without mathematics (see Sarantakos, 2002).

> PLEASE NOTE: Statistical analysis is conducted using SPSS version 11 or 12; version 10 can be used, although some adjustments may be required. Version 10 contains practically the same computation procedures as versions 11 and 12, except that it sets some measures in locations other than those of the two newer versions.

1 STEPS OF DATA ANALYSIS

Given that data analysis is now conducted almost exclusively with the assistance of computers, our discussion in this chapter will focus on electronic data analysis only. For this a computer and the SPSS computer program (version 11 or 12) are required.

Data analysis begins where data collection ends; and this is when the instruments of data collection that contain the data (e.g. questionnaires) are completed. From this point on, the researcher will follow a systematic process that begins with preparing the data for computer entry, followed by entering the data in the computer and then by data processing and analysis. The researcher may be interested in getting a brief overview of the general trends regarding the research question. There are many ways of doing this; tables, graphs and statistical coefficients are a few examples. What follows from this stage is interpretation and drawing conclusions. In the following sections we shall address these steps in detail.

Box 16.1

Tasks of quantitative analysis

- *Data preparation.* Checking, editing and coding.
- *Data entry.* Entering the data in the computer.
- *Graphic presentation.* For example, presenting the findings in the form of graphs or tables.
- *Data processing and analysis.* Conducting statistical analysis.
- *Interpretation of the findings.* Explaining the meaning of data individually.
- *Conclusions.* Proposing direct answers to the research question.

1.1 Data preparation

Data preparation first involves checking, editing and coding. Hence information gathered through the study should be checked and edited so that it is clear, legible, relevant and appropriate. Editing is done where necessary; if answers are missing and/or illegible, the researcher will decide whether to accept or to reject them.

Coding is the process of converting verbal responses to numerical codes. For instance, 'Male' may be given the code 1, and 'Female' code 2. Coding can be performed before data collection (pre-coding) or after it (post-coding). The numbers expressing the codes (e.g. 1 and 2) are called *values*, and the concepts they represent (e.g. 'Male' and 'Female') the *value labels*.

In quantitative analysis, coding can also be employed when open-ended questions are employed. This involves first the development of categories, and second the assignment of the corresponding value label and the value to each question. For instance, when the open-ended question deals with the question of how power issues are handled in families, the categories may be 'patriarchal', 'democratic', and 'matriarchal', and the values 1, 2, and 3 respectively. This is followed by a careful reading of the answer, identification of the appropriate category, and entering the corresponding number in the designated place next to the answer. Value labels will be used when entering the data in the computer. Usually, category construction is conducted before the commencement of the study, and the relevant codes are presented in the code book, which is generally made available to coders.

Missing answers to questions, or inaccurate responses (e.g. when the tick indicating the gender has been placed ambiguously between 'Male' and 'Female') must also be recorded. They are called missing values and are represented by '9', '99', or '999', depending on whether the expected value has one, two or three figures.

Finally, investigators are expected to monitor coding in order to prevent errors or bias. Coder reliability is significant and is usually checked in two contexts, the

Box 16.2

Perception of Marriage Questionnaire (extract)

Please tick the option that reflects fully your views on the issues listed below

Office use only

1. What is your gender?

Male (✓) 1
Female ( ) 2

1

2. What is your age?

Below 25 ( ) 1
26 - 50 (✓) 2
50 - 75 ( ) 3

2

3. Would you consider yourself...

Very religious ( ) 1
Religious ( ) 2
Not religious (✓) 3
Anti-religious ( ) 4

3

4. Are you currently...

Single (✓) 1
Married ( ) 2
Cohabiting ( ) 3
Divorced/separated ( ) 4
Widowed ( ) 5

1

5. Are you in favour of de-institutionalising marriage?

Strongly in favour ( ) 1
In favour ( ) 2
No opinion ( ) 3
Against ( ) 4
Strongly against (✓) 5

5

6. Are you in favour of polygamy?

Yes ( ) 1
No (✓) 2
I don't know ( ) 3

2

7. Should the state take over the responsibility for children?

I think so ( ) 1
I don't think so ( ) 2
I don't know (✓) 3

3

8. Overall, are families as happy as they used to be?

I think so ( ) 1
I don't think so (✓) 2
I don't know ( ) 3

2

9. Are you in favour of prohibiting abortion

Yes (✓) 1
No ( ) 2
I don't know ( ) 3

1

reliability of the coder (i.e. that the coder maintains a stable and uniform pattern of coding, and that variability in coding is avoided) and inter-coder reliability (checked by testing how uniform the pattern of coding is when performed by several coders).

1.2 Data entry in the computer

The first step of electronic data processing is to enter the checked and coded answers in the computer. As noted above, for this a computer, equipped with the statistical package SPSS Version 10, 11 or 12 (see Miller et al., 2002) is required. This program is powerful, student-friendly and relatively inexpensive. The process of entering data in the computer includes two basic steps. These are defining the variables, and entering the data. In the following, we shall address these steps in turn.

Defining the variables

The procedure of defining the variables is like building 'boxes' inside the computer, adequately labelled and prepared, to accommodate the data that belong to that variable. You will tell the computer, for instance, to construct a box; to call it, say, 'Gender'; to divide it into two parts, labelled 'Male' and 'Female'; and to assign them the values 1 and 2 respectively. This is where the answers will be placed when the actual data are entered. You repeat this process for each variable. Let us examine an example.

Suppose we conducted a study including a questionnaire containing several questions. Let us see how the first nine questions (and the nine variables they entail) will be defined. The variables gender, age, religiosity, marital status, marriage, polygamy, children, happiness, and abortion are shown in the questionnaire (see Box 16.2), and are to be entered in the computer.

To demonstrate how variables are defined, we shall use the variable *Gender*, and show how this is done. All other variables are defined in the same way. To define the variable *Gender*, we follow the following steps.

a. Go to SPSS Data Editor and Click on Variable View (at the bottom of the screen).
b. Type 'Gender' under Name (first column, first line of the screen).
c. Move right to Type, and click on the shaded box and set the type to the option you consider appropriate. In our case 'numeric' is adequate.
d. Move right to Width, and leave it at 8; this is sufficient.
e. Move right to Decimals and change it to 0, by clicking on the arrow that points down. Given that our responses are 1 or 2, decimals are not required.
f. Move right to Label and type in the full name of the variable, e.g. sex of subjects. You can use up to 60 characters, but short expressions are preferable.
g. Move right to Values and click on the shaded box next to it.
   ■ In the box Value, type the number of the value or code for the first answer. Our options are male and female with their respective codes being 1 and 2. Hence, type in 1 for male, and move to Value Label.
   ■ In the box Value label type 'Male' and click Add.
   ■ Go back to Value and enter 2 (for Female), and then go to Value label, and enter 'Female'; click Add again, and then OK.
h. Move right to Missing and click on the shaded box. In the new window:

- ■ Activate 'Discrete missing values'.
- ■ Type in '9' in the Discrete missing values box.
- ■ Click OK.
- i. Move right to Columns, and set the width to your preference (8 is sufficient).
- j. Move right to Align and leave it as is (right)
- k. Move right to Scale and change it to 'nominal'; if the variable is ordinal or interval, we set Scale accordingly.

Now, the variable *Gender* has been defined, and the computer is ready to accept relevant data. Following the same path, you define the remaining variables, which will be set below *Gender*.

Entering the data

So far, we have set the context in which the data will be entered. This contains the variables corresponding to each question and the corresponding response options. Hence, the computer knows where to set the answers. We now turn our attention to the responses marked on the questionnaire (Box 16.2). Briefly, the values corresponding to the nine questions are 1, 2, 3, 1, 5, 2, 3, 2, and 1.

The first step towards entering data is to move to the Data Editor. The scores must now be placed appropriately, each under its corresponding variable name. This is very simple: The 1 goes under 'Gender', the 2 under 'Age', the 3 under 'Religion' (note that you can use only 8 characters) and so on. We repeat this process until all questionnaires have been read and entered. Having completed the entry of data, the computer is ready to conduct any statistical tests we wish.

2 PRESENTATION OF GROUPED DATA

There are many ways of presenting the findings; the two most common ways are tables and graphs, and will be introduced briefly below.

2.1 Tables

The most common types of tables are univariate tables, containing one variable, such as the number of children per family; bivariate tables, containing two variables, such as the number of children of British and Irish families, and multivariate tables (containing more than two variables, such as the number of children by nationality, maternal age, maternal education, and maternal ethnic background). Tables contain certain elements which distinguish them from each other. The most common elements are shown in Box 16.3.

Rules of presentation

Data presentation is based on a set of rules. The rules most frequently listed by a number of writers (see Becker, 1989; and Mahr, 1995) are shown in Box 16.4.

The main elements of tables

- The class interval is that part of the range ordered into a group; for example, in the age distribution 1–5, 6–10, 11–15 and 16–20. The four subdivisions (1–5, 6–10 etc.) are the class intervals.
- The class width is the difference between the lower and the upper interval level.
- Class limits are the numbers that define the boundaries of a class interval. For example, in the class interval 1–5, 1 is the lower and 5 the upper class limit.
- The midpoint is the value that lies between the upper and the lower limits of a class interval. For instance the midpoint in the class interval 1–5 is 3.
- Frequency is the number of observations in each item, category or class interval.
- An open-ended class is a class that has only one limit. The classes 'under 5 years', 'under $2.00', '65 years and over' are open-ended classes.

Table construction using SPSS

The easiest way of constructing tables is to use the computer. SPSS (the statistical programs for social scientists discussed earlier) have a number of ways of presenting tables, for example frequency tables for one variable or crosstabs for two or more variables. The steps followed to construct a table are shown below.

Univariate tables

1. Select Analyze/Descriptive Statistics/Frequencies.
2. Transfer the variable you wish to display in the table to the Variable(s) box.
3. Activate Display frequency tables, and click OK.

In a table showing the annual income of public servants in the United Kingdom, the computer may show how many respondents earn below £20,000, and how

---

Rules of data presentation

- *Clarity.* Information should be presented clearly, and without ambiguity or confusion.
- *Simplicity.* Information should be easily readable.
- *Economy of space.* Neither excessive spacing nor undue crowding should occur in data presentation.
- *Order of variables.* Independent and dependent variables should be presented in their correct places.
- *Appearance.* Tables and graphs should have a pleasant appearance.
- *Accuracy.* Marginals should accurately correspond with cell values, and footnotes with relevant references.
- *Objectivity.* Figures contained in tables or graphs should not be misleading and should not encourage erroneous conclusions.

many above £20,000 per year, including value, frequency, percentage, valid percentage and cumulative percentage.

Bivariate tables

To obtain bivariate tables – those that contain two variables, such as the number of students attending a class, grouped for instance by place of birth (country–city) and gender (Male–female) – we proceed as follows:

1. Go to Data Editor and select Analyze/Descriptive Statistics.
2. Click Crosstabs.
3. Set one variable in the Rows box, and the other in the Columns box.
4. Click OK.

Using the example of the annual income of public servants in the United Kingdom, this table can also include another variable, for example gender, and present information related to how much male and female public servants earn annually. For instance, how many males and how many females earn less or more than £20,000 per year. When you instruct the computer to produce bivariate tables, you need to specify whether you require percentages, and if so, whether you need them in the rows, the columns or in both.

2.2 Graphs

Graphs are figures that offer a visual presentation of the results. Some consist of a skeleton and a body. While the skeleton in such graphs is the same, the shape of the body usually varies from one type to the other. Other graphs use circles, bars, columns, maps, pictures or other figures to display relevant information.

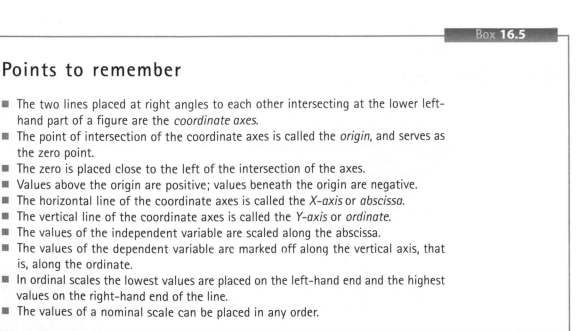

Box **16.5**

Points to remember

- The two lines placed at right angles to each other intersecting at the lower left-hand part of a figure are the *coordinate axes*.
- The point of intersection of the coordinate axes is called the *origin*, and serves as the zero point.
- The zero is placed close to the left of the intersection of the axes.
- Values above the origin are positive; values beneath the origin are negative.
- The horizontal line of the coordinate axes is called the *X-axis* or *abscissa*.
- The vertical line of the coordinate axes is called the *Y-axis* or *ordinate*.
- The values of the independent variable are scaled along the abscissa.
- The values of the dependent variable are marked off along the vertical axis, that is, along the ordinate.
- In ordinal scales the lowest values are placed on the left-hand end and the highest values on the right-hand end of the line.
- The values of a nominal scale can be placed in any order.

Types of graphs

There are many types of graphs employed by researchers to display their findings visually. This section will introduce some of the most common graphs, and explain their structure and purpose. Those are line graphs, histograms, bar graphs (clustered and stacked), scattergrams, and pie charts. You may try the other graphs listed in the computer and compare results.

Line graphs

Line graphs (or line charts) contain a number of dots joined with straight lines. Line charts can be simple, or multiple. Each line represents one variable. To present the number of children per family we only need one line showing how many families have one, two, three, four etc. children. More lines are used if more variables are to be presented in the graph.

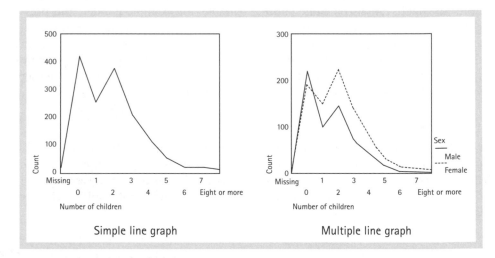

Figure 16.1 Line graphs

Histogram and bar graph

A *histogram* is a graph plotted on the coordinates and shows the form, breadth, centre and height of the distribution. Histograms display continuous scale values; hence, bars are set adjacent to each other, without space between them.

   Bar graphs are similar to histograms in that they consist of bars that indicate the magnitude of the values of the variable in question; however, the bars are not joined together but are set apart from each other. They are employed to present nominally scaled variables including values with discrete intervals. They can be vertical (bars running vertically) or horizontal (bars running horizontally).

   There are *simple* bar graphs (presenting single values), *clustered* bar graphs (presenting sets of bars side-by-side), and *stacked* bar graphs (presenting bars stacked on top of each other), as shown in Figure 16.3.

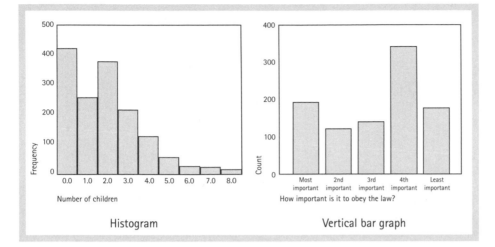

Figure 16.2 Histogram and vertical bar graph

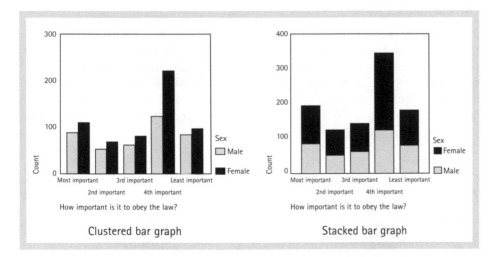

Figure 16.3 Clustered bar graph and stacked bar graph

The scattergram

A scattergram is a graph employed when correlations are computed, and describes the relationship between two variables. This relationship is expressed in the shape of the dots it contains. Scattergrams indicate whether there is a relationship between the two variables, and if so, whether the relationship is positive, negative, strong or weak. The closer the dots are to a straight line, the stronger the relationship. Dots gathered around a line starting from the origin and cutting the angle of the two axes in the middle indicate a positive correlation. Dots like those in Scattergram B indicate a negative correlation. Scattergram A shows no correlation between the variables.

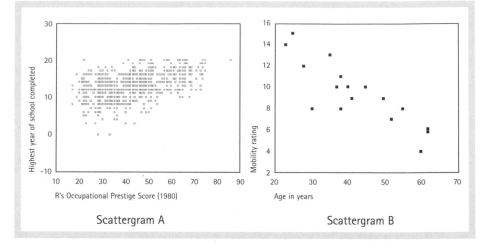

Figure 16.4 Scattergrams

The pie chart

Pie charts are used to describe one categorical variable, and to present the size of their parts. In pie charts, variables are presented in the form of a circle (pie), with each of their part occupying a segment of the pie that is proportional to its real size. Pie charts are an easy way of displaying relationships between the whole and its parts as well as comparisons between the parts. The racial composition of a population (see Figure 16.5), and the number of children per family can easily be presented in pie charts.

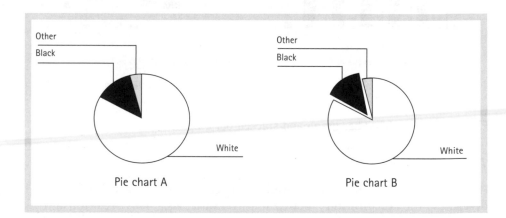

Figure 16.5 Pie charts

Chart construction using SPSS

Provided that the computer has access to files with relevant data, SPSS can instantly construct one or more charts at will. In all charts, the construction process follows the same path; hence, the construction of such charts is very simple. To construct a simple bar chart, you proceed as follows:

1. Go to SPSS Data Editor and click Graphs.
2. Click Bar, and then activate 'Summaries for groups of cases'.
3. Click the chart that stands before Simple.
4. Click Define and activate 'N of cases'.
5. Transfer the variable you wish to display to the Variable box.
6. Click OK.

Following this, a bar chart will appear on screen. To construct other charts, specify their name in Line 2 above. The procedure is the same. For more advanced choices you may need to explore the SPSS options in your computer.

3   STATISTICAL PROCESSING

Statistical processing includes techniques that allow a detailed analysis of the data. One such technique will offer general descriptions of the data, and is known as *descriptive analysis* (descriptive statistics). Another technique focuses on relationships between variables, looking for associations (correlations), and is known as *relational analysis* (relational statistics). The third form of statistical processing is *significance testing*, which informs us about the extent to which our findings reflect the criteria of the (target) population, and whether the study allows generalisation of the findings.

We begin our exploration with some elementary techniques of descriptive statistics.

Box **16.6**

Relational measures and their function

Measures	Description and examples
Rate	The rate compares the computed frequency of a variable with the possible frequency. It is obtained by dividing the former by the latter.
Ratio	Ratio is the relationship of parts of a variable to each other (e.g. males to females). It is obtained by dividing the former (e.g. males) by the latter (e.g. females). If the numbers were 26 and 37 respectively, the ratio of males would be (26/37=0.7) 0.7, or there are 7 males for every 10 females; the ratio of females is (37/26=1.4) 1.4, i.e. there are 14 females for every 10 males.
Percentage	Percentage describes the relationship between a subgroup (n) to the total group (N) and is obtained by using the formula n/N x 100. In the example above, the percentage of males is 41.26% (26/63 x 100 = 41.26), and of females 58.73% (37/63 x 100 = 58.73).

3.1 Relational measures

Numerical figures alone have little informative power in quantitative research. They become informative and significant when they are interrelated. For instance, 500 respondents thinking in a particular way is a large number if it is a part of a sample of 600, but relatively small if it comes from a sample of 10,000 respondents. Relational measures serve to relate figures to each other or to the whole. The measures considered here are rate, ratio and percentage; the latter in particular is extensively used not only in research but in everyday life. These measures are briefly described in Box 16.6.

3.2 Measures of central tendency

These measures are used when we need to know about the average, most common or typical value in a distribution. The most useful measures that give such values are the mean, the mode and the median. Their application depends on the nature of the data they describe. Their features are shown in Box 16.7.

Using SPSS (version 10, 11 or 12), mean, median and mode can be computed separately or together, depending on your choice in Line 4 below. Use the following steps to have the computer display the values of all three measures.

1. Select Analyze/Descriptive statistics/Frequencies.
2. Transfer the variable of your choice to the Variable(s) box.
3. Activate Display frequency tables.
4. Click Statistics and then activate Mean, Mode, and Median.
5. Click Continue, and then click OK.

Box **16.7**

Measures of central tendency

Measure	Description and examples
Mean	Is the average of all observations. It is obtained by adding up all scores and dividing the sum by the number of scores. → IS USED in interval and ratio data
Median	Is the point on a (rank-ordered) distribution that divides the observations (not their values) into two equal parts. In the distribution 36, 33, 30, 28, 26, 23, 18, 12, 11, 8, 4, the median is 23 (there are five observations on each side of 23). → IS USED in ordinal, interval and ratio data
Mode	Is the category with the largest number of observations. If in a test 6 students received an A, 9 a B, 16 a C, and 7 a P, the mode is C. → IS USED in nominal, ordinal, interval and ratio data

---

All measures have a purpose, and are therefore equally useful. Their suitability depends very much on the nature of distribution they measure and other factors, as shown in Box 16.8 (Foddy, 1988; Pfeifer, 2000):

Box **16.8**

When to use the mean, the mode and the median

- The mode is used if the variable is nominally scaled, although it can be used for all types of data.
- The mean is chosen if the variable is ordinal, interval or ratio.
- If the distribution shows a central tendency, the mean or median is a better measure; if there is no central tendency the mode is preferable.
- If the distribution is skewed, the median is a better measure. This is particularly so for distributions of interval data. When the skew is extreme, and if the distribution contains ordinal data, the mode may be a better choice.
- If a quick but rough measure is acceptable, the mode can be helpful.
- If information about the central trend is wanted, the mean is the best choice.
- If information is needed about the location of cases in the two halves of the distribution, the median is a better measure.

Of these measures, the mean has many very important mathematical properties, and is a stable measure, not easily affected by shifts of a few data. It is therefore the most commonly used measure of central tendency. Trends in the findings are usually presented by using means, which are more common than other measures of central tendency.

3.3 Measures of dispersion

These measures are employed when we need to know how far the scores are spread around the mean, and about the average deviation of the scores from the mean. The measures of dispersion considered in this discussion are the *variance, standard deviation* and *range*. Their main features are briefly described in Box 16.9.

The computation of the measures of dispersion follows the steps shown below. Note that, since variance and standard deviation serve the same purpose, only standard deviation will be considered in this section. Note also that these measures can be computed together with the measures of central tendency. Following the steps given below, the screen displays the mean, median, mode, range and standard deviation.

1. Select Analyze/Descriptive statistics/Frequencies.
2. Transfer the variable of your choice to the Variable(s) box.
3. Click Statistics and then activate Range and Std deviation.
4. Click also Mean, Median and Mode.
5. Click Continue, and click OK.

3.4 Comparing scores: z–scores

Assume two students took a test in social research, one in a psychology class and the other in a sociology class. Student A obtained 65/100 and Student B

Box 16.9

Variance, standard deviation and range

Measure	Description and examples
Variance	Is the average of the distances of the individual scores from the mean, OR the mean of the squared deviations of the observations from the mean.
Standard deviation	Is the square root of variance. E.g. in a class of students with a mean IQ of 120, a standard deviation (SD) of 5 means that the average deviation of these students from the mean IQ is 5 points, i.e. most students have an IQ between 115 and 125.
Range	Is the distance between the highest and the lowest score of a distribution. E.g. if the lowest maths score is 45 and the highest 90, the range is (90 – 45 = 45) 45.

70/100. The question here is: Can we conclude that Student B performed better than Student A? The z-score answers this question by taking into consideration the mean. A possible answer is that score 65 comes from a distribution with a mean of 60, showing that Student A is an above-average student, and that score 70 comes from a distribution with a mean of 70, whereby Student B is an average student. Hence, Student A performed better than Student B.

In statistical terms, z-scores transform raw scores into scores measured in a distribution where the mean is 0 and the SD is 1, and where the scores are measured in SD units. Hence, in such a computation a z-score of +1.5 means that the raw score that corresponds to this z score is one-and-a-half standard deviations above the mean; in other words, it is a relatively good score. Likewise, a z-score of –.5 means that the corresponding raw score is one-half SD below the mean.

To compute the z-scores for a set of data, using SPSS, we proceed as shown below. Note that you need computer data containing a variable with scores, which you intend to convert to z scores.

1. Click the name of the variable (with scores that are to be converted) in the Data Editor.
2. Choose Analyze/Descriptive statistics/Descriptives.
3. Transfer the variable to be converted to the Variable(s) box.
4. Activate 'Save standardised values as variable'.
5. Click OK.

Following these steps, the computer will display another variable next to the one you wanted to convert, including the corresponding z-scores. These scores can be statistically treated like any other set of data. To compare two scores, both distributions must be converted to z-scores.

4 ASSOCIATIONS

4.1 Nature of association measures

A correlation is a method that examines the relationship between two variables. More specifically, correlations examine three major aspects of relationships. These are:

- the presence or absence of a correlation, that is, whether or not there is a correlation between the variables in question
- the direction of correlation, that is, whether an existing correlation is positive or negative
- the strength of a correlation, that is, whether an existing correlation is strong or weak.

The presence, direction and strength of correlation are demonstrated in the coefficient of correlation. In general, the coefficient ranges from −1 to +1. A zero correlation indicates that there is no correlation between the variables. The closer the coefficient is to 1 (+1 or −1), the stronger the correlation; and the closer it is to 0, the weaker the correlation.

The direction of correlation is indicated by the sign that stands in front of the coefficient. When it is positive (+) it means that variables change in the same direction (positive correlation); in other words, when one variable is high (e.g. income) the other (e.g. quality of life) is also high. A negative (−) sign indicates that the variables move in opposite directions (negative correlation): when one (e.g. income) decreases, the other (e.g. criminality) increases. It must be stressed that correlation does not imply causation.

Box **16.10**

Measuring correlations

A correlation is:

- very low if the coefficient has a value under 0.20
- low if the coefficient has a value between 0.21 and 0.40
- moderate if the coefficient has a value between 0.41 and 0.70
- high if the coefficient has a value between 0.71 and 0.91
- very high if the coefficient is over 0.91.

(Pfeifer, 2000)

4.2 Available options

There are three different types of test, each containing a number of specific tests. The choice of the type of test depends on the type of distribution (whether continuous or discrete), the structure and characteristics of the distribution, and the level of measurement. Table 16.1 displays a few popular measures, grouped according to level of measurement.

Table 16.1 Association tests by level of measurement

Level	Association tests
Nominal	ϕ coefficient, Cramer's V, Contingency coefficient (C), Tschurprow's T, Yules Q, and Lambda test
Ordinal	Spearman's rank correlation; Tau-a, Gamma coefficient, Sommer's d, and Tau-b
Interval-ratio	Pearson's product-moment correlation

In this section only one measure for each level of measurement will be introduced. These are ϕ coefficient and Cramer's V, Spearman's rho and Pearson's r.

4.3 Nominal measures of association

Nominal measures are employed when the relationship examined relates to nominal variables. It is important to remember that coefficients here range from 0 to 1, with 0 being the lowest level of their value; negative values have no meaning.

Box 16.11

Testing nominal association: an example

A survey shows that 70 of the 100 male students and 55 of the 100 female students are against examinations. Can we argue that the differences between these two groups are large enough to allow the conclusion that gender is associated with their position on examinations? Knowing the student's gender, can we predict their attitude to examinations?

Phi (ϕ) coefficient and Cramer's V

Phi is employed with 2×2 tables, while Cramer's V can be used also for larger tables. In SPSS, both are computed together and also produce similar results. Still, when used in larger tables, phi values can exceed 1; in such cases we use Cramer's V. To compute phi and Cramer's V we proceed as shown below:

1. Select Analyze/Descriptive statistics/ Crosstabs.
2. Transfer one variable to Row(s) box, and the other to Column(s) box.
3. Click Statistics and then activate 'Phi and Cramer's V'.
4. Click Continue, and then click OK.

Using one of the examples listed above, the computer displays the table shown below including the values of ϕ and Cramer's V, and their significance level.

Symmetric measures: Phi & Cramer's V

	Measures	Value	Approx. Sig
Nominal by Nominal	Phi	.145	.041
	Cramer's V	.145	.041
N of Valid Cases		200	

The value of ϕ is .145, and the approximate significance level is .041. This means that the association between the two variables is 'very low', almost negligible, and that this is statistically 'very significant' (.041 is below the set limit of .05); hence there is no association between the two variables in question.

4.4 Ordinal measures of association

Ordinal measures are employed when ordinal data is tested, that is, with ranking pairs. Of the various measures employed in ordinal data, Spearman's rho is the most common, and will be introduced next.

Testing ordinal association: an example

The 15 students of a tutorial class were ranked twice, once according to their participation in sport (RANK 1) and once according to their academic performance (RANK 2). Using these rankings, can we say that there is a correlation between participation in sport and academic performance?

Spearman's rank-order correlation coefficient

This is a product-moment, non-parametric correlation coefficient which deals with ranks (not magnitudes), and measures the strength of the linear association between variables. Unlike other ordinal measures, rho is a correlation-based measure. Using the example above, we instruct the computer as follows:

1. Select Analyze/Correlate and click on Bivariate.
2. Transfer the two variables to be correlated to the Variable(s) box.
3. Activate Spearman by clicking on the square box in front of it.
4. Activate One-tailed or Two-tailed as required.
5. Activate Flag significant correlations, and then click OK.

The computer responds with a set of tables containing relevant information, of which the following is the most relevant.

Spearman's correlation

			Acad. ranking	Sport ranking
Spearman's rho	Academic ranking	Correl coeff.	1.000	.952 **
		Sig. (2-tailed) N	 15	.000 15
	Sport ranking	Correl. Coeff. Sig. (2-tailed) N	.952 ** .000 15	1.000 15

The results show that the correlation coefficient is .952, and its significance level .000. Hence, there is a very high and dependable association between the two variables. Simply stated, those students ranked highly in one area were also highly ranked in the other, and vice versa.

4.5 Interval/ratio measures of association

Box 16.13

Testing interval/ratio association: an example

A journalist interviewed 500 public servants employed in the same department (Criminal Justice) and of the same educational background. The question was whether there was a correlation between length of service and yearly income. Can one say that the longer the service, the higher the income?

Pearson's product-moment correlation coefficient, r

This is the most common measure of association of variables scaled on an interval level. It is a symmetric test that deals with pairs of scores and with magnitudes of observations; it tests whether there is a linear correlation between the variables and if so whether the correlation is positive, negative, strong or weak. Pearson's r is computed as follows:

1. Choose Analyze/Correlate and click on Bivariate.
2. Transfer the variables Years and Income to the Variable(s) box.
3. Activate Pearson by clicking on the square box in front of it.
4. Activate One-tailed or Two-tailed as required.
5. Activate Flag significant correlations, and then.

Using the data of the survey described above, the computer shows the following display.

Pearson correlation

			Years of service	Level of income
Years of service	Pearson correlation		1	.883**
	Sig. (2-tailed) N	.	500	.001 500
Level of income	Pearson correlation Sig. (2-tailed) N		.883 ** .001 500	1 500

The table shows, first, that there is a positive correlation (.883 has no negative sign); second, a strong correlation (.883); and third, a very significant correlation (shown in .001 and **). (Note that two stars next to .883 indicate a very significant correlation). Hence we can conclude that there is a very strong association between years of service and level of income.

Coefficient of determination

The coefficient of determination describes the common variance, that is, the degree of variability shared by the two variables. It is the square of the coefficient of correlation (r^2), and offers an index of predictability: it allows the researcher to make predictions about one variable if the degree of determination is known. For example, an r of .7, which in most cases is as high as one is expected to obtain in real situations, can only explain 49 per cent of the changes that can be explained by the independent variable.

5 TESTS OF SIGNIFICANCE

5.1 Introduction

Tests of significance are employed when we want to know about the significance of our findings, that is, about the extent to which the findings of the study reflect or are consistent with what happens in the target population. For example: Are our findings a truthful reflection of what happens in the population or the result of methodological or of other problems? Or better: Can our findings be generalised? (See Box 16.16).

What are we talking about here? Assume that a study of 200 students found that female students cheat in the examinations to a higher degree than male students do. The question that concerns the researcher is: Is this result a true reflection of what happens in the target population? Do female students in general cheat more than male students? H_o (null hypothesis) proposes that there is no difference in examination cheating of male and female students. Significance tests will show whether H_o is correct.

There are several types of test of significance, depending on three factors:

- whether the distributions are scaled on a nominal, ordinal or interval/ratio level
- whether the study includes one or more samples (one-sample tests, two-sample tests, k-sample tests)
- whether the samples are related (matched) or independent.

Box 16.14

What is a significant level?

Level of significance is a measure which indicates the extent to which the findings of a study are significant. This level is provided by the computer when relevant tests are conducted. The level of significance ranges from 0 to 1. A significance level of 0 means that there is a very high probability that our results reflect those of the target population. The risk of making a mistake in this conclusion is 0 in 100. The exact opposite means a significance level of 1. Here the chance of making a mistaken conclusion is 100 in 100. In the statistical jargon, a significance level indicates the risk of rejecting the null hypothesis (H_o), when it should have been accepted, which we are prepared to take. This is referred to as alpha (α).

The α values most commonly accepted by social researchers are 0.05 and 0.01. In these cases, we accept that there is a 5 per cent (for 0.05 level) or 1 per cent (for 0.01 level) probability of rejecting a true H_o. In other words, if we were to randomly take a number of samples from the same population, a difference as great as that given in the findings at the 0.05 level would occur by chance only five times in 100 samples; the remaining 95 times the differences will reflect differences in the target population. The study is obviously more precise if the differences are significant at the 0.01 level, where the chance of rejecting a true H_o is 1 in 100. Briefly, what we have to remember is that coefficients are significant if their level is between 0.05 and 0.000.

The main types of significance test are shown in Table 16.2. These tests follow a strict procedure, beginning with setting a research hypothesis, formulating the null hypothesis (H_o) and the alternative hypothesis, computing test statistics and then checking whether the null hypothesis can be accepted or rejected. In the discussion that follows we shall consider only a few tests, introducing their purpose and relevance, showing briefly how their values are derived and interpreted. Hence, the main points that will be covered when discussing these tests will be:

- when and under what conditions specific tests are employed
- how they are computed (using SPSS)
- how their values are interpreted.

More information on these tests can be found in the workbook accompanying this text, and in relevant literature.

Table 16.2 Overview of tests of significance

Non-parametric tests		Parametric tests	
Number and type of samples	Nominal level	Ordinal level	Interval/ ratio level
One	χ^2-test (Goodness-of-fit test)	Kolmogorov-Smirnov test	t-test
Two independent	χ^2-test of independence Fisher's exact test z-test for proportions	Mann-Whitney U-test Wald-Wolfowitz runs test	t-test
Two dependent	McNemar test	Sign test Wilcoxon test	t-test
More than two independent	χ^2-test	Kruskal-Wallis H-test	ANOVA
More than two dependent	Cochran Q-test	Friedman test	ANOVA

Table 16.3 Some nominal-level tests of significance

Number of samples	Type of samples	Significance test
One sample	N/A	χ^2 goodness of fit
Two samples	Independent	χ^2 test of independence Fisher exact test
	Dependent	McNemar test
k-samples	Independent	χ^2 test
	Dependent	Cochran Q test

5.2 Nominal-level tests: chi-square tests

Researchers employ a number of nominal-level tests. The choice of a particular test depends on a number of factors, such as type of samples and degree of dependence between them. Examples of such tests are listed in Table 16.3. In the following discussion we shall introduce chi-square (χ^2) only. Information on the other tests can be found in the relevant literature.

Chi-square (χ^2) tests (pronounced *kye square*) are the most popular and most frequently used tests of significance in the social sciences; they provide information about whether the collected data are close to the value considered to be typical and generally expected, and whether two variables are related to each other. There are two types of chi-square tests, namely the goodness-of-fit test and the test of independence.

Box 16.15

A chi-square test is:

a nominal-level test of significance applied to ascertain the degree to which findings produced by a sample-based study can be generalised. For instance, if a study of 500 (of the 5,000) first-year students of the local university found that 350 of the respondents are against examinations, chi-square tests can tell us whether or not this is a true reflection of what the majority of the 5,000 first year students prefer.

Goodness-of-fit test: one variable

This test is employed when the study includes one variable only. Consider the example shown in Box 16.16.

Box 16.16

One-variable goodness-of-fit test: an example

Of 300 female nurses surveyed, 100 were found to support fully the administration of their hospital, 150 to tolerate it, and 50 to be openly against it. Are the numerical differences here significant enough to justify the conclusion that, overall, female nurses in the target population think likewise?

Assuming that in general the views of the nurses are equally divided among the three options, we proceed as shown below:

1. Select Analyze/Non-parametric tests and click Chi-square.
2. Transfer variable to the Test variable list box.
3. Activate All categories equal.
4. Click Options and activate Descriptive.
5. Click Continue and then OK.

Following this, the computer displays the table shown below, which contains the value of chi-square, the degrees of freedom, and the significance level. The figure that is most relevant to us is the significance level, which is .000. The meaning of this finding was explained earlier in Box 16.14.

Test statistics: t-test goodness-of-fit test

	Attitudes
Chi square	50.000
df	2
Asymp. Sig.	.000

Simply, this indicates a very high level of significance, the highest one can obtain. Hence we reject H_0, and conclude that the differences between the three groups of nurses identified in the study reflect differences in the population and are not caused by other factors.

Let us now repeat the computation, this time taking the option that the expected frequencies are not equal, but that, say, 50 per cent are expected to be in favour, 30 per cent tolerant, and 20 per cent against:

- Select Analyze/Non-parametric tests and click on Chi-square.
- Transfer variable to the Test variable list box.
- Activate Values then enter 50 and click Add.
- Enter 30 and click Add; then enter 20 and click Add.
- Click Options and activate Descriptive.
- Click Continue, and then on OK.

The computer shows that the chi-square value is 41.667, and that with 2 degrees of freedom $p = .000$. Interpretation of the figures is the same as that of the previous case, and requires no further comment.

Chi-square test of independence: two variables

This test is employed when two nominal-level variables are being studied. The main question regarding this test is not about the 'fit' of the observed values of one variable in the theoretical model, but whether the two variables are independent from or related to each other. H_0 states that the variables are independent.

Box 16.17

Chi-square test of independence: two variables: an example

The results of a survey on attitudes to abortion, including 100 males and 100 females found that many more men than women were against abortion. Can we say that they are sufficiently different to reject the zero association between them, and the assumed independence of the variables? Are attitudes to abortion independent from gender?

To compute the chi-square test of independence we proceed as follows:

1. Select Analyze/Descriptive statistics/Crosstabs.
2. Transfer abort to the Row(s) box and gender to the Column(s) box.
3. Click Statistics and activate Chi-square.
4. Click Continue, and then click OK.

On the computer screen we read the following table. The relevant point for us here is the level of significance, noted in the table as 'Asymp. Sig. (2–sided)'.

Chi–square tests

	Value	df	Asymp. sig. (2–sided)	Exact sig. (2–sided)	Exact sig. (1–sided)
Pearson chi–square	10.666	1	0.001		
Continuity correction	9.759	1	0.002		
Likelihood ratio	10.767	1	0.001		
Fisher's exact test				0.002	0.001
Linear-by-linear Association	10.613	1	0.001		
N of valid cases	200				

Given the high significance level [Asymp. Sig (2-sided)= 0.001], we reject the H_o, and with it the assumption that the variables (attitudes to abortion and gender) are independent. Thus it is reasonable to conclude that the variables are dependent; consequently, men and women have different attitudes to abortion.

5.3 Ordinal–level tests

Ordinal-level tests deal with ordinal data, and serve the same purpose that nominal-level tests serve in their context. There are many such tests; a list of some popular ordinal-level tests is given in Table 16.4.

In the social sciences, ordinal-level tests are not used as frequently as nominal and interval/ratio tests. For this reason, in this section only a brief description of these tests will be given. In the following we shall describe the main characteristics of the tests, where and how they are employed and how to interpret their findings. Their computation is simple, particularly when using SPSS, as we shall see next.

Table 16.4 Ordinal-level tests

Number of samples	Type of samples	Significance tests
One sample	N/A	Kolmogorov-Smirnov test
Two samples	Independent	Wald-Wolfowitz runs test Mann-Whitney U-test
	Dependent	Sign test Wilcoxon test
k-samples	Independent	Kruskal-Wallis H-test
	Dependent	Friedman test

SPSS groups these tests under the general name of *non-parametric tests*. Consequently the path you need to follow to find these measures is Analyze > Nonparametric tests. This leads you to a list of measures containing the following: chi-square, binomial, runs, one-sample K-S, 2 independent variables, k independent variables, 2 related samples and k related samples. Each of these items contains one or more of the tests introduced in this section. A list of these tests per list item is given below:

List items	Non-parametric tests
Chi-square	Chi-square test
Binomial	Binomial test
Runs	Runs test
One sample K-S	One sample Kolmogorov-Smirnow test
2 independent variables	Man-Witney U; Wald-Wolfowitz; Kolmogorow-Smirnov Z, etc.
k independent samples	Kruskal-Wallis H; Median
2 related samples	Wilcoxon; Sign; McNemar
k related samples	Friedman; Kendall's W; Cochran's Q.

This list shows where to find each test and how to address it. For instance, the McNemar test is in the two-related-samples group; consequently the path to this test is Analyze> Nonparametric tests > 2 related samples > McNemar. In a similar fashion, the path you will use to get to Friedman's test is Analyze> Nonparametric tests > k related samples > Friedman. From there, you only need to follow the program instructions. Coefficients are interpreted using the same standards employed in other tests.

5.4 Interval/ratio-level tests

This section addresses two of the most common interval/ratio-level tests. They are also called *parametric tests of significance*, as they are based on the assumption that the population is normally distributed, adhering to the principles of normal curve. Table 16.5 displays the interval/ratio significance tests that will be presented or referred to below, arranged according to the number of types of samples tested.

Table 16.5 Interval/ratio-level significance tests

Number of samples	Type of samples	Significance tests
One sample	N/A	t-test
Two samples	Independent or dependent	t-test
k-samples	Independent	Simple ANOVA
	Dependent	Multiple ANOVA

The t-test

The t-test is a very popular and useful test, used predominantly for small samples, although it is also thought to be appropriate for large samples (Argyrous, 1996: 223). There are two types of t-tests; the one-sample test, and the two-sample test.

Box **16.18**

What is a t-test?

A t-test is an interval/ratio test of significance which has the purpose of ascertaining whether or not the findings of a sample-based study are significant, that is, also valid for the target population. It checks the degree of generalisability of the findings of this study. The t-test serves the same purpose as chi-square tests, except that it is suitable for interval/ratio variables.

The one-sample t-test

A single-sample t-test compares the sample mean with the population mean, and tests whether there is a significant difference between them. Consider the following example.

Box **16.19**

One-sample t-test: an example

A lecturer has grounds to believe that female nurses at her institution are more conservative than female nurses at other institutions. To test this assumption she ascertains the scores of 26 female nurses using a conservatism scale, and computes the mean (5.715) and standard deviation (1.384). Given that the average conservatism score of female nurses is known to be 4.4, can she argue that the differences are significant?

The lecturer employs the one-sample t-test to test her hypothesis. The steps to follow are shown below (the variable name is 'conserv'):

1. Select Analyze/Compare means/One-sample T Test.
2. Transfer 'conserv' to the Test variable(s) box.
3. Type 4.4 in the Test value box.
4. Click Options and set Confidence interval to 95 per cent.
5. Activate Exclude cases analysis by analysis (in Missing values sector).
6. Click Continue, and then OK.

The computer displays the following table:

One-sample test

	Test value = 4.4				95% confidence interval of the difference	
	t	df	Sig. (2-tailed)	Mean difference	Lower	Upper
Conservatism	4.846	25	.000	1.32	.76	1.87

The decisive figure is the significance level (Sig.), which is very high (.000). On the basis of the high significance we can reject the null hypothesis. This means that the differences between the means are not due to methodological influences or problems but due to differences in the target population. Hence, the conservatism score of the female nurses in question is significantly different from that of their counterparts in the target population.

The two-sample t-test for dependent samples

Two-sample tests are used to check the differences between the means of two samples. These samples can be dependent or independent; hence there is a test for independent samples, and one for dependent samples. In this discussion we focus on the dependent samples test. The t-test is employed here to examine the differences between each pair of data.

Box **16.20**

Two-sample t-test: an example

A journalist interviews ten respondents twice, first at an initial meeting, and then after they have attended a symposium on homosexuality. The point of investigation was to ascertain whether the views of the subjects on this matter changed significantly after the symposium. The scores of the two surveys were entered in the computer. The null hypothesis states that there are no differences between the scores. Is this correct?

Let us consider an example, and see what the results of the t-test suggest. We begin with the computation, which proceeds as follows:

1. Choose Analyze/Compare means, and click Paired-samples T test.
2. Highlight both variables and transfer them to the Paired variable(s) box.
3. Click Options.
4. Set Confidence interval to 95 per cent and Missing values as required.
5. Click Continue, and click OK.

The computer displays a table which contains relevant information, especially the value of t, and the level of significance.

Paired samples test

| | | Paired differences | | | | | | | |
| | | | | | 95% confidence interval of the differences | | | | |
		Mean	St. dev	Std error of mean	Lower	Upper	t	df	Sig. (2-tailed)
Pair 1	Pre-test/ Post-test	1.80	1.033	.327	1.06	2.54	5.511	9	.000

Given the very high significance level (.000), the H_o that the means are equal is rejected. Hence the mean obtained after the symposium is significantly different from the first mean. Consequently, the differences between the means are significant. It is therefore reasonable to suggest that the symposium and the contact the respondents had with delegates had an impact on their views on homosexuality.

Analysis of variance (ANOVA)

This is one of the most powerful and most common tests employed in the social sciences, and is suitable for interval/ratio-level distributions. It is known either as *analysis of variance* or as the *F-test* and is used as a simple factorial, general factorial or multivariate factorial test; these tests are also known as single or one-way (when one criterion is used), as two-way (when two criteria are used), or as N-way (factorial) analysis (when more criteria are used). It is called the F-test after its creator, Sir R. D. Fisher.

Box **16.21**

Analysis of variance is:

an interval–ratio test of significance, suitable for comparing two or more samples. It appears in a variety of models and operates in the same way and has the same purpose as t-tests, except that the latter are suitable for comparisons of two samples. ANOVA is considered to be more powerful than t-tests.

ANOVA is employed if certain conditions are met. The following are the most important:

- *Random sampling*. The sample is taken randomly.
- *Independence*. Scores are independent from each other.
- *Normality*. Scores are normally distributed.
- *Homogeneity*. Variances are equal.

The two most common tests are one-way and two-way ANOVA. In this section, the nature and use of the former will be explained. One-way analysis of variance is employed when there is one factor (acting like an independent variable) and one dependent variable. The factor is a nominal variable (males, females; ethnic groups, marital status etc.); the dependent variable is a quantitative variable. Although there are two variables being tested, one-way ANOVA looks at whether the sample groups vary systematically in one way, or with regard to one aspect only. Examples of such variable arrangements in one-way analysis of variance are:

Factor (qualitative variable)	Quantitative-dependent variable?
Marital status Levels: single, married, divorced etc.	Overall happiness very happy, happy, unhappy, very unhappy
Gender Levels: male, female	Scholastic achievement very high, high, moderate, low, very low
Ethnicity Levels: Greek, German, British, Irish	Educational aspirations very high, high, moderate, low, very low
Education Level: primary, secondary, tertiary	Familism very high, high, moderate, low, very low

A two-way analysis of variance includes two criteria of classification as well as two independent variables and one dependent variable. For instance, if we ask about the effects of social class on overall happiness we employ a one-way analysis of variance; but if we relate social class and marital status to overall happiness we employ a two-way analysis. In the first example there is one factor: social class. In the second there are two factors: social class and marital status.

Computing ANOVA

As stated above, a one-way analysis of variance is employed when there are two variables, one factor and a one-way classification. To explain the way in which ANOVA tests are conducted we use the example in Box 16.22.

Box **16.22**

One-way ANOVA: an example

A group of students from five countries were surveyed to establish their attitudes to the family. Questionnaires were completed and accurate figures were gathered for each country. The question here is whether there are significant differences in the family attitudes of students of these countries. ANOVA will assist us to answer these question.

After the data are entered in the computer, we proceed as follows:

1. Select Analyze/Compare means.
2. Click One-Way ANOVA.
3. Transfer independent variable Familism to the Dependent List box.
4. Transfer factor Country to the Factor box.
5. Click Options and then Descriptive.
6. Click Continue, and then OK.

Upon completion of these steps we obtain the display including the ANOVA table (also known as F-Table), and the 'Descriptives' table. The ANOVA table contains the information that is most important for us at this stage at least, the significance level, which is .010. As in other cases of significance testing, so here, given that our significance value is .010, the null hypothesis of equality of the means is rejected. Hence, the various groups studied have different attitudes to families. More precisely, we can say that it is reasonable to assume that *at least one group differs* from the others.

ANOVA

Source of variation	Sum of squares	df	Mean squares	F	Sig.
Between groups	35.760	4	8.940	4.382	.010
Within groups	40.800	20	2.040		
Total	76.560	24			

MAIN POINTS

- Quantitative and qualitative research employ different types of data analysis.
- Quantitative analysis employs advanced statistics to process quantitative data.
- Most quantitative researchers conduct statistical analysis using computers.
- Quantitative researchers present summaries of their findings in tables and graphs.
- The rate, the ratio and the percentage are relational measures. They relate parts of a group to each other or to the group.
- The mean, the mode and the median are measures of central tendency.
- The variance, the standard deviation and the range are measures of dispersion.
- The most common correlation measures are Pearson's r and Spearman's rho.
- Tests of significance relate statistics to parameters; they ask: Does the sample reflect accurately the target population?
- The most common tests of significance are chi square, t-tests and ANOVA.

WHERE TO FROM HERE?

Before you leave this chapter, visit the companion website for the third edition of *Social Research* at http://www.palgrave.com/sociology/sarantakos to review the main concepts introduced in this chapter and to test yourself on the major issues discussed.

FURTHER READING

Betts, K., Hayward, D. and Garnham, N. (2001) *Quantitative Analyses in the Social Sciences: An Introduction*. Croydon, Victoria: Tertiary.

Brace, N., Kemp, R. and Snelgar, R. (2000) *SPSS for Psychologists. A Guide to Data Analysis using SPSS for Windows*. Houndmills: Palgrave.

Field, A. (2000) *Discovering Statistics Using SPSS for Windows: Advanced Techniques for the Beginner*. London: Sage.

Foster, J. J. (2001) *Data Analysis Using SPSS for Windows New Edition: Editions 6–10*. London: Sage.

Miller, R. L., Acton, C., Fullerton, D. A. and Maltby, J. (2002) *SPSS for Social Scientists: Versions 9, 10 and 11*. Houndmills: Palgrave Macmillan.

Sarantakos, S. (2000) *Basic Stats Without Maths*. Sydney: Harvard Press.

Publication

17 Reporting

Reporting

- offers guidelines as to how to construct a research report
- outlines the structure and content of a research report
- describes research reports in specific contexts
- considers the writing styles of reports
- discusses reports in qualitative and quantitative research.

KEY HEADINGS

INTRODUCTION

The final step of the research process is publication of the findings, that is, the dissemination of information gathered during the investigation. This is an important step because it informs the community of the state of affairs in the area of the study and offers an opportunity to interest groups and the government to take notice of the findings, and more importantly, to act upon them. For the community, and even the experts, research reports *are* 'the research'; and research is what is contained in these reports. The research report is 'the face of the investigation'. Hence, reports must be prepared in a manner that will present the findings as clearly and as constructively as possible.

In this chapter we shall discuss the construction of research reports. We shall see among other things what report writing entails, and how reports can become a crucial, beneficial and constructive way of communicating the findings clearly and accurately to the readers. We will introduce some of the ways in which reports can be presented, the factors which must be taken into account when research reports are prepared, and the items they should contain to be complete, useful and effective.

1 THE CONTEXT OF REPORTING

Report writing is 'engineered writing' (Murray and Hay-Roe, 1986), that is, systematic and disciplined writing. More specifically, a report is expected to describe the research process and to present the research outcomes accurately, adequately and effectively. In the first instance, any report, regardless of its nature and content, has to be prepared with its context in mind. The minimum elements of this context to be taken into account when preparing a report are ethical standards, the kind of people to whom it will be addressed, its purpose, and the reporting outlets. We shall see later that the context is larger and more complex. But in the first instance, the reporter will have to begin thinking about these four factors, even before the writing has begun.

1.1 Ethics

To begin with, research must adhere to ethical standards, and this pertains also to the manner in which reports are written. As noted above, the report is the 'face of the study', and the way the findings are reported affects the quality and credibility of the whole study. The underlying standards of a report should reflect professionality, fairness and justice, which researchers are expected to respect. Disrespect of ethical standards, such as plagiarism, fabrication of the data, cheating and the like, constitutes misconduct that is punishable by law.

1.2 The reader

The report must also be written in a manner that will make it accessible to the intended reader. Readers have different linguistic competencies and their knowledge of scientific terminology varies significantly. Consequently, it is important that the language in which the report is prepared is that of the consumer. In a

Box **17.1**

Basic ethical requirements in reporting

- Research reports are required to present an accurate, honest and realistic account of the findings, without misrepresentation and without misleading the reader.
- Anonymity and confidentiality must be faithfully observed; the text should not contain information that could betray the identity of the respondents and should not publish confidential information.
- Key informants, mediators and gatekeepers should be duly protected.
- Plagiarism is misconduct: the works of others as well as contributions to the research and/or to the preparation of the report should be duly acknowledged.
- Cheating while preparing the report is a violation of ethical and professional standards and a punishable offence.
- Fabrication of the findings is unethical and a serious offence.
- Concealing findings is equally unethical and unprofessional and violates research standards.
- Limitations of the research caused by any reason must be disclosed in the report.
- Persons who contributed to the completion of the study and/or of the report must be duly acknowledged.
- The report should be prepared in a professional manner, and should not harm the reputation or interests of the respondents or the sponsors.

similar fashion, the length of the report, the amount of detail it contains, the extent to which technical aspects are included and the depth of analysis and discussion will vary according to the capacity of the reader. Obviously talks given to concerned community groups will be different from reports submitted to a sponsor, papers presented in conferences or articles published in professional journals. In all cases, the report is expected to be clear, honest, thorough and informative, always with the specific reader in mind.

1.3 Purpose

The nature and content of reports vary according to the purpose of the research and of the report. Descriptive studies result in publications presenting descriptive findings, and exploratory studies generate reports containing exploratory data. In a similar fashion studies based on action research will entail plans of action, which will show interest groups and the government what needs to be done to achieve the goals supported by the research. The purpose of the report underlies its structure and content, and should be clearly stated. Whether the report aims to inform the reader, to advise the sponsor or the government, or to generate public debate or public action, has a strong impact on the manner in which it is presented as well as on the content and structure of the report.

1.4 Reporting outlets

For some, thinking at this stage of writing about the form in which a report will be published may seem out of place. Normally, you will expect this issue to be resolved after the report is written. Although logical, this consideration is not correct. The reason for this is that the nature, content, purpose, readership and length of the report depend very much on the publication channel. Hence, the publication outlet needs to be determined at this stage. In summary, the findings usually appear in one or more of the following outlets:

- *Newspapers*. This medium addresses the general public, and is interested in reports that describe the central trends of the findings. In most cases, such reports are brief, are written in a simple language and style, are prepared by journalists and not by the researcher, and hence adhere to the publication standards of the newspaper.
- *Newsletters*. Findings published in newsletters address readers with a special interest and/or a certain ideological orientation. The language and style are adjusted to the level of the reader, and the report, which is not prepared by the researcher, offers a brief summary of the essence and significance of the findings.
- *Conferences*. More specific and more complex are the findings presented at conferences, where experts in specific areas are addressed. The presentation offers a detailed discussion of preliminary or final findings in the language of the audience, and it is prepared by the researcher.
- *Monographs*. This outlet allows for larger reports, which are detailed and contain a full discussion of the issue in question. Monographs are serious publications, sometimes a part of a series, are prepared by the researcher, and are treated in all aspects as a kind of book.
- *Journals*. This medium provides an outlet for summarised, concise, detailed and critical research reports prepared by the researcher, and is the most common way of bringing the results to the critical attention of academic specialists. In most cases, the research findings are published in a series of journal articles, with each focusing on one aspect of the findings. Given the nature of the outlet, reports are fully professional in nature, and are written in the style prescribed by the journal editor.
- *Books*. Books provide perhaps the best and most highly respected method of publishing research findings. The wider boundaries and focus allow for more scope and more complete coverage of the findings. The only limitation for reporting findings in a book is that its publication is often not supported by market conditions; hence only a few studies will be published in this form. Many research reports that are specialised and do not attract enough readers to make the publication viable find this medium a rather inaccessible outlet.

There are many more outlets for publishing findings. Workshops for interested people and/or the sponsors and seminars are two of them. Media interviews, particularly for radio or television stations, are other ways to disseminate the knowledge obtained through research. However, most researchers would rank books and monographs as the preferred form of publication, followed by refereed journal articles and conference papers. As we saw earlier, whether a report reaches the status and level of publication it deserves does not depend on quality alone. Politics and economic considerations are equally (and sometimes more) important.

2 STRUCTURE AND CONTENT

Having set the scene for the writing in terms of knowing what the report aims to achieve, who the readers are, where it is to be published and whether ethical standards are guaranteed, the reporter will begin writing. The discussion that follows relates to the professional standards (Wolcott, 1990) that guide the preparation of reports. Briefly, researchers preparing reports have to decide about, first, the content of the report, considering which parts of the findings to include, the amount of detail, the inclusion of statistics and narratives and so on; second, the structure of the report; and third, the text style. All three elements of the report are equally important, should be well integrated and need to be given adequate consideration before the writing begins. These points will be discussed briefly below. Since structure and content are closely related to each other, they will be discussed together.

The content of the report is expected to adhere to certain rules, and meet certain standards set by peers and the industry (see Fine, 1988). The content of the report is expected to reflect the points listed in Box 17.2.

Box **17.2**

General attributes of the report content

The report content:

- communicates and discusses the findings of the project, as well as problems and frustrations experienced during the study
- is presented in a simple and orderly way, with every aspect of the project being properly introduced and explained, with the presentation directed towards pre-set aims and the whole structure organised according to accepted standards and practices
- adheres to the accepted standards and practices of the social sciences, for example in its structure and composition.

Many of the rules for writing reports in quantitative research also apply in qualitative research. The overall structure (introduction, main body, conclusion), as well as issues of accuracy and ethics, will be as important in qualitative as they are in quantitative research. However, there are types of qualitative research which deviate somewhat from this model. As noted earlier, when discussing certain types of qualitative research, there are cases in which presentation of the findings in qualitative research can take the form of poetry, painting, or drama. These are perhaps at the opposite extreme of the spectrum from reports in quantitative research, but are nonetheless a part of it.

Another aspect of report writing in qualitative research is that reporting is not a task that comes after the research is completed but a central part of the research: so central, indeed, that some writers see it as the place where the final analysis takes place. Writing up is the last part of the project but also the final stage of analysis. Matt (2000: 581), for instance, notes on this that the presentation of reality is always also a construction of reality. The way in which data, statements, and results are set creates a relevant interpretation of the world. The same author notes 'it is even allowed on the way from experience to text presentation to write different versions of a plausible text' (p. 583).

Whether this impression is acceptable to the majority of qualitative researchers is questionable. There are many and different views on this within the domain of qualitative research, as we shall see later. For our discussion in this section we contrast qualitative and quantitative research, note their differences, and shall discuss their practice in reporting research findings separately.

3 THE REPORT IN QUANTITATIVE RESEARCH

There are usually five main parts in a report: the introduction, methodology, findings, discussion and conclusion. These parts are expected to be presented in a symmetrical and proportional manner. Although all parts of the report are important, the sections 'Findings' and 'Discussion' are usually the most important, simply because they present the essence of the results and a critical evaluation of their quality. For this reason, the other sections of the report are generally smaller. As a general guide, the introduction and method usually do not exceed 10 per cent of the report, except when relevant literature or methodology are controversial and require special attention (in which case they may be presented in a separate section entitled 'Literature review'), or when a complicated methodology is used. Similarly, conclusions and recommendations make up only a small proportion of the report.

3.1 Abstract

An abstract is an accurate, comprehensive, concise and informative summary of the report. It provides a useful summary (of between 150 and 200 words), allowing the reader to gain a brief overview of the findings of the study. An abstract is a mini-report where the reader will find sufficient information about the purpose and the outcome of the study to decide whether to read the report or not. More specifically, an abstract answers the questions listed in Box 17.3.

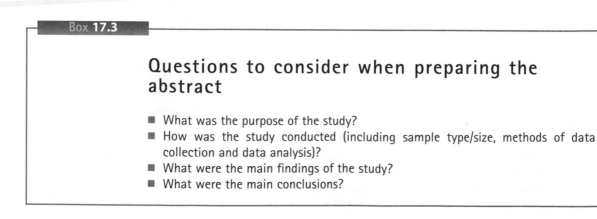

Box 17.3

Questions to consider when preparing the abstract

- What was the purpose of the study?
- How was the study conducted (including sample type/size, methods of data collection and data analysis)?
- What were the main findings of the study?
- What were the main conclusions?

Abstracts are required with reports which are submitted to professional journals, and are gradually becoming more common than before. The types of publications in which abstracts are not required are books, journal articles, monographs and newsletters. In a number of cases, reports contain what is referred to as Executive Summary. This is an abstract that is more detailed and somewhat larger than usual.

3.2 Introduction

Here, the author describes, explains and introduces: the topic of the report; the purpose and significance of the research; the findings of the exploratory study (if any); a review of the literature; problems encountered; and adjustments made to arrive at the topic ultimately studied and presented in the report. Briefly the main questions considered in this section of the report are those shown in Box 17.4.

Box **17.4**

Questions to consider when preparing the introduction

- What is the research topic?
- Why is there a need to research this topic, and who will benefit from this?
- What has been found/said by other researchers/writers in this area?
- Is everything said/done in the past on this topic correct?
- Are there gaps, deficiencies etc. that justify the research introduced in this report?
- What is the view of the researcher on past research and policy on the research topic?
- What is hypothesised by the researcher?
- What are the expected outcomes of this study?

These questions are expected to set the research topic in the context of current research, debates and policies, and show why the reader should be interested in the report, why the report is important and what the reader will gain from studying this report.

3.3 Method

This section informs the reader in clear and specific terms about the manner in which the research was conducted. Many professional journals have already established set patterns regarding how this section should be referred to and what to include. Some call this section 'Method', others 'Methodology'. In a similar fashion some are strict about the elements that are to be included in the section, as well as the names of the sections used, while others are less strict about names and aspects contained in this section. Overall, this section covers issues regarding the methodological framework, sampling procedures, instrumentation, methods of data collection, analysis and interpretation, and problems encountered by the researcher during the study. Briefly, this entails all the steps introduced when discussing the steps of the research process. To sum up, the methodology section will include the following.

- Choice of the topic and methodology.
  - What is the research topic?
  - How has the research question been addressed?
  - What type of methodology has been employed in the study?
  - What is the overall framework that contains the research process?
- Instrumentation.
  - What precisely is the research topic, and what are the relevant variables?
  - How were the variables operationalised?
  - What types of instruments were used to measure the variables?
  - What type of scales and response categories were used in the research?
  - What are the working hypotheses, null hypothesis and alternative hypotheses?
- Sampling.
  - Who were the respondents who took part in the study?
  - What was the size and composition of the sample?
  - What sampling procedures were used to select the sample?
  - What measures were employed to avoid errors?
  - What degree of generalisability was expected?
  - What were the characteristics of the population?
- Methods of data collection.
  - What methods of data collection were employed in the study and why?
  - What were the actual procedures of data collection, including ways of preventing or correcting non-response?
  - How were validity and reliability ensured in the study?
  - What types of pre-tests and pilot studies were employed in the investigation, and what were their findings?
- Data analysis.
  - How were data analysed?
  - Were statistical measures and computing employed?
  - What precautions were taken to ensure validity and reliability?
  - Are there any concerns that need to be taken into account?
- Ethics.
  - How were ethical issues addressed in the study?

3.4 Findings

This is where the results are presented. It is usually the largest part of a report, and its specific content depends on the nature of the topic and the methodology employed and the extent to which presentation is supposed to go (whether to offer a brief summary of the findings, for example, or a detailed analysis of the data). Its chief component is a direct description of variables and relationships between variables in the form of statements, tables, figures, graphs and/or other types of presentation. The findings are presented here, point-by-point, and step-by-step, following the structure of the instrument used or the order of the topics as categorised by the researcher.

Findings are presented in a summary form so that a general impression of trends is created. A common way of presenting the findings is in the form of central tendency and dispersion, aided by frequency tables and graphs integrated in the text. Following this, cross-tabulations and estimations of associations between the variables are undertaken. This will show whether factors of the issue in question are interrelated or interdependent. If regression analysis was used in the study, the findings will be presented in this section. Finally, the results of significance tests, if employed, will be provided here to strengthen the significance of relationships or differences reported in this section. The issues considered in this section are listed in Box 17.5 in question form.

Box 17.5

Questions to consider when writing the findings

- What are the direct answers to the research questions?
- How can the findings be presented in a summary form?
- What techniques can be used to present visually the trends identified in the study?
- Are there any associations evident in the study that can explain interdependence between relevant factors?
- Can the findings allow predictions to be made on the basis of the findings?
- How significant are differences reported in this study?
- Why should we trust the findings?
- Are there any problems that may affect the validity and reliability of the study?
- Does the presentation of the findings conform to ethical standards?

The presentation of the findings and the associated quantitative and ideological/ethical considerations will provide a platform for further critical elaboration. This is presented in the next section.

3.5 Discussion

The presentation of the findings is followed by a discussion of the most important points. The findings are summarised, explained and interpreted, establishing more general trends beyond individual observations and data. Without repeating the findings or departing fully from the facts identified in the study, this section will facilitate a more general debate of the significance of the findings and comparisons with other studies. Such a discussion takes place in a logical, theoretical, comparative and political context, and attempts to integrate the findings into theories, into the purpose of the study, and into its main hypotheses. Ultimately, the discussion of the findings offers some more general answers to the research questions and explains many issues included in the research problem. In addition, eventual weaknesses of the methods employed in the study will be explained adequately, and possible effects on the results and the resulting limitations of the study will be disclosed. The main issues, which are usually addressed in this section, are summarised in Box 17.6.

There are cases in which findings are presented and discussed in the same section. In such cases the sections 'Findings' and 'Discussion' are merged into one, usually labelled 'Findings and discussion' or 'Presentation and discussion of the findings'. In either case, the discussion section should not introduce data not previously presented in the 'findings' section. Discussion means just that: discussion of the results presented in the previous section of the report.

Box 17.6

Questions to consider when writing the discussion

- What is the general meaning of the findings?
- How do the findings relate to the main assumptions/questions introduced earlier in the report?
- How do the findings fit with trends reported in the relevant literature?
- What theories, views or opinions do these findings support or reject?
- Do the findings support plans and programmes related to the issue in question?
- Do the findings support the hypotheses formulated by the researcher at the outset?

3.6 Conclusions and recommendations

Most reports contain a section headed 'Conclusions', 'Summary and conclusions' or 'Conclusions and recommendations'. This section summarises the basic answer(s) that emerged out of the research data, and stresses the implications these findings have for the study object, the theory and the community in general. In addition, attention is given to gaps in our knowledge identified in the study which deserve further attention.

Following the formulation of conclusions, researchers usually make recommendations about action that is required to respond to the situation identified in the study. Here the author puts the results of the study in a normative context and makes some general or specific recommendations, the implementation of which is expected to solve the problems studied in the project. Action theorists will of course put more emphasis on this point than positivists, but the general trend is for the researcher to take a stance on the issue in question, to consider the conclusions made and to state, directly or indirectly, what action is recommended in this area. In summary, the questions listed in Box 17.7 are some of the issues that are addressed in this section of the study:

This section is one that readers will study very carefully, and one that policy makers and critics will give special consideration. It is therefore wise to construct this section in a way that offers an accurate, legitimate and fair reflection of the study and of the research report. Most of all, conclusions should reflect only the findings of the study, and should not go beyond what the research can support.

3.7 References

Every report is expected to contain a list of references: literature referred to in the report should be adequately documented and listed in alphabetical order at

Box **17.7**

Questions to consider when presenting the conclusion

- What is the answer to the research question?
- Does the study answer the question fully and convincingly?
- Does the answer require further empirical support?
- Does the study point to deficiencies in theory and research?
- What are the implications of the findings for the issue in question and the community in general?
- Are there any gaps in our knowledge of the issue in question and relevant theory?
- What can be done to improve the state of affairs in this area of study?
- Who should take action in this context: the individual, interest groups, the community or the government?

the end. Referencing can be done in many ways. The style used depends on the guidelines adopted by the publisher, or on the author's preference if no restrictions are set to the topic. Hence, the question here is not about whether such references should be made or not, but rather in what way. Journals and publishers, as well as other academic bodies (universities or professional bodies), already have established ways of referencing which are widely used. The Harvard system is one example, but others are equally popular. Using one or the other seems to be a matter of preference rather than a reflection of the quality of the system.

3.8 Optional elements

Finally, the report may include acknowledgements, a list of contents and an appendix. All three parts are optional and are included in the report only if required or relevant.

Acknowledgements may be given in a separate section or as a footnote attached either to the title of the paper or to some part of the introduction. A list of contents is generally required when large reports are produced, and may provide detailed information or just the main points or chapters of the report. Appendices provide an opportunity for the researcher to place in the report elements of the study which, although important, do not fit into the main body. Such elements might include the full questionnaire, pictures, maps, lengthy tables and other peripheral material that can help the reader to understand the findings fully, and to offer additional evidence, clarification or support.

4   THE REPORT IN QUALITATIVE RESEARCH

Most aspects of report writing in quantitative research that were described in the previous section are also relevant to the qualitative report. The structure and overall flow of the main body are almost the same in both contexts. Both begin with an abstract and an introduction, both present the main body, findings and conclusions, cite relevant literature and make acknowledgements to those who helped with the completion of the project (although other parts of a qualitative report may in a number of cases vary considerably from the quantitative format).

In addition, with respect to reports referring to studies conducted within a fixed qualitative model, the report will be similar to that of quantitative researchers. The actual content may not entail statistical figures and significance tests but the overall format and the standards of presentation, regarding parts of the report, styles, ethics and so on, will be the same. However, in the case of a study developed within a grounded theory model, the report is rather different. As noted above, there may be a few extra parts and there will certainly be basic differences in their content and underlying argumentation.

One basic characteristic of qualitative reports is their diversity. Reports vary not only according to the nature of the research topic and the research model, but also according to the underlying paradigm. The report of the findings of a text analysis based on hermeneutic or postmodernist principles will be constructed in a different manner from one reporting the findings of a case study. This is the reason that some writers who present guidelines on report writing in qualitative research suggest separate reports for each research domain, rather than constructing one to be applied in all research models.

It must be noted at this stage that despite the differences in length, nature and detail of the various steps of the report, the overall structure of the report demonstrates many commonalities. Above all, many researchers present their report in a manner that does not vary significantly from that employed in field research, while others prefer to pledge affiliation to grounded theory but produce reports that do not vary from those prepared by field researchers. In the following sections we shall describe a few other examples.

4.1 Report writing in field research

An example of reporting in field research is described by Bailey (1996) and is summarised in Box 17.8. Although in structural terms it is similar to that of quantitative researchers, it is lengthier and contains no explicit section on discussion of the findings. The nature of qualitative research, the reciprocal interaction between the researcher and the respondents, is reflected fully in the structure and content of the report.

Having discussed the structure and process of field work, it is easy to understand the tasks that are included in the steps of the report outlined above.

Types of presentation

Referring to ethnographic research, van Mannen (1988; see also Matt, 2000: 584–5) introduces a more diverse approach to report writing. In this context, reference is made to the observation that ethnographic texts are permeated by what he calls *realist tales*, which are the most common writing styles in this context, and which guide the presentation of the content of the report. In

Box **17.8**

Main items of the field-research report

1. *Introduction*
2. *History.* This reports the history of the setting or the group.
3. *Narrative.* This describes the research in chronological order.
4. *Supporting documentation.* This includes supportive material, verbatim quotations, pictures, maps and the like.
5. *Retaining the speaker's voice.* This relates to the perception, views and behaviour of the speaker.
6. *Locating oneself.* Has the researcher influenced the outcomes? Is the researcher insecure or ambivalent as to the extent of his/her influence on the outcome?
7. *Methodological details.* This section describes methods, entry, exit, problems, and limitations.
8. *Sharing results with the members.* A draft of the report is shared with key informants for comment and reactions are invited.
9. *Ethical issues.* These are similar to those in other types of research.
10. *Conclusions and appendices.* These are as discussed in other report types.

(Bailey, 1996)

addition, there are another two tales (*self-confidential tales* and *impressionistic tales*), which are reported to be less popular. These three models are shown below.

Types of presentation

- Realist tales:
    - written in the third person
    - written in a realistic style, using the language of the facts
    - stresses the typical, which is presented in the foreground
    - a production of objective reality
    - the author stands in the background as an uninvolved observer.
- Self-confessional tales:
    - entails the researcher being fully involved in and talking from the field
    - personal style of the researcher is employed
    - researcher describes all possible experiences with, and outcomes of, ethnographic work
    - contains methodological accounts and experiences about entry into, experience with, feelings, and changes in the field
    - written in the first person; includes also personal assumptions, prejudices etc.; presents researcher's version
    - findings presented in a realistic form.
- Impressionistic tales:
    - highly personal presentation of an 'expansive recall of fieldwork experience' (van Mannen, 1988: 102)
    - attempts to bring the public to the world of the researched

- attempts to present a moving and unusual story from the field
- researcher stands in the foreground
- written in essay form
- impressionist tales are presented within a realist or on impressionist model (ibid: 106).

The presentation of the styles listed above demonstrates the diversity of reports not only within the qualitative paradigm but also within the domain of individual research models. It goes without saying that this diversity should not be seen as a problem but rather as an advantage. Each version serves a purpose, which other models cannot serve equally adequately and equally accurately.

Sets of formats

These are not the only forms of data presentation in field research. There are several equally respected and accepted types of report writing in this area. Burgess (1984: 182) refers to three different types of qualitative reports. These are *descriptive*, *analytic* and *substantive* reports.

- *Descriptive reports.* These present summaries of the experiences the researcher recorded while conducting the research in a set format, mostly without adding personal evaluations and without deviating from what the researcher believes was happening in that setting.
- *Analytic reports.* These present descriptions but also discuss the concepts that emerge from the research. Comparisons, evaluations, and explanations are part of the content of this type of reporting.
- *Substantive reports.* These are similar to analytic reports, with the added attribute that they entail discussions that contribute to the development of general theories.

From a different perspective, other researchers and writers (Richardson, 1994; Pfeifer, 2000) note that field reports employ a number of set formats of writing, of which the following three are worth mentioning.

- *Member-centred writing.* Reports written within this format present findings from the point of view of the respondents. They present the findings as realistically (i.e. as closely to reality) as possible, with elements such as typical activities, and personal input on the part of the respondents, set in a time context and in a social context. The views of the respondents are presented verbatim, and interpretations of situations, events, relationships and so on are presented as perceived by the members of the community.
- *Writer-centred writing.* Reports employing this format focus on the writer, who presents reality as seen and interpreted by him or herself. Accounts of life in the setting are not necessarily 'realistic' (i.e. not necessarily as they really happened). The writer in this format has a great deal of freedom to present reality at will. Richardson (1994) gives the following examples of writing styles employed in this context: narrative of the self, ethnographic fictional presentations, poetic representation, ethnographic drama and mixed genres (see Box 17.9).

- *Mixed-format*. Within this format, reporting the results of a field study is accomplished by means of a combination of member-centred and writer-centred guides. Reporting life in the setting 'realistically', as well as presenting personal views and the like is considered to offer a stereoscopic view of life in the field.

Box **17.9**

Writer–centred writing styles in field research

- *Narrative of the self.* The writer employing this format is allowed to 'exaggerate, swagger, entertain, make a point without tedious documentation, relive the experiences, and say what might be unsayable in other circumstances' (Richardson, 1994: 521).
- *Ethnographic fictional presentations.* Reports here resemble fictional stories, making fiction out of field research experiences. The writer feels free to create scenes with characters, events and other aspects, and write about them.
- *Poetic representation.* The setting that was studied by the researcher is perceived as a place where field conversations are a form of poetry. Hence the report is presented as a long poem.
- *Ethnographic drama.* In this context, field experiences are recorded and presented in a form of drama. The summary of these experiences are then presented in a form of drama; in other words, they are performed rather than published in the conventional way.
- *Mixed genres.* This model does not prescribe a singular format but rather encourages the use of more than one of the four writing styles listed above.

(Richardson, 1994)

Although field researchers use all writing formats, the mixed-format report seems to be the most popular. For some writers (e.g. Bailey, 1996: 108), many field researchers situate their writing between respondent-centred and writer-centred writing.

4.2 Case studies

The models of report structure and presentation described above with regard to field studies research are also employed by many researchers in case studies research. The report may appear as a single case narrative with descriptions, tables, graphs, pictures and so on. It may appear as a multiple-case report with multiple narratives, as a question–answer report or as a cross-case report presenting a separate theme in each chapter rather than a case per chapter. How the details will be set within the context of the report depends on many factors; hence the report format may vary, and take the form of one of those presented in Box 17.10 (see Yin, 1991).

Box 17.10

Structures of case study reports

- *Analytical structure.* The report progresses from introduction to information regarding the topic, the setting and so on, presentation of data and analysis, followed by a discussion of the results.
- *Theory-building structure.* The presentation of the material is guided by the underlying paradigm. Elements of the theory constitute the main points of the book, presented in separate chapters together with the relevant data that support the theory.
- *Comparative structure.* This entails multiple examinations of cases conducted from various standpoints and in a comparative context to allow an assessment of the possible options and to choose the most appropriate option.
- *Chronological structure.* The content is presented in chronological order, following the development of the case history. Apart from anything else, this encourages the identification of changes over time and eventually the relationship between social events and experiences.
- *Suspense structure.* This is the inverse of that presented in the analytical model. The central findings of the study are presented first, and the details, plus the methodological explanations, follow later. Knowledge of the parameters of the social context presented first allows a better understanding of the details and a better frame for assessment of the conclusions.
- *Unsequented structure.* In this model, the chapters are presented as separate entities without a particular relationship to the each other. Their order can change without a loss of quality.

---

5 THE REPORT IN MULTIPLE-PARADIGM RESEARCH

The report format employed by researchers employing a multi-paradigm research model varies according to the nature of this model. As noted in Chapter 2, the structure of research models employing both the quantitative and the qualitative methodology is quite diverse, and we may expect this to be reflected in the resulting report. In addition to what was reported in Chapter 2, the dominant methodology plays an important role in the construction of the research design, and hence it is expected to play an equal role during the stage of report writing.

5.1 Successive-paradigm triangulation

In cases where one methodology is employed as a stepping-stone for the conduct of another, the construction of the report usually follows the guidelines of the latter. For instance, when a qualitative study is employed before a quantitative study, aiming to provide vital information for the construction of the latter, the researcher will prepare a quantitative report. In this case, the results of the qualitative study will be presented in the methods section of the report. Whether this section will follow the format of a qualitative study or not depends on the nature of the study. Preliminary findings, such as those of the qualitative study, are usually presented in a summary form, but still in a manner that will offer both sufficient results to guide the quantitative study and adequate justification of the validity and reliability of the instruments of the study.

It goes without saying that the same logic will be employed when the first study is quantitative. Here the report will most likely be qualitative, with the results of the quantitative study presented in summary form in the introduction or methods section of the qualitative report. It must, finally, be noted that if the first study is extensive and produces results that deserve special consideration, its findings can be presented in a separate report. In such cases, the project will produce two separate reports, one for each of the studies.

A similar approach will be employed when more than two studies are employed consecutively. The most likely expectation is that the report will follow the format of the final study, with the results of the others being incorporated in the report of that study.

5.2 Concurrent-paradigm triangulation

The nature of the report of a study employing two methodologies concurrently is rather complex. This is because it depends on the nature of the study and the intent of the researcher. In most cases, one of the studies is more dominant than the other, but other options are equally open, even if only theoretically.

When the project contains a major and a minor study, the report format will naturally be that of the major study. The information of the minor study will be inserted in the report in a manner that will fill in the gaps of the larger study. One study may include a large structured questionnaire and twenty-five in-depth interviews, in a quantitative and a qualitative context respectively. The report here will most likely be quantitative, with inserts of narratives from the interviews to explain more accurately the points made by the quantitative study. The same applies when the last study is qualitative; the final report will most likely be qualitative.

5.3 Step-wise conversion

This option comprises a design in which a study is conducted that produces qualitative data, which in turn are converted to quantitative. One example might be a study employing unstructured observation resulting in a set of brief statements on the same topics for each of the respondents, in which the researcher decides after completion of the study to quantify the answers and analyse the data using a quantitative paradigm. The way in which the report of this study will be constructed depends on the purpose of the study and the intent of the researcher.

A possible – and also logical – scenario is for the researcher to prepare a qualitative report, and to incorporate the converted data in its structure, most likely in the 'results' section. Given that the initial study was designed within a qualitative paradigm, it is logical to assume that the researcher was interested in qualitative data and aimed to produce qualitative findings; hence the quantitative data seem to serve the purpose of expanding the applicability of the qualitative findings and/or of allowing more accurate comparisons within and outside the main study.

Another possible – but less likely – scenario is that the researcher produces two reports, one containing the qualitative data and following the qualitative format, and another containing the quantitative data and following the quantitative model. This is, for instance, the case when the reports are directed to different groups of readers, and also when the researcher wishes to address different aspects of the results in the reports.

In conclusion it must be noted that the discussion in this section relates to a small minority of cases. In actual fact, first, almost all researchers prefer to work within one paradigm at a time; second, those who opt to employ qualitative and quantitative research work predominantly within one research paradigm, using the other only secondarily; and third, those who give equal weight to both methodologies are in the minority. Given the diverse paths of research design employed by the two methodologies, the intensive work required to complete both studies within a project, and the innate incompatibility of the paradigms, the likelihood of occurrence of multi-paradigm studies – and hence multi-methodological reports – is rather slim.

6 THE STUDENT PROJECT REPORT

As shown above, a research report is framed according to the methodological context in which the research was developed. Different methodologies set different parameters of report construction, resulting in the reports being either qualitative or quantitative in nature. The structure and content of these reports may vary to some extent, but in principle they adhere to basic theoretical standards which assign reports the status of being 'scientific': that is systematic, disciplined, following specific theoretical rules and principles, and adhering to ethical and professional codes.

The nature of the reports is independent of the status of the researcher. The researcher has two options: either to produce a report according to professional standards, or to construct a report outside these parameters. These conditions apply to all those who produce results by means of research procedures: to the professional researchers, to the professors who publish their results professionally, to other academics and to students conducting research as part of their postgraduate work or otherwise.

Students, more than anyone else, have to demonstrate in their reports that they are in command not only of methods of acquiring knowledge, but also of the methods of sharing their findings with their fellow academics, in a manner that is as professional as any other respectable writer. The report will be constructed in a scientific manner, and beyond this, in either a qualitative or a quantitative context.

Following this, the student's report will not differ substantially from any other report. The only considerations which can motivate students to modify their report are the specifications set by their institution, the advice of their supervisor, and, if their report is to be published, the requirements of the publisher. This means that the discussion presented in the previous sections of this chapter and that which follows apply also to the reports of students.

7 PRESENTATION

7.1 Conveying the message

If content denotes what is included in the report, presentation refers to how the content is displayed. In both research paradigms, reports are expected to meet certain criteria, which are set by peers, by academic standards, by the nature of the recipients and by market demands. Ultimately, the purpose of the report is to convey the information, and this implies that the readers are in a position to understand its content fully, not to mention that they find the report easy to read and interesting. Some practical hints as to how a report can be presented in a successful manner are given below (see Farber, 2001: 238); the main points to consider are that the report should be:

- *Concise.* That is, compact and to the point. Large reports are not more effective than smaller ones that convey the same information.
- *Readable.* Written at the level of the user. Academics, public servants, politicians and policy makers have different standards of how a report is to be presented, have different expectations, and are accustomed to different language. Reports should be adjusted to the needs of the readers. It is not unusual for researchers to compile a report for a local council, and an article for a professional journal, both presenting the findings of the same study, but presented differently.
- *Well-written.* This relates not only to style and grammar but also to the general construction of the content. Academics will expect a report to comply with the standards of the journal or publisher, which they are accustomed to; policy makers will expect a brief 'executive summary', a straight and simple presentation of the results (usually with a low level of statistics and no academic jargon), charts, diagrams, tables, and summary information (using bullets, for example, where reasonable and possible).
- *Interesting.* Presented in a manner that relates constantly to the point of analysis, engaging the reader, relating to community needs, raising important questions, suggesting possible solutions, and addressing critical and topical issues.
- *Timely.* A report should be brought out as soon as the results become available. Aged data may be of interest to academics but not so much to politicians and policy makers.

These appear to be the minimum requirements of a research report. Most researchers and readers expect more in such reports, particularly with regard to substance and professional standards. The standards presented in Box 17.11 are considered (e.g. Becker, 1989; Martin, 1988; Puris, 1995) to be most significant.

While these points are generally accepted among many researchers, there is controversy about the validity of some of these guidelines. Critical theorists and feminists will consider them inappropriate, particularly in regard to objectivity, detachment and impersonality. Nevertheless, many qualitative researchers adhere to standards of objectivity, and as we saw above, objectivity is an aspect of research reports of qualitative research.

Box 17.11

Research report: minimum requirements

- *Clarity.* Reports should be written clearly; confusing and ambiguous statements should be avoided.
- *Precision.* The author should avoid generalities and vague statements.
- *Appropriacy.* The report should be comprehensible not only to academics and specialists but to all intended readers.
- *Completeness.* No parts of the study should be left out of the report. All issues should be given adequate emphasis.
- *Objectivity.* Subjectivity and emotionality should be avoided. Reports are expected to convey information about the findings of the research; opinions and subjective views should be presented so that they are clearly identifiable as such. Facts and value judgements should be separated.
- *Fairness.* Findings should be presented in a fair and unbiased manner.
- *Verifiability.* Information presented in the report must be readily verifiable.
- *Impersonality.* It is advised that reports should be written in the third person.
- *Ethics.* The report should comply with the code of ethics.

7.2 Writing style

Writing styles vary considerably. The style used in a conference presentation is different from that used when writing for a professional journal or a book intended for the general reader. The styles are different, but legitimate and acceptable in their context. As stated above, the criterion that makes the difference is the reader, along with the accepted standards of the context in which the work is published.

Nevertheless, there are some common stylistic standards agreed upon by many writers. Although agreement on such standards is becoming weaker with time, and standards seem to be accepted more by some groups of writers than by others, these standards seem to be preferred by most writers and deserve to be mentioned.

First or third person?

Many writers, editors and publishers insist that the third person is used. It is preferable to say 'It has been found in the present study . . .' rather than 'I found in my study . . .'. In both cases, the message is the same but conventions support the former rather than the latter.

Active or passive voice?

In a similar manner, conventions prescribe that the passive voice is preferred to the active voice. Many writers would say 'Women were found to suffer more than men . . .' rather than 'The researcher found that women suffer more than . . .'. As in the previous example, the message is the same, but the expression varies. However, there is a gradual shift from passive to active expression. More journals are coming to accept 'active' expressions more than before, while others do not seem to pay attention to this point. Either is accepted as long as the usage is consistent throughout the report.

Past or present tense?

Whether the writer uses the past or present tense depends on the issues referred to in the text. The rule, however, is that reports of research findings are made in the past tense. This is logical given that the research being reported happened in the past. It is logical to say that 'There were more women than men in favour of censorship' than 'There are more women than men in favour of censorship'; apart from the fact that the latter is incorrect (women were in favour of equality at the time of the study five years ago, but are they now?), it seems to imply a generalisation of the finding, which may not be supported by the research.

Sexist language?

There is a general expectation that sexist language should not be used in the reports. This requirement was initiated by the women's movement, and has been institutionalised in all parts of the Western world. There are many reasons for this. Apart from the fact that sexist language violates standards of equity and reflects discriminatory practices, it is also unacceptable on ethical grounds. More to the point, using a single descriptor for both sexes – male or female – is ambiguous and inaccurate, and fails to reflect the information contained in the data fairly and fully. To simplify the point, was he (the criminal) a male or a female? In such cases, the report misrepresents the content of the findings and hence it is inaccurate.

Box **17.12**

Think critically! (On *he* and *she* and *human*kind)

The argument: if most feminists are constructionists, and if constructionism values meanings rather than 'objects' – such as words – why is it so important to replace certain words (such as *he*, *man*kind etc.) with others (*he or she*, *human*kind etc.) that are literally different, but have the same meaning? Moreover, the meanings of the objectionable words, first, represent both genders anyway (*he* means both men and women; and *man*kind refers to all human beings), and second, have meanings that can and will be reconstructed.

There must be a deeper reason for this! What is it?

The valid point made by feminists is that researchers and respondents are male and female; there is therefore no justification for referring to them uniformly and consistently as he or she. Using both pronouns (he or she, he/she or (s)he) may be awkward and tedious to read but is the proper alternative nonetheless. Using pronouns in plural may be a preferred alternative. The sentence 'The respondent has the right to be asked for his/her consent' can be better written as 'Respondents have the right to be asked for their consent'. Alternatively, writers may use the pronouns he and she interchangeably.

However, there are others who find the 'good old model' harmless and more comfortable to read. Susan Haack (1995: 8), for instance, explaining her writing style in the introduction of her book on epistemologies, notes that she has neither complicated her 'presentation by replacing the 'he' of standard English by 'he or she', nor restructured sentences so as to avoid the need for any pronoun.' She stresses, however that 'It should go without saying . . . that of course I think that women, no less than men, are knowing subjects.'

Writing style is not an integral part of the social research process and of the creation of knowledge. Nevertheless it is a part of the research process, and indeed an important one. It is the part that will help disseminate findings to the interested parties in a clear, accurate and acceptable manner, and in this sense it deserves as much attention as any other part of the research process.

8 SELF-ASSESSMENT

It is wise that, before it leaves the hands of the author, the report is subjected to a final check, to ensure that it presents a true reflection of the findings, that it meets the general writing standards, and that it is free of errors or omissions. Writers (e.g. Becker, 1989; Judd et al., 1991; Puris, 1995; Selltiz et al., 1976) have referred to a number of points that, in their opinion, deserve to be considered during such an assessment. These points make up the detailed and useful list given below.

8.1 The abstract

- Is the abstract relevant, adequate, complete and concise?
- Does it overstate/understate the findings?
- Is it objective and informative?
- Is the language/style clear and adequate, and consistent with that employed in the other parts of the report?

8.2 The main body of the report

- Is the structure symmetrical and proportionately divided?
- Is it complete, readable, clear, precise, objective, fair, verifiable and impersonal?
- Does it comply with ethical standards?
- Does each part of the report fulfil its purpose?

The introduction

- – Is the research topic introduced clearly and adequately?
- – Is the literature review pertinent, exhaustive and accurately reported and evaluated?
- – Is the purpose of the study explained adequately?
- – Has the need for the study been adequately justified?

The method

- Are populations and research units clearly defined?
- Are the variables operationalised and the indicators explicitly stated?
- Are methods and instruments adequately chosen, explained, employed and justified?
- Are methods and instruments sufficiently guarded against bias, violation of the code of ethics and errors to ensure validity and reliability?
- Have extraneous variables been controlled adequately?
- Are the hypotheses clearly stated, pertinent to the main issues of the study and verifiable?

Findings

- Are the findings complete, readable, and adequately organised and presented?
- Do they correspond to the research hypotheses and the basic points of the research question?
- Are visual displays of the data well integrated in the text and easy to read?

Discussion

- Are the findings adequately interpreted and generalised?
- Are the interpretations legitimate in terms of the nature of the study?
- Are all issues presented in the previous sections equally considered?
- Is the discussion free of bias and violations of the ethical code?
- Were the limitations of the study considered when generalising the findings?

Conclusions

- Are the conclusions clear, logical and convincing?
- Are the conclusions related to the main elements of the research question?
- Are they justified by the research and its limitations?
- Do they cover all the important aspects of the study?

8.3 The references/bibliography

- Are the references presented consistently and according to accepted and relevant standards and guidelines set by the publisher?
- Does this section include only sources that are referred to in the report?
- Are all sources cited in the text included in the bibliography?
- Have all sources listed in the text and bibliography been directly consulted?

8.4 General

- Do the presentation of the report and the information provided allow replication?
- Does it show flow and continuity?
- Is the title relevant and adequate?
- In objective terms, is the report worth publishing?

The report is often given to colleagues for comments and criticism. A second opinion regarding the soundness of the procedures, methods, analysis and interpretation is most useful. In certain cases, writers show parts of their report to persons who were studied or key informants for comments; such comments have been found to be very helpful indeed.

9 LAST BUT NOT LEAST: THE FATE OF THE REPORT

9.1 The politics of publication

Almost without exception, the ultimate goal of report writing is publication. Researchers are interested in publishing their reports in a way that will guarantee a wide distribution of the findings so that the research is communicated to the largest range of readers. After all, the slogan 'publish or perish' is not merely empty words. One's reputation as a publishing academic and another citation on one's CV count more than writing a perfect report.

However, publishing is more than putting words in print; it entails intensive political and ideological manoeuvring, negotiation and politicking (Brown, 1992). Whether manuscripts will be accepted for publication in book form or not depends on many factors, of which quality of the report, social relevance, economic considerations and ideological imperatives are a few. Publication in journals is easier, in the sense that market factors and (to a lesser extent) social relevance are less significant. Similarly, publication in newspapers depends more on social relevance than on quality of the study, while newsletters and monographs published by the author or sponsor of the study find no difficulties with publication.

The quality of the report is an important factor: high-quality manuscripts are more likely to reach the shelves of a bookseller or to be accepted by journals for publication than poor ones. However, this is not always the case. Publication is a function of more than one of the above listed factors. With regard to journal articles, the decisive factor is reviewers' reports; and this constitutes a possible problem for many reports. When biased reviewers infiltrate the editorial boards of journals and publishing houses, this issue becomes critical. Personal interests, economic considerations and ideological convictions are a few reasons why some valid and relevant research findings remain unpublished. Groups or individuals who consider the findings critical of their personal interests or ideological principles usually do not support the publication, and where possible do not 'allow' the report to be published. Academic quality is not of primary importance in such cases.

In a similar fashion, companies or political parties that have contracted the research may not publish the report unless it supports their views and practices. For instance, an organisation that receives a contracted report proving that the waste it produces is toxic, contaminates the surrounding area within a radius of 50 km and causes severe damage to flora, animals and people will ensure that this report remains unpublished.

Interest groups too may make a strong effort to keep reports from being published if they are not consistent with their expectations. This may be done either in a direct or an indirect way; it may also be done on the basis of ideological standards or economic principles. Individuals who review manuscripts may decide the fate of a report on the basis of personal and ideological convictions rather than on academic grounds.

As far as books are concerned, publishers are interested in manuscripts that are of high quality and promise high returns for their investment. And while a combination of academic quality and business interests is the ideal, some publishers emphasise the former while others consider the latter to be more important. Publication proposals are often rejected on the grounds of a weak market. To overcome this problem and to allow the publication of less marketable (i.e. specialist literature) but academically sound and vigorous studies, specialist publishers have been established. Some universities have organised their own publishing operations (referred to as university presses) for this purpose.

It must be born in mind that the success of a research project is not always reflected in the amount or type of publication. The success of projects is measured in terms of their soundness and the type of findings they produce. It is not unusual to see excellent research findings in self-published reports or in sponsor-supported publications. Success is also measured in terms of the extent to which publications have initiated structural and/or political changes. Action research may not reach the shelves of booksellers but may have a stronger impact on social policies than books and articles combined.

9.2 From research findings to policy and practice

The practical goal of report writing is to bring findings to the attention of the public, the stakeholders and the policy makers. But publishing the reports does not imply that the research findings will have an influence on public policy. Even bringing the findings to the attention of the authorities does not necessarily guarantee that relevant action will be taken. To encourage and stimulate such action, some investigators employ intervention tactics, such as those employed in action research.

Such tactics entail emancipation, raising awareness, focus, and guidance. In other words, action informs people of the nature of the problem, raises their awareness as to their rights as citizens and the ways they are violated, points out the areas where they should focus their concern, and shows them how to 'encourage' government authorities to take into consideration the content of the report and to act accordingly.

The way in which such action and intervention tactics are facilitated varies widely. In some cases, it involves active debate of the issue directly with the relevant authorities. Such debates do not primarily involve the researcher but rather are conducted between the stakeholders as a group and members of relevant government departments. Such debates are repeated until they prove to be fruitful. When the results are not satisfactory, active debates are shifted to higher authorities and take on a confrontational stance, where stakeholders become more conscious of their rights and the presence of problems, and more confrontational, demonstrating that they will not stop acting until the issue is satisfactorily resolved.

Political involvement is another tactic. This entails visiting the local representatives of the governing party, holding active debates and confrontations, asking for relevant action to be taken. When pressure groups find the outcome of such debates and consultations unsatisfactory, an alternative is to approach members of the opposition. This in itself is most promising because it forces the governing parties to reconsider their position on the issue, and be more forthcoming to the stakeholders' requests.

Use of the media is another intervention tactic, usually employed in conjunction with other methods. Community groups inform other people through media campaigns about the research findings, often juxtaposed with the response of the authorities, demonstrating not only the needs of the community but also the attitude of the government towards the community. Media campaigns are often very successful.

When all else fails to achieve satisfactory results, pressure groups may plan street demonstrations where members of the community actively demand that the issue in question be given due attention and consideration. In this and other tactics, the most important achievement is that the research issue contained in the report becomes a public issue, a community matter and a political concern. In an environment dominated by political agendas and party interests, this is more than a researcher can generate through a research report.

Action or pressure groups are very useful, not only because they provide ideas and suggestions about how to proceed further, but also because such action helps unite members of the community, makes them realise their strength and political power, and encourages them to act as a group so they can bring about social change. When many people become aware of the presence and significance of a problem, they share feelings and concerns, and finally establish networks of like-thinking individuals who can exert pressure upon the government to take action. And the government is more sensitive to public pressure than to reports which can be hidden away and often become invisible.

For those who see social research as a way of emancipation, and who consider action as an element of the research process, the planning of action after the findings have been established is as important as planning research before it has begun. The problem is that action research constitutes only a small proportion of social inquiry. All other researchers have to rely on the commitment and good will of those who care to read and understand the research findings and their role in people's lives.

MAIN POINTS

- Reporting is the channel for communicating the findings of a study to interested groups.
- Of the factors that affect the writing of the report, the most important are ethical considerations, the reader and the purpose of the report.
- The structure of the report varies with the type and nature of publication.
- The most common outlets for the results of a study are newspapers, newsletters, conferences, monographs, journal articles and books.
- The main parts of a report are the abstract, introduction, method, results, discussion, conclusion, recommendation and references. Some of these parts are optional.
- The criteria that mark a good report are clarity, precision, appropriate language, completeness, objectivity, fairness, verifiability, impersonality and ethics.

- In quantitative research, reports are more structured than in qualitative research.
- With regard to presentation, consideration must be given to whether to use the first or third person, active or passive voice, and past or present tense, and to the type of language.
- Reports are expected to avoid using sexist terms of any kind.
- The politics of publishing constitutes a very important factor and requires due consideration.

WHERE TO FROM HERE?

Before you leave this chapter, visit the companion website for the third edition of *Social Research* at http://www.palgrave.com/sociology/sarantakos to review the main concepts introduced in this chapter and to test yourself on the major issues discussed.

FURTHER READING

Bowden, J. (2002) *Writing a Report : How to Prepare, Write and Present Effective Reports*. Oxford: How To Books.

Brause, B. S. (2000) *Writing Your Doctoral Dissertation: Invisible Rules for Success*. London: Falmer.

Budestam, K. E. and Newton, R. R. (2001) *Surviving Your Dissertation: A Comprehensive Guide to Content and Process*. Thousand Oaks, Calif.: Sage.

Clough, P. and Nutbown, C. (2002) *A Student's Guide to Methodology*. London: Sage.

Evans, D. and Gruba, P. (2002) *How to Write a Better Thesis*. Carlton South, Vic.: Melbourne University Press.

Johnstone, M-J. (2004) *Effective Writing for Health Professionals: A Practical Guide to Getting Published*. Crows Nest, N.S.W.: Allen & Unwin.

Lester, J. D. and Lester, J. Jr (2001) *Writing Research Papers: A Complete Guide*. New York: Longman.

Punch, P. D. (2000) *Developing Effective Research Proposals*. London: Sage.

Waters, K. (2000) *Researching, Writing and Presenting Reports*. Croydon, Vic.: Eastern House.

Glossary

Abscissa: The horizontal line of a graph in which the independent variable is presented.

Abstat: A computer program for statistical analysis of research data, mainly for IBM PCs and CP/M operating computers.

Accretion measure: A methodological tool employed in the study of physical traces, focusing on accumulation of residue on certain objects or places.

Action research: Applied research orientated towards bringing about change, involving respondents in the process of investigation, and particularly in the implementation of the findings.

ANOVA: Analysis of variance. A parametric test of significance, which compares the means of two or more samples.

Analytic induction: A method of qualitative data analysis whereby the universality of explanations of phenomena is tested through establishing hypothetical explanations and testing them through new data. Universality of the explanation is established when all new cases are consistent with the hypothetical explanation.

Anonymity: Systematic protection of personal identity of the respondents.

Applied research: A research type focusing on practical issues and seeking solutions.

Arbitrary zero: An arbitrary zero does not indicate the total absence of the criterion in question. Zero opinion (no opinion) does not mean absence of opinion; no opinion is an opinion. The opinion of that person is 'no opinion'.

Archival research: Studies of people or organisations based on collected documents produced by them.

Association: A relationship between two variables displaying joint variation.

Attrition: The loss of members of a sample, e.g. due to inability or unwillingness to take part in the study.

Authenticity: The state of being original, natural, not influenced (qualitative research).

Basic research: A research type focusing purely on discovering new knowledge; it is pure research.

Bias: A systematic error when planning or conducting research.

Bivariate statistics: The type of statistics that studies two variables.

Bivariate tables: Tables presenting data relating to two variables.

BMDP ('Biochemical programs'): A statistical program for computer-assisted analysis of research data, mainly for the medical profession.

Bogardus Social Distance Scale: A scale used to measure attitudes toward certain groups, such as ethnics, gay people or immigrants.

Boomerang effect: The condition where a measure achieves the opposite of what it was intended to achieve.

Canonical correlation: A form of correlation between two groups of variables employing factor analysis.

Case study: A research method (or design) focusing on the study of single cases.

Category: A group of people demonstrating the same or similar attributes, although they may not have face-to-face contacts.

Causal relationship: A relationship where one variable causes changes in another.

Causal research: A form of research aimed at confirming or testing causal relationships between variables.

Causality: The state of relationships between two variables, where the one causes changes in the other.

Central tendency: An attribute of distributions showing the general trend of the data and measured by means of the mean, median and mode.

'Chart': A statistical package for computer analysis of research data.

Chicago School: A school of thought founded by Mead, Park and Thomas which established a theoretical and methodological direction known as symbolic interactionism.

Chi-square test: A test of significance for nominal values that compares observed with expected frequencies, employing a null hypothesis of no relationship.

Clinical interviews: Interviews used to provide information about specific causes of problems or types of illness, employed predominantly by psychologists and social workers.

Closure: A situation in experimental research in which all variables except the independent variable are controlled (closed off).

Cluster analysis: A form of analysis developed by Tyron, Holzinger and Harman used to study variables by integrating similar objects and grouping them together into clusters.

Cluster sampling: A form of sampling procedure in which the primary selection unit is a 'cluster' (a school, a hospital, a soccer team or similar entity).

Code: A symbol or set of symbols used in measurement and analysis in place of responses collected through social research. In grounded theory: the result of coding, which may be a category or a relationship of categories.

Code book: A book containing a set of rules and guidelines for coding.

Coding: The process of transforming raw data for the purpose of analysis. In grounded theory: the process of conceptualising data.

Coefficient of determination: A statistic expressing the amount of variation in the dependent variable explained by the independent variable.

Cohort: A group of subjects sharing a common characteristic (e.g. date of birth).

Cohort study: A study of cohorts to ascertain trends and developments over time.

Communality: A common factor variance; a measure of the degree to which variables change in a similar way.

Community impact assessment: Evaluation research focusing on the impact programmes or policies are expected to have on the community.

Community studies: Empirical studies employing a variety of methods and techniques that focus on communities as whole units.

Compunication: A new concept developed to describe communication involving computers.

Computer interviews: Computer-aided interviews in which the interviewer is replaced partly or wholly by a computer.

Concept: A word that labels or classifies an object, event or experience.

Conduit: A statistical program for computer-assisted analysis of research data.

Confidentiality: Systematic protection of the nature of information supplied by respondents.

Constant: An attribute that remains unchanged within the study.

Constructionism: The epistemological doctrine that maintains that the world is not objective and discovered but socially constructed.

Content analysis: A research method or design that focuses on the content of documents, based on diverse research paradigms, and employing a variety of research methods.

Content validity: The type of validity that refers to the extent to which it covers all possible aspects of the research topic.

Contextual research: Research that addresses subjects within their social context.

Contingency: A type of correlation related to nominal data.

Contingency analysis: A method developed by Osgood in the area of content analysis, employed to study relationships between parts of text.

Contingency table: A table containing a numerical presentation of two variables.

Continuous variable: A variable that can take unlimited numerical values within a unit of measurement. (Opposite: discrete variable)

Control: A procedure employed in experimental research to prevent external factors or variables from affecting the dependent variable in any way. (See also Closure)

Control group: The group selected in experimental studies that is not exposed to the experimental stimulus.

Control question: A question employed to test the validity of the response given to another question.

Convenience sample: A sample constructed by enlisting easily accessible and willing persons.

Convergent interview: A type of unstructured interview involving respondents with divergent views, where interviewers jointly plan the process of interviewing, and discuss the results of each interview before they proceed with the next.

Correlation: A general term for the statistical analysis of the degree to which two variables co-vary (synonymous with association).

Correlation matrix: A matrix containing the values of the coefficient of correlation between the variables in question.

Cost–benefit analysis: An evaluation of programmes or policies involving an analysis of their costs and benefits and exploring whether they are worth continuing.

Co-variance: A measure of the degree of common variance between variables.

Criterion variable: Another name for the dependent variable.

Cross-sectional study: A study containing units from different sections of the community, but studied over the same period of time.

Cross-validation: A method of ascertaining validity by checking groups of data against other groups of data from the same study.

CSS ('Complete statistical system'): A statistical computer package employed in analysis of data.

Cumulative data: Frequencies established by adding low-value scores to the score with next highest value.

'Daisy professional': A computer program for statistical analysis of research data, suitable for Apple II computers.

Data: Items or units of information collected through social research.

data-x: A statistical package for statistical analysis of research data for PET computers.

Deception: Lying to the respondent about the true nature and intentions of the study.

Deduction: The process of establishing logical conclusions by proceeding from general and abstract to specific and concrete phenomena (the opposite of induction).

Delphi method: A method of data collection that relies on the opinion of experts.

Demography: A method of study introduced for the first time by Guillard in 1855 to describe and/or analyse the structure and change of populations.

Demoscopy: A method of study employed to study opinions and attitudes, using mainly survey research. Formally developed in 1920 in the United States by Gallup.

Dependent variable: A variable that is explained or affected by another variable.

Depth interview: Unstandardised, roughly structured interview; also known as a clinical interview.

Design: The research plan that contains all steps of the research process (e.g. survey design, experimental design).

Diagnostic interviews: Interviews employed to diagnose aspects of reality.

Discourse: A socially constructed framework of meanings which serves to guide people like guiding rules, norms or conventions, and informs people as to what is appropriate or inappropriate, allowed or not allowed, acceptable or not acceptable, valued or not valued.

Discrete variable: A variable containing a number of distinct attributes with no continuity between them. (Opposite: continuous variable.)

Dispersion: The degree to which items of distribution are spread around the mean.

Disproportional sampling: A form of stratified sampling in which the units included in the sample are disproportional to those of the population.

Dogmatic hermeneutics: A branch of hermeneutics that adheres to certain dogmatic principles, such as religion or ideology.

Double-barrelled question: A question containing two points that require an answer.

Ecological fallacy: The logical extrapolation of evidence established at the group level onto its members, hence explaining the behaviour of individuals by way of rules holding true in groups.

Elite interviews: Interviews with elites, that is, well-known, prominent and influential people.

Empirical data: Data gathered by means of sensory experience.

Empiricism: The notion that knowledge comes through factual research based on direct experience gathered through the senses.

Epistemology: (Gr. *Episteme* = science) The science of science; deals with the nature of knowledge; studies grounds and modes of knowledge acquisition.

Equivalence reliability: Reliability across indicators.

Erosion measure: A methodological tool employed in the study of physical traces or artefacts, focusing on deterioration or otherwise of certain objects.

Ethnocentrism: The tendency to see one's own culture as the centre of life and its elements as the standards for evaluating other cultures.

Ethnography: The discipline that describes cultures; common among cultural anthropologists. A branch of field studies referring to in-depth study of people in their natural setting. The report of ethnographic research.

Ethnology: A discipline that studies social structures and cultures of primitive societies (in Europe) but also of modern societies (United States and England, where it is known as social anthropology or cultural anthropology).

Ethnomethodology: A sociological discipline developed by Garfinkel (1967) that emphasises the methods and procedures employed by people when they define and interpret everyday life through talk and interaction. It is the study of common-sense knowledge, its creation and use in natural settings.

Evaluation research: A type of applied research which is employed to assess the implementation, operation and ultimate effectiveness of policies and programmes.

Experiment: A research method that studies predominantly causal relationships under systematic and controlled conditions.

Experimental group: The group selected in an experimental study that is exposed to the experimental stimulus.

Exploration: A method of data collection and a research model employed in quantitative and qualitative studies.

Extrapolation: Estimation of missing external values by means of knowledge of internal values.

Factor analysis: A method of multivariate statistical analysis of variables.

Factorial design: An experimental design including more than one independent variable.

Factors: In ANOVA, factors are the independent variable(s).

Falsification: The process of disproving the validity of a hypothesis.

Feasibility studies: Research undertaken to establish the economic or other viability of a proposed programme.

Field experiment: An experiment conducted in the field, a natural setting.

Field study: A study conducted in a natural setting (e.g. field research, field experiments).

Fieldwork: The part of field research that is conducted in the field.

Fine analysis: A method employed in the context of objective hermeneutics.

Focus group: A group of people used as a research unit, constructed for the purpose of studying a particular issue.

Focused interviews: Semi-structured interviews conducted to explore a specific object or a certain point of the research topic in depth.

Formal theory: The final step of theory development employed in the context of grounded theory.

Formative evaluation: A type of evaluation research that aims to reform or improve a programme.

Free interviews: Another name for unstructured, unstandardised and open interviews.

'General inquirer': A computer program employed in content analysis to compute various indices.

Generalisability: The quality of a study that justifies conclusions drawn from studies of samples to large populations. Applicable with regard to space and time.

genstat ('general statistical program'): A statistical program for computer analysis of research data.

'Graph/stats II': A statistical package for computer-assisted analysis of research data for BBC microcomputers.

Grounded theory: A qualitative research model, introduced by Glaser and Strauss, where data collection and analysis are conducted together, and where the research design is guided by the emerging theory. Also a theory that is grounded on data generated when using the grounded theory model. Offers one of the bases of qualitative or interpretative research.

Group discussion: A method of data collection in which information is collected in the context of a group by means of some form of discussion.

Guided interview: A form of semi-structured interview.

Gutman scale: An ordinal scale suitable for attitude measurement.

Halo effect: The influence that the response to a question has on the way other questions of the same context will be answered.

Hard interviews: Interviews in which structure and presentation are authoritarian and resemble formal interrogation.

Hawthorne effect: An expectation effect; reflects the situation where the respondents' knowledge of being observed affects their behaviour.

Hermeneutics: A school of thought interested in studying and interpreting texts and other manifestations of cultures.

Heterogeneity: A group characteristic reflecting the diversity of the group's elements.

Histogram: Graphic presentation of a distribution consisting of blocks equal to the values of the units of the distribution.

Historicism: The school of thought that states that the course of society is governed by historical laws; the discovery of these laws can help to predict the future of a society.

Holism: Referring to the whole; being interested in and studying a group or case as a whole.

Homogeneity: A group characteristic reflecting the sameness or similarity of the group's elements or attributes.

Hypothesis: An assumption, an educated guess, which can be tested.

Idiographic approach: Approaching reality through description (opposite of nomological approach).

Independent variable: The variable that is set to exert an influence on another variable.

Index: A composite measure comprising a combination of aspects of a concept, the values of which are summed up to provide a numerical score. It is a summary of indexes of theoretical and arithmetic nature.

Indicator: A directly observable trait used to construct an operational definition of a concept.

Individual interviews: Interviews with one interviewee at a time.

Induction: The process of drawing conclusions by proceeding from the specific and concrete to the general and abstract (the opposite of deduction).

Inductive statistics: Inferential statistics.

Inferential statistics: The type of statistics that constructs conclusions based on data derived from parts of the population (samples) which are projected onto the target population.

Informant: An individual, usually a member of the group under study, who assists the researcher with accessing vital information about the group.

Informative interviews: A term used to designate interviews that are conducted to provide information of a descriptive nature.

Informed consent: Consent granted after all parameters of a study and its potential effects are fully and accurately explained to the research participants.

Inquiring interviews: A concept used to designate interviews in which the respondent is an informant with a lot of freedom and opportunities to offer data.

Instruments: Tools of research employed in the context of gaining and analysing data.

Intensive interview: A form of interviewing employing an unstructured and unstandardised approach, emphasising informal questioning, searching for deep and accurate information, and considering the needs and preferences of the interviewee.

Interaction analysis: A model of studying patterns of interaction in small groups, developed in the 1950s by Bales.

Inter-cohort analysis: Analysis of two or more cohorts in the same or in different period(s) of time.

Interpolation: Estimation of missing internal values on the basis of knowledge of external values.

inter-stat: A computer program for statistical analysis of research data, mainly for Apple II computers.

Interval-level measurement: This form of measurement names and orders subjects, setting them in a continuum containing equal intervals, stating also the distance between the values.

Interview: A method of data collection that gathers information through oral questioning.

Interviewer bias: An undesirable effect of interviewing, stemming from the mere presence of and/or certain traits of the interviewer, and leading to distortions.

Interviewer guide: A set of questions and instructions used by the interviewer during interviewing.

Intra-cohort analysis: Analysis of internal attributes of particular cohorts, in the same or different period(s) of time.

Invasion of privacy: Intrusion into the life of the respondents, which is ethically wrong.

Items: Elements of a scale or questionnaire. May be a question, a statement or stimulus, about which the opinion of the subjects is sought.

Laboratory experiments: Experiments conducted in a laboratory under strictly controlled conditions.

Lambda coefficient: A measure of association between nominally scaled variables.

Leading questions: Questions formulated in a way that encourages the respondent to answer them in a specific way.

Likert scale: A scale introduced by Likert employing a set of response categories ranging from very positive to very negative, one of which the respondent has to choose.

Linear regression: A method of estimating the value of a dependent variable when the values of two intervally scaled and normally distributed variables are known.

Linguistic repertoires: Clusters of terms, descriptions and figures of speech; they are the building blocks used to make constructions or versions of cognitive processes, actions, policies and other phenomena.

Logical positivism: A branch of positivism known as empiricism, according to which reality can be experienced only through the senses.

Longitudinal studies: Research designs or methods of data collection that are carried out more than once (e.g. panel studies and trend studies).

Marginals: The row and column totals of a table.

Matching: A method of choosing subjects for experimental testing, whereby subjects are appropriately matched in pairs and then assigned to study groups.

Mean: The average value.

Median: The value that divides an ordinally ranked distribution into two equal parts.

Meta-analysis: A statistical method that collectively analyses the findings of other related studies, employing standardisation of the results.

Meta-theory: The theory that explores the ways in which other theories must be formed in order for them to assume credibility and validity.

Methodology: The science of methods; the theory of methods.

Missing data: Unanswered questions and hence lack of data for a variable, usually recorded by using 9, 99, 999, etc.

Mode: The value, in a distribution, with the highest number of observations; the most frequent value.

'Modistat': A statistical package for statistical analysis of research data for MSDOS, PCDOS and Compaq computers.

Multiple-choice question: A question with a set of given responses.

Multiple-choice test: A test containing multiple-choice questions.

Multiple correlation: A form of correlation between a dependent variable and a group of independent variables.

Multiple operation(al)ism: A method employing more than one measure, group of subjects, time and paradigm to address the object of study; often referred to as triangulation of measurement.

Multivariate statistics: Statistical methods dealing with more than one variable.

Narrative interviews: These interviews encourage the respondent to describe in detail or reconstruct a part of his/her life. They involve a low-level participation of the interviewer in this process, and focus on the way interviewees conceptualise experiences and events of their lives in their accounts.

Natural experiments: Experiments studying people in their natural social context, not in one constructed by the researcher for this purpose.

Neutral interviews: Those interviews that lie between hard and soft interviews and in which the interviewer takes a factual, distant, friendly and impersonal position.

Nominal-level measurement: Nominal-level measurement involves classification of events into categories that must be distinct, uni-dimensional, mutually exclusive and exhaustive.

Nominal scales: Scales in which items can only be defined as equal or unequal/same or different.

Nomological: Being based on, related to or accepting law-like, generally valid standards; endeavouring to establish law-like statements.

Non-parametric statistics: Part of inferential statistics that assumes no metric, but topological data or normal distribution.

Null hypothesis (H_0): A hypothesis that defines traits of a sample and on which hypothesis testing is based; H_0 usually states that differences in the samples are caused by chance or methodological procedures and that they have the same traits as the population.

'Number cruncher stat system': A computer program for statistical analysis of research data, for Macintosh computers.

Objective hermeneutics: A research model that deals with text interpretations, interactions in text, and with the reconstruction of objective structures of meaning.

Objectivity: The notion that in their work social scientists and researchers should exclude values and subjective judgements.

Objectivism: The belief in an objective knowable reality that is distinct from the knowing individual.

Observation: A method of data collection employing vision as the main medium of collection.

Ontology: (Greek *On* = The being) The science of being; deals with the nature of reality.

Open-ended questions: Questions without a given set of response options.

Open interviews: Unstructured and unstandardised interviews.

Openness: The notion held by qualitative researchers proposing that research should be open to changes according to the requirements of the research process.

Operationalisation: The process of translating abstract concepts into workable (operational) indicators.

Ordinal-level measurement: The type of measurement that categorises elements into groups, ordering and ranking them according to magnitude from the lowest to the highest.

Ordinal scales: Scales in which elements are arranged according to their relationship to each other (e.g. greater, smaller, older).

Osiris: A statistical package for computer-assisted analysis of research data.

Outlier: Extreme values of a distribution that lie outside the rest of the distribution.

P-stat ('Princeton statistical package'): A computer program for statistical analysis of research data.

Panel studies: Studies using the same sample and the same techniques carried out more than once (longitudinal studies).

Paradigm: (From the Greek: *paradigma*) The underlying presuppositions and world views scientists share in their discipline.

Parameters: Attributes of the population, symbolised by Greek letters. (Equivalent to statistics.)

Partial correlation: A form of correlation computed under the assumption that all other variables are held constant.

Participant observation: A form of observation in which the observer becomes a member of the group or a part of the situation he/she observes.

PAR (Participatory action research): A form of research characterised by participation of members of the community in the research process.

Path analysis: A statistical method employing multiple regression to study causal relationships in recursive models.

Percentile: A measure of dispersion.

Personal interviews: Interviews during data collection in which the interviewer and interviewee communicate with each other in a close, face-to-face situation.

Phenomenology: The doctrine that deals with the way people make sense of their world and how they construct their everyday world.

Phi: A measure of association (ϕ) for qualitative data and 2×2 tables.

Physical traces: Products of human endeavour, such as erosion or accretion, often studied to infer aspects of their creators.

Pictograms: A form of graphic presentation of data using pictures, such as pictures of coins, people, animals, cars.

Pie graph: Graphic presentation of data in the form of a circle ('pie') divided into sections, each corresponding to the measured value of the variable.

Pilot study: A complete replica of the main study employed in a fraction of the sample.

Placebo effect: The effect thought to be caused by a stimulus that has no power to produce such effects.

Plagiarism: Including the work of others in one's publication without due acknowledgment, hence presenting it as one's own.

Positivism: A school of thought developed by Comte that sees reality as the sum of sense impressions, employs a deductive logic and quantitative research methods, and assumes that life is regulated through natural laws, which social sciences have to uncover and document.

Positivist research: The type of research that focuses on accumulation and analysis of facts as the way of establishing explanations.

Postmodernism: A paradigm that rejects all principles and standards of modernism. In its extreme form it rejects the presence of absolute truths or knowledge, and the ability of science to explain social phenomena. Moderate postmodernists accept standard methods of social research with some hesitation.

Predictor variable: Another name for the independent variable.

Predictive validity: The quality of a measure to predict the results of another.

Pre-test: A small-scale test administered before the introduction of a study aiming to measure the suitability of one or more elements of the main study.

Priestly sociology: A sociology working in and for the status quo of an established order.

Probe: A question type that follows a primary question; it aims to encourage the respondent to elaborate, amplify and expand on a previous answer, and hence enhances the quality of information gathered.

Product-moment correlation: A form of correlation measuring the relationship between intervally scaled variables.

Prophetic sociology: A sociology critical of the status quo, interested in discovering system deficiencies and inconsistencies, and aimed at informing the community and achieving a more humane society.

Proportional stratification: Is employed in stratified sampling, and relates to setting the size of sub-samples to represent proportionally the size of the relevant strata of the population.

Propositions: A set of logically interrelated concepts establishing some degree of regularity.

Purposive sample: A non-probability sample, in which respondents are chosen according to the researcher's judgement as to their suitability for the project. Also referred to as judgmental sample.

Pygmalion effect: The effect caused by the tendency of respondents to adapt to structures and conditions previously defined by the researcher.

Qualitative methods: Methods of social research based principally on theoretical and methodological principles of interpretivism, as expressed in paradigms such as symbolic interactionism, hermeneutics and ethnomethodology.

Quantification: The process of converting qualitative data to numbers.

Quantitative methods: Methods employing quantitative theoretical and methodological principles and techniques, including statistics.

Quota sampling: A sampling procedure that includes quotas of people, often chosen by the interviewers, as specified by the research design.

Random sampling: A type of sampling that employs the theory of probability as the basis of choice of respondents.

Randomisation: The process of randomly choosing and ordering subjects for experimental and control groups.

Range: A measure of dispersion describing the distance from the lowest to the highest value of the distribution.

Rating scale: An ordinal scale in which respondents assign values to a research object according to a set of response categories.

Ratio-level measurement: This is the same as interval-level measurement with the difference that it entails a true zero as its lowest value.

Reactivity: Any form of change in the behaviour of research participants resulting from the process of measurement.

Reductionism: The tendency to reduce the explanation of phenomena to single causes; explaining group behaviour by means of individual personality attributes.

Regression analysis: A method employed to study the relationship between variables, especially the extent to which a dependent variable is a function of one or more independent variables.

Regression curve: The graphic presentation of the regression equation.

Reliability: The capacity of an instrument to produce consistent results. It measures objectivity, precision, stability and consistency.

Reliability tests: Tests designed to measure reliability (e.g. retests, split-half tests, parallel-tests).

Replication: This is the attribute of a study that allows repetition of the research, and with this, validity checking and comparisons.

Representative reliability: Reliability across groups.

Representativeness: The capacity of a sample to reflect all relevant elements of the population, and so to represent the population in the research study.

Research ethics: A set of standards and principles displaying what is acceptable and right and what is wrong and unacceptable when conducting social research.

Residual category: The response category in a set of responses that is intended to cover all unspecified answers (e.g. 'other'); the set of influences that cannot be specified or controlled further.

Response rate: The rate of people responding to a survey. It is computed by dividing the number of those taking part in the survey by the number of those included in the sample frame.

Retest: A reliability test based on testing identical respondents, using identical methods as those of the original study.

Rho: The name of Spearman's coefficient of correlation.

Rotation: A technique of rotating factors in factor analysis in order to determine the optimal matrix of factor loading.

Sample: A group of units chosen to be included in a study.

Sampling: The procedure of choosing samples.

Sampling frame: A list containing all members of the target population, from which a sample will be drawn.

SAS ('Statistical analysis system'): A statistical computer package for social scientists.

Saturation study: A study that includes all members of the target population.

Scaling: The process of constructing the scales commonly used to study attitudes and opinions.

Secondary analysis: Analysis of data previously collected by another study.

Self-destroying prophesy: A prediction that failed to come true because it became known.

Self-fulfilling prophesy: A prediction that came true because it became known.

Semantic differential: A scaling method employing standardised pairs of concepts marking the ends of a seven-point continuum on which the respondents are expected to place their responses.

Semi-standardised interviews: Interviews in which the questions are only partly standardised.

Semi-structured interviews: Interviews with a given structure but with relative freedom to formulate the questions and to determine their order and presentation.

Semiotics: The study of Semeia (Greek Σημεια) namely signs. It focuses on discovering the central and deeper meanings of social phenomena and on the construction of meanings.

Sensualism: The notion held by positivists that the only valid sources of knowledge are the senses.

Significance: A criterion related to the validity of data.

Simple random sampling: A method of sampling employing probability in the selection of the units.

Snowball sampling: A sampling technique in which the respondents are chosen on the basis of information supplied by already studied subjects.

Social distance scale: The Bogardus scale.

Sociogram: Graphic presentation of sociometric data.

Sociomatrix: Tabular presentation of sociometric data.

Sociometry: A method of studying social preferences between members of a group, developed by Moreno.

Soft interviews: A form of interview in which the interviewer exercises no control over the interviewee, but offers guidance and assistance only in the task of answering the questions.

Spearman's rho: The coefficient of Spearman's correlation.

'Spida': A computer program for statistical analysis of research data.

Split-half method: Method of testing reliability by halving the data and comparing the correlation coefficients of the halves.

SPSS ('Statistical programs for social scientists'): A popular method of statistical analysis by means of computers.

Spurious correlation: A correlation that does not hold when conditions change or another variable is introduced.

Stability reliability: Reliability across time.

Stakeholders: Those with an interest in the research and its outcomes.

Standard deviation: The square root of the variance.

Standardised interview: A form of interview using strict content and procedures, ensuring uniformity in approaching the respondents and in collecting the data.

'Statease': A statistical program for computer analysis of research data, devised for Apple computers.

'Statfast': A statistical package for analysis of research data, mainly for Macintosh computers.

'Statflow': A statistical program for computer-assisted analysis of research data.

Statistics: Numerical values of a sample displayed using English letters (the opposite of parameters).

'Statpak': A computer package for statistical analysis of research data.

'Statpro': A computer program employed for statistical analysis of research data.

'Statworks': A computer statistical package for analysing research data.

Stratified sampling: A sampling technique in which the population is divided into strata, and samples are taken from each stratum. These partial samples constitute the sample of the study.

Substantive theory: A type of initial theory developed as a prelude to a formal theory; employed in grounded theory.

Survey: A method of data collection employing a systematic and structured verbal or written questioning.

Summative evaluation: A type of evaluation research which assesses the outcome of a completed programme.

System of coordinates: A two-dimensional graph employed to display research data.

t-test: A parametric test of significance, comparing the means of two samples.

Target population: The part of the general population for which research data are required.

Taxonomy: A systematic classification of units into groups or categories.

Teleology: The theoretical presupposition that social behaviour, structures and phenomena are explained by their purpose or ends.

Telephone interviews: Interviews conducted by phone.

Test of significance: A method testing the probability of a set of statistics reflecting the parameters of the population from which the sample was taken.

Theory: A set of logically and systematically interrelated propositions describing and explaining social phenomena.

Thick descriptions: Descriptions pertaining to settings, people and interaction that are rich, natural, accurate and vivid enough to bring the reader close to the natural life of the study object. It is most common in qualitative research.

Thurstone scale: A scale employed to measure attitudes and opinions, developed by Thurstone.

Trend studies: Longitudinal studies monitoring a given issue over time and using different samples at each stage of investigation.

Triangulation: The practice of using more than one methodology, method, sample, times, and/or researcher within the context of the same study.

True zero: A true zero indicates the total absence of the criteria or values in question. Zero income or zero children means no income, and no children. (Compare arbitrary zero.)

Unobtrusive methods: The type of methods which collect data without the knowledge or awareness of the respondents of being studied.

Validity: A property of a research instrument which measures its relevance, precision and accuracy.

Value-free: The research position according to which researchers should avoid using values in their work.

Variable: An empirical construct that takes more than one value.

Variance: A measure of dispersion; the average distance of the scores of a distribution from the mean.

Verification: The process of empirical validation, mainly of hypotheses.

Bibliography

Abercrombie, N., Hill, S. and Turner, B. (1988) *The Penguin Dictionary of Sociology*. Harmondsworth, UK: Penguin.

Adams, S. (2001) *Interviewing for Journalists*. London: Routledge.

Alcoff, L. (1988) 'Cultural Feminism vs Post-structuralism: The Identity Crisis in Feminism'. *Signs*, 13(3): 405–36.

Alcoff, L. (1996) *Real Knowing: New Versions of Coherence Epistemology*. Ithaca: Cornell University Press.

Alcoff, L. and Potter, E. (1993) *Feminist Epistemologies*. London: Routledge.

Altheide, D. L. (1996) *Qualitative Media Analysis*. Thousand Oaks, Calif.: Sage.

Althoff, M., Bereswill, M. and Riegraf, B. (2001) *Feministische Methodologien und Methoden. Tradition, Konzepte und Erörterungen*. Opladen: Leske & Burdich.

American Sociological Association (1997) *American Sociological Association Code of Ethics*. http//www. asanet. org/members/ecoderev. html.

Anderson, G. (1989) 'Critical Ethnography in Education: Current Status, and the New Directions'. *Review of Educational Research*, 59(3): 249–70.

Argyrous, G. (1996) *Statistics for Social Research*. Melbourne: Macmillan.

Arlek, P. L. and Settle, R. B. (1995) *The Survey Research Handbook: Guidelines and Strategies for Conducting a Survey*. New York: McGraw-Hill.

Assiter, A. (1996) *Enlightened Women: Modernist Feminism in a Postmodern Age*. London: Routledge.

Atkinson, J. M. and Heritage, J. (1984) *Structure of Social Action: Studies in Conversational Analysis*. Cambridge: Cambridge University Press.

Atkinson, P. (1990) *The Ethnographic Imagination: Textual Construction of Society*. London: Routledge.

Atkinson, P. and Hammersley, M. (1994) 'Ethnography and Participant Observation'. In N. K. Denzin and Y. S. Lincoln (eds), *Handbook of Qualitative Research*. Thousand Oaks, Calif.: Sage, pp. 248–61.

Aufenanger, S. and Lenssen, M. (eds) (1986) *Handlung und Sinnstruktur: Bedeutung und Anwendung der objektiven Hermeneutik*. Munich: Kindt.

Australian Vice Chancellors Committee (1990) *Guidelines for Responsible Practices in Research and Dealing with Problems of Research Misconduct*.

Babbie, E. (1995) *The Practice of Social Research*. Belmont, Calif.: Wadsworth.

Bailey, C. A. (1996) *A Guide to Field Research*. London: Pine Forge.

Bailey, K. D. (1982) *Methods of Social Research*. New York: Free Press.

Bailey, K. D. (1988) 'Ethical Dilemmas in Social Research: A Theoretical Framework'.

American Sociologist, 19: 121–37.

Bakeman, R. and Gottman, J. M. (1997) *Observing Interaction: An Introduction to Sequential Analysis*. Cambridge: Cambridge University Press.

Barton, A. H. and Lazarsfeld, P. F. (1979) 'Einige Funktionen von qualitativer Analyze in der Sozialforschung'. In C. Hopf and E. Weingarten (eds), *Qualitative Sozialforschung*. Stuttgart: Clett-Cotta, pp. 41–89.

Baudrillard, J. (1983) *Simulations*. New York: Semiotext.

Bauer, W. (1994) *Qualitative Forschung mit Gastarbeitern*. Weimar: Ganz Verlag.

Bechhofer, F. and Paterson, L. (2000) *Principles of Research Design in the Social Sciences*. New York: Routledge.

Becker, B. (1989) *Grundlagen soziologischer Methodologie*. Frankfurt: Selbstverlag.

Beere, C. A. (1990) *Gender Roles: A Handbook of Tests and Measures*. New York: Greenwood.

Benini, A. (2000) *Construction of Knowledge*. Rome: Gnome.

Berg, B. L. (1995) *Qualitative Research Methods for Social Sciences*. Boston and London: Allyn and Bacon.

Berger, H., Wolf H. F. and Ullmann, E. (eds) (1989) *Handbuch der Sozialistischen Forschung: Methodologie, Methoden, Technicken*. Berlin: Akademie Verlag.

Bergmann, B. (1991) *Sozialtheorie und Soziologie*. Stuttgart: Selbstverlag.

Bergmann, J. R. (1991) 'Konversationsanalyse'. In U. Flick et al. (eds) *Handbuch Qualitative Sozialforschung*. Munich: Psychologie Verlags Union, pp. 213–18.

Berk, R. A. (1995) 'Publishing Evaluation Research'. *Contemporary Sociology: A Journal of Reviews*, 24(1): 9–12.

Betts, K., Hayward, D. and Garnham, N. (2001) *Quantitative Analyses in the Social Sciences: An Introduction*. Croydon, Victoria: Tertiary.

Blaikie, N. (1988) 'Triangulation in Social Research: Origins, Use and Problems'. Paper presented at the Conference of the Sociological Association of Australia and New Zealand, Canberra.

Blaikie, N. (1993) *Approaches to Social Inquiry*. Cambridge: Polity.

Blaikie, N. (2000) *Designing Social Research*. Cambridge: Polity.

Blumer, H. (1969) *Symbolic Interactionism: Perspectives and Method*. Englewood Cliffs, N.J.: Prentice-Hall.

Blumer, H. (1973) 'Der methodologische Standort des Symbolischen Interaktionismus'. In Arbeitsgruppe Bielefelder Soziologen (eds), *Alltagswissen, Interaktion und gesellschaftliche Wirklichkeit*. Reinbek bei Hamburg: Rowohlt, pp. 80–146.

Blumer, H. (1979a) *Critiques of Research in the Social Sciences*. New Brunswick, N.J.: Transaction.

Blumer, H. (1979b) 'Methodologische Prinzipien empirischer Wissenschaft'. In K. Gerdes (ed.), *Explorative Sozialforschung*. Stuttgart: Enke, pp. 41–62.

Bogdan, R. C. and Bilken, S. K. (1992) *Qualitative Research for Education: An Introduction to Theory and Methods*. Boston, Mass.: Allyn and Bacon.

Bogumil, J. and Immerfall, S. (1985) *Wahrnehmungsweisen empirischer Sozialforschung: Zum Selbstverständnis des sozialwissenschaftlichen Forschungsprozesses*. Frankfurt am Main: Campus Verlag.

Böhm, A. (2000) 'Theoretisches Codieren: Textanalse in der Grounded Theory'. In U. Flick, E. von Kardorff and I. Steinke (eds), *Qualitative Forschung: Ein Handbuch*. Reinbek bei Hamburg: Rowohlt, pp. 475–85.

Bohnsack, R. (1993) *Rekonstructive Sozialforschung: Einfürung in Methodologie und Praxis qualitativer Forschung*. Opladen: Leske and Budrich.

Bohnsack, R. (1999) *Rekonstruktive Sozialforschung: Einführung in Methodologie und Praxis*. Opladen: Leske and Budrich.

Bolton, B. F. (2001) *Handbook of Measurement and Evaluation in Rehabilitation*. Gaithersburg, Md.: Aspen.

Boniface, D. R. (1995) *Experiment Design and Statistical Methods for Behavioural and Social Research*. London: Chapman and Hall.

Bordens, K. S. and Abbott, B. B. (1999) *Research Design and Methods: A Process Approach* (4th edn). Mountain View, Calif.: Mayfield.

Boruch, R. (1997) *Randomized Experiments for Planning and Evaluation: A Practical Guide*. Thousand Oaks, Calif.: Sage.

Bouma, G. D. (2000) *The Research Process* (4th edn). New York: Oxford University Press.

Bowden, J. (2002) *Writing a Report: How to Prepare, Write and Present Effective Reports*. Oxford: How To Books.

Bowling, A. (1997) *Measuring Health: A Review of Quality of Life Measurement Scales*. Buckingham: Open University Press.

Boyatzis, R. E. (1998) *Transforming Qualitative Information: Thematic Analysis and Code Development*. Thousand Oaks, Calif.: Sage.

Brace, N., Kemp, R. and Snelgar, R. (2000) *SPSS for Psychologists: A Guide to Data Analysis using SPSS for Windows*. Houndmills: Palgrave.

Bradburn, N. M. and Sudman, S. (1988) *Polls and Surveys: Understanding What They Tell Us*. San Francisco: Jossey-Bass.

Brause, B. S. (2000) *Writing Your Doctoral Dissertation: Invisible Rules for Success*. London: Falmer.

Brieschke, P. A. (1992) 'Reparative Praxis: Rethinking the Catastrophe that is Social Science'. *Theory into Practice*, 31(2): 173–80.

British Association of Social Workers (1996) *The Code of Ethics for Social Work*. Birmingham: British Association of Social Workers.

British Psychological Society (2000) *Code of Conduct, Ethical Principles and Guidelines*. Leicester: British Psychological Society. http//www. bps. org. uk, accessed 18 February 2004.

British Sociological Association (n. d.) Statement on Ethical Practice. http//www. britsoc. org. uk/about/ethic. html, accessed 18 February 2004.

Bromley, D. B. (1986) *The Case-Study Method in Psychology and Related Disciplines*. New York: Wiley.

Brown, R. H. (1992) *Writing the Social Text: Poetics and Politics in Social Science Discourse*. New York: Allyn and Bacon.

Bryman, A. (1984) 'The Debate about Quantitative and Qualitative Research: A Question of Method or Epistemology?' *British Journal of Sociology*, 35, pp. 75–92.

Bryman, A. (1988) *Quantity and Quality in Social Research*. London: Unwin Hyman.

Bryman, A. and Burgess R. (1994) *Analyzing Qualitative Data*. London: Routledge.

Bude, H. (1984) 'Rekonstruktion von Lebenskonstruktionen: eine Antwort auf die Frage, was die Biographieforschung bringt'. In M. Kohli and G. Robert (eds), *Biographie und soziale Wirklichkeit: Neue Beiträge und Forschungsperspektiven*. Stuttgart: Metzler, pp. 7–28.

Budestam, K. E. and Newton, R. R. (2001) *Surviving your Dissertation: A Comprehensive Guide to Content and Process*. Thousand Oaks, Calif.: Sage.

Bühler-Niederberger, D. (1985) 'Analytische Induction als Verfahren der qualitativen Methodologie'. *Zeitschrift für Soziologie*, 6: 475–85.

Bullock, R. (1998) *Research in Practice: Experiments in Development and Information Design*. Sydney: Ashgate.

Burgard, W. and Lueck, H. E. (1991) 'Nichtreactive Verfahren'. In U. Flick et al. (eds), *Handbuch Qualitative Sozialforschung*. Munich: Psychologie Verlags Union, pp. 198–202.

Burgess, R. G. (1982) *Field Research: A Sourcebook and Field Manual*. London: Allen & Unwin.

Burgess, R. G. (1984) *In the Field: An Introduction to Field Research*. London: Allen & Unwin.

Burns, R. B. (1990) *Introduction to Social Research in Education*. Melbourne: Longman Cheshire.

Butler, J. (1990) *Gender Trouble: Feminism and the Subversion of Identity*. New York and London: Routledge.

Caria, M. (2000) *Measurement Analysis*. London: Imperial College Press.

Carspecken, P. F. and Walford, G. (eds) (2001) *Critical Ethnography and Education*. London: Elsevier Science.

Charmaz, K. (2000) 'Grounded Theory: Objectivist and Constructivist Methods'. In N. K. Denzin and Y. S. Lincoln (eds), *Handbook of Qualitative Research* (2nd edn). Thousand Oaks, Calif,: Sage.

Cheek, J. (2000) *Postmodern and Poststructural Approaches to Nursing Research*. Thousand Oaks, Calif.: Sage.

Chelimsky, E. and Shadish, W. R. (eds) (1997) *Evaluation for the Twenty-first Century: A Handbook*. Thousand Oaks, Calif.: Sage.

Chen, S.-Y. (1997) *Measurement and Analysis in Psychological Research: The Failing and Saving of Theory*. Aldershot: Arebury.

Cicourel, A. (1970, 1974) *Methode und Messung in der Soziologie*. Frankfurt am Main: Shurkamp.

Clark, J. (1995) 'Ethical and Political Issues in Qualitative Research from a Philosophical Point of View'. Paper presented to the annual meeting of the American Educational Research Association, San Francisco.

Clarke, A. (1999) *Evaluation Research: An Introduction to Principles, Methods and Practice*. London: Sage.

Clough, P. and Nutbown, C. (2002) *A Student's Guide to Methodology*. London: Sage.

Cobb, G. W. (2002) *Introduction to Design and Analysis in Experiments*. Emeryville, Calif.: Key College Publishing.

Code, L. (1991) *What Can She Know? Feminist Theory and the Construction of Knowledge*. Ithaca: Cornell University Press.

Coffee, A. (1999) *The Ethnographic Self: Fieldwork and the Representation of Reality*. London: Sage.

Coffey, A. and Atkinson, P. (1996) *Making Sense of Qualitative Data: Complementary Research Strategies*. Thousand Oaks, Calif.: Sage.

Collins, C. A. (1999) *Statistical Experiment Design and Integration: An Introduction with Agricultural Examples*. New York: Wiley.

Collins, E. C. (1992) 'Qualitative Research as Art: Toward a Holistic Process'. *Theory into Practice*, 31(2): 181–6.

Contrad, P. and Reinharz, S. (1984) 'Computers and Qualitative Data'. *Qualitative Sociology*, 7, pp. 4–15.

Converse, J. M. and Presser, S. (1986) *Survey Questions: Handcrafting the Standardised Questionnaire*. Beverly Hills, Calif.: Sage.

Cook, J. A. and Fonow, M. M. (1990) 'Knowledge and Women's Interests: Issues of Epistemology and Methodology in Feminist Sociological Research'. In J. M. Nielsen (ed.), *Feminist Research Methods: Exemplary Readings in the Social Sciences*. London: Westview, pp. 69–93.

Cook, T. D., Cooper, H., Cordray, D. S., Hartman, H., Hedges, L. V., Light, R. J., Louis, T. A. and Mosteller, F. (1992) *Meta-analysis for Explanation: A Casebook*. New York: Russell Sage Foundation.

Cook, T. and Reinhardt, C. S. (eds) (1979) *Qualitative and Quantitative Methods in Evaluation Research*. Beverley Hills, Calif.: Sage.

Cooper, H. M. (1998) *Synthesizing Research: A Guide for Literature Reviews*. London: Sage.

Corman, J. (1978) 'Foundational versus Nonfoundational Theories of Empirical Justification'. In G. Pappas and M. Swain (eds), *Essays on Knowledge and Justification*. London: Cornell University Press.

Couper, M. P. (2000) 'Web Surveys: A Review of Issues and Approaches'. *Public Opinion Quarterly*, 64: 464–94.

Coulthard, M. (1994) *Advances in Written Text Analysis*. London: Routledge.

Crabtree, B. F. and Miller, W. L. (1992) *Doing Qualitative Research*. Newbury Park, Calif.: Sage.

Crawford, H. J. and Christensen, I. B. (1995) *Developing Research Skills: A Laboratory Manual*. Boston: Allyn and Bacon.

Creswell, J. W. (1998) *Qualitative Inquiry and Research Design*. Thousand Oaks, Calif.: Sage.

Creswell, J. W. (2003) *Research Design: Qualitative, Quantitative, and Mixed Method*. Thousand Oaks, Calif.: Sage.

Crotty, M. (1995) 'The Ethics of Ethics Committees'. Paper presented at the second Colloquium on Qualitative Research in Adult Education, September–October, University of Melbourne.

Crotty, M. (1998). *Foundations of Social Research: Meaning and Perspective in the Research Process.*, Thousand Oaks, Calif.: Sage.

CSWS (Committee on the Status of Women in Society) (1986) *The Treatment of Gender in Research*. Washington D.C.: American Sociological Association.

Cunningham, J. B. (1993). *Action Research and Organisational Development*. London: Praeger.

Danner, H. (1979) *Methoden Geisteswissenschaftlicher Pädagogik*. Munich: E. Reinhardt.

Davies, C. A. (1999) *Reflexive Ethnography: A Guide to Researching Selves and Others*. London: Routledge.

De Laine, M. (2000) *Fieldwork, Participation and Practice: Ethics and Dilemmas in Qualitative Research*. Thousand Oaks, Calif.: Sage.

Denscombe, M. (1998) *The Good Research Guide for Small-scale Social Research Projects*. Buckingham: Open University Press.

Denzin, N. K. (1970, 1978, 1989) *The Research Act: A Theoretical Introduction to Sociological Methods* (3rd edn). Englewood Cliffs, N.J.: Prentice-Hall.

Denzin, N. K. (1991) *Images of Postmodern Society*. London: Sage.

Denzin, N. K. (1997) Int*erpretive Ethnography: Ethnographic Practice for the Twenty-first Century*. London: Sage.

Denzin, N. K. (2000) 'Symbolischer Interaktionismus'. In U. Flick, E. von Kardorff and I. Steinke (eds), *Qualitative Forschung: Ein Handbuch*. Reinbek bei Hamburg: Rowohlt, pp. 136–50.

Denzin, N. K. and Lincoln, Y. S. (1994) 'Introduction: Entering the field of qualitative research'. In N. K. Denzin and Y. S. Lincoln (eds), *Handbook of Qualitative Research*. Thousand Oaks, Calif.: Sage, pp. 1–22.

Derrida, J. (1976) *Die Schrift und die Differenz*. Frankfurt: Suhrkamp.

de Vaus, D. (2001) *Research Design in Social Research*. London: Sage Publications.

de Vaus, D. (2002a) *Analyzing Social Science Data*. London: Sage.

de Vaus, D. (2002b) *Surveys in Social Research*. London: Routledge.

Diekmann, A. (1995) *Empirische Sozialforschung*. Reinbeck bei Hamburg: Rohwolt.

Dillman, D. (2000) *Mail and Internet Surveys: The Tailored Design Method* (2nd edn). Chichester: Wiley.

Dimas, K. (2003) *Research, Hermeneutics and Theory* [in Greek] Leipzig: Selbstverlag.

Dreher, M. and Dreher, E. (1991) 'Gruppendiscussionverfahren'. In U. Flick et al. (eds), *Handbuch Qualitative Sozialforschung*. Munich: Psychologie Verlags Union, pp. 186–8.

Drew, C. J., Hardman, M. L. and Hart, A. W. (1996) *Designing and Conducting Research Inquiry in Education and Social Science*. London: Allyn and Bacon.

Duran, J. (1995) *Towards a Feminist Epistemology*. Lanham, Md.: Rowan & Littlefield.

Edwards, A. A. (1957) *Techniques of Attitude Scale Constructions*. New York: Appleton-Century-Crofts.

Eichler, M. (1988) *Non-Sexist Research Methods: A Practical Guide*. Boston: Allen & Unwin.

Eichler, M., Lenton, S., Bridribb, S., Haddad, J. and Ross, B. (1985) *A Selected Annotated Bibliography on Sexism in Research*. Ottawa: Social Sciences and Humanities Research Council of Canada.

Ellgring, H. (1991) 'Audiovisuell unterstützte Beobachtung'. In U. Flick et al. (eds) *Handbuch Qualitative Sozialforschung*. Munich: Psychologie Verlags Union, pp. 203–8.

Ellis, L. (1993) 'Operationally Defining Social Stratification in Human and Nonhuman Animals'. In L. Ellis (ed.), *Social Stratification and Socioeconomic Inequality: A Comparative Biosocial Analysis*. New York: Präger, pp. 15–35.

Ellis, L. (1994) *Research Methods in the Social Sciences*. Oxford: Brown and Benchmark.

Engel, U. and Weggenig, U. (1991) 'Statistische Auswertungsverfahren nominalskalierter Daten'. In U. Flick et al. (eds) *Handbuch Qualitative Sozialforschung*. Munich: Psychologie Verlags Union, pp. 237–42.

Evans, D. and Gruba, P. (2002) *How to Write a Better Thesis*. Carlton South, Victoria: Melbourne University Press.

Ezzy, D. (2002) *Qualitative Analysis: Practice and Innovation*. Crows Nest, N.S.W.: Allen and Unwin; London: Routledge.

Farber, W. (2001) *Kunstlehre der Erklärung*. Graz: Selbstverlag.

Fawcett, B. (ed.) (2000) *Practice and Research in Social Work: Postmodern Feminist Perspectives*. New York: Routledge.

Fay, B. (1980) *Social Theory and Political Praxis*. London: Allen & Unwin.

Fay, B. (1987) *Critical Social Science: Liberation and its Limits*. Ithaca, N.Y.: Cornell University Press.

Fee, E. (1986) 'Critiques of Modern Science'. In R. Bleier (ed.), *Feminist Approaches to Science*. New York: Pergamon, pp. 42–56.

Feyerabend, B. K. (1976) *Wider den Methodenzwang*. Frankfurt: Suhrkamp.

Feyerabend, B. K. (1981) *Enkenntnis für freie Menschen*. Frankfurt: Suhrkamp.

Feyerabend, B. K. (1989) *Irrwege der Vernunft*. Frankfurt: Suhrkamp.

Field, A. (2000) *Discovering Statistics Using SPSS for Windows: Advanced Techniques for the Beginner*. London: Sage.

Fielding, N. G. and Lee, R. M. (1998) *Computer Analysis and Qualitative Research*. London: Sage.

Fine, G. A. (1988) 'The Ten Commandments of writing'. *The American Sociologist*, 19: 152–60.

Fink, A. (1995) *How to Sample in Surveys*. Thousand Oaks, Calif.: Sage.

Fink, A. (1998) *Conducting Research Literature reviews: From Paper to the Internet*. London: Sage.

Firestone, W. A. (1993) 'Alternative Arguments for Generalizing from Data as Applied to Qualitative Research'. *Educational Researcher*, 22(4): 16–23.

Fischer, W. and Kohl, M. (1987) 'Biographieforschung'. In W. Voges (ed.), *Methoden der Biographie- und Lebenslaufforschung*. Opladen: Leske und Buderich, pp. 23–50.

Fisher, M. (1997) *Qualitative Computing: Using Software for Qualitative Data Analysis*. Aldershot: Avebury.

Flick, U. (1995) *Qualitative Forschung: Theorien, Methoden, Anwendung in Psychologie and Sozialwissenschaften*. Reinbek bei Hamburg: Rowohlt.

Flick, U. (1998) *An Introduction to Qualitative Research*. London: Sage.

Flick, U. (2000a) 'Konstruktivismus'. In U. Flick, E. von Kardorff and I. Steinke (eds), *Qualitative Forschung: Ein Handbuch*. Reinbek bei Hamburg: Rowohlt, pp. 150–64.

Flick, U. (2000b) 'Design und Prozess qualitativer Forschung'. In U. Flick, E. von Kardorff and I. Steinke (eds), *Qualitative Forschung: Ein Handbuch*. Reinbek bei Hamburg: Rowohlt, pp. 252–65.

Flick, U. (2000c) 'Triangulation in der qualitativen Forschung'. In U. Flick, E. von Kardorff and I. Steinke (eds), *Qualitative Forschung: Ein Handbuch*. Reinbek bei Hamburg: Rowohlt, pp. 309–18.

Flick, U., Kardorff, E. von, Keup, L., Rosenstiel, V. and Wolf, S. (eds) (1991) *Handbuch Qualitative Sozialforschung*. Munich: Psychologie Verlags Union.

Flick, U., Kardorff, E. and Steinke, I. (2000) 'Was ist qualitative Forschung? Einleitung und Überblick'. In U. Flick, E. von Kardorff and I. Steinke (eds), *Qualitative Forschung: Ein Handbuch*. Reinbek bei Hamburg: Rowohlt, pp. 13–29.

Foddy, W. H. (1988) *Elementary Applied Statistics for Social Sciences*. Sydney: Harper and Row.

Foddy, W. H. (1992) *Constructing Questions for Interviews and Questionnaires*. Melbourne: Cambridge University Press.

Foddy, W. H. (1993) *Constructing Questions for Interviews and Questionnaires: Theory and Practice in Social Research*. Melbourne: Cambridge University Press.

Foster, J. J. (2001) *Data Analysis Using SPSS for Windows New Edition: Editions 6–10*. London: Sage.

Foster, N. (1995) 'The Analysis of Company Documentation'. In C. Cassell and G. Symon (eds), *Qualitative Methods in Organisational Research*. London: Sage, pp. 147–66.

Frey, J. H. (1989) *Survey Research by Telephone*. Newbury Park, Calif.: Sage.

Frey, J. H. and Oishi, S. M. (1995) *How to Conduct Interviews by Telephone and in Person*. Thousand Oaks, Calif.: Sage.

Friedrichs, J. (1987) 23. *Soziologentag 1986: Sektions- und Ad-hoc Gruppen*. Opladen: Westdeutscher Verlag.

Fuchs, W. (1984) *Biographische Forschung: Eine Einführung in Praxis und Methoden*. Opladen: Westdeutscher Verlag.

Gadamer, H.-G. (1960, 1975) *Wahrheit und Methode, Grundzüge einer philosophischen Hermeneutik*. Tübingen: Mohr.

Galavotti, M. C. (2003) *Observation and Experiment in the Natural and Social Sciences*. Boston: Kluwer Academic.

Garfinkel, H. (1967) *Studies in Ethnomethodology*. Englewood Cliffs, N.J.: Prentice-Hall.

Gash, S. (2000) *Effective Literature Searching for Research*. Aldershot, UK: Gower.

Geer, J. G. (1988) 'What Do Open-ended Questions Measure?'. *Public Opinion Quarterly*, 52: 365–71.

Geldsthorpe, L. (1992) 'Response to Martyn Hammersley's Paper on Feminist Methodology'. *Sociology, Journal of the British Sociological Association*, 26(2): 213–18.

Gergen, K. J. (1994) *Realities and Relationships: Soundings in Social Construction*. Cambridge, Mass.: Harvard University Press.

Gergen, K. J. (1999) *An Invitation to Social Construction*. London: Sage.

Gibbs, B. (2001) *Qualitative Data Analysis: Explorations with Nvivo*. Buckingham: Open University Press.

Ginevan, M. and Splitstone, D. E (2004) *Statistical Tools for Environmental Quality Measurement*. Boca Raton, Fla.: Chapman & Hall.

Girtler, R. (1984) *Methoden der qualitativen Sozialforschung: Anleitung zur Feldarbeit*. Wien: Böhlau.

Glaser, B. G. (1992) *Emergence vs. Forcing: Basics of Grounded Theory Analysis*. Mill Valley, Calif.: Sociology Press.

Glaser, B. G. and Strauss, A. L. (1967) *The Discovery of Grounded Theory: Strategies for Qualitative Research*. Chicago: Aldine.

Glaser, B. G. and Strauss, A. L. (1979) 'Die Entdeckung genenwartsbezogener Theorie: Eine Grundstrategie qualitativer Sozialforschung'. In C. Hopf and E. Weingarten (eds), *Qualitative Sozialforschung*. Stuttgart: Enke.

Glasersfeld, E. v. (1987) *Wissen, Sprache und Wirklichkeit: Arbeiten zum radikalen Konstruktivismus*. Braunschweig: Vieweg.

Glasersfeld, E. v. (1992) 'Aspekte des Konstruktivismus: Vico, Berkeley, Piaget'. In G. Rush and S. J. Schmidt (eds), *Konstruktivismus: Geschichte und Anwendung*. Frankfurt am Main: Shurkamp, pp. 20–33.

Glass, G. V. (1976) 'Primary, Secondary and Meta-analysis of Research'. *Educational Researchers*, 5: 3–8.

Glick, P. and Fiske, S. T. (1996). 'The Ambivalent Sexism Inventory: Differentiating and Hostile Benevolent Sexism'. *Journal of Personality and Social Psychology*, 70: 491–512.

Goldman, A. H. (1988) *Empirical Knowledge*. Berkeley, Calif.: University of California Press.

Goode, E. (1996) 'The Ethics of Deception in Social Research: A Case Study'. *Qualitative Sociology*, 19: 11–33.

Gooding, D. (1990) *Experiments and the Making of Meaning: Human Agency in Scientific Observation and Experiment*. Boston: Kluwer Academic.

Greene, J. C. (1994) 'Qualitative Program Evaluation: Practice and Promise'. In N. K. Denzin and Y. S. Lincoln (eds), *Handbook of Qualitative Research*. Thousand Oaks, Calif.: Sage, pp. 530–54.

Greene, J. C. and Caracelli, V. J (eds) (1997) *Advances in Mixed-Method Evaluation: The Challenges and Benefits of Integrating Diverse Paradigms*. San Francisco: Jossey Bass.

Greenwood, J. (1994) 'Action Research and Action Researchers: Some Introductory Considerations'. *Contemporary Nurse*, 3(2): 84–92.

Guba, E. G. (1990) *The Paradigm Dialog*. Newbury Park, Calif.: Sage.

Guba, E. G. and Lincoln, Y. S. (1989) *Fourth Generation Evaluation*. Newbury Park, Calif.: Sage.

Guba, E. G. and Lincoln, Y. S. (1994) 'Competing Paradigms in Social Research'. In N. K. Denzin and Y. S. Lincoln (eds), *Handbook of Qualitative Research*. Thousand Oaks, Calif.: Sage, pp. 104–17.

Gubrium, J. F. and Holstein, J. A. (1997) *The New Language of Qualitative Method*. Oxford: Oxford University Press.

Gubrium, J. F. and Holstein, J. A. (eds) (2001) *Handbook of Interview Research: Context and Method*. Thousand Oaks, Calif.: Sage.

Haack, S. (1995) *Evidence and Inquiry: Towards Reconstruction in Epistemology*. Cambridge: Blackwell.

Haig, B. D. (1997) 'Feminist Research Methodology'. In J. P. Keeves (ed.), *Educational Research, Methodology, and Measurement: An International Handbook*. Oxford: Elsevier, pp. 180–5.

Hakim, C. (1987) *Research Design: Strategies and Choices in the Design of Social Research*. London: Allen & Unwin.

Hakim, C. (2000) *Research Design: Successful Designs for Social and Economic Research* (2nd edn). London: Routledge.

Hammersley, M. (1991) *Reading Ethnographic Research: A Critical Guide*. London: Longman.

Hammersley, M. (1992a) 'On Feminist Methodology'. *Sociology, Journal of the British Sociological Association*, 26(2): 187–206.

Hammersley, M. (1992b) *What is Wrong with Ethnography?* London: Routledge.

Hammersley, M. (1996) 'The Relationship between Qualitative and Quantitative Research: Paradigm Loyalty versus Methodological Eclecticism?' In J. T. E. Richardson (ed.), *Handbook of Research Methods for Psychology and the Social Sciences*. Leicester: BPS Books.

Hammersley, M. and Atkinson, P. (1983) *Ethnography: Principles in Practice*. New York: Vintage.

Hammersley, M. and Atkinson, P. (1995) *Ethnography: Principles in Practice* (2nd edn). London: Routledge.

Harding, S. (1986) *The Science Question in Feminism*. Ithaca, N.Y.: Cornell University Press.

Harding, S. (ed.) (1987a) *Feminism and Methodology*. Bloomington: Indiana University Press.

Harding, S. (1987b) 'Conclusion: Epistemological Questions'. In S. Harding (ed.), *Feminism and Methodology*. Milton Keynes: Open University Press, pp. 181–90.

Harding, S. (1987c) 'The Instability of the Analytical Categories of Feminist Theory'. In S. Harding and J. F. O'Barr (eds), *Sex and Scientific Inquiry*. Chicago, Ill.: University of Chicago Press, pp. 283–302.

Harding, S. (1990) 'Feminism, Science, and the Anti-enlightenment Critiques'. In L. Nicholson (ed.), *Feminism/Postmodernism*. New York: Routledge, pp. 83–106.

Harding, S. (1991) *Whose Science? Whose Knowledge? Thinking from Women's Lives*. Ithaca: Cornell University Press.

Harding, S. (1998) *Is Science Multicultural? Postcolonialisms, Feminisms, and Epistemologies*. Bloomington: Indiana University Press.

Harding, S. (1999) *Feministische Wissenschaftstheorie: Zum Verhältniss von Wissenschaft und sozialem Geschlecht*. Hamburg: Argument Verlag.

Harreé, R. (1972) *The Philosophies of Science*. Oxford: Oxford University Press.

Hart, C. (1998) *Doing a Literature Review: Releasing the Social Science Imagination*. Thousand Oaks, Calif.: Sage.

Hart, C. (2001) *Doing a Literature Review*. London: Sage.

Harvey, L. (1990) *Critical Social Research*. London: Unwin Hyman.

Hawe, P., Degeling, D. and Hall. J. (1993) *Evaluating Health Promotion: A Health Workers Guide*. Sydney: Mclennan and Petty.

Hayes, N. (1997) *Doing Qualitative Analysis in Psychology*. Hore, UK: Psychology Press.

Heinze, T. (1987, 1992, 1995) *Qualitative Sozialforschung: Erfahrungen, Probleme und Perspektiven*. Opladen: Westdeutscher Verlag.

Henry, G. T. (1990) *Practical Sampling*. Newbury Park, Calif.: Sage.

Hermans, H., Tkocz, C. and Winkler, H. (eds) (1984) *Berufsverlauf von Ingenieuren: biographieanalytische Auswertung narrativer Interviews*. Frankfurt am Main: Campus Verlag.

Hermanns, N. (1991) 'Narratives Interview'. In U. Flick et al. (eds), *Handbuch Qualitative Sozialforschung*. Munich: Psychologie Verlags Union, pp. 182–5.

Hicks, C and Hennessy, D. (1997) 'The Use of Customised Training Needs Analysis Tool for Nurse Practitioner Development'. *Journal of Advanced Nursing*, 26: 389–98.

Hicks, C., Hennessy, D. and Bawell, F. (1996) 'Development of a Psychometrically Valid Framing Needs Analysis Instrument for Use with Primary Health Care Teams'. *Health Services Management Research*, 9: 262–72.

Hildebrand, B., Müller, H., Beyer, B. and Klein, D. (1984) 'Biographiestudien in Rahmen von Milieustudien'. In M. Kohli and G. Robert (eds), *Biographie und soziale Wirklichkeit: Neue Beiträge und Forschungsperspektiven*. Stuttgart: Metzler, pp. 29–52.

Hitzler, R. and Honer, A. (1997) *Sozialwissenschaftliche Hermeneutic*. Opladen: Leske and Budrich.

Hodson, L. (1999) *Analysing Documentary Accounts*. Thousand Oaks, Calif.: Sage.

Holzkamp, K. (1968) *Wissenschaft als Handlung*. Berlin: de Gruyter.

Holzkamp, K. (1972) *Kritische Psychologie*. Frankfurt: Fischer.

Holzkamp, K. (1981) *Theorie und Experiment in der Psychologie*. Berlin: de Gruyter.

Homan, R. (1991) *The Ethics of Social Research*. London: Longman.

Honer, A. (1999) 'Bausteine zu einer Lebensweltorientierten Wissenssoziologie'. In R. Hitzler, J. Reichertz and N. Schröer (eds), *Hermeneutische Wissenssoziologie*. Konstanz: UVK, pp. 51–67.

Honer, A. (2000) 'Lebensweltanalyse in der Ethnographie'. In U. Flick, E. von Kardorff and I. Steinke (eds), *Qualitative Forschung: Ein Handbuch*. Reinbek bei Hamburg: Rowohlt, pp. 194–204.

Hopf, C. (1991) 'Qualitative Interviews in der Sozialforschung: Ein Überblick'. In U. Flick et al. (eds) *Handbuch Qualitative Sozialforschung.* Munich: Psychologie Verlags Union, pp. 177–81.

Hopf, C. (1996) 'Hypothesenprüfung und qualitative Sozialforschung'. In R. Strobl and A. Böttger (eds), *Wahre Geschichten? Zur Theorie und Praxis qualitativer Interviews.* Baden-Baden: Nomos.

House, E. R. (1993) *Professional Evaluation.* Thousand Oaks, Calif.: Sage.

Huber, G. L. (1991) 'Computerunterstützte Auswertung qualitativer Daten'. In U. Flick et al. (eds), *Handbuch Qualitative Sozialforschung.* Munich: Psychologie Verlags Union, pp. 242–8.

Hughes, J. A. (1990) *The Philosophy of Social Research* (2nd edn). London: Longman.

Hügli, A. and Lübcke, P. (1997) *Philosophielexikon.* Hamburg: Rohwolt.

Humphreys, L. (1970) *Tearoom Trade: Impersonal Sex in Public Places.* Chicago: Aldine.

Hunston, S. and Thompson, G. (2000) *Evaluation in Text: Authorial Stance and the Construction of Discourse.* Oxford: Oxford University Press.

Hunter, J. E. (1990) *Methods of Meta-analysis: Correcting Error and Bias in Research.* Newbury Park, Calif.: Sage.

Husserl, E. (1950) *Gesammelte Werke.* The Hague: M. Nijhoff.

Jacob, E. (1987) 'Traditions of Qualitative Research: A Review'. *Review of Educational Research,* 51: 1–50.

Jacob, E. (1988) 'Classifying Qualitative Research'. *Educational Researcher,* 17, pp. 16–24.

Janesick V. J. (2004) *'Stretching' Exercises for Qualitative Researchers.* Thousand Oaks, Calif.: Sage.

Jankowski, N. W. and Wester, F. (1991) 'The Qualitative Tradition in Social Science Inquiry: Contributions to Mass Communication Research'. In K. B. Jensen and N. W. Jankowski (eds), *A Handbook of Qualitative Methodologies for Mass Communication Research.* London: Routledge, pp. 44–74.

Johnstone, M.-J. (2004) *Effective Writing for Health Professionals: A Practical Guide to Getting Published.* Crows Nest, N.S.W.: Allen & Unwin.

Jorgensen, D. L. (1989) *Participant Observation: A Methodology for Human Studies.* Newbury Park, Calif.: Sage.

Judd, C. K., Smith, E. L. and Kidder, L. H. (1991) *Research Methods in Social Relations.* New York: Harcourt, Brace, Jovanovich.

Jupp, V. (1996) 'Documents and Critical Research'. In R. Sapford and V. Jupp (eds), *Data Collection and Analysis.* London: Sage, pp. 298–316.

Kahn, R. L. and Cannell, C. F. (1957) *The Dynamics of Interviewing: Theory, Technique, and Cases.* New York: Wiley.

Kardorff, E. v. (2000) 'Qualitative Evaluationsforschung'. In U. Flick, E. von Kardorff and I. Steinke (eds), *Qualitative Forschung: Ein Handbuch.* Reinbek bei Hamburg: Rowohlt, pp. 238–50.

Keats, D. (1993) *Skilled Interviewing.* Hawthorn, Victoria: Acer.

Kelle, U. and Erzberger, C. (1999) 'Integration qualitativer und quantitativer Methoden: methodologische Modelle und ihre Bedeutung für die Forschungspraxis'. *Kölner Zeitschrift für Soziologie und Sozialpsychologie,* 51: 509–31.

Kelle, U. and Erzberger, C. (2000) 'Qualitative und quantitative Methoden: kein Gegensatz'. In U. Flick, E. von Kardorff and I. Steinke (eds), *Qualitative Forschung: Ein Handbuch.* Reinbek bei Hamburg: Rowohlt, pp. 299–309.

Kellehear, A. (1993) *The Unobtrusive Researcher: A Guide to Methods.* Sydney: Allen & Unwin.

Keller, E. F. (1985) *Reflections on Gender and Science.* New Haven, Conn.: Yale University Press.

Kellner, D. (1988) 'Postmodernism as a Social Theory: Some Problems and Challenges'. *Theory, Culture and Society,* 5: 239–70.

Kellner, D. (1992) 'Popular Culture and the Construction of Postmodern Identities'. In S. Lash and J. Friedman (eds), *Modernity and Identity*. Oxford: Blackwell, pp. 141–77.

Kimmel, A. J. (1988) *Ethics and Values in Applied Social Research*. Newbury Park, Calif.: Sage.

Kimmel, A. J. (1996) *Ethical Issues in Behavioural Research: A Survey*. Cambridge: Blackwell.

Kirk, J. and Miller, M. L. (1986) *Reliability and Validity in Qualitative Research*. Beverley Hills, Calif.: Sage.

Kleining, G. (1982) 'Umriss zu einer Methodologie qualitativer Sozialforschung'. *Kölner Zeitschrift für Soziologie und Sozialpsychologie*, 34(2): 224–53.

Kleining, G. (1986) 'Das qualitative Experiment'. *Kölner Zeitschrift für Soziologie und Sozialpsychologie*, 38(4): 724–50.

Kleining, G. (1988) *Das rezeptive Interview*. Bielefeld: University of Bielefeld.

Kleining, G. (1991) 'Das qualitative Experiment'. In U. Flick et al. (eds), *Handbuch Qualitative Sozialforschung*. Munich: Psychologie Verlags Union, pp. 263–5.

Köckeis-Stangl, I. (1980) 'Methoden der Sozialisationsforschung'. In D. Ulrich and K. Hurrelmann (eds), *Handbuch der Sozialisationsforschung*. Opladen: Beltz, pp. 312–70.

Kohli, M. (1987) 'Normalbiographie und Individualität: Zur institutionellen Dynamik des gegenwärtigen Lebenslaufregimes'. In J. Friedrichs (ed.), *23. Soziologentag 1986: Sektions- und Ad-hoc Gruppen*. Opladen: Westdeutscher Verlag, pp. 432–5.

Kohli, M. and Robert, G. (eds) (1984) *Biographie und soziale Wirklichkeit: Neue Beiträge und Forschungsperspektiven*. Stuttgart: Metzler.

Konegen, N. and Sondergeld, K. (1985) *Wissenschaftstheorie für Sozialwissenschaftler*. Opladen: Leske und Budrich.

Krämer, H. C. and Thieman, S. (1987) *How Many Subjects? Statistical Power Analysis in Research*. London: Sage.

Krebs, D. and Schmidt, P. (1993) *New Directions in Attitude Measurement*. Berlin and New York: W. de Gruyter.

Krejcie, R. V. and Morgan, D. W. (1970) 'Determining Sample Size for Research Activities'. *Educational and Psychological Measurement*, 30: 607–10.

Kromrey, H. (1986) *Empirische Sozialforschung*. Opladen: Fernuniversität Gesamthochschulen.

Krüger, B. (1983) *Theoretische Methodologie*. Leipzig: Selbstverlag.

Krüger, H. (1983) 'Gruppendiskussion. Überlegungen zur Rekonstruktion sozialer Wirklichkeit aus der Sicht der Betroffenen'. *Soziale Welt*, 34: 90–109.

Krüger, R. A. (1998) *Moderating Focus Groups*. Thousand Oaks, Calif.: Sage.

Krüger, R. A. and Casey, M. A. (1998) *Focus Groups: A Practical Guide for Applied Research*. Thousand Oaks, Calif.: Sage.

Küchler, M., Wilson, T. P. and Zimmerman, D. H. (eds) (1981) *Integration von qualitativen und quantitativen Forschungsansätzen*. Manheim: ZUMA-Arbeitsbericht 81/19.

Kuhn, T. (1970) *The Structure of Scientific Revolutions*. Chicago: University of Chicago Press.

Kulik, J. A. and Kulik, C. C. (1992) 'Meta-analysis: Historical Origins and Contemporary Practice'. *Advances in Social Science Methodology*, 2: 53–79.

Kuzel, A. J. (1992) 'Sampling in Qualitative Inquiry'. In B. F. Crabtree and W. L. Miller (eds), *Doing Qualitative Research*. Newbury Park, Calif.: Sage, pp. 31–44.

Kvale, S. (1996) *InterViews: An Introduction to Qualitative Research Interviewing*. Thousand Oaks, Calif.: Sage.

Laatz, W. (1993) *Empirische Methoden*. Frankfurt am Main: Harri Deutsch.

Lamnek, S. (1988) *Qualitative Sozialforschung. Band 1: Methodologie; Band 2: Methoden und Techniken*. Munich: Psychologie Verlags Union.

Lamnek, S. (1993, 1995) *Qualitative Sozialforschung. Band 1: Methodologie; Band 2: Methoden und Techniken*. Weinheim: Psychologie Verlags Union.

Lancy, D. E. (1993) *Qualitative Research in Education: An Introduction to the Major Traditions*. New York: Longman.

Laster, P. E. and Bishop, L. K. (2000) *Handbook of Tests and Measurement in Education and the Social Sciences*. Lanham, Md.: Scarecrow Press.

Lather, P. (1991) *Getting Smart: Feminist Research and Pedagogy with/in the Postmodern*. New York: Routledge.

Lather, P. (1992) 'Critical Frames in Educational Research: Feminist and Post-structural Perspectives'. *Theory into Practice*, 31(2): 87–99.

Lather, P. (1993) 'Fertile Obsession: Validity after Post-Structuralism'. *Sociological Quarterly*, 35: 673–93.

Lavrakas, P. (1993) *Telephone Survey Methods: Sampling Selection and Supervision*. Beverley Hills: Sage.

Lauth, B. and Sareiter, J. (2002) *Wissenschaftliche Erkenntnis*. Paderborn: Mentis.

LeCompte, M. D. and Goetz, J. P. (1982) 'Problems of Reliability and Validity in Ethnographic Research'. *Review of Educational Research*, 52: 31–60.

Lee, R. M. (2000) *Unobtrusive Measures in Social Research*. Buckingham: Open University Press.

Legewie, H. (1991) 'Feldforschung und teilehmende Beobachtung'. In U. Flick et al. (eds), *Handbuch Qualitative Sozialforschung*. Munich: Psychologie Verlags Union, pp. 189–92.

Lehrer, K. (1974) *Knowledge*. Oxford: Clarendon.

Lenssen, M. and Aufenanger, S. (1986) 'Zur Rekonstruktion von Interaktionsstrukturen. Neue Wege zur Fernsehanalyze'. In S. Aufenanger and M. Lenssen (eds), *Handlung und Sinnstruktur: Bedeutung und Anwendung der objektiven Hermeneutik*. Munich: Kindt, pp. 123–204.

Lester, J. D. and Lester, J. Jr (2001) *Writing Research Papers: A Complete Guide*. New York: Longman.

Likert, R. A. (1932) 'A Technique of Measurement of Attitudes'. *Archives of Psychology*, 140: 44–53.

Lincoln, Y. S. (1995) 'Emerging Criteria for Quality in Qualitative and Interpretive Research'. *Qualitative Inquiry*, 1: 275–89.

Lincoln, Y. S. and Guba, E. G. (1985) *Naturalistic Inquiry*. Beverley Hills, Calif.: Sage.

Lincoln, Y. S. and Guba, E. G. (1986) 'Research, Evaluation and Policy Analysis: Heuristics in Disciplined Inquiry'. *Policy Studies Review*, 5: 546–65.

Lofland, J. and Lofland, L. (1994) *Analyzing Social Settings: A Guide to Qualitative Observation and Analysis* (2nd edn). Belmont, N.J.: Transaction.

Longino, H. E. (1990) *Science as Social Knowledge*. Princeton: Princeton University Press.

Lueger, M. (2000) *Grundlagen qualitativer Feldforschung*. WUV-Universitätsverlag Wien.

Luhmann, N. (1997) *Die Gesellschaft der Gesellschaft*. Frankfurt am Main: Shurkamp.

Lunt, P. and Livingstone, S. (1996) 'Rethinking the Focus Group in Media and Communications Research'. *Journal of Communication*, 46: 79–98.

Lyotard, J. F. (1984) *The Postmodern Condition: A Report on Knowledge*. Manchester: Manchester University Press.

Machamer, P. (2002) 'A Brief Historical Introduction to the Philosophy of Science'. In P. Machamer and M. Silberstein (eds), *The Blackwell Guide to the Philosophy of Science*, Oxford: Blackwell, pp. 1–17.

MacIntyre, A. (1996) *A Short History of Ethics*. London: Macmillan.

Madron, T. W., Tate, C. N. and Brookshire, R. G. (1987) *Using Microcomputers in Research*. Beverley Hills, Calif.: Sage.

Mahr, W. (1995) *Politische Struktur der Sozialforschung*. Leipzig: Selbstverlag.

Maindok, H. (1996) *Professionelle Interviewführung in der Sozialforschung*. Pfaffenweiler: Centaurus Verlagsgesellschaft.

Maisel, R. and Hodges Persell C. (1996) *How Sampling Works*. Thousand Oaks, Calif.: Sage.

Mangione, T. W. (1995) *Mail Surveys: Improving the Quality*. Thousand Oaks, Calif.: Sage.

Mann, C. (1990) 'Meta-analysis in the Breech'. *Science*, 249: 476–80.

Manning, P. K. (1982) 'Analytic induction'. In R. B. Smith and P. K. Manning (eds), *Qualitative Methods: Vol. II of Handbook of Social Research Methods*. Cambridge, Mass.: Ballinger.

Mariner, J. (1986) *Anwendung von Gruppendiscussion in Soziologie*. Munich: Blasaditch.

Marshall, C. and Rossman, G. B. (1989) *Designing Qualitative Research*. Beverley Hills, Calif.: Sage.

Marshall, H. (1995) 'Discourse Analysis in an Occupational Context'. In C. Cassell and G. Symon (eds), *Qualitative Methods in Organisational Research*. London: Sage, pp. 91–106.

Martin, K. (1988) *Methodologisches Denken*. Hamburg: Selbstverlag.

Mason, J. (1997) 'Social Work Research: Is there a Feminist Method?' *Affilia: Journal of Women and Social Work*, 12: 12–32.

Matt, E. (2000) 'Darstellung qualitativer Forschung'. In U. Flick, E. von Kardorff and I. Steinke (eds), *Qualitative Forschung: Ein Handbuch*. Reinbek bei Hamburg: Rowohlt, pp. 578–87.

Maxwell, J. A. (1992) 'Understanding and Validity in Qualitative Research'. *Harvard Educational Review*, 62(3): 279–300.

May, T. (2001) *Social Research: Issues, Methods and Process*. Buckingham, UK: Open University Press.

Maynard, M. (1994) 'Methods, Practice and Epistemology: The debate about Feminism and Research'. In M. Maynard and J. Purvis (eds), *Researching Women's Lives from a Feminist Perspective*. London: Taylor and Francis.

Maynard, M. (1998) 'Feminists' Knowledge and the Knowledge of Feminisms: Epistemology, Theory, Methodology and Method'. In T. May and M. Williams (eds), *Knowing the Social World*. Buckingham: Open University Press.

Mayring, P. (1983) *Grundlagen und Techniken qualitativer Inhaltsanalyze*. Dissertation, University of Munich.

Mayring, P. (1985) 'Qualitative Inhaltsanalyze'. In H. Jüttemann (ed.), *Qualitative Forschung in der Psychologie: Grundfragen, Verfahrensweisen, Anwendungsfelder*. Weinheim: Beltz, pp. 187–211.

Mayring, P. (1988) *Qualitative Inhaltsanalyse: Grundlagen und Techniken*. Munich: Dt Studien Verlag.

Mayring, P. (1991) 'Qualitative Inhaltsanalyse'. In U. Flick et al. (eds), *Handbuch Qualitative Sozialforschung*. Munich: Psychologie Verlags Union, pp. 209–12.

Mayring, P. (2000) 'Qualitative Inhaltsanalyse'. In U. Flick, E. von Kardorff and I. Steinke (eds), *Qualitative Forschung: Ein Handbuch*. Reinbek bei Hamburg: Rowohlt, pp. 468–75.

McCall, G. J. (1979) 'Qualitätskontrolle der Daten bei teilnehmender Beobachtung'. In K. Gerdes (ed.), *Explorative Sozialforschung*. Stuttgart: Enke, pp. 141–57.

McDowell, I. and Newell, C. (1996) *Measuring Health: A Guide to Rating Scales and Questionnaires*. New York: Oxford University Press.

McNiff, J. (1992) *Action Research: Principles and Practice*. London: Routledge.

McQuarrie, E. F. (1996) *The Market Research Toolbox: A Concise Guide for Beginners*. Thousand Oaks, Calif.: Sage.

Meinefeld, W. (1997) 'Ex-ante-Hypothesen in der qualitativen Sozialforschung: Zwischen "fehl am Platz" und "unverzichtbar"'. *Zeitschrift für Soziologie*, 26: 22–34.

Meinefeld, W. (2000) 'Hypothesen und Vorwissen in der qualitativen Sozialforschung'. In U. Flick, E. von Kardorff and I. Steinke (eds), *Qualitative Forschung: Ein Handbuch*. Reinbek bei Hamburg: Rowohlt, pp. 265–75.

Menard, S. (1991) *Longitudinal Research*. Newbury Park, Calif.: Sage.

Menzel, A. (1936) *Griechische Soziologie*. Vienna and Leipzig: Hölder-Piechlor-Tempsky.

Merten, K. (1983) *Inhaltsanalyse: Einführung in Theorie, Methode und Praxis*. Opladen: Westdeutscher Verlag.

Merton, R. K., Fiske, M. and Kendall, P. L. (1990). *The Focused Interview: A Manual of Problems and Procedures* (2nd edn). London: Collier MacMillan.

Michell. J. (1999) *Measurement in Psychology: Critical History of a Methodological Concept*. New York: Cambridge University Press.

Miles, M. B. and Huberman, A. M. (1994) *Qualitative Data Analysis: An Expanded Sourcebook*. Beverley Hills, Calif.: Sage.

Miller, C. and Treitel, C. (1991) *Feminist Research Methods: An Annotated Bibliography*. New York: Greenwood.

Miller, R. L. (2000) *Researching Life Stories and Family Histories*. London: Sage.

Miller, R. L., Acton, C., Fullerton, D. A. and Maltby, J. (2002) *SPSS for Social Scientists: Versions 9, 10 and 11*. Houndmills, UK: Palgrave Macmillan.

Mills, C. W. (1959) *The Sociological Imagination*. London: Oxford University Press.

Minichiello, V., Aroni, R., Timewell, E. and Alexander, L. (1990) *In-Depth Interviewing: Researching People*. Melbourne: Longman Cheshire.

Mitchell, M. and Jolley, J. (2004) *Research Design Explained*. Belmont, Calif.: Thomson/Wadsworth.

Mohr, M. (1996) *Ethics and Standards for Teacher Research: Drafts and Decisions*. Conference paper delivered at AERA Conference, New York.

Morgan, D. L. (1996) 'Focus Groups'. In J. Hagan and K. S. Cook (eds), *Annual Review of Sociology, Vol. 22*. Palo Alto, Calif.: Annual Reviews, pp. 129–52.

Morgan, D. L. (1997) *Focus Groups as Qualitative Research*. Newbury Park, Calif.: Sage.

Morgan, D. L. (1998a) *Planning Focus Groups*. Thousand Oaks, Calif.: Sage.

Morgan, D. L. (1998b) 'Practical Strategies for Combining Qualitative and Quantitative Methods'. *Qualitative Health Research*, 8: 362–76.

Moser, C. A. and Kalton, G. (1971) *Survey Methods in Social Investigation*. London: Heinemann.

Mucchielli, R. (1973) *Das Gruppeninterview: Theoretische Einführung*. Salzburg: Müller.

Mullen, B. and Miller, N. (1991) 'Meta-analysis'. In C. K. Judd, E. L. Smith and L. H. Kidder (eds), *Research Methods in Social Relations*. New York: Harcourt, Brace, Jovanovich, pp. 425–49.

Murray, M. J. and Hay-Roe, H. (1986) *Engineered Writing: A Manual for Scientific, Technical and Business Writers*. Tulsa, Okla.: PennWell.

Nagler, K. and Reichertz, J. (1986) 'Kontaktanzeigen: Auf der Suche nach dem anderen den man nicht kennen will'. In S. Aufenanger and M. Lenssen (eds), *Handlung und Sinnstruktur: Bedeutung und Anwendung der objektiven Hermeneutik*. Munich: Kindt, pp. 84–122.

Nebraska Sociological Feminist Collective (1988) *A Feminist Ethic for Social Science Research*. Lewiston: Edwin Mellen.

Nelson, L. H. (1990) *Who Knows: From Quine to Feminist Empiricism*. Philadelphia: Temple University Press.

Nelson, L. H. (2002) 'Feminist philosophy of science'. In P. Machamer and M. Silberstein (eds), *The Blackwell Guide to the Philosophy of Science*. Oxford: Blackwell, pp. 312–31.

Neuendorf, K. A. (2002) *The Content Analysis Guidebook*. Thousand Oaks, Calif.: Sage.

Nicholson, L. (ed.) (1990) *Feminism/Postmodernism*. New York: Routledge.

Nielsen, J. M. (ed.) (1990) *Feminist Research Methods: Exemplary Readings in the Social Sciences*. London: Westview.

Oakley, A. (1981) 'Interviewing Women: A Contradiction in Terms'. In H. Roberts (ed.), *Doing Feminist Research*. London: Routledge, pp. 30–61.

Oakley, A. (1998) 'Gender, Methodology and People's Ways of Knowing: Some Problems with Feminism and the Paradigm Debate in Social Science'. *Sociology*, 32: 307–31.

Oakley, A. (2000) *Experiments in Knowing: Gender and Method in the Social Sciences*. Cambridge: Polity.

Oja, S. and Smulyan, L. (1989) *Collaborative Action Research: A Developmental Approach*. London: Falmer.

Olesen, V. (1994) 'Feminisms and Models of Qualitative Research'. In N. K. Denzin and Y. Y. Lincoln (eds), *Handbook of Qualitative Research*. Thousand Oaks, Calif.: Sage.

Oppenheim, A. N. (1992) *Questionnaire Design, Interviewing and Attitude Measurement*. London: Pinter.

Orr, L. L. (1999) *Social Experiments: Evaluating Public Programs with Experimental Methods*. Thousand Oaks, Calif.: Sage.

Övermann, V., Allert, T., Konav, E. and Krambeck, J. (1979) 'Die Methodologie einer "objectiven Hermeneutik" und ihre allgemeine forschungslogische Bedeutung in der Sozialwissenschaften'. In H.-G. Söffner (ed.), *Interpretative Verfahren in der Sozial- und Textwissenschaften*. Stuttgart: Metzler.

Övermann, V., Allert, T., Konav, E. and Krambeck, J. (1983) 'Die Methodologie einer "objectiven Hermeneutik"'. In P. Zedler and H. Moser (eds), *Aspekte qualitativer Sozialforschung: Studien zu Aktionsforschung empirischer Hermeneutik und reflexiver Sozialtechnologie*. Opladen: Leske und Budrich, pp. 95–123.

Pannas, N. (1996) *Politiki kai Koini Gnomi* [Politics and Public Opinion]. Leipzig: Selbstverlag.

Parten, M. (1950) *Survey Polls and Samples*. New York: Harper and Row.

Patton, M. (1990) *Qualitative Evaluation and Research Methods*. Newbury Park, Calif.: Sage.

Patton, M. Q. (1986) *Utilisation-Focused Evaluation* (2nd edn). Newbury Park, Calif.: Sage.

Patzer, G. L. (1996) *Experiment–research Methodology in Marketing: Types and Applications*. Westport, Conn.: Quorum.

Pawson, R. and Tilley, N. (1997) *Realistic Evaluation*. London: Sage.

Pelz, D. C. (1981) *Use of Innovation in Innovating Processes by Local Governments*. Ann Arbor: CRUSK, Institute for Social Research, University of Michigan.

Pfeifer, L. (2000) *Sachverhalte, Konstruktion und Wirklichkeit*. Wien: Selbstverlag.

Pink, S. (2001) *Doing Visual Ethnography: Images, Media and Presentation in Research*. London: Sage.

Pilcher, J. and Coffey, A. (eds) (1996) *Gender and Qualitative Research*. Aldershot, UK: Avebury.

Plake, B. S. and Impara, J. S. (eds) (2001) *The Fourteenth Mental Measurements Yearbook*. Lincoln: Buros Institute.

Platt, J. (1996) *A History of Sociological Research Methods in America, 1920–1960*. Cambridge: Cambridge University Press.

Pollock, J. (1979) 'A Plethora of Epistemological Theories'. In G. Pappas (ed.), *Justification and Knowledge*. London: Reidel.

Pollock, J. (1986) *Contemporary Theories of Knowledge*. London: Rowman and Littlefield.

Poser, H. (2001) *Wissenschaftstheorie*. Stuttgart: Reclam.

Posovac, E. J. and Carey, R. G. (1997) *Program Evaluation: Methods and Case Studies*. Upper Saddle River, N.J.: Prentice-Hall.

Potter, J. (1996) *Representing Reality: Discourse, Rhetoric and Social Construction*. London: Sage.

Potter, J. (1997) 'Discourse Analysis as a Way of Analyzing Naturally Occurring Talk'. In D. Silverman (ed.), *Qualitative Research: Theory, Method and Practice*. London: Sage.

Potter, J. and Wetherell, M. (1994) 'Analyzing Discourse'. In A. Bryman and R. G. Burgess (eds), *Analyzing Qualitative Data*. London: Routledge, pp. 47–66.

Punch, P. D. (2000) *Developing Effective Research Proposals*. London: Sage.

Puris, X. (1995) *The Complexity of Research Measure* [in Greek]. Paris: Ajax.

Ragin, C. C. (1987) *The Comparative Method*. Berkley: University of California Press.

Ragin, C. C. (1994) *Constructing Social Research*. Thousand Oaks, Calif.: Sage.

Ragin, C. C. and Becker, H. S. (1989) 'How the Microcomputer is Changing our Analytic Habits'. In G. Blank et al. (eds), *New Technology in Sociology: Practical Applications in Research and Work*. New Brunswick, N.J.: Transaction.

Ramazanoglu, C. (1992) 'On Feminist Methodology: Male Reason versus Female Empowerment'. *Sociology, Journal of the British Sociological Association*, 26(2): 207–12.

Ramazanoglou, G. (2002) *Feminist Methodology: Challenges and Choices*. London: Sage.

Rassenberger, J. (1989) *Computerintegrierte Informationsverarbeitung in der empirischen Sozialforschung*. Nürnberg: Institut für Freie Berufe.

Reason, P. and Bradbury, H. (2001) *Handbook of Action Research: Participative Inquiry and Practice*. London: Sage.

Reed, M. (2000) 'The Limits of Discourse Analysis in Organisational Analysis'. *Organisation*, 7: 524–30.

Reichertz, J. (1991) 'Objective Hermeneutik'. In U. Flick et al. (eds), *Handbuch Qualitative Sozialforschung*. Munich: Psychologie Verlags Union, pp. 223–7.

Reichertz, J. (2000) 'Objektive Hermeneutik und hermeneutische Wissenssoziologie'. In U. Flick, E. von Kardorff and I. Steinke (eds), *Qualitative Forschung: Ein Handbuch*. Reinbek bei Hamburg: Rowohlt, pp. 514–24.

Reid, S. (1987) *Working with Statistics*. Cambridge: Polity.

Reinecker, H. (1987) 'Einzelfallstudie'. In E. Roth (ed.), *Handbuch Qualitative Sozialforschung*. Munich: Psychologie Verlags Union, pp. 277–91.

Reinharz, S. (1983) 'Experiential Analysis: A Contribution to Feminist Research'. In G. Bowles and R. Dülli-Klein (eds), *Theories of Women's Studies*. Boston: Routledge and Kegan Paul, pp. 162–91.

Reinharz, S. (1992) *Feminist Methods in Social Research*. New York: Oxford University Press.

Rescher, N. (2002) *Rationalität, Wissenschaft und Praxis*. Würzburg: Königshousen & Neuman.

Richards, L. and Richards, T. (1987) 'Qualitative Data Analysis: Can Computers Do It?'. *Australian and New Zealand Journal of Sociology*, 23(1): 23–35.

Richards, T. (1986) *NUDIST: User's Manual*. Melbourne: Replee.

Richards, T. and Richards, L. (1994) 'Using Computers in Qualitative Analysis'. In N. Denzin and Y. Lincoln (eds), *Handbook of Qualitative Research*. Thousand Oaks, Calif.: Sage.

Richardson, L. (1992) 'The Consequences of Poetic Representation'. In C. Ellis and M. Flaherty (eds), *Investigating Subjectivity*. Thousand Oaks, Calif.: Sage.

Richardson, L. (1994) 'Writing: A Method of Inquiry'. In N. K. Denzin and Y. S. Lincoln (eds), *Handbook of Qualitative Research*. Thousand Oaks, Calif.: Sage, pp. 516–29.

Riessman, C. K. (1993) *Narrative Analysis*. Newbury Park, Calif.: Sage.

Riffe, D., Lacy, F. and Fico, F. G. (1998) *Analyzing Media Messages: Using Quantitative Content Analysis in Research*. Mahwah, N.J.: Lawrence Erlbaum.

Roberts, C. W. (ed.) (1997) *Text Analysis for the Social Sciences: Methods for Drawing Statistical Inferences from Texts and Transcripts*. Hove, UK: Laurence Erlbaum.

Roberts, H. (1981) *Doing Feminist Research*. London: Routledge and Kegan Paul.

Robinson, E. and Robinson, S. (2003) *What does it Mean? Discourse, Text, Culture: An Introduction*. Sydney: McGraw-Hill.

Robinson, J. P., Shaver, P. and Wrightsman, L. S. (1999) *Measures of Political Attitudes.* San Diego: Academic Press.

Robson, C. (1994) *Experiment, Design and Statistics in Psychology.* Harmondsworth, UK: Penguin.

Robson, C. (2000) *Small-Scale Evaluation: Principles and Practice.* London: Sage.

Rodriguez, N. and Ryave, A. (2002) *Systematic Self-observation.* Thousand Oaks, Calif.: Sage.

Rolfe, G. (2000) *Research, Truth, and Authority: Postmodern Perspectives on Nursing.* Basingstoke, UK: Macmillan.

Rorty, R. (1985) 'Solidarity or Objectivity?'. In J. Rajchman and C. West (eds), *Post-analytic Philosophy.* New York: Columbia University Press, pp. 3–19.

Rosenau, P. M. (1992) *Postmodernism and the Social Sciences.* Princeton, N.J.: Princeton University Press.

Rosnow, R. L. and Rosenthal. R. (1997) *People Studying People: Artifacts and Ethics in Behavioural Research.* New York: Freeman.

Rossi, P. H. and Freeman, H. E. (1993) *Evaluation: A Systematic Approach* (5th edn). Newbury Park, Calif.: Sage.

Roth, E. (ed.) (1987) *Sozialwissenschaftliche Methoden: Lehr- und Handbuch für Forschung und Praxis.* Munich: Oldenburg.

Rubin, H. J. and Rubin, I. S. (1995) *Qualitative Interviewing: The Art of Hearing Data.* Thousand Oaks, Calif.: Sage.

Salamun, K. (2001) 'Neopositivismus'. In K. Salamun (ed.), *Was ist Philosophie.* Tübingen: Mohr Siebek, pp. 1–11.

Sanders, J. R. (ed.) (1999) *Handbuch der Evaluationstandards, Joint Committee on Standards for Educational Evaluation.* Opladen: Leske and Budrich.

Sanger, J. (1996) *The Compleat Observer? A Field Research Guide to Observation.* Thousand Oaks, Calif.: Sage.

Sapsford, R. (1999) *Survey Research.* London: Sage.

Sapford, R. and Abbott, P. (1996) 'Ethics, Politics and Research'. In R, Sapford and V. Jupp (eds), *Data Collection and Analysis.* London: Sage, pp. 317–42.

Sarantakos, S. (1984) *Living Together in Australia.* Melbourne: Longman Cheshire.

Sarantakos, S. (1987) *For a Caring Care.* Wagga: Keon.

Sarantakos, S. (1992) *Cohabitation in Transition.* Sydney: Keon.

Sarantakos, S. (2000a) *Basic Stats Without Maths.* Sydney: Harvard Press.

Sarantakos, S. (2000b) *Same-Sex Couples.* Sydney: Harvard Press.

Saulwick, W. (1987) *Sex Role Portrayal of Women in Advertisements: A Content Analysis.* Canberra, ACT.: Office of the Status of Women.

Sayers, J., Evans, M. and Redclift, N. (eds) (1987) *Engels Revisited: New Feminist Essays.* London: Tavistock.

Scheele, B. (1991) 'Dialogische Hermeneutic'. In U. Flick et al. (eds), *Handbuch Qualitative Sozialforschung.* Munich: Psychologie Verlags Union, pp. 274–8.

Schensul, J. J. and Schensul, S. L. (1992) 'Collaborative Research: Methods of Inquiry for Social Change'. In M. D. LeCompte, W. L. Millroy and J. Preissle (eds), *The Handbook of Qualitative Research in Education.* New York: Academic Press, pp. 161–200.

Scheurich, J. J. (1997) *Research Method in the Postmodern.* London: Falmer.

Schmidt, S. J. (1998) *Die Zähmung des Blicks: Konstruktivismus–Empirie–Wissenschaft.* Frankfurt am Main: Shurkamp.

Schnädelbach, H. (2002) *Erkenntnistheorie.* Hamburg: Junius.

Schofield, J. W. (1993) 'Increasing the Generalizability of Qualitative Research'. In M. Hammersley (ed.), *Social Research: Philosophy, Politics and Practice.* London: Sage, pp. 200–25.

Schrag, F. (1992) 'In Defence of Positivistic Research Paradigms'. *Educational Researcher,* 21(5): 5–8.

Schütz, A. (1971) *Gesammelte Aufsätze, Band 1: Das Problem der sozialen Wirklichkeit.* Den Haag: Nijhoff.

Schütze, F. (1977) *Die Technik des narrativen Interviews in Interactionsfeldstudien – dargestellt an einem Project zur Erforschung Kommunalen Machtstrukturen, Arbeitsberichte und Forschungsmaterialien, Nr. 1.* Bielefeld: University of Bielefeld.

Schütze, F. (1979) *Die Technik des narrativen Interviews in Interaktionsstudien. Dargestellt an einem Projekt von kommunalen Machtstrukturen, No. 1.* Bielefeld: University of Bielefeld, Arbeitsberichte und Forschungsmaterialien.

Schütze, F. (1981) 'Prozeßstrukturen des Lebenslaufs'. In J. Mathes, A. Pfeifenberger and M. Stosberg (eds), *Biographie in Handlungswissenschaftlicher Perspective.* Nürnberg: University of Erlangen-Nürnberg, pp. 55–156.

Schütze, F. (1982) 'Narrative Repräsentation kollektiver Schiksalsbetroffenheit'. *Erzählungen,* 4: 568–90.

Schütze, F. (1983) 'Bibliographieforschung und narratives Interview'. *Neue Praxis,* 13(3): 283–93.

Schütze, F. (1987) *Das Narrative Interview in Interactionsfeldstudien, Kurs 3755.* Hagen: University of Hagen.

Schwandt, T. A. (1994) 'Constructivist, Interpretivist Approaches to Human Inquiry'. In N. K. Denzin and Y. S. Lincoln (eds), *Handbook of Qualitative Research.* Thousand Oaks, Calif.: Sage, pp. 118–37.

Seale, C. (1999) *The Quality of Qualitative Research.* London: Sage.

Seiber, J. E. (1992) *Planning Ethically Responsible Research: A Guide for Students and Internal Review Boards.* Beverley Hills, Calif.: Sage.

Selener, D. (1997) *Participatory Action Research and Social Change.* Ithaca, N.Y.: Cornell University Press.

Selltiz, C., Wrightsman, L. J. and Cook, S. W. (1960, 1976) *Research Methods in Social Relations.* New York: Holt, Rinehart and Winston.

Shaw, C. R. (1930, 1966) *The Jack Roller: A Delinquent Boy's Own Story.* Chicago: University of Chicago Press.

Shaw, I. (1999) *Qualitative Evaluation.* Thousand Oaks, Calif.: Sage.

Shepherd, J. C. (1994) 'Training Needs Analysis: Necessity or Luxury?' *Journal of Nursing Management,* 3: 319–22.

Silverman, D. (1985) *Qualitative Methodology and Sociology.* Aldershot, UK: Gower.

Silverman, D. (2001) *Interpreting Qualitative Data in Methods for Analysing Talk, Text and Interaction.* London: Sage.

Simons, H. (ed.) (1989) *Rhetoric in the Human Sciences.* Beverley Hills, Calif.: Sage.

Smith, D. D. E. (1992) 'Sociology from Women's Experience: A Reaffirmation'. *Sociological Theory,* 10: 88–98.

Smith, J. K. (1990) 'Alternative Research Paradigms and the Problem of Criteria'. In E. Guba (ed.), *The Paradigm Dialog.* Newbury Park, Calif.: Sage, pp. 167–87.

Smith, J. K. (1992) 'Interpretive Inquiry: A Practical and Moral Activity'. *Theory into Practice,* 31(2): 100–6.

Smith, M. J. (1998) *Social Science in Question.* London: Sage.

Söffner, H.-G. (2000) 'Sozialwissenschaftlice Hermeneutik'. In U. Flick, E. von Kardorff and I. Steinke (eds), *Qualitative Forschung: Ein Handbuch.* Reinbek bei Hamburg: Rowohlt, pp. 164–75.

Sofos, N. (1990) *Quantitative Analyse.* Berlin: Selbstverlag.

South Australian Community Health Research Unit (1991) *Planning Healthy Communities: A Guide to doing Community Needs Assessment.* Adelaide: Flinders.

Spector, P. E. (1992) *Summated Rating Scale Construction: An Introduction.* Newbury Park: Sage.

Spinello, R. A. (2003) *Case Studies in Information Technology Ethics.* Upper Saddle River, N.J.: Prentice-Hall.

Spitznagel, A. (1991) 'Projective Verfahren'. In U. Flick et al. (eds), *Handbuch Qualitative Sozialforschung*. Munich: Psychologie Verlags Union, pp. 272–4.

Sprague, J. and Zimmerman, M. K. (1989) 'Quality and Quantity: Reconstructing Feminist Methodology'. *American Sociologist*, 20: 71–86.

Sproull, N. L. (1988) *Handbook of Research Methods: A Guide to Practitioners and Students in the Social Sciences*. London: Scarecrow.

Stake, R. E. (1994) 'Case studies'. In N. K. Denzin and Y. S. Lincoln (eds), *Handbook of Qualitative Research*. Thousand Oaks, Calif.: Sage, pp. 236–47.

Stake, R. E. (1995) *The Art of Case Study Research*. Thousand Oaks, Calif.: Sage.

Stanley, L. (ed.) (1990) *Feminist Praxis: Research, Theory and Epistemology in Feminist Sociology*. London: Routledge.

Stanley, L. and Wise, S. (1983) *Feminist Consciousness and Feminist Research*. London: Routledge and Kegan Paul.

Stanley, L. and Wise, S. (1993) *Breaking out Again: Feminist Ontology and Epistemology*. London: Routledge.

Stapf, K. H. (1995) 'Laboruntersuchungen'. In E. Roth (ed.), *Sozialwissenschaftliche Methoden*. Wien: R. Olenbourg Verlag, pp. 228–44.

Steinke, I. (1999) *Kriterien qualitativer Forschung: Ansätze zur Bewertung qualitativ-empirischer Sozialforschung*. München: Juventa.

Steinke, I. (2000) Gütekriterien qualitativer Forschung'. In U. Flick, E. von Kardorff and I. Steinke (eds), *Qualitative Forschung: Ein Handbuch*. Reinbek bei Hamburg: Rowohlt, pp. 319–31.

Stergios, L. (1991) *Theory Construction and Social Research*. [In Greek.] Athens: Selbstverlag.

Stewart, D. W. and Shamdasani, P. N. (1990) *Focus Groups: Theory and Practice*. Newbury Park, Calif.: Sage.

Strauss, A. L. (1987, 1990) *Qualitative Analysis for Social Scientists*. New York: Cambridge University Press.

Strauss, A. L. (1991) *Grundlagen qualitativer Sozialforschung: Datenanalyse und Theoriebildung in der empirischen Sozialforschung*. Munich: Wilhelm Fink Verlag.

Strauss, A. L. and Corbin, J. M. (1998) *Basics of Qualitative Research: Techniques and Procedures for Developing Grounded Theory*. Thousand Oaks, Calif.: Sage.

Stroker, E. (1998) 'Wissenscaftstheorie'. In A. Pieper (ed.), *Philosophische Disziplinen*. Leipzig: Reclam Verlag, pp. 437–50.

Sudman, S. and Blair, E. (1999) 'Sampling in the Twenty-first Century'. *Journal of the Academy of Marketing Science*, 27(2): 269–77.

Suls, J. M. and Rosnow, R. L. (1988) 'Concerns about Artifacts in Psychological Experiments'. In J. G. Morawski (ed.), *The Rise of Experimentation in American Psychology*. New York: Yale University Press, pp. 153–87.

Tashakkori, A. and Teddlie, C. (1998) *Mixed Methodology: Combining Qualitative and Quantitative Approaches*. Thousand Oaks, Calif.: Sage.

Taylor, S. (ed.) (2001) *Ethnographic Research: A Reader*. London: Open University Press.

Terhardt, E. (1981) 'Intuition–Interpretation–Argumentation: Zum Problem der Geltungsbegründung von Interpretationen'. *Zeitschrift der Pädagogik*, 27(5): 769–93.

Tesch, R. (1989) 'Computer Software and Qualitative Analysis: A Reassessment'. In Blank et al. (eds), *New Technology in Sociology: Practical Applications in Research and Work*. New Brunswick, N.J.: Transaction Books.

Tesch, R. (1990) *Qualitative Research: Analysis, Types and Software Tools*. New York: Falmer.

Thomas, J. (1993) *Doing Critical Ethnography (Qualitative Research Methods Series, No. 26)*. Newbury Park, Calif.: Sage.

Thomas, W. J. and Znaniecki, F. (1958) *The Polish Peasant in Europe and America*. New York: Octagon.

Thorndike, R. M. (1997) *Measurement and Evaluation in Psychology and Education*. Upper Saddle River, N.J.: Merrill.

Torres, R. T., Preskill, S. H. and Piontek, M. E. (1996) *Evaluation Strategies for Communicating and Reporting: Enhancing Learning and Organisations*. London: Sage.

Usher, R., Bryant, I. and Johnston, R. (1997) *Adult Education and the Postmodern Challenge: Learning Beyond the Limits*. London: Routledge.

Van Mannen, J. (1988) *Tales of the Field: On Writing Ethnography*. Chicago: University of Chicago Press.

Vlahos, N. (1984) *Κοινωνικη Ερευνα* [Sociological Methodology; in Greek]. Athens: Phantom.

Voges, W. (ed.) (1987) *Methoden der Biographie- und Lebenslaufforschung*. Opladen: Leske und Budrich.

Volcott, H. F. (1990) 'On seeking – and rejecting – validity in qualitative research'. in W. Eisner and A. Peshkin (eds), *Qualitative Inquiry in Education: The Continuing Debate*. New York: Teachers College Press, pp. 121–52.

Volmerg, U. (1983) 'Validität im interpretativen Paradigma: Dargestellt an der Konstruktion qualitativer Erlebensverfahren'. In P. Zedler and H. Moser (eds), *Aspekte qualitativer Sozialforschung. Studien zu Aktionsforschung empirischer Hermeneutik und reflexiver Sozialtechnologie*. Opladen: Leske und Budrich, pp. 124–43.

Wachter, K. W. (1988) 'Disturbed by Meta-analysis?' *Science*, 241: 1407–8.

Wadsworth, Y. (1984) *Do It Yourself Social Research*. Melbourne: Victorian Council of Social Service.

Wadsworth, Y. (1991) *Everyday Evaluation of the Run*. Melbourne: Action Research Issues Association.

Walker, R. (ed.) (1985) *Applied Qualitative Research*. Aldershot, UK: Gower.

Wallace, R. A. and Wolf, A. (1986) *Contemporary Sociological Theory*. Englewood Cliffs, N.J.: Prentice-Hall.

Wandmacher, J. (2002) *Einführung in die psychologische Methodenlehre*. Heidelberg: Spectrum Akademischer Verlag.

Wang, M. and Mahoney, B. (1991) 'Scales and Measurement Revisited'. *Health Values*, 15: 52–6.

Warren, C. A. D. and Hackney, J. K. (2000) *Gender Issues in Ethnography* (2nd edn). London: Sage.

Waters, K. (2000) *Researching, Writing and Presenting Reports*. Croydon, Victoria: Eastern House.

Webb, E. J., Campbell, D. T., Schwartz, R. D. and Sechrest, L. (2000) *Unobtrusive Measures*. Thousand Oaks, Cal.: Sage.

Weber, R. P. (1990) *Basic Content Analysis*. Newbury Park, Calif.: Sage.

Weitzman, E. and Miles, M. B. (1993) *Computer-aided Qualitative Data Analysis: A Review of Selected Software*. New York: Center for Policy Research.

Weitzman, E. A. and Miles, M. B. (1994, 1995) *Computer Programs for Qualitative Data Analysis*. Thousand Oaks, Calif.: Sage.

Weiss, C. H. (1997) 'How Can Theory-based Evaluation Make Greater Headway?' *Evaluation Review*, 21(4): 501–24.

Weiss, C. H. (1998) *Evaluation: Methods for Studying Policies and Programmes*. New York: Prentice-Hall.

Wells, L. E. and Rankin, J. H. (1991) 'Families and Delinquency: A Meta-analysis of the Impact of Broken Homes'. *Social Problems*, 38: 71–93.

Westkott, M. (1990) 'Feminist Criticism of Social Sciences'. In J. M. Nielsen (ed.), *Feminist Research Methods: Exemplary Readings in the Social Sciences*. London: Westview Press, pp. 58–68.

Wetherell, M. and Potter, J. (1992) *Mapping the Language of Racism*. Hemel Hempstead: Harvester Wheatsheaf.

Whyte, W. F. (ed.) (1991) *Participatory Action Research*. Newbury Park, Calif.: Sage.

Wilhoit, G. and Weaver, D. (1980) *Newsroom Guide to Polls and Surveys*. Washington, D,C.: American Newspaper Publishers Association.

Wilkinson, S. (1999) 'Focus Groups: A Feminist Method'. *Psychology of Women Quarterly*, 23: 221–44.

Winter, R. (1987) *Action Research and the Nature of Social Inquiry: Professional Innovation and Educational Work*. Avebury: Gower.

Witzman, E. A. and Miles, M. B. (1995) *Computer Programs for Qualitative Data Analysis*. London: Sage.

Wolcott, H. F. (1990) *Writing up Qualitative research*. Newbury Park, Calif.: Sage.

Wolcott, H. F. (1992) 'Posturing in Qualitative Research'. In M. D. LeCompte, W. L. Millroy and J. Preissle (eds), *The Handbook of Qualitative Research in Education*. San Diego: Academic Press, pp. 3–52.

Wolcott, H. F. (1994) *Transforming Qualitative Data: Description, Analysis, Interpretation*. Thousand Oaks, Calif.: Sage.

Wood, L. A. and Kroger, R. O. (2000) *Doing Discourse Analysis: Methods for Studying Action in Talk and Text*. Thousand Oaks, Calif.: Sage.

Yin, R. K. (1991) *Case Study Research: Design and Methods*. Newbury Park, Calif.: Sage.

Yin, R. K. (2003) *Case Study Research: Design and Methods* (3rd edn). Thousand Oaks, Calif.: Sage.

Zeller, R. A. and Carmines, E. G. (1980) *Measurement in the Social Sciences*. Cambridge: Cambridge University Press.

Index

Chelt